THE SIXTH
OLD HOUSE CATALOGUE

Front entrance of the William Pepperrell House (1720-23), Kittery (Kittery Point), Maine. Photograph by Jack E. Boucher, Historic American Buildings Survey.

THE SIXTH
OLD HOUSE CATALOGUE

Compiled by Lawrence Grow

Beth Kalet and Ned Smith
General Editors

A Sterling/Main Street Book
Sterling Publishing Co., Inc.   New York

Compiler: Lawrence Grow

General Editors: Beth Kalet
Ned Smith

Staff Writers: Martin Greif
Beth Kalet
Ned Smith

Art: Bruce H. Baker
M. Henri Katz
Ronald R. Misiur

10 9 8 7 6 5 4 3 2 1

A Sterling/Main Street Book

Published in 1990 by Sterling Publishing Company, Inc.
387 Park Avenue South, New York, N.Y. 10016
© 1988 by The Main Street Press
Distributed in Canada by Sterling Publishing
⅋ Canadian Manda Group, P. O. Box 920, Station U
Toronto, Ontario, Canada M8Z 5P9
Manufactured in the United States of America

Sterling ISBN 1-55562-065-5 Paper

Library of Congress Cataloging-in-Publication Data

Grow, Lawrence.
   The sixth old house catalogue.

   Includes index.
   1. Historic buildings—United States—Conservation
and restoration—Catalogs. 2. Buildings—United States—
Conservation and restoration—Catalogs. I. Title.
II. Title: 6th old house catalogue. III. Title: Old
house catalogue.
TH3411.G7634 1988   728.3′7′0288029473   88-13385
ISBN 1-55562-065-5 (pbk.)

Contents

Introduction

There is an even greater need for an *Old House Catalogue* today than there was a dozen years ago when this biennial source book was first published. Although preservation and restoration have become socially acceptable and economically viable concepts during this time, it is no less difficult now to locate the well-wrought and fitting object or material for the old house than it was in 1976. Today nearly every major manufacturer of building and furnishings materials promotes a line of old-fashioned products that have the semblance of age, but not its character. "Authentic" has become an almost meaningless term. Talented craftsmen and artisans who know how to produce authentic goods, however, persevere against the competition of these mass-merchandisers to maintain themselves, their standards, and a market for their goods. Hopefully, *The Sixth Old House Catalogue* will be of help to them and to you the reader.

The assembly of a book of this sort is an extremely complex operation. From hundreds of sources, the names of craftsmen, manufacturers, suppliers, distributors, artists, dealers in old materials, and consultants and architects are meticulously gathered. As important as the search is the evaluation of products and services. Approximately twenty-five percent of these are selected for write-ups, with another twenty-five percent listed at the end of each chapter. Fifty percent are rejected completely. In the evaluation process, several considerations are paramount. Someone who renders a service must be available on a regular basis and must possess the credentials required to do a proper job; manufacturers and craftsmen must prove that the objects they can supply are designed and executed in a stylistically proper or documented manner and are made of materials which are both durable and fitting. As best we can, we also try to determine whether products and supplies are sold and delivered in an efficient and honest manner.

After all materials and information are properly evaluated, the task of compiling the write-ups in a useful format gets underway. Since we want the book to be as fresh and up-to-date as possible, it is necessary to rush to print as quickly as we can. Lists can be assembled almost instantly, but the writing of textual material requires careful and thoughtful consideration. Advice on how and when to use various products or services is interwoven with the individual write-ups. Additional lists of suppliers are included for each category covered in the various chapters.

Each biennial *Old House Catalogue* is a thoroughly revised book. New sources are included on nearly every page, and many products or services from a source previously acknowledged are new as well. At the same time, we are summing up in every chapter—either in the text itself or in the list of additional suppliers at the end of each chapter— many objects or services previously featured. One book thus builds on another in a way that we think is most useful.

The search for original and reproduction old-house materials is guided by three major considerations—time, money, and effort. The urge is always to "improve" things just as quickly as possible with the least possible effort and cost. The temptation to seize on what is readily available and easily worked into place is very difficult to resist if the price is right. But patience has its rewards. The question of whether an item is appropriate in style and form should be answered first, but this is by no means the only matter of importance. How durable is the object? How much maintenance will it require? Is it something integral to the expression of a period style or merely a passing fancy to be consigned to the attic or a garage sale ten years hence? The answers to these questions cannot be fully given in *The Sixth Old House Catalogue.* Each house has its own particular problems and needs. The process of finding, evaluating, and using a wide variety of materials, however, can be made a much less frustrating exercise with the use of this book. The process of restoring a room or a complete house should be an invigorating and satisfying project. We're still learning, sweating, and, yes, even smiling, after twelve years of tackling the legacy of the past, its problems and its pleasures.

Once again we must express our thanks to the many people who have assisted in the compilation of this biennial publication. Ned Smith and Beth Kalet have guided the Main Street staff in locating new sources of supply and in evaluating and organizing material. Together they have written thousands of letters and made countless calls to produce an avalanche of information that is thoroughly up-to-date. The assistance of friends and associates in the restoration field who have shared their knowledge so freely is greatly appreciated. Some of these are craftsmen or professionals who have offered their own evaluations of particular products, and, in a number of cases, recommended the work of competitors.

Lawrence Grow
Pittstown, New Jersey
October, 1988

THE SIXTH
OLD HOUSE
CATALOGUE

1.

Structural Products and Services

The most important chapter in any old house resource book is correctly devoted to such fundamentals as doors, windows, stairways, and basic building materials. These are the nuts-and-bolts elements which give form to a building, along with a good percentage of its style. If a building is not structurally sound, corrective work must be done before rehabilitation or replacement of the decorative elements. But sound construction, in our book, is more than a skeletal matter: a building should "hang together," its proportions should be right, the structural members should relate well to one another, and they must also be able to bear the weight or stress intended for them without difficulty.

Many old buildings acquire an odd look over a period of time. Ill-conceived "add-ons" are thrown up on one side or another. Rather than restoring the basic framework, a choice is made to cover the frame with another coating, perhaps of asphalt or vinyl siding, thereby obliterating the old lines. Possibly the most common horror perpetrated on the old building is the destruction of windows and doors. Segmented picture windows, for example, are often cut to replace a double-hung sash window without any thought given to the rest of the façade. In the pursuit of comfort, double-glazed vinyl windows which only yellow with age are substituted for leaky old wooden sashes. It needn't be so. There are now many manufacturers of air-tight, double-glazed windows of an appropriate material and style.

The sources given in this chapter can provide some of the basic elements which may need replacement or restoration. There are also many craftsmen listed who specialize in making the old as good as new. We would urge the reader to make use of real period building materials as often as aesthetically and economically feasible. If copies have to be made, however, make sure that the artisan you choose is willing to be a bit old-fashioned in his approach. It is tempting to accept the easy "period" solutions offered by many manufacturers: styrofoam-like beams, veneered rather than solid doors, and yes, even plastic shutters. It may take just a little more time to find something better, but it will be a bit more durable, and, in the long run, more satisfying to live with.

Façade detail, Derby House (1761-62), Salem, Massachusetts. Photograph by Eric Muller, Historic American Buildings Survey.

Architectural Salvage

Architectural antiques used to be known as "junk" or "salvage." And in some communities, thoughtless people still call in a wrecking team to finish off their decrepit old houses. Salvage dealers, however, know that there is money to be made from old windows, doors, flooring, paneling, etc., and some dealers, unbeknownst to the seller, make arrangements to place at least the better pieces with a big-city treasure hunter. The competition for even run-of-the-mill decorative pieces is growing more fierce each year. Increasingly, even reproduction objects are being presented as antique. It is important, then, that the buyer of old house materials deal with only the most reputable dealers, such as those presented in the following listings.

The Architectural Antique Warehouse

This company demonstrates the principle of *multum in parvo*. It usually carries some objects retrieved from old homes, although it's better known for its collections of reproduction items—bath and lighting fixtures, wood and metal ornamentation, furniture, fencing, mantels, tin ceilings, and doors. A selection of new beveled glass doors and windows in traditional styles is also available. The Architectural Antique Warehouse even does some consulting for renovation and restoration projects and will prepare blueprints or supervise the implementation of repairs or changes.

Literature available.

Architectural Antique Warehouse
PO Box 3065
Ottawa, Ontario, Canada K1P 6H6
(613) 526-1818

Architectural Antiques

How better to inspire a design for an authentic interior than by walking through authentic antique rooms? Architectural Antiques has preserved several such complete interiors in its 18,000-foot showroom. Standard offerings of mantels, hardware, lighting fixtures, columns, and woodwork are joined by entire staircases, a roomful of plumbing fixtures, entryways, and a prize pair of leaded-glass doors, topped by a matching fan transom. Architectural Antiques will send photographs upon individual requests and provides a locator service if existing stock doesn't satisfy your needs.

Architectural Antiques
121 E. Sheridan Ave.
Oklahoma City, OK 73104-2419
(405) 232-0759

Architectural Antiques Exchange

Some stores feature a little bit of everything; Architectural Antiques Exchange features a lot of everything, or at least it seems as if it does. The 30,000-square-foot warehouse is stuffed with fascinating antiques from the 1700s to the 1940s, although the emphasis is on Victorian artifacts. Pine, oak, cherry, walnut, chestnut, and mahogany doors and mantels abound; lustrous oak, mahogany, and walnut paneling is waiting to be used again. If you can't find an original piece that meets your criteria, you can purchase a reproduction door or ask the in-house woodworking shop to make something special. It's easy to spend hours looking at the other antique items in the store, which usually include stained glass, front and back bars, mirrors, lighting fixtures, balustrades, newel posts, columns, pedestal sinks, ironwork, ornate frames, marble carvings,

and fretwork. Architectural Antiques Exchange will be happy to pack its merchandise and to ship it anywhere.

Literature available.

Architectural Antiques Exchange
709-15 N. 2nd St.
Philadelphia, PA 19123
(215) 922-3669

Architectural Salvage Co.

Warmth isn't just a temperature with an antique mantel from Architectural Salvage. Reclaimed mantels enrich a vintage interior with historic woodwork. Cherry pieces, carved with vines or flowers, are among the more ornate selections. Designs in oak may include shelves, beaded columns, or even a repeating ornament of wooden owls. Other services from Architectural Salvage include carpentry and building with architectural antiques, as well as restoration of antiques (with special expertise in stained glass).

Brochure available.

Architectural Salvage Co.
103 W. Michigan Ave., Box 401
Grass Lake, MI 49240
(517) 522-8516

The Bank

You have to visit The Bank's 42,000 square-foot collection of architectural antiques to believe it. The company specializes in items from the rich architectural heritage of New Orleans and the Mississippi delta. Recently, The Bank has expanded its offerings to include building materials from other areas of the U.S. and the world—Mexico, Central America, Portugal, and Spain included.

Doors, doorways, mantels, moldings, staircases, porches, stained glass, gratings, plumbing fixtures, and an almost infinite variety of other architectural antiques are all stored according to a unique system that facilitates on-site buying as well as mail-ordering. With the addition of an adjoining mill and woodworking shop, The Bank is able to restore any damaged treasure in the ever-changing inventory. With careful and precise state-of-the-art stripping and restoration techniques, none of the character or quality of an original item is lost to time or wear.

The Bank also offers assistance with design matters, whether a customer is seeking to authen-

tically restore a home or desires to fit out a newly constructed office or house in a period style.

Literature available.

The Bank, Architectural Antiques
1824 Felicity St.
New Orleans, LA 70113
(504) 523-2702

The Brass Knob

Specializing in late 19th- and early 20th-century brass hardware and lighting fixtures, The Brass Knob is a useful resource for anyone searching for a proper Victorian or Edwardian period piece. The lighting devices are of all kinds, most being quite ornamental; the hardware is similarly ornate.

In addition to this basic stock, The Brass Knob also carries an ever-changing inventory of ironwork, columns, tiles, mantels, doors, and stained, beveled, and leaded glass.

Visits are recommended, but written inquiries about particular types of items are always welcome. No catalogue is available.

The Brass Knob
2311 18th St., N.W.
Washington, DC 20009
(202) 332-3370

Canal Company

Opened originally in Georgetown, The Canal Company is now located in downtown Washington, D.C., near historic Logan Circle. Dealing in architectural antiques, the company primarily serves customers in the D.C. area, but the mailing list includes every state and Canada. No catalogue is available since the inventory is in constant flux, but inquiries are handled promptly by telephone or mail.

The company offers interior and exterior doors, door hardware, fireplace mantels and accessories, pedestal sinks, interior and exterior shutters, tiles, vintage lighting and parts, both restored and "as is." The Canal Company

13

is also a retail outlet for many manufacturers specializing in antique reproductions.

The Canal Company
1612 14th St., N.W.
Washington, DC 20009
(202) 234-6637

E. Cohen's Architectural Heritage

Recently relocated in Ottawa, Ontario, Eric Cohen's collection of architectural antiques spans 300 years of history. There are thousands of doors, mantels, and stained glass, beveled, and etched windows. Even more interesting is the selection of architectural components such as stairs and newel posts, wood scrollwork, and columns.

Cohen's inventory is drawn from all over North America and is representative of many period styles. The stock is in unusually good condition as there is a workshop on site.

The company ships throughout the world and will provide photographs of requested items for 50¢ each.

A flyer is available with a SASE.

E. Cohen's Architectural Heritage
1240 Bank St.
Ottawa, Ontario, Canada K1S 3Y3
(613) 729-4427

Governor's Antiques

The New York area's United House Wrecking is matched in the South by Governor's Antiques. Located outside Richmond, Virginia, Governor's sprawls across 20,000 square feet chock-a-block with architectural antiques of every variety. There are more than one million items for sale on its 4.5-acre site.

Governor's specialty is wrought-iron fencing, but there is considerable depth in other areas as well. Currently there are more than 400 marble mantels and 500 old and reproduction doors in stock. Lighting fixtures also number in the hundreds.

Governor's has been in business for more than seventeen years

and offers such auxiliary services as refinishing and repair of all variety of items, marble cutting, glass etching and bending, the duplication of hardware, and wood carving.

Great American Salvage

From a cramped garage to showrooms in Vermont, New York, Florida, and Connecticut, Great American Salvage has spent its half dozen years growing, building, adding, finding. French doors, beveled glass, lighting fixtures, stonework, mantels, and bars only begin the catalogue of Great American Salvage's inventory. Request the in-house newspaper for quarterly updates on Great American Salvage's unusual discoveries during reclamation and salvage jobs.

Literature available quarterly.

Great American Salvage Co.
34 Cooper Sq.
New York, NY 10003
(212) 505-0070

Whit Hanks

A newly expanded, 15,000-foot showroom makes Whit Hanks one of the largest retailers of architectural antiques in Texas. Specializing in massive, oversized

JACK PURYEAR & ASSOCIATES

Brochure available.

Governor's Antiques Ltd.
6240 Meadowbridge Rd.
Mechanicsville, VA 23111
(804) 746-1030

pieces like a terrific street clock from London and this oversized entryway of beveled glass and Belgian pine, Whit Hanks also offers 1000 unique mantels, iron gates, and general antiques. After working with architectural antiques for many years, Whit Hanks now restores antiques as well as selling them. The firm will respond to all inquiries with photographs and information on one-of-a-kind pieces.

Whit Hanks
1009 W. 6th St.
Austin, TX 78703
(512) 478-2101

Irreplaceable Artifacts

Evan Blum takes the business of saving architectural ornamentation very seriously. He has filled fifteen floors in New York City with architectural art and ornaments, proof enough of his dedication. Few other dealers would have tackled such gigantic salvage as interior ornamentation from New York's Helen Hayes Theater, a movie theater marquee, and copper facing from the Commodore Hotel in New York.

Visiting Irreplaceable Artifacts' showrooms is always an exciting and eye-opening experience. Many of the customers are interior designers, builders, and contractors seeking conversation pieces that will impress and perhaps improve the exterior or interior of a building. But there are also the homeowners who want something a bit less grandiose. Blum can supply almost anything needed if it was made in the late 1800s or early 20th century.

Both antique and reproduction garden furniture and ornaments are a specialty of the company.

Literature available.

Irreplaceable Artifacts
14 Second Ave.
New York, NY 10003
(212) 982-5000

Howard Kaplan Antiques

In addition to antique furnishings, Kaplan stocks a wide variety of architectural elements and period and reproduction sinks, tubs, water closets, bidets, and bath accessories. There are four floors of showrooms at the firm's Broadway location in New York City.

Included in the supply of components are etched glass doors, enameled leaded windows, sets of French doors with beveled glass, balcony railings, and ironwork.

Illustrated are two examples of Kaplan's bath fixtures—a French china pedestal sink, c. 1890, and an American pedestal tub, c. 1900.

Information on bathroom fixtures, $2.

Howard Kaplan Antiques
827 Broadway
New York, NY 10003
(212) 674-1000

Materials Unlimited

Both new and antique period accessories and architectural elements are available through Materials Unlimited. Much of the inventory has been drawn from Midwestern sources. Included are such items as doors and entrances, windows, mantels, lighting fixtures, hardware, and stained, beveled, and etched glass.

Because of the ever-changing inventory, it is impossible for the company to issue a comprehensive catalogue. Individual photographs are available, however, for a charge of $1 (which will be refunded with a purchase). Prospective customers should be very specific about what they are seeking and provide some idea of size, style, wood/metal type, and price range.

Materials Unlimited employs talented craftsmen who will repair

or restore antique pieces or reproduce such items as bookshelves, room dividers, and stained glass panels.

General brochure on the company, $3.

Materials Unlimited
2 W. Michigan Ave.
Ypsilanti, MI 48197
(313) 483-6980

New Jersey Barn

Barns are fast disappearing from the Delaware valley, as they are nationally, but some of the best examples are being saved for new sites and uses. Conversion of barns for residential use has been popular for many years and the supply of really fine timber-framed structures is beginning to dwindle. New Jersey Barn specializes in massively-framed structures with hand-hewn oak timbers, joined by mortise and tenon and secured with wooden pegs. Unlike the softwood barns of New England, New Jersey and Pennsylvania barns were fashioned almost exclusively of oak. The framing is usually of an English or New World Dutch style.

The company's interest is only in the frame which it disassembles,

cleans, and transports either for storage or to be raised on a new site. Foundation, flooring, sheathing, roofing, etc., is left to the customer and his contractor or architect. New Jersey Barn, nevertheless, can offer useful advice in planning a barn-house.

Barns have been transported to sites within New Jersey and to New York, Pennsylvania, Connecticut, Maryland, and Massachusetts. Longer moves can also be made.

Illustrated are two barns, the first from Cream Ridge, New Jersey, and the second from Bucks County, Pennsylvania.

Literature available.

The New Jersey Barn Company
PO Box 702
Princeton, NJ 08542
(609) 924-8480

North Fields Restorations

This is a company that claims to have "everything conceivable for your restoration needs." This would appear to be the truth—if antique Colonial architectural elements are what is being sought.

North Fields dismantles houses and barns, many for reassembly on new sites. At the same time, the firm stocks such items as

doors, mantels, random-width flooring, beams, paneling, complete room ends, wainscoting, moldings, fencing, brick, granite, cupboards, staircases, and complete entranceways. Several items from the company's continually changing inventory are illustrated.

North Fields makes weekly

deliveries to locations in Massachusetts, New Jersey, Connecticut, and Long Island. The company will also arrange motor freight shipments to other areas.

North Fields Restorations
Box 741
Rowley, MA 01969
(617) 948-2722

Ohmega Salvage

Poke around in the yard at Ohmega Salvage and you'll turn up an eclectic selection of rebuilt kitchen fixtures, marble mantels, Peerless, Hajoca, and John Douglas toilets, among other treasures. Ohmega takes special pride in its antique and contemporary stained and beveled glass doors, which the firm repairs, restores, or reproduces to order.

Ohmega Salvage
2407 San Pablo Ave., Box 2125
Berkeley, CA 94702
(415) 843-7368

Pelnik Wrecking

A doomed building may seem an unlikely candy shop, but for sixty years Pelnik Wrecking has been salvaging "all the goodies" from buildings slated for demolition. Pelnik's has amassed a phenomenal collection of mantels, sinks, corbels, railings, heart pine timbers, and more. Especially choice are windows—beveled, etched, and stained glass. This slender window of zipper-cut beveled glass is a valuable prize of architectural salvage. Lodge a specific request for photographs and see what Pelnik's offers you from its trove.

Pelnik Wrecking Co., Inc.
1749 Erie Blvd. E.
Syracuse, NY 13210
(315) 472-1031

PHOTOGRAPHY BY JULES

Queen City Architectural Salvage

Doors, mantels, and hardware are among the major categories regularly stocked by Queen City, a leading Rocky Mountain states dealer in architectural salvage. In business for over twelve years, Tom Sundheim is confident that he can provide almost any kind of object or service required for a restoration project.

Flyer available.

Queen City Architectural Salvage
4750 Brighton Blvd.
Denver, CO 80216
(303) 296-0925

Tullibardine Enterprises

Unlike many dealers in architectural salvage, John Molholm of Tullibardine handles *only* antique building materials. Reproductions, however good, he leaves to others. And he is an expert at finding just the right thing—from floor joists to a square nail.

In the process of salvaging building materials, Molholm tries to research the history of the building as much as possible; everything is photographed. In

the coming year he will be dismantling three Federal brick houses, one of which has a handsome cherry staircase.

As the illustrations show, a wide variety of building materials is presently available. Shown are two Ohio black walnut four-panel doors with original hardware. These date from the mid-1800s. The second photograph is of sandstone foundation stones from a barn in Licking County, Ohio, c. 1850.

Tullibardine is also a good source of handmade bricks, mantels, hand-hewn beams, and staircases. And if anyone is interested in a

complete barn, log cabin, or old house, each can be supplied when available.

Call or write for specific items.

Brochure, $3.25

Tullibardine Enterprises
5900 Dublin Rd.
Dublin, OH 43017
(614) 889-6307

United House Wrecking

Several generations of New York-area residents have explored the grounds of the famous United House Wrecking company. The grandfather of architectural salvage dealers, United House has recently moved into new quarters in Stamford, Connecticut. It is a 30,000 square-foot building stocked with just the kind of objects that will inspire old-house owners as well as designers, architects and contractors.

Marble and wood mantels, doors, windows, hardware, lighting and plumbing fixtures, wood ornamentation, outdoor statuary, furniture, and accessories—all are to be found at United House in a wide variety of styles and ages. Gazebos and iron fencing and gates are also part of the inventory.

General literature available.

United House Wrecking
535 Hope St.
Stamford, CT 06906
(203) 348-5371

Urban Archaeology

Some say the Parisian department store Au Bon Marché was the apogee of Art Deco. Decide for yourself by visiting the complete circa 1920 interior, preserved at Urban Archaeology. The grand staircase, bronze balconies, leaded-glass skylights, plaster moldings, and copper railings are typical of the items available from this firm. The unusual showroom and four warehouses contain Art Deco, Art Nouveau, and Victorian relics, as well as antique slot machines, barber shops, and ice cream parlors. Urban Archaeology can replicate some items if your demands exceed what is available. The firm employs an excellent mold maker and carver for just this purpose. Make your request, or visit New York City and Urban Archaeology directly.

Urban Archaeology
137 Spring St.
New York, NY 10012
(212) 431-6969

Wrecking Bar

Based on a commitment to rescue the past for the future, Atlanta's Wrecking Bar has one of the country's largest collections of authentic architectural elements from both domestic and foreign sources. Created solely to supply restoration and preservation materials, the company offers wood carvings, American and European statuary, wrought-iron objects, lighting fixtures, brass and copper hardware, and beveled, stained, and etched glass.

Obviously no literature can provide up-to-date information on this huge and constantly changing inventory, but details and photographs can be supplied of requested items that are in stock. The Wrecking Bar also offers extensive restoration, design, and installation services for the customer wishing to make use of various types of architectural elements.

The Wrecking Bar
292 Moreland Ave., N.E.
Atlanta, GA 30307
(404) 525-0468

Brick and Stone; Roofing Materials

Locating supplies of the type of masonry material originally used in an older building is a task requiring considerable patience. Whether your aim is to patch up a small area, restore a whole expanse of wall, or add a complementary addition, you will have to seek out the specialty dealer or producer. Architectural antiques suppliers sometimes carry an inventory of old brick; salvage yards are another good source. Manufacturers of old-style brick may be able to help you if you forward a sample to them. Stone is somewhat easier to come by, as most varieties popular in the past, such as brownstone, slate, marble, and granite, are still quarried today.

A good roofing material is indispensable for any old house, and its application must be carefully done. A leaking roof can cause no end of structural problems which may be extremely expensive to correct. Although a roofing material is often out of sight, it cannot be out of mind. This is especially true in the majority of North American regions where a roof is traditionally included to ward off the elements. Only in arid regions, such as the Southwest, where rainfall is slight and snow rare, are roofs traditionally flat. Many modern builders have learned to their regret that flat roofs collect rather than shed the elements. Why they couldn't figure this out in advance is puzzling. But, then, who ever said that modern builders have it over the old?

Aged Woods

It's very difficult to find good fieldstone today, except in the foundations of old farm buildings, so that's where Aged Woods goes to get it. Dismantling structures that cannot be used safely, the company salvages all the building materials that it can—including multicolored fieldstones which can be used for facing surfaces, fireplaces, interior walls, and some floors. Aged Woods also sells blue-gray Peach Bottom slate for roofs or walls.

Brochure available.

Aged Woods
RD 3, Box 80
Delta, PA 17314
(800) 233-9307

Blue Ridge Shingle

Blue Ridge Shingle explains that unfinished shingles, known as "shakes", will soon deteriorate. Choose hard, durable white oak shingles that weather to a silvery gray. Blue Ridge issues three grades of these recommended shingles, differing in texture and percentage of heartwood in their

composition but each an investment in the weatherproofing of your old house.

Brochure available.

Blue Ridge Shingle Co.
Montebello, VA 24464
(703) 377-6635 or
(919) 395-5333

C. & H. Roofing

Country Cottage is the descriptive trade name given the unusual curved roof developed by C. & H.

Roofing. It is not the thatched roof of Europe, but one that makes use of an all-American product, Western red cedar. The shingles are steamed and bent to fit the shape of the roof's frame.

The shingles can be applied in a random pattern or in several carefully designed, waved styles. As in the photograph, the shingles may envelop eyebrow dormers, vents, gables, and eaves.

C. & H. offers a variety of color schemes for the shingles, each of which is stained with a preservative available in various colors. Installation, the company claims, is not as difficult as it might seem and involves only conventional roofing procedures and simple additions to any existing frame.

The firm offers on-site consultation, a free estimate, and a drawing of how the customer's house would look with a Cottage Country roof. For each project under contract, C. & H. provides roof framing drawings and other specifications.

Catalogue, $10.

C. & H. Roofing, Inc.
1305 E. 39th St. N.
Sioux Falls, SD 57104
(800) 327-8115
(605) 332-5060 (SD)

Cedar Valley

Cedar Valley's first priority is effectiveness; this company knows that the most important aspect of roofing is to function well. That doesn't mean, however, that Cedar Valley has neglected aesthetics; on the contrary, the

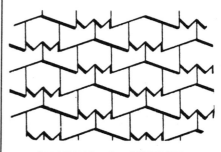

DIAGONALS & SAWTOOTH

company produces a line of decorative cut shingles that are as attractive as any wood shingles you'll find. Made of western red cedar, they can be coated with a

ROUNDS, SAWTOOTH & OCTAGONS

clear stain, painted with oil-base or acrylic paints, or left to weather to a natural gray. They are sold in boxes of about 100 pieces, but they are also available in two-

ROUNDS & ARROWS

course panels with a maximum exposure of 7½". Cedar Valley suggests combining different shingle

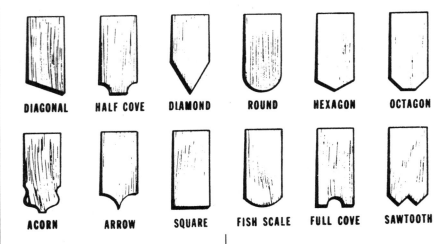

DIAGONAL HALF COVE DIAMOND ROUND HEXAGON OCTAGON

ACORN ARROW SQUARE FISH SCALE FULL COVE SAWTOOTH

types to create unusual designs; a few examples are shown here.

Literature available.

Cedar Valley Shingle Systems
985 S. 6th St.
San Jose, CA 95112
(408) 998-8550

Cushwa

For five generations the Cushwa family has lead one of the foremost brickmaking firms in the United States, and the company's product has been featured in many foreign buildings as well. The distinctive bricks they manufacture are known by the trade name of Calvert Colonials.

Cushwa produces three basic types or brick—hand-molded facing, machine-molded facing, and paving brick. There is a large variety of colors and stock shapes in all three categories. The most frequently used brick for restoration projects, the hand-molded, is available in rose, birch, dark red, provincial brown, Virginia, Ole' Maryland, and medium red

shades. This brick is made in only one size—4″ by 2¾″ by 8½″. Machine-molded bricks are available in three sizes—3⅝″ by 2¼″ by 8″ (standard), 3⅝″ by 2¼″ by 7⅝″ (modular), and 3⅝″ by 2¾″ by 8″ (oversize). The colors available are red, rose red, medium brown, Tiber Island, dark red, pastel rose, medium red, provincial brown, rose, and terra blend.

Cushwa fashions arches and surrounds for decorative purposes. Two examples of the company's standard surround combinations are illustrated. The B-4IN and B-4 combine to create a slightly rounded edge while the J-2 and J-2X together give a more angular feeling to the same opening. Cushwa will also make custom

brick from detailed drawings in a variety of shapes, sizes, and colors.

When antique brick is not available for paving purposes, Cushwa can supply the need. There are two colors available in pavers—rose and medium red. And there are three sizes: 3⅝″ by 2¼″ by 7⅝″ (modular), 3⅝″ by 1⅚″ by 7⅝″ (Baby Roman), and 8″ by 2¼″ by 8″ (Dutch).

Catalogue, $2.

Victor Cushwa & Sons, Inc.
PO Box 160
Williamsport, MD 21795
(301) 223-7700

Glen-Gery

If it's made of brick, Glen-Gery is likely to have it; if the company doesn't have it, it will probably make it. For nearly 100 years, Glen-Gery has been making bricks, so it's not surprising that it manufactures the basics very well. Its machine-made, sand-molded

bricks are among the finest available and come in a multitude of sizes, colors, and textures

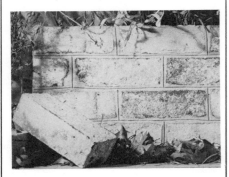

suitable for traditional homes. What's special about Glen-Gery, however, is that it doesn't simply make fine standard bricks. It also makes handmade bricks formed

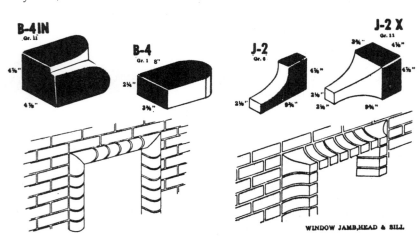

B-4IN
Gr. 11

B-4
Gr. 1 8″

J-2
Gr. 6

J-2X
Gr. 11

WINDOW JAMB,HEAD & SILL

in wooden molds, each unlike any other. Measuring 2¾" high by 4" wide by 8½" long or 2¼" high by 3⅝" wide by 7⅝" long, and thus larger than standard bricks, they are available in a rainbow of reds, burgundies, tans, browns, whites, buffs, and pinks.

Glen-Gery also offers a design and technical assistance service which enables you to consult with an engineer. Finally, for solving design problems, adding interest to a surface, or re-creating traditional detailing, the company offers a large selection of molded and extruded brick shapes. Wall caps, coping, bullnoses, watertable, sills, corners, step treads, and arches are among the standard shapes, and the company will execute custom designs on request.

Literature available.

Glen-Gery has branches in several mid-Atlantic, northeastern, and midwestern states. For further information or to locate the branch nearest you, contact:

Glen-Gery Corp.
Rte. 61, PO Box 340
Shoemakersville, PA 19555
(215) 562-3076

Mad River Woodworks

Why think of your house's roof as merely a device for keeping out the rain? Properly covered, it can be a festive decoration as well as a durable shelter. Mad River's attractive redwood shingles can help your roof contribute to your

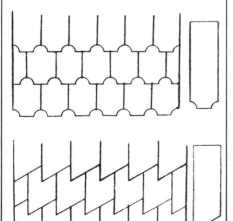

home's appearance of authenticity; such shingles have been protecting homes in California for over 100 years. A number of shingles, measuring either 5" or 6" in length, are available in several styles, including hexagons,

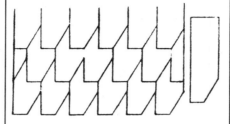

diamonds, and octagons. The indented Halfcove, sharp Diamond, and unusual Sawtooth versions are shown here.

Catalogue, $2.

Mad River Woodworks
Box 163
Arcata, CA 95521
(707) 826-0629

Mister Slate

Chuck Smid, known from coast to coast as Mr. Slate, has been working with reclaimed Vermont slate since 1974, providing inventory for roofers and restorers throughout the U.S. The company's roofing slate is very durable and attractive. It is offered in black, greens, purples, grays, and even hard-to-find reds. Long-lasting, the slate tiles are available in any sizes and can be trimmed in diamond, octagonal, scallop, and other shapes for more ornamental roofing.

Smid, who can supply new slate as well, does custom cutting and color-matching on request.

Literature available.

Mister Slate
Smid, Inc.
Sudbury, VT 05733
(802) 247-8809

New York Marble Works

The veins of impurities that render marble so delicate are, ironically, the source of striking colors that recommend its use in protected indoor spaces. Hues of red, black, green, and gold,

polished to a high sheen, are rare luxuries for tabletops, pedestals, and floors. New York Marble Works offers marble and granite in over 400 colors, in tile sizes ranging from 6" by 6" to 20" by 20". Custom designs, restoration (often using color-matched epoxies), and replacement for everything from fireplaces and furniture to handsome marble floors issue unrivaled from the inventory of this firm.

Brochure available.

New York Marble Works, Inc.
1399 Park Ave.
New York, NY 10029
(212) 534-2242

W. F. Norman

Galvanized steel or solid copper, Norman's shingles and tiles are back in production. This company began manufacturing roofs in 1908. Many of the very first roofs still exist, attesting to the supreme durability of Norman's functional, elegant product. Resilient and practical, these roofs withstand hail and fire, winter and broiling summer weather. Spanish and Mission tiles maintain their

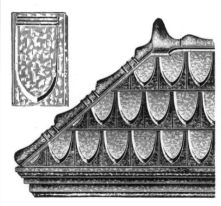

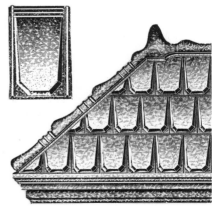

popularity, and Victorian and slate-like Normandie shingles enjoy a healthy following as well.

Brochure available.

W. F. Norman Corp.
Box 323
214-32 N. Cedar St.
Nevada, MO 64772-0323
(800) 641-4038

Missouri customers, call collect:
(417) 667-5552

Rising and Nelson

For more than a century, Rising and Nelson has been producing colored slate from its Vermont quarries. The slate's density, fire and water resistance, low maintenance cost, and ability to be installed over other roofing materials make it effective and practical. Its various colors, including black, gray, sea green, dark emerald, dark reddish purple, and red, make it a wise choice from an aesthetic standpoint as well. Some of the colors soften or acquire a brown or buff patina with age, and others remain unchanged by exposure to the elements. Lengths run from 10" to 24" in 2" increments; widths are random. Two textures are available. The smooth slate ranges from ³⁄₁₆" to ¼" in thickness, and the rough slate from ³⁄₁₆" to 1". If you wish, Rising and Nelson will make use of its capable design service to help you plan your roof.

Literature available.

Rising and Nelson Slate Co., Inc.
West Pawlet, VT 05775
(802) 645-0150

Superior Clay

For superior structural protection, top walls with coping formed from vitrified clay. Unfazed by harsh weather, the tough clay surface pieces from Superior Clay sport special features such as grooved tail inserts that guarantee tight bonds between pieces. Reinforcing drop sides also cleave to mortar in waterproof joints. Single slant, double slant, streamline,

and camelback styles provide the variety to suit any architectural style.

Brochure available.

Superior Clay Corp.
Box 352
Uhrichsville, OH 44683
(800) 848-6166

Terra Cotta Productions

The decades around the turn of the century were the heyday of terra-cotta construction. Authentic and economical restoration of historic structures from that era is now possible with help from Terra Cotta Productions. Experts in ceramic design, backed by thorough historic research and mass production capabilities, Terra Cotta Productions manufactures strong, solid terra cotta with

buff clay from its own clay mine. The plant capacity of Superior Clay Corporation, representing half a century's experience, allows production of custom terra cotta, matched to originals by size, color, and design, as well as stock architectural tile. Terra cotta cleans easily, and proper maintenance renders it proof against fire, natural elements, and pollution for centuries. Terra Cotta Productions assesses what each job will require by using photographs, sketches, measurements of pieces needed, and a sample of the original terra cotta for analysis.

For further information, contact:

Terra Cotta Productions, Inc.
Box 99781
Pittsburgh, PA 15233
(412) 321-2109

Ceilings

Ceilings in most period rooms are fairly simple. They may contain a center medallion or rosette but little else. Nineteenth-century Americans often attempted to spice up overhead space with special printed papers. This was an inexpensive way to make up for the lack of plasterwork or carved ornament. Another way of decorating the ceiling was to use composition or plaster borders and corners along with a center medallion.

In the late 1800s metal ceilings became quite popular for commercial spaces. They were decorative and inexpensive. Fortunately, they have been rediscovered; unfortunately, they have been overused in theme-park-like restaurants. A metal ceiling might be used in the kitchen of a private home or in an urban railroad flat, but the historical precedent for much residential use is difficult to document.

AA-Abbingdon Affiliates

Compared with the fanciful metal ceilings of the late 19th century, today's ceilings seem unbearably

dull. AA-Abbingdon's Prestplate metal ceilings were designed to reproduce the interesting lighting effects of those older surfaces. Over twenty styles, all sold in 2' by 8' sheets, feature pineapples, bold sharp lines, delicate beading, classical motifs, geometric designs, and intricate floral patterns. It's easy to find something you like. Ten cornice patterns increase the variety of this company's stock. The ceilings can be finished with any oil-base paint, clear lacquer, or polyurethane.

Brochure available.

AA-Abbingdon Affiliates Inc.
2149-51 Utica Ave.
Brooklyn, NY 11234
(718) 258-8333

In Canada, AA-Abbingdon's products can be obtained from:

The Architectural Antique Warehouse
1583 Bank St.
Ottawa, Ontario, Canada K1H 7Z3
(613) 526-1818

Chelsea Decorative Metal

Chelsea has recently introduced three new designs to its line of pressed tin ceilings. Each design is impeccably Victorian. The top design (#707) is a cornice molding, 7½" wide by 4'. The other two designs are available in 2' x 4' sheets, as are remaining Chelsea patterns. At left is a 6" multiple plate (#202) and, at right, a 24" multiple plate (#524).

Chelsea asserts that its electroplytic tin plate is more rust resistant, fire retardant, and retentive of paint than many other metal types.

Installation instructions are included with every order—for use by the homeowner or contractor. The panels are lightweight but they are also somewhat difficult to handle. If a homeowner is going to choose between a drop acoustical ceiling or a period metal one, there is no question but that the extra effort is well worth the investment in time.

Catalogue, $1.

Chelsea Decorative Metal Co.
9603 Moonlight
Houston, TX 77096
(713) 721-9200

Heart-Wood

Wainscotted ceilings became popular in the late 1800s for kitchens and pantries. Composed of tongue-and-groove wooden slats, these ceilings were an inexpensive alternative to the use of plaster. This type of ceiling has held up well over the years. It can be cleaned easily, effectively absorbs sound, and is aesthetically pleasing. Often the same type of wainscotting was used on the walls of a kitchen or pantry.

Heart-Wood is one supplier that specializes in wood for wainscotted or beaded ceilings. The principal wood offered is Southern yellow heart pine although heart cypress and Southern red cherry are also available. The cypress would be as appropriate as the pine; the cherry would be rather expensive to use overhead.

Most of the lumber has been salvaged or recycled and is now stored in Heart-Wood's Florida warehouse. With shipping charges being relatively low, it may make sense to buy from the company directly rather than trying to find an equivalent stock closer to home.

Brochure available.

Heart-Wood, Inc.
Rte. 1, Box 97-A
Jasper, FL 32052
(904) 792-1688

W. F. Norman

Popular with today's designers and builders, decorative pressed metal ceilings are also appropriate for some period rooms. These ceilings are lightweight, fire-resistant, reasonable in price, and they also serve as attractive and effective covering for fatally cracked and damaged plaster.

W. F. Norman has been stamping out decorative metal ceiling panels since the late 1800s. The company has revived an extensive collection of patterns ranging from late Victorian to Art Deco. The main panels are 2' x 4' or smaller; borders, fillers, moldings, center medallions, cornice pieces, and wainscotting are available as well to add to the flavor of any composition.

Brochure available.

W. F. Norman Corp.
Box 323, 214-32 N. Cedar St.
Nevada, MO 64772-0323
(800) 641-4038
Missouri customers, call collect:
(417) 667-5552

Doors and Windows

Finding a good door can be as difficult as finding a good man to hang it proper-ly. There are aluminum exterior doors with a baked finish that look all right but pull right away from their frames in a year or two; there are hollow interior wood doors which are light as a feather to handle but won't stay shut for very long. We've tried lots of doors, inside and out, and we're ready to settle for a good, solid wood door—as thick as possible. The same goes for screen and storm doors. Since they are particularly exposed to the elements, it is important that they be well made. Aluminum or vinyl may be easy to put up and take down but until these materials are proven to take more than a few years wear and tear, we'll stick with properly treated wood, thank you.

Windows are like doors. They are never easy to handle. In hot weather they stick and in cold they leak. Windows that are properly framed, that have sash with panes that are well puttied, and that are provided with suitable hardware shouldn't stick and won't leak. But they still do both. We don't know any solu-tion to the problem. We do know we'd just as soon have handsome, solidly built windows that add character to the house. Most old houses don't look right with modern sash. There are lots of suppliers who will help you to maintain the old image in good shape.

Anderson Pulley Seal

It's frustrating to know that heat is seeping from your house. You know that you're paying more than you should to warm your home, and there's nothing you can do about it. Anderson Pulley Seal, however, has invented an in-expensive way to save quite a bit of money. The company's little white or brown seals fit quickly and easily over the pulleys in old windows, covering the slots and reducing heat loss by as much as thirty-five percent. When properly caulked, weatherstripped, and sealed with Anderson's products, your old windows will be as energy-efficient as good-quality new windows.

Brochure available.

Anderson Pulley Seal
920 W. 53rd St.
Minneapolis, MN 55419
(612) 827-1117

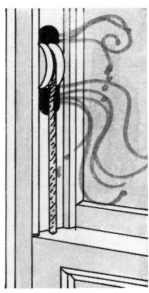

Architectural Components

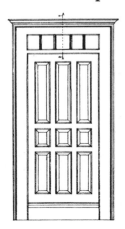

Workmanship of the 18th and 19th centuries may be inimitable, but it's not necessarily any less painstaking than museum-quality contemporary work by Architec-tural Components. Using con-struction techniques based on research into Georgian, Federal,

and Revival styles, the firm pro-duces sturdy doors which come in double thicknesses or insulated designs. Cut from eastern white pine, pieces are milled and dried,

mortise and tenon joined, and held with square pegs. In addi-tion to its doors, Architecural

Components stocks plank window frames, small pane window sash, and moldings styled after Connecticut Valley originals. Custom work includes French doors, paneled items, sash, and cameo, casement, or fanlight windows. Contact Architectural Components with your specific requests.

Brochure, $3.

Architectural Components
Box 249
Leverett, MA 01054
(413) 367-9441

Beech River Mill

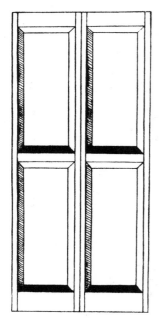

Founded in 1856, the Beech River Mill still uses genuine water-powered, Victorian mortisers, planers, and an antique rabbeting and beading machine. Custom

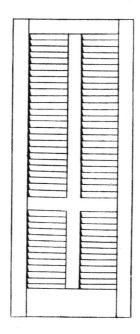

sized, the wooden doors that Beech River Mill turns out are of unquestionably high quality. A folding door shows an upper section of narrow panels over a single raised panel at the bottom. The door may be 1⅛" or 1⅜"

thick, and the cross rail may be positioned at the height you specify. This four-panel louver door is also available with raised solid panels across the bottom. Clear, dry pine is the standard material, but Beech River Mill can use ash, cherry, cypress, mahogany, and oak as well.

Catalogue, $3.

Beech River Mill Co.
Old Route 16
Centre Ossipee, NH 03814
(603) 539-2636

Bright Star Woodworking

French doors are a specialty of Bright Star Woodworking. Happily, aluminum sliding glass doors are now out of fashion, thus enabling craftsmen such as Bright Star's Tim Kretzmann and Jay Redmond to make a good living. Their doors may be suitable for either new or old buildings.

The standard door is 1¾" thick and is made of red oak. There are also other woods available, including mahogany, white oak, cherry, walnut, redwood, Douglas fir, Philippine mahogany, pine, and poplar.

There are over a dozen different models to choose from. Bright Star will also execute other types of doors as well as almost any type of window.

Brochure available.

Bright Star Woodworking
14618 Tyler Foote Rd.
Nevada City, CA 95959
(916) 292-3514

Combination Door Co.

For all their Old-World appeal, vintage homes are usually none too energy efficient. Windows and doors will guarantee drafty chill in winter and steep bills for summer air conditioning, unless you turn to such firms as the Combination Door Company for help. Sound doors of solid ponderosa or sugar pine (wood doesn't conduct the chill) feature aluminum screen and tempered glass inserts in order to function as screen or storm doors. Each door is fitted

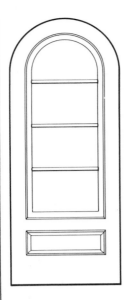

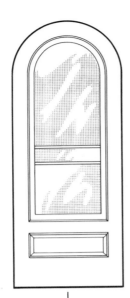

with an adjustable vinyl and aluminum sweep that nestles at the sill to keep heated or air-conditioned air from escaping. The Combination Door Company cuts every door from 1¹¹⁄₁₆″ thicknesses of clear, kiln-dried wood treated with preservative and water-repelling compounds. Use paint, or keep a natural finish as you wish. The circle-top door, shown with both sets of seasonal hardware, demonstrates the "Easy Change" system at work. Another door is shown with four panels of airy screen. Also shown are variations on a charismatic octagonal window, both equipped with ⅛″ thick tempered glass.

Brochure available.

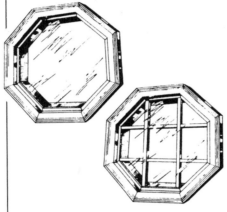

Combination Door Co.
Box 1076
Dept. OH
Fond du Lac, WI 54935
(414) 922-2050

rust. Styles include Victorian, Colonial, Mission, and many other period designs. Storm window inserts can equip the doors for foul weather, and Creative Openings can often match screen doors with solid doors, some with hand-beveled or stained glass.

Brochure available.

Creative Openings
Box 4204
Bellingham, WA 98227
(206) 671-6420

Dovetail Woodworking

Few things are more irritating than knowing what you want and being unable to find it. All too frequently, old house lovers encounter this sort of frustration when looking for doors and windows. The craftsmen who built houses 200, 100, or even 50 years ago brought individuality to their work; today, standardization has left sashless, doorless gaps in fine old structures. Dovetail Woodworking attempts to solve the problem by specializing in hard-to-find, irregular shapes and sizes. The company can reproduce almost any design, and it makes its sashes, storm windows, and doors from solid wood for efficient insulation and natural beauty.

Creative Openings

"Screeeek . . . . . . slam!" According to Creative Openings, that (and not the dry rattle of cheap aluminum) is the inimitable sound of an authentic hardwood screen door. From kiln-dried walnut, teak, mahogany, old growth Douglas fir, and ash, Creative Openings assembles and finishes each door by hand. Hand-turned spindles, a tradition from the 1880s, accent the doors with spokes of ebony, maple, cherry, purpleheart, and other woods. Hardware is brass, bronze, or chrome. Easily replaceable bronze insect screens accompany all doors and can accept protective coatings to resist

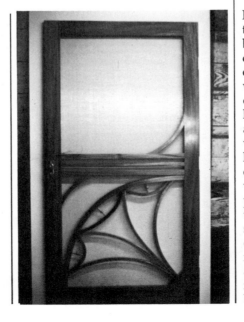

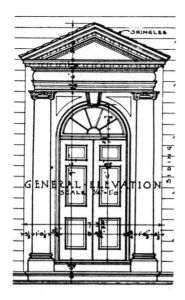

Brochure available.

Dovetail Woodworking
550 Elizabeth St.
Waukesha, WI 53186
(414) 544-5859

Eagle Plywood & Door

Eagle doors are built to last for years. They may be especially useful for commercial buildings where security can be a problem. These doors are not designed in a period style but are what are known as architectural doors. They range anywhere from $1\frac{3}{8}$" to 3" in thickness. With the addition of a veneer—available through Eagle's subsidiary, Artistry in Veneers—a sturdy, conventional door can be transformed.

Eagle is prepared to fulfill any specification—from the selection of a veneer to the final completion of the project. Information on Eagle doors is available through architects, contractors, and wood-workers, or from the company.

Eagle Plywood & Door
Manufacturing, Inc.
450 Oak Tree Ave.
South Plainfield, NJ 07080
(201) 668-1460

Entrances

Doors and windows from Entrances, Inc., display the uncommon intelligence and skill of their designers. These are modern pieces insulated in the most effective way possible but built in a traditional manner. The principal product offered is the Warm Door, a corner cross section of which is illustrated. It is a practical sandwich of foil-faced urethane with a plastic vapor barrier over which sheathing of knotty pine, clear pine, clear cedar, or redwood is applied. All of this is encased in a frame of clear red oak. The door is then pre-hung in a solid wood $\frac{1}{4}$" thick single rabbeted frame and sealed with foam weather-stripping.

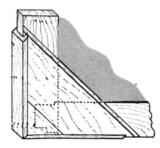

The design of the standard Warm Door incorporates vertical boards. There are other designs, however, which make use of horizontal or herringbone pattern sheathing. Standard windows are individual lights of safety glass glazed by hand with a beveled wood strip. Entrances, Inc., also has its own leaded glass workshop where opaque, clear, or opalescent stained glass windows are made for doors and sidelights. The company will also supply hand-blown bull's-eye glass for doors or transoms.

Unlike most door manufacturers, Entrances, Inc., makes use of hand-forged hardware that is suitable for a well-crafted door. Four different latch sets are supplied by blacksmith Richard Sargent; Sargent will also supply a dead bolt and heavy strap hinges.

Entrances, Inc., is also a good supplier of French doors, screen doors, and two types of storm doors. The storm door is not necessary for a Warm Door but may be a useful addition in other situations. Illustrated is a handsome 12-light storm door. The $2\frac{1}{2}$ board storm door is a Colonial design made from rough sawn pine boards that range up to 18"

wide. All of these specialty doors have mortise and tenon frames.

Standard widths and heights for the Warm Doors and most of the other doors range from 2'6" by 6'6" to 3'0" by 6'8".

Brochure available.

Entrances, Inc.
RFD 1, Box 246A
Westmoreland, NH 03467
(603) 399-7723

Fypon

Fypon's "entrance systems" showcase the company's exceptional Molded Millwork, a dense polymer that you can work with drills, nails, or field carpenter tools. Don't worry about warping or rotting—and insects can't harm Molded Millwork, either. Different crossheads, or Peaked, Ram's Head, Acorn, or Sunburst pediments crown openings that

vary by several feet within different styles of entrances. Pilasters trim to the desired height, and the entire system is easily installed. A creamy barrier coating takes oil-base primer and top coats, and the completed system requires very little upkeep. Other Molded Millwork items include custom bay and bow window roofs, window heads, door trim, moldings, and brackets.

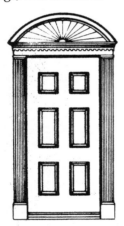

Catalogues and sample sections available.

Fypon, Inc.
22 W. Pennsylvania Ave.
Stewartstown, PA 17363
(717) 993-2593

Glass Arts

Best known for its wide selection of elaborate beveled-glass panels, Glass Arts also makes nine styles of handsome doors from solid Appalachian red oak. All measure 6'8" high by 3' wide by 1¾" thick and are designed to accommodate

single beveled panels or triple-glazed tempered glass. Mortise and tenon construction and oak pegging make the doors strong enough to be treasured by future generations. If red oak doesn't suit your needs, or if you'd like to match the design of another door in your house, Glass Arts will build a door to your specifications or execute its standard styles in oak, mahogany, walnut, or soft maple. Particle core veneer doors are also available for those who'd prefer to avoid the high cost of solid wood.

Catalogue available.

Glass Arts
30 Penniman Rd.
Boston (Allston), MA 02134
(617) 782-7760

Grand Era Reproductions

Screen and storm doors that will last for many seasons are standard products from Grand Era. A new firm, it has already proved its skill in design and production. All of the doors are crafted from kiln-dried select hardwood and not from lightweight pine, cypress, or fir. Frames are mortise and tenon joined for additional strength. Each of the standard models is 1⅛" thick and is shipped unfinished so that it can be painted or stained as the customer desires.

Many of Grand Era's doors incorporate Victorian spandrels, corner brackets, or decorative moldings. There are a few plain doors suitable for earlier style buildings.

Double doors are custom orders and Grand Era is prepared to execute them. The firm will also custom craft transom frames that will match any of its doors, complete with storm and screen inserts.

Standard door sizes are either 32" by 81" or 36" by 81". Delivery time is approximately two weeks from receipt of order.

Any old house owner with carpentry skills can arrange to order one of Grand Era's screen doors in kit form. All parts are precut and some are preassem-

bled. There is a savings of 20% off the assembled price.

Catalogue, $2 (refundable with purchase).

Grand Era Reproductions
PO Box 1026
Lapeer, MI 48446
(313) 664-1756

Historic Windows

Beauty, styling in the spirit of the 18th century, and the natural effectiveness of wood as an insulator make interior paneled shutters a wise choice. Historic Windows makes several designs to your size specifications, including the three-paneled Annapolis. The company recommends that it be used only on windows at least 48" high to maintain the shutter's classic proportions. Half and Dutch shutters are also available. Four half shutters are usually required for each window; eight Dutch sections are needed—four for the bottom and four for the top. Windows narrower than 26" may need only two or three half shutters or four to six Dutch shutters. All of Historic Windows' products are

nnapolis

available in white oak, rustic knotty oak, red oak, rustic knotty walnut, rustic knotty cherry, knotty pine, white oak, white maple, white birch, natural birch, pecan, and hickory. Wormy chestnut, clear walnut, and clear cherry are sometimes available. All shutters are ¾" thick. If you'd like to see a sample of a particular wood, a single raised panel measuring 8" by 12" is available for inspection. The price of the sample is refundable if it is returned within sixty days of the shipping date.

Half & Dutch

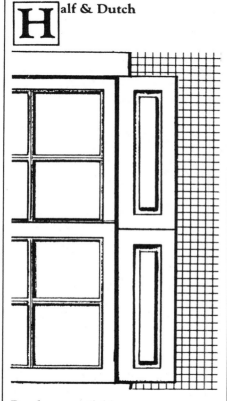

Brochure available.

Historic Windows
Box 1172
Harrisonburg, VA 22801
(703) 434-5855

Humberstone Woodworking

Humberstone offers different types of architectural components, including Colonial door entrances. Made of laminated pine, these are available in various heights and widths. The entrances are shipped in three pieces ready for nailing. The standard model is a broken pediment design.

Free brochure.

Humberstone Woodworking
PO Box 104
Georgetown, Ontario L7G 4T1
Canada
(416) 877-6757

The Joinery Company

Authenticity is paramount in the manufacture of The Joinery Company's six-panel heart pine doors. Like the antique originals, these doors are hand pegged, raised on one side and flat on the other, and equipped with panels which are all made from the same plank. The panels are floating to help prevent splitting or fracturing due to the gain or loss of moisture. They are positioned in such a way as to reveal symmetrical, aligned graining. A choice of hand-planed or sanded surfaces is available. The Joinery Company also makes fine board-and-batten heart pine doors.

Brochure, $5.

The Joinery Co.
Box 518
Tarboro, NC 27886
(919) 823-3306

KU/2 Specialties

Marc Coutu claims to "own and operate what just may be the smallest sash building company in the world." In this case, small is beautiful. He makes only historically accurate, true divide wood sash with insulated glass for both residential and commercial uses.

Coutu is prepared to provide sash only, glazed sash, or sash glazed and primed. Sizes range from as small as 1" to huge units.

One of his most recent commercial projects for a company located in a Massachusetts historic district is illustrated.

If requested, Coutu will also build pre-hung window units, storm panels, and exterior shutters.

Brochure available.

KU/2 Specialties, Marc Coutu
Box 618
Munsonville, NH 03457
(603) 847-9749

Kenmore Industries

Kenmore owes its excellent reputation to superb doorways like the ones described here. Model 510 has cast leaded paterae at the joints, an elliptical leaded fanlight, carved capitals and pilasters, and a closed triangular pediment. Model 610 is an Adam-style entrance using a carved, draped frame with a choice of four half rounds and leaded sidelights surrounded by columns

with carved capitals. Kenmore is in the process of adding several new designs to its line, including

a doorway with a pineapple motif and carved bolection molding and two broken-pediment doorways with horizontal leaded glass in a choice of sunburst or gothic styles.

Brochure, $3.

Kenmore Industries
Box 34, One Thompson Sq.
Boston, MA 02129
(617) 242-1711

Mad River Woodworks

Delicate white stencilwork or ornamental gingerbread woodwork turns Mad River's screen doors into decorative treasures. The company has reproduced four designs that were popular in the 1860s and manufactures them using double-doweled corner joints and knives ground especially for the cutting of the framework parts. All doors are built to your specifications, and a charcoal-gray aluminum screen is included. Plexiglass can be easily installed to make an all-weather storm door. To enable you to match the door to your exterior color scheme, it is left unfinished, ready for the paint or stain of your choice.

Catalogue, $2.

Mad River Woodworks
Box 163
Arcata, CA 95521
(707) 826-0629

Marvin Windows

Windows and doors made by this nationally known manufacturer are used in thousands of homes, new and restored. Marvin gained its reputation because of consistently good design and quality. All of the windows are made of solid Ponderosa pine with either insulated glass or what is termed Low E glass combined with Argon gas.

The Retro patio door is typical of the traditional-appearing units

made by Marvin. It is difficult to visualize a sliding door as being "authentic," but Marvin comes as close as any manufacturer to achieving this effect. If the bar handle were eliminated and replaced with more classic hardware, the unit would be a most appropriate substitute for aluminum, single-panel sliding doors.

Marvin Windows has distributors throughout North America. For information regarding all of the company's special designs and sizes, contact the firm.

Literature available.

Marvin Windows
PO Box 100
Warroad, MN 56763
(800) 346-5128
(800) 552-1167 (MN)

Materials Unlimited

This firm offers both new and antique building materials and serves as a distributor of a number of national door manufacturers. Especially interesting is a line of interior doors in cedar, knotty pine, or oak. The doors are available in $1\frac{3}{8}$", $1\frac{3}{4}$", or 2" thickness. There are a dozen models in what is termed the Standard Series and they are offered in one basic height—80"—and fourteen widths ranging from 1' to 3'.

Materials Unlimited is also the distributor of a line of bifold doors which is complementary to the simple interior door series. The same materials are available. One thickness—$1\frac{3}{8}$"—is offered. The height is 80" and the width of these four-hinged models can be 24", 30", 32", or 36".

Exterior doors available through Materials Unlimited embrace several types. There are mahogany designs featuring beveled glass ovals from Architectural Antiques West, arched doors made by Caoba in red oak or mahogany appropriate for Spanish Colonial houses, and carved door and sidelight designs from International Wood Products.

Package of reproduction products literature, $8.

Materials Unlimited
2 W. Michigan Ave.
Ypsilanti, MI 48197
(313) 483-6980

Maurer and Shepherd Joyners

An entranceway can enhance or destroy a home's period look. It naturally draws the eye, and it must withstand more scrutiny than most other parts of a house's exterior. Maurer and Shepherd's entranceways prove more than a match for close examination. The one illustrated here is a splendid example of the company's work. All surfaces are hand-planed; all joints are mortise and tenon, held together by wooden pegs. Maurer and Shepherd also makes mantels, wainscoting, flooring, shutters, window sashes, window frames, and $^{15}/_{16}$"-thick interior doors in any panel configuration desired. All work is custom-made and done by hand.

Brochure available.

Maurer and Shepherd Joyners, Inc.
122 Naubuc Ave.
Glastonbury, CT 06033
(203) 633-2383

Midwest Wood Products

Midwest Wood's restoration projects include rebuilding paneled doors, porch windows, and screens. Attention to historic detail is a prime goal, and, with that priority in mind, Midwest Wood qualifies as a superb source for authentic window sash, an important element in recreating a period façade.

Send SASE for brochure.

Midwest Wood Products
1051 S. Rolff St.
Davenport, IA 52802
(319) 323-4757

North Pacific Joinery

This manufacturer of fine millwork offers a handsome line of windows and doors. The double-hung windows of solid all-heart redwood employ full mortise and tenon joinery. They can be milled to any size and have the strength and traditional lines appropriate for many older buildings. Hardware and insulated glass are standard and each unit is pre-hung in a solid redwood frame ready for installation. Matching interior trim, including two bull's-eye corner blocks, is optional.

Specialty windows include old-fashioned casement pairs with solid brass hardware; octagonal, circular, and triangular windows; and multi-light, sidelight, and sunburst combinations. All of these models are pre-hung in solid redwood frames.

Doors also run the gamut from the traditional solid paneled to complete entrance systems. Doors are generally available in oak, mahogany, redwood, or fir. Each is pre-hung in a matched jamb and fitted with the customer's choice of hardware. Specialty glass—stained, etched, beveled leaded, and glue ship—is available for many of the interior and exterior models. North Pacific will also custom mill and assemble sliding, French, and bifold doors.

Literature available.

North Pacific Joinery
76 W. 4th St., Dept. OHC
Eureka, CA 95501
(707) 443-5788

Lumber

If you are searching for boards or beams or even a small heavy strip of wood to replace a threshold or door saddle, you probably won't find what you want at a local lumberyard or home center. The usual response to a question concerning the availability of something other than composition or the softest pine is that the better grade woods are simply not available any longer. That is not true. The truth is that the average building materials supplier makes his money from plywood, various types of composition board, and pine durable enough to frame a house. Consequently, specialty lumber dealers have established themselves throughout North America. All stock quantities of newly cut domestic and foreign timber such as quality white pine and oak, and many also keep a supply of recycled Southern heart pine. These dealers usually maintain an inventory of the more elegant woods used for interior work. If you need to have boards milled and finished in a particular manner, the specialty supplier probably can help.

Aged Woods

Few things are more appropriate to an old house than the time-enhanced beauty of old wood. Used for exposed beams, furniture, cabinets, doors, flooring, or paneling, old wood has a comfortable and solid look that's hard to match. Aged Woods offers several species salvaged from old buildings, inspected, treated for insects if necessary, and cleaned with water or steel brushing. Planks or beams are usually available in pine, oak, walnut, and rare American chestnut. Twenty-five-year-old cypress is also sold for use in damp areas. You can purchase samples of various woods if you like; the price will be refunded if you place an order.

Brochures available.

Aged Woods
RD 3, Box 80
Delta, PA 17314
(800) 233-9307

Carlisle Restoration Lumber

Carlisle is a source of wide-board lumber that you might have trouble locating near your home. Expertly milled square-edged pine ranges from 14" to 21" in width. It can be obtained with shiplapped edges in widths between 8" and 12" as well. Oak planks are milled in 5" to 10" widths. All three types of lumber range from 8' to 16' in length. Carlisle also sells pine feather-edge clapboards.

Literature available.

Carlisle Restoration Lumber
Rte. 123
Stoddard, NH 03464
(603) 446-3937

Cedar Valley

When it comes to shingle siding, the combination of easy installation and superb weather protection is hard to beat, and Cedar Valley's products excel in both categories. Two-course or three-course panels, attached to ⁵⁄₁₆"-thick plywood with special staples, make mounting the shingles simple and precise. The problem of uneven nailing is eliminated, and stress is better distributed. The placement of a 30/30/30 Kraft paper barrier between the shingles and the plywood eliminates the need for a separate sheet of building paper.

Cedar Valley's shingles are attractive as well as functional. They are made of western cedar, which weathers to a rustic gray; the staples are invisible, and there's little need for obtrusive face nailing. A patented system hides joints between panels, and you can choose the exposure length of the shingles. Standard lengths are 6", 7", 8", 12", and 14"; custom lengths may be specified.

Literature available.

Cedar Valley Shingle Systems
985 S. 6th St.
San Jose, CA 95112
(408) 998-8550

Conklin's

Leo Conklin salvages siding, hand-hewn beams, planks, and flooring from old barns in the Northeast. All of the timber has been trimmed and denailed so that it is ready for reuse.

Maintained at all times is anywhere from 50,000 to 100,000 square feet of barnwood in gray, gray silver, red, and brown gold. The material is pine or hemlock and is available in random lengths and widths. Flooring and plank lumber also varies in length and width and is of pine or hemlock.

The size of the beams varies, the best material being oak but with hemlock and pine also on hand. Conklin always has 8,000 to 10,000 running feet in stock.

Conklin's Authentic Antique Barn-
wood and Hand-Hewn Beams
RD 1, Box 70
Susquehanna, PA 18847
(717) 465-3832

Craftsman Lumber

Charles Thibeau's Craftsman Lumber has long been one of the most reliable suppliers of pine clapboards, Victorian wainscotting in pine or oak, and wide pine boards for paneling, flooring, and colonial wainscotting. The principal material offered is Eastern white pine or knotty pine, a common grade (classed #3 or better). Two better grade boards are also available: a #1 or #2 common finish board with smaller and few knots and a clear pine with only one or two knots.

Craftsman's pine boards for most uses range from 1' to 32" in width—much wider than the stock carried by many lumber dealers. The nominal thickness is 1″. Clear or knotty white pine clapboards can be supplied in any width and with any edge configuration, a beaded edge or Victorian scallop being two possibilities.

Craftsman, of course, is also a good supplier of pine or oak flooring, wainscotting, and custom moldings in pine, poplar, oak, walnut, cherry, mahogany and plain, curly, or bird's-eye maple.

Literature, $1.

Craftsman Lumber Co.
PO Box 222
Groton, MA 01450
(508) 448-6336

Diamond K.

Bill Krawski of Diamond K. is well known for his recycled building materials, in particular barn siding in various weathered shades, hand-hewn chestnut and pine beams, and old pine clapboards. Diamond K. also supplies new Canadian wide plank pine in widths of 1′ to over 20″ and in random lengths ranging from 6′ to 16′.

Deliveries can be made anywhere in the United States by motor freight.

Literature available.

Diamond K. Co., Inc.
130 Buckland Rd.
South Windsor, CT 06074
(203) 644-8486

Donnell's Clapboard Mill

A restored clapboard mill in Sedgwick, Maine, has given new life to old-fashioned methods of producing siding. The basic principles behind the production of clapboards have changed greatly in this century, but not at Donnell's. Radially-sawn boards known as "quarter-sawn" were produced until the early 1900s. In the colonial period they were hand sawn from a log with the growth rings running parallel to the board's length. These edge-grained clapboards would not

warp or twist, thus making for a flatter, tighter fit.

The 19th century witnessed the development of machinery to saw the logs in the same manner. It is thought that Donnell's mill is the only one ever built to take 8′ logs. All the machinery used there today is authentic.

Logs are first "rossed," or turned on a large lathe until a smooth dowel, 8′ long and at least 15″ in diameter is produced. This dowel is then stabilized at the center, on each end, and set over a blade. Each cut goes a little less than one-half of the way through the log. After the log is completely sawn in this manner, the boards are then detached from the core

of the log and piled to air dry. Later they are planed and cut to various lengths.

Eastern white pine is the material most frequently used by Donnell's. Pine has long been considered a much better wood for siding than spruce or hemlock. According to Donnell's, it is not unusual to find radially-sawn pine clapboards in excellent condition after two hundred years of exposure to the elements.

Two grades of boards are supplied—#1 premium clear, recommended for restorations and new buildings; and #2 New England Cape which is ideal for repair work and for small outbuildings or modest cottages. The

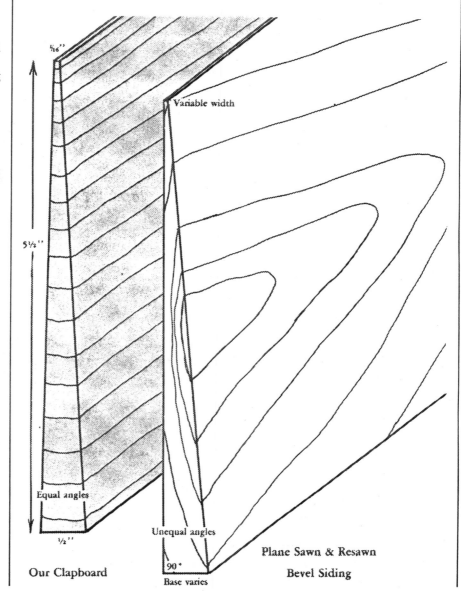

⁵⁄₁₆″

Variable width

5½″

Equal angles

½″

Unequal angles

90°

Base varies

Our Clapboard

Plane Sawn & Resawn
Bevel Siding

standard board size is 5½"; Donnell's, however, also produces 3½", 4½", and 6" clapboards by special order.

Brochure available.

Donnell's Clapboard Mill
County Rd., RR Box 1560
Sedgwick, ME 04676
(207) 359-2036

Goodwin Lumber

Southern longleaf yellow pine is the principal recycled wood available through this Florida firm. This is lumber that was timbered over 100 years ago. Goodwin saws the logs, kiln-dries them, and then planes and finishes the lumber at its own facility.

This special pine is used for flooring, paneling, and beams. The customer specifies the width and length needed. Goodwin also has a limited supply of Rosemary or curly heart pine on hand.

For exterior siding and decking, Goodwin recommends its red cypress, recycled heart cypress, or pecky heart cypress. These Southern-timbered woods were used in many Victorian homes and have a fine grain.

Brochure available.

Goodwin Lumber Co.
Rte. 2, Box 119-AA
Micanopy, FL 32667
(904) 373-WOOD

Granville Manufacturing

The last machine for manufacturing quartersawn clapboards was built in 1910. Only three mills still operate to produce these boards today. Granville, Vermont's mill has turned out clapboards since 1857, and many of them, even unpainted, still cover and protect New England homes. Quartersawn boards, each a tapered section reaching from the log's center to its surface (minus bark), result in straight grain for each board, while the easier "resawing" methods of manufacturing clapboards yield a warp-prone curved grain. Straight grain, furthermore, holds stains and paints better. Select from four widths of white and red spruce and white pine, in 2' to 6' lengths. Three grades are available: clear clapboard; boards with no more than one blemish or knot each; or the "cottage" grade, with a rustic look engendered by numerous knots and blemishes (guaranteed not to impair use).

Catalogue, $1.

Granville Manufacturing Co., Inc.
Rte. 100
Granville, VT 05747
(802) 767-4747

Mad River Woodworks

Mad River Woodworks has fallen in love with Victorian millwork—its ornate and fanciful style and its special grace. Work from these craftspeople will have you charmed, too. Of particular interest is Mad River's many styles of decorative siding. Majestic redwoods yield a naturally enduring

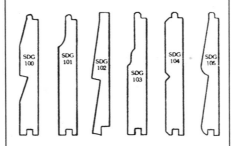

wood. Clear kiln-dried sections of this material, cut in various decorative patterns for distinctive and practical siding, take stain and paint or show to advantage in a natural finish.

Catalogue, $2.50.

Mad River Woodworks
Box 163
Arcata, CA 95521
(707) 826-0629

E. T. Moore, Jr.

Tongue-and-groove flooring, beams, treads, and risers are among the items available in Southern longleaf yellow pine from Moore. In the recycled lumber business for some time now, owner Taylor Moore mills only custom orders in his Richmond plant. He offers three grades. Select, 95-100 percent heart with small tight knots and small nail holes, is used primarily for cabinets and fine furniture. The most popular lumber is #1, 90-100 percent heart with sound knots about the half-dollar size and 5-10 percent nail-hole content. It is available in various sizes and thicknesses and is useful for flooring, paneling, and as beams. The lowest grade material, #2, is 30 percent heartwood and 70 percent sapwood. There is much color variation and the wood is very rustic in appearance.

Moore has also developed a line of stock moldings, chair rails and caps, hand rails, panel moldings, door and window casings, and wainscotting.

Literature available.

E. T. Moore, Jr., Co.
3100 N. Hopkins Rd., Suite 101
Richmond, VA 23224
(804) 231-1823

Mountain Lumber

Longleaf heart pine is Mountain Lumber's specialty. Retrieved from structures built before 1900, this fine wood can be used for floors, paneling, beams, doors, moldings, cabinets, and mantels. Rough-sawn boards and rough-sawn or hand-hewn beams are available, as well as stair treads and risers. Paneling comes in several types: ⁷/₁₆"-thick panels with flush shiplap joints and random lengths of 4" to 8"; ¾"-thick panels with tongue and groove flush joints and random lengths of 4" to 10" in what Mountain Lumber calls its "naily grade," and ¾"-thick panels in random lengths of either 4" to 8" or 4" to 10". The latter two sizes have tongue and groove construction with a choice of beaded or "V" joints. The company's president, William G. Drake, welcomes visits to the showroom, which is located five minutes from the Charlottesville airport. If you call ahead, someone will be glad to pick you up at the airport and drive you back afterward.

Brochure available.

Mountain Lumber Co.
Rte. 2, Box 43-1
Ruckersville, VA 22968
(804) 985-3646 or
(804) 295-1922

Oak Crest

Anyone considering the use of oak shakes or shingles should consult Oak Crest. This is a supplier that understands the history and use of white oak in American buildings for siding and roofing and appreciates how much more durable this material is than the commonly used cedar. Oak Crest guarantees its product for twenty years against any defects in workmanship and quality.

Oak Crest finds its hardwood in the forests of eastern Tennessee and uses only white or chestnut oak logs. The roofing shingles are available either split sawn or smooth sawn. There is a consistent thickness and grain structure to the shingles which makes installation much easier. Shakes are available in one form, are not tapered, and have a rough, rustic look. The wood for the shakes

comes only from the best portions of the large butt of a tree.

Oak Crest will tell every customer that shakes should be applied only when the moon is waning. Tradition has it that if they are applied when the moon is full, they will curl up. And, believe it or not, this has been found to be true.

Literature available; samples, $5.

Oak Crest Mfg., Inc.
1405 E. Emory Rd.
Knoxville, TN 37938
(615) 938-1315

Ramase

Hand-hewn beams, wall boards, random-width flooring, and weathered barn siding are just some of the building materials available from Ramase. Owner Harold Cole is also known for his large collection of 18th- and 19th-century mantels, window glass, old brick, hardware, and cupboards.

Cole is available by appointment only.

Harold Cole
Ramase
Rte. 47
Woodbury, CT 06798
(203) 263-3332 (office)
(203) 263-4909 (home)

Woods Co.

Owner and craftsman Barry Stup says it well: "The old wood business has graduated from weathered barn boards on the rec room wall." Quality recycled lumber is needed for more serious uses—room ends, flooring, staircases, and structurally as beams and joists. Stup finds oak, wormy chestnut, and longleaf heart pine in old barns, log houses, mills, and factories which have already crumbled or are due for demolition.

Heart pine is the principal material supplied and is offered in three grades ranging from the best clear, "Select," to the rustic, "Cabin." Illustrated is an installa-

tion of antique heart pine flooring and stair base supplied by Stup.

Woods can also provide such new woods as redwood, cedar, and poplar for various types of jobs. Most jobs, new or old, are milled to order.

Brochure and price list available.

Woods Co.
123 S. Main St.
Brownsville, MD 21715
(301) 432-8419

Stairways

A stairway can be the most dramatic element in a house: how many Hollywood movies feature a stairway scene, with the heroine descending into the arms of romance or danger? While a stairway must be sturdy, it should also have some flair—if not grandeur. Old house builders understood this and were not satisfied with constructing a straight up-and-down path. Nearly every old stairway curves gracefully at some point—top, bottom or middle. All of the suppliers (of complete staircases and of parts) in the following listings understand something of the charm of the well-wrought bridge between floors.

Dahlke Studios

Tom Dahlke's art demands he play the hybrid of sculptor-engineer. A custom designer and builder of curving wooden staircases, Dahlke came to stair design through Oakland's California College of Arts and Crafts, experience in sailboat maintenance that taught him laminating techniques for delicately curved wood, and a penchant for getting the best of tough design problems.

Dahlke delves deep with his research, and when he uncovers the suitable historical motifs, he uses them imaginatively in his work to produce pieces that cleave to the period without plagiarizing designs. Using laminations of wood slivered to thicknesses of $\frac{3}{32}$", Dahlke bends and glues dozens of layers, with a resulting curved piece that looks like a twist of solid wood. The staircase shown here bespeaks Tom Dahlke's talent and delivers a breathtaking effect in the house it graces.

Brochure, $2.

Dahlke Studios
Box 1128
Glastonbury, CT 06033
(203) 659-1887

H and M Stair Builders

This group of woodworkers, affiliated with The Fireplace Mantel Shop and distributors of Prebuilt Wood Stairs, builds several types of period staircases. Among the most attractive is the curved stair, C-1 model. This uses clear oak treads, risers, brackets, and railings. H and M also produces sets of box stairs.

This firm is also a good supplier of balusters, newel caps, oak landing tread, moldings, and various types of other fittings.

Literature available.

H and M Stair Builders, Inc.
4217 Howard Ave.
Kensington, MD 20895
(301) 564-1550

The Iron Shop

Perfect for tight spaces and simple in design, spiral staircases can often solve difficult problems. If you like the look of metal, take a look at The Iron Shop's easily assembled kit for a steel staircase with a vinyl handrail. All fasteners are included, and all parts are primed flat black. The Iron Shop even includes a spray can of the primer in case the finish is scratched during shipping. Available options include oak or embossed treads, an oak

handrail, fancy spindles, and assorted parts that give your staircase a custom look.

If you prefer the warmth of wood, however, the company's oak staircase kit may be to your liking. Made of beautifully grained, kiln-dried solid oak from Kentucky, Indiana, and Tennessee, it has 1¼"-thick treads supported by dovetailed gussets, a hollow central hub that measures 5" in diameter, and a 2½"-high by 1⅜" wide curved railing.

The metal staircase kit comes in eight sizes, ranging from 3' 6" to

7' in diameter; the oak staircase is available only in 4' and 5' sizes. Both kits are custom-built to meet your floor-to-floor height specifications.

Brochure, $1.

The Iron Shop
Dept. OHCF
Box 128, 400 Reed Rd.
Broomall, PA 19008
(215) 544-7100

The Joinery Company

The beauty of a solidly built wooden staircase can make an entrance hall a majestic sight, and for most 17th- and 18th-century homes, its authenticity is undeniable. The Joinery Company manufactures heart pine stair parts that will enable you to achieve a look that only fine materials and painstaking craftsmanship can bestow. At the Joinery Company, everything is manufactured by hand, and you'll find everything you need. Stair

treads are made of 1¼"-thick by 12" deep boards milled to 1" by 11" with nosing profiles, and they can be hand-planed or sanded, depending on your preference. Treads with vertical grain are also available. Risers, which may also have vertical graining, are made of 1" by 8" boards milled to ¾" by 7¾" with square-edged profiles.

The company also sells scotia molding for use between treads and risers, Georgian-style hand rails, turned or 1" square by 36"-high pickets, and newel posts. Two standard posts are made—Georgian, with a square post, raised panel cap, and ogee molding; and Deerfield, with a square base and hand-carved top. Turned newel posts are made on request. The Joinery Company invites visits to its showroom.

Brochure, $5.

The Joinery Co.
Box 518
Tarboro, NC 27886
(919) 823-3306

North Pacific Joinery

Known primarily as a manufacturer of windows and doors, North Pacific is also a good West Coast source for staircases in the Victorian style. The firm will work with the customer to determine the proper design and materials to be used. North Pacific has executed handsome staircases in Brazilian mahogany and red oak, but other woods may be used. The company can also provide posts and wainscotting.

Brochure available.

North Pacific Joinery
76 W. 4th St.
Eureka, CA 95501
(707) 443-5788

Perkins Architectural Millwork

Most homes do not have the space for a grand staircase and even fewer for a double staircase. But if there is room, why not? Kenneth Perkins is not afraid to tackle this most dramatic element in architectural design, and to oversee its execution. His grand staircase, as illustrated, is an eclectic composition of Victorian and Georgian colonial elements. All of the elements are available through Perkins, as are others intended for much simpler staircases.

Catalogue and videos available.

Perkins Architectural Millwork
Rte. 5, Box 264-W
Longview, TX 75601
(214) 663-3036

Schwartz's Forge

If the staircase you want seems impossible to find, have a talk with Joel A. Schwartz. Schwartz uses his extensive training, research, and experience to create ironwork that is durable, attractive, and rich in detail; his work has been exhibited at the Museum of Contemporary Crafts in New York City and at the Renwick Gallery of the Smithsonian Institution. His commissions for New York residences have included an imposing two-story spiral staircase, an undulating stair railing with a wild vine motif, and a five-story stairway that features a smoothly curving top rail and gently bending posts ending in spirals at their tops and bottoms.

Literature available.

Schwartz's Forge & Metalworks
Forge Hollow Rd.
Box 205
Deansboro, NY 13328
(315) 841-4477

Somerset Door & Column

Best known for its wood columns, Somerset also makes an attractive circular stairway. Built of solid hardwood, the stairway has a gentle curve that lends elegance to a room or to an entrance hallway. Its simplicity and grace make it appropriate for most decors. Somerset also does custom work.

Brochure available.

Somerset Door & Column Co.
Box 328
Somerset, PA 15501
(800) 242-7916
(800) 242-7915 (PA)

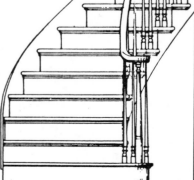

Stair Specialist

Circular and elliptical stairways for homes or commercial establishments are the only items built by this firm. The greater the space allowed for a staircase, the more elaborate it is likely to be. Stair Specialist, however, can also design and fabricate elegant small radius stairways.

Oak, cherry, walnut, rosewood, teak, and mahogany are some of the woods used. A hardwood is always employed for balusters and risers. Many of the stairways incorporate hand-carved brackets or other decoration.

Each stairway is a custom order project for Stair Specialist.

Brochure available.

Stair Specialist
2257 W. Columbia Ave.
Battle Creek, MI 49017
(616) 964-2351

Steptoe & Wife

Victorian-style cast-iron staircases are Steptoe & Wife's specialty. In addition to two spiral staircases, the 5'-diameter Barclay and the 4'3"-diameter Albany, the company makes an elegant straight model, the Kensington. Perfect for front entrances, patio exits, porch steps, and interior applications, cast-iron staircases are a welcome alternative to unsightly concrete. Measuring 36" wide, each elaborate open fretwork riser is composed of four castings bolted together. Order as many risers as you need; if you're using more than three, steel channels will provide extra support. If you like, you can add brass and steel railings or decorative cast-iron balusters.

Catalogue available.

Steptoe & Wife Antiques Ltd.
322 Geary Ave.
Toronto, Ontario, Canada M6H 2C7
(416) 530-4200

Vintage Lumber

Only centuries of slow, steady growth could produce the tight-grained heartwood of the longleaf pine. Naturally immune to insects and decay, the wood was coveted, cut for homes, bridges . . . even the keel of the *U.S.S. Constitution.* Retrieved wood from these structures seems to be quite a prize, since lumbermen have felled the great pine forests, destroying the needed conditions for them ever to grow again.

Vintage Lumber offers stair parts from this reclaimed heart pine. Treads, risers, landing and return nosing, etc.—all have been resawn from antique timbers.

Vintage Lumber & Construction Co.,
  Inc.
9507 Woodsboro Rd.
Frederick, MD 21701
(301) 898-7859

Whitten Enterprises

Although basically contemporary in design, Whitten's spiral staircases are graceful and useful sculptures which will fit into many different types of houses. Since they are of one-piece construction, these are very sturdy and fairly easy to install. There are two models, the solid steel Model 10 being more expensive than the Model 20. Either one can be fitted with solid oak treads rather than steel and an oak rail can be substituted for steel. There are also scroll and fleur-de-lis designs in cast iron which can be used as ornamental filler between the spindles as well as a cast-iron design for spindles themselves.

Whitten also supplies spiral stair units in kit form. There are optional stair layouts such as a one-half turn 5'6" diameter spiral stair kit and a combination stair kit with one-quarter turn. There are obvious economic advantages to ordering a kit, but the customer should be confident of his ability to see the staircase properly installed.

Literature available.

Whitten Enterprises, Inc.
PO Box 1121
Bennington, VT 05201
(802) 442-8344

The Woods

Planning, designing, and fabricating the parts for a staircase is something Barry Stup of The Woods Co. does well. Although he no longer installs these components himself, he will arrange for the work to be done properly. All of the elements necessary— treads, risers, balusters, rails, moldings, and stringers—can be supplied by Stup.

Brochure and price list available.

The Woods Co.
123 S. Main St.
Brownsville, MD 21715
(301) 432-8419

Consultants, Architects, and Contractors

Almost everyone needs advice in putting an old house back together or in renovating some part of it. Consultants and architects can help tremendously with such preliminary steps as inspecting a building before it is purchased, digging out the building's history, and drawing up a recommended list of restoration or renovation steps to be taken. Once the direction is clear and the plans have been drawn up, a contractor is usually called in to perform most of the work. The architect or consultant need not step out of the picture entirely at this point; he is usually willing to supervise the contractual work.

Builders with the skills necessary to execute restoration or renovation work successfully can be difficult to find. Nearly every area of North America, however, has at least a few of these talented individuals. In addition to basic construction techniques, the old house contractor must be very familiar with various period styles, old-fashioned building methods, and the types of materials which can be appropriately used. How to locate such a history-sensitive contractor? The listings that follow will be helpful, and, if one individual cannot help you, he may be able to lead you to another who can assist.

Abatron

Concrete has been used in American residential and commercial buildings for many years. Abatron is a supplier of structural adhesives useful in repairing concrete floors, walls, and ornamentation. Abatron's principal product is Abocrete, an epoxy patching and resurfacing cement. Mainly used for industrial purposes, it has the strength and ease of application which also recommends it for repairing columns, railings, posts, stairs, and other architectural elements originally worked in cement.

Abocrete is distributed nationally. The firm also supplies epoxies for masonry and wood restoration.

For further information, contact the company.

Literature available.

Abatron Inc.
141 Center Dr.
Gilberts, IL 60136
(312) 426-2200

Anderson Building Restoration

The expert craftsmen at Anderson Building Restoration return aged structures to their original glory, cleaning and restoring antique masonry with state-of-the-art techniques. These photographs show details of a Newport, Kentucky metamorphosis. The James Wiedemann House, a building on

the National Register of Historic Places, showed massive injury to red sandstone decoration, demanding artistic and scientific skill to repair. Using patch material from Edison Chemical Systems, Anderson transformed cracked details, often rebuilding missing segments of the original, until no sign of damage remained. The artistic talent is obvious; the technological back-up was crucial.

Anderson has found Diedrich Chemicals' cleaning products ideal for most jobs. Surfaces cleaned with Diedrich products skirt the pitting, erosion, dulling, and general deterioration wreaked through sandblasting by using water-soluble, biodegradable substances that preserve finely carved detail and even protect the masonry skin that repels water and dirt. By using only the safest products of restoration

technology, Anderson respects history and devotes itself to preserving architectural legacies for the future.

For further information, contact:

Anderson Building Restoration
923 Marion Ave.
Cincinnati, OH 45229
(513) 281-5258

For further information on Edison products, contact:

Edison Chemical Systems, Inc.
25 Grant St.
Waterbury, CT 06704
(203) 597-9727

For information on Diedrich, contact:

Diedrich Chemicals Restoration
* Technologies, Inc.*
300A E. Oak St.
Milwaukee, WI 53154
(800) 323-3565

The San P[...] town tha[...] than an[...] II event[...] black powde[...] Hercules. After [...] down and even the s[...] had grazed the area (to c[...] chance of disastrous grass fire[...] were gone, a score of Colonial Revival and Queen Anne homes still stood. A baker's dozen of these buildings, relocated in a nationally listed historic district, still display their classic architecture,

Architectural Preservation Trust

In addition to reproduction outbuilding kits, marketed under the name of New England Outbuildings, the Architectural Preservation Trust disassembles and offers authentic New England buildings for sale. Most of the structures date from the 18th and early 19th centuries.

Parmelee House is a good example of the Trust's buildings. The original house dates from 1740; it was enlarged in 1827. Built in Killingworth, Connecticut, it is now seeking a proper setting. The Trust will add a large country kitchen addition designed to the buyer's requirements.

For information regarding this property and others, contact:

Architectural Preservation Trust
152 Old Clinton Rd.
Westbrook, CT 06498
(203) 669-1776

to the work of the Architectural Resources Group. [...]nal wood shingles and [...]lwork were restored. [...]ecessary replacements were matched to antiques. Interior work, such as the ornate decoration of Colonial Revival entrance halls, was faithfully preserved. Modern additions, sometimes entailing complete plumbing systems, were executed to leave the village basically undisturbed. Architectural and design services from Architectural Resources Group make projects like this one feasible. Contact the firm for further information.

Architectural Resources Group
Pier 9
The Embarcadero
San Francisco, CA 94111
(415) 421-1680

Architectural Reclamation

Andy and Bruce Stewart comprise the heart of Architectural Reclamation. They have worked for over ten years as general contractors specializing in the restoration and rehabilitation of historic structures, building up a large, varied, and respectable clientele in and around Ohio. These two are the troubleshooters of the reclamation industry, experts in finding solutions to the many problems that come up when adapting historic buildings to modern uses, simultaneously preserving the unique character and construction of each structure.

The company uses modern materials off-the-shelf, newly fabricated reproductions, and salvaged materials in most projects. When necessary the craftsmen have even made use of antique tools.

One of the more interesting projects is the restoration of the Wright Brothers Cycle Shop in Cleveland, Ohio. The work has included reconstruction of the storefront, fabrication of new doors and windows, brick replacement and repointing, and a great deal more. Architectural Reclamation undertakes both commercial and residential projects.

Literature and photographs available.

Architectural Reclamation
312 S. River St.
Franklin, OH 45005
(513) 746-8964

Biltmore, Campbell, Smith

This enterprising restoration firm has built an enviable reputation over the years for very fine work. Most of its clients are private institutions or government agencies able to afford to have extensive work done. Among places in which Biltmore, Campbell, Smith has undertaken projects are the Pennsylvania state capitol, Flagler College in Florida, the Smithsonian Institution, and the Valentine Museum in Richmond.

The firm, headquartered in Asheville, North Carolina, mastered many of its restoration techniques at Biltmore House, the Vanderbilt mansion and estate in Asheville. Projects, however, are carried out throughout North America by the firm's conservators, artists, and craftsmen.

Newsletter available.

Biltmore, Campbell, Smith
  Restorations, Inc.
1 N. Pack Sq.
Asheville, NC 28801
(704) 255-1776 or 255-1788

Carson, Dunlop

The house captures your heart, but how do you squelch doubts about antique constructions, nuances of maintenance over the years that may harbor impending costly repairs? Let Carson, Dunlop & Associates ease your mind with the information to make an expertly informed decision. Partial or full inspections, conducted six days a week, yield honest evaluations; an on-site verbal report precedes the prompt written summary. Carson, Dunlop is the first Canadian firm in the American Society of Home Inspectors and holds certification from the Association of Professional Engineers of Ontario.

Brochure available.

Carson, Dunlop & Associates
597 Parliament St., Suite B-5
Toronto, Ontario, Canada M4X 1W3
(416) 964-9415

Clio Group

Calling itself "Clio" after the Greek muse of history suggests the historical foundations of this group's work. Over 100 buildings and a score of historic districts have been placed on the National Register of Historic Places by Clio. The group has also planned and supervised over 250 certified rehabilitations, ten historic site surveys, and numerous historic structure reports, restoration projects, and exhibits.

The company provides professional services to meet the standards of federal, state, and local governments. In addition, Clio performs adaptive reuse studies, materials analysis, structural reports, and real estate development consultation. The academic credentials of the firm's principals qualify them to present a wide range of lectures and seminars, too. Other useful and hard-to-find services include architectural photography (to facilitate drafting, marketing, and publicity) and computer-based research and data analysis.

Brochure available.

Clio Group, Inc.
3961 Baltimore Ave.
Philadelphia, PA 19104
(215) 386-6276

Community Services Collaborative

Older buildings not only provide a link with the past but comprise a visual statement that gives each community its character. Community Services Collaborative is an architectural and planning firm that has specialized in historic preservation for over ten years. The company offers an integrated approach to problem solving that is invaluable and hard to come by.

Services include developing a base of support for preservation within the community, handling National Register nomination and tax certification, performing historic materials analysis, establishing design guidelines, and supervising restoration work.

The company's other services include all types of planning, architectural design, and landscape architecture. Community Services Collaborative will respond by letter to serious inquiries.

Community Services Collaborative
1315 Broadway
Boulder, CO 80302
(303) 442-3601

Dell

Buildings which have suffered some degree of wood deterioration profit greatly from the attention of the experts from Dell. A general contracting firm, it has special expertise in such areas as timber construction, epoxy uses, and marine restoration. Dell will handle a job from survey and evaluation through to the end—and has done so many times.

Planning and budgeting for work can be almost as important as the execution of the project. Dell has a customized computer database which can provide a cost analysis of a project after it is surveyed and specifications are outlined. Prices can be determined with respect to expectations of quality and quantity of work.

Dell will also perform maintenance work, if that is all that is required. In addition, it can develop a maintenance program to be followed in the future so that deterioration does not become a crippling problem.

The company has the advantage of being the exclusive North American distributor of the Beta Epoxy System for wood restoration. This is a patented process using epoxy mortar with specially fabricated polyfiber reinforcement rods for restoring and strengthening beams and other structural wood members.

Literature available upon request.

Dell Corp.
1045 Taft St., PO Box 1462
Rockville, MD 20850
(301) 279-2612

Jamie Gibbs and Associates

Eleven years of experience, nine of them as the head of his own private practice, have taken Jamie Gibbs across three continents. His specialty is the creation of traditional interiors, and his work in this field has encompassed a wide range of architectural styles. Gibbs has also written several books and

frequently gives lectures and conducts study tours through famous houses, many of which are not usually open to the public.

Jamie Gibbs and Associates
Landscape Architects and Interior
* Designers*
340 E. 93rd St., Suite 14C
New York, NY 10128
(212) 722-7508

Koeppel/Freedman Studios

Formerly Ornamental Plaster Restoration, Koeppel/Freedman is a small specialized company dedicated to the art of preservation, custom architectural restoration, and design. The firm's services include moldmaking from existing elements, hand remodeling by skilled artists, re-creation of lost detail from photographs, drawings, or blueprints, and the creation of new ornaments for appropriate application within the context of existing architecture. Interior work is hand-modeled or cast in plaster and reinforced for structural durability. Plaster/fiberglass composites are available where lighter weight is advised. Most exterior casts are done in epoxy-fiberglass, cement, or a combination of both elements. Marble repair, as well as terracotta repair, is also available. Koeppel/Freedman can serve as consultants in any of these areas, both to the individual homeowner, and to other professionals within the restoration and design fields.

In addition to these three-dimensional services, the firm also provides painting services, which include color matching and re-creation of original processes, as well as decorative painting of restored plasterwork. Koeppel/Freedman also specializes in trompe l'oeil painting of wall murals, floors, screens, and furniture.

Since all work is customized, the firm offers no literature, but mail and telephone inquiries are welcome.

Koeppel/Freedman Studios
386 Congress St.
Boston, MA 02210
(617) 426-8887

Steven P. Mack Associates

From the authentic whitewash he mixes himself to barnraising parties (bluegrass band included), Steven P. Mack's restorations of antique houses and barns are rife with authenticity. Ever since he fell in love with a windowless shambles that seemed more an oversized bird roost than a house—entailing a restoration of its rotting floor that was "like replacing the soles in your shoes while standing in them" — Mack's been hooked on historic preservation. Mack's services include design, architectural work, the supply of building materials, and preservation. He specializes in rescuing old structures facing demolition, dismantling them (with photographic documentation), and storing them to be erected again.

Steven P. Mack Associates
Chase Hill Farm
Ashaway, RI 02804
(401) 377-8041

M. J. May

From the most minutely detailed Victorian fretwork or trim to the most complex wood floor and ceiling installations, M. J. May is ready to help. The firm handles all aspects of repair and replacement involved in building restoration. May will also locate any replacement structural antiques needed and, of course, will install them on-site. The company offers competitive rates, free estimates, and its principals are ready to travel outside of their home region.

Brochure available.

M. J. May Antique Building
*   Restoration*
505 Storle Ave.
Burlington, WI 53105
(414) 763-8822

Tom Moore's Steeple People

High or hard-to-reach places are just like home to the Steeple People. Cupolas, rooftops, steeples, ceilings, and bell towers receive the benefit of this company's restoration know-how. Some tasks frequently performed are restoring gold leaf, repairing metal ceilings, making and installing copper gutters and downspouts, and fixing roofs made of slate, metal, or Spanish tile. Although most of the company's work is done in New England, where it will issue

written estimates free of charge, commissions are accepted from anywhere in the country.

Tom Moore's Steeple People
21 Janine St.
Chicopee, MA 01013
(413) 533-9515

North Fields Restorations

In addition to supplying antique building materials, North Fields dismantles 18th-century New England houses and barns and offers them for sale. Some of the properties offered in the past year include a c. 1730-40 center-hall colonial, a c. 1687 Rhode Island stone-ender, a 40 by 18 carriage shed, a c. 1730 half house from E. Andover, Mass., and a c. 1720 saltbox. Many of the buildings include such fine details as paneled room ends, original two- and four-panel doors with authentic hardware, and hard pine flooring.

For further information, contact Mark Phillips at:

North Fields Restorations
Box 741
Rowley, MA 01969
(617) 948-2722

Old World Restorations

When an heirloom piece of porcelain is chipped or an antique stained-glass window broken, it can be heart-wrenching. Fortunately, there's a company that specializes in restoring such objects to their former beauty. Old World Restorations restores and conserves oil paintings, frames, porcelain, glass, china, ivory, stone, wood, pottery, gilding, sculpture, stained glass, metal, marble, and other materials. In most cases the repairs are invisible to the naked eye. Just send the object to Old World; a brochure available from the company gives good packaging and shipping instructions. An examination of the object will take place and a written estimate will be prepared before any work is begun.

Literature available.

Old World Restorations, Inc.
Columbia/Stanley Bldg.
347 Stanley Ave.
Cincinnati, OH 45226
(513) 321-1911

Preservation Associates

Let Preservation Associates guide you through the maze of planning, revitalizing, and registering necessary for protecting historic structures. Providing a substantial fund of information and records of restoration and preservation materials and methods, as well as the expertise to ascertain what must be preserved in a vintage building, Preservation Associates is obviously prepared to help fanciers of old homes. The firm is expert in readying applications for certification with the National Register of Historic Places.

Preservation Associates
207 S. Potomac St.
Hagerstown, MD 21740
(301) 791-7880

Preservation Partnership

From grant applications and tax advice to architectural design, historic structure reports, preservation planning and education, The Preservation Partnership offers comprehensive services in the preservation field. A staff of eight architects, historians, and conservators is experienced in serving private, institutional, and government clients throughout the Northeast. Whatever problems or questions have arisen or are anticipated, this company is equipped and qualified to help.

One important project the company performed was for the Nantucket Historical Association. The Partnership provided architectural services for the restoration of the Macy warehouse, Hawden House, and the 1800 House, authored a study of all the association's properties, and studied the climatological factors affecting the group's various collections.

The breadth of The Preservation Partnership's expertise is further illustrated by the work done for the Preservation Society of Newport County, Rhode Island. The company compiled a conservation study of all eight mansion-museums followed by extensive conservation work on The Breakers, The Elms, Marble House, Kingscote, and Rosecliffe.

Architectural services included supervision of masonry restoration, copper roofing, waterproofing, wood conservation, and other complex repairs.

Literature available.

The Preservation Partnership
345 Union St.
New Bedford, MA 02740
(508) 996-3383

Preservation Services

Best known as a color-consultant firm that other consulting firms turn to when working on historic interiors and exteriors, Preservation Services is also able to meet most other preservation and restoration needs. Working primarily in the Midwest, the company can serve as architect, architectural historian, architectural conservator, designer, historic craftsman, grant writer, tax consultant, and researcher.

Preservation Services directed the restoration of the Villa Katherine, built in 1899 in the Moorish tradition in Quincy, Illinois. Hardly an average job, this building incorporates authentic Middle Eastern details. Often consultations begin prior to the purchase of a property, and then continue through the actual restoration, as was the case here. Using state funds, the villa was perfectly restored and is now partially open to the public as a tourist information center.

Literature available.

Preservation Services
1445 Hampshire
Quincy, IL 62301
(217) 224-2300

Restorations Unlimited

Beth and Jim Facinelli are so confident of the work that they perform that their home is their showroom. Consultants and master craftsmen in the field of old house restoration, they work in a seventeen-room, 6,000 square-foot mansion built in 1903 which has been completely restored. If a client has questions about particular aspects of a job, his answer may be found within the walls of the Facinelli office-residence.

Restorations Unlimited services begin in the planning stages and extend through education and contracting. The Facinellis are experts in interpreting regulations and laying the proper groundwork for tax certification. The company will also alter existing plans to meet the standards set by enabling government agencies.

Contracting services include millwork and fine cabinetry, wood flooring and refinishing, stenciling, brick and stone masonry, pointing, and others. Restorations Unlimited also serves as a retail source for such suppliers as W. F. Norman and Rich Craft.

Literature available.

Restorations Unlimited, Inc.
24 W. Main St.
Elizabethville, PA 17023
(717) 362-3477

River City Restorations

Is Lincoln turning over in his grave worrying about the restoration and repair work that his Springfield home is now undergoing? Certainly not with River City Restorations as the principal contractor.

Its goal is to assure the stability of the 149-year-old building in which the Lincoln family lived for seventeen years. The restoration has revealed many details of the home which were previously unknown. And state-of-the-art research and technology have made possible a fuller understanding of the types of materials used in furnishing the home.

River City's contracting services include structural repair and stabilization, masonry restoration, roofing and metalwork, moisture control, plastering, mechanical systems, decorative painting and finishing, and a great deal more. In addition, the company serves as consultant and planner both before and after the completion of any restoration work, providing service and developing maintenance programs often omitted by other firms.

Consulting services range from building inspection to structural analysis, feasibility studies and cost projections, establishment of priorities, architectural and historic research and design, construction drawings and specifications, and development of cyclical maintenance programs.

Literature available.

River City Restorations
PO Box 1065, 623 Collier Rd.
Hannibal, MO 63401
(314) 248-0733

Riverbend Timber Framing

Riverbend Timber Framing reinstates the historic timber framing of the first North American colonial houses as a dramatic exposed element in homes today. The great strength of this framing allows huge open spaces and breathtaking high-ceilinged rooms. The exacting craftsmanship and durable materials in timber-framed colonial American homes have sustained these buildings for 350 years—a duration dwarfed by a thousand-year-old Japanese temple and by European buildings over twice the age of their American relatives. An added merit—timber framing makes efficient use of wood resources, requiring less raw lumber than stud framing or log construction, and generating much less sawdust waste than results from sawing two-by-fours.

Riverbend's custom sheathing panels, with laminated foam cores, strengthen and insulate the timber-frame homes that contain them. The use of stress-skin panels converts the work of laying exterior sheathing, insulation, and drywall into one economical step.

To accommodate growing interest in timber framing methods, Riverbend presents lectures and provides several informative books and periodicals on timber framing for the owner-builder. Riverbend's design services will guide you in adapting timber framing to suit your particular needs.

Brochure available.

Riverbend Timber Framing, Inc.
Box 26
Blissfield, MI 49228
(517) 486-4566

Russell Restoration of Suffolk

When a craftsman has mastered his medium, it's made obvious by his versatility, the quality of his work, and his willingness to accept challenging projects. It's apparent that Dean M. Russell has achieved this level of skill in plaster construction. From restoring a ceiling to making his own jigs for drawn moldings, he seems able to handle almost any aspect of the craft. Working for local museums and historical societies as well as for individuals, Russell makes flexible molds, niches, curved moldings, domes, arches, various ornaments, and even complete interiors with nothing but bare walls as a starting point. His company also produces ornaments cast in Portland cement, epoxies, fiberglass-reinforced plastic, and other synthetic materials.

Russell Restoration of Suffolk
5550 Bergen Ave.
Mattituck, NY 11952
(516) 765-2481

Traditional Line

Drawing on museum restoration work of exceptionally high quality, James Boorstein and Peter Strasser established Traditional Line in 1984. Since that time they have completed the restoration of a number of houses and apartments in the New York area. These have included several apartments in the landmark Dakota and a Greek Revival townhouse.

The partners bring to their work a high level of technical skill and a love of quality materials, especially fine woods. This is illustrated in two of their projects for the Metropolitan Museum: the Rococo Revival room and the Frank Lloyd Wright room.

In addition to their work as restoration craftsmen, Boorstein and Strasser will serve as consultants and will oversee a project. This may involve everything from structural analysis to planning the work of electricians and plumbers so that the modern improvements do not disturb the true period character of a dwelling.

Traditional Line also restores and refinishes fine furniture and architectural components.

Brochure available.

Traditional Line Architectural Restoration Ltd.
35 Hillside Ave.
Monsey, NY 10952
(914) 425-6400

Victorian Collectibles

The Grand Opera House in Oshkosh, Wisconsin, was built in 1883 by local businessmen who saw that a public theater was much needed in the city. With its heyday lasting almost fifty years, the Grand gradually fell into disuse. By the time the building was bought by the city in 1980, the opera house had spent several years as an X-rated movie house. The restoration of the building was completed in 1987 after three million dollars was spent on both interior and exterior renovations. Victorian Collectibles provided the necessary historical research as well as the design of the interior which follows as closely as possible to the original appearance.

The various ceiling surfaces have been repainted by hand and the wallpaper patterns were drawn from Victorian Collectibles's archives of 1,379 different antique Victorian designs.

In addition to contract work, Victorian Collectibles can also supply a variety of reproduction furnishings—ceramic tiles, fabrics, murals, hand-woven rugs, stenciled floorcloths, plaster moldings—all of which are complementary in style to the firm's wallpaper patterns.

Catalogue, $3.

Victorian Collectibles, Ltd.
845 E. Glenbrook Rd.
Milwaukee, WI 53217
(414) 352-6910

Reproduction Period Homes

The rediscovery since World War II of the clean, honest lines of early American architecture has been marked by the diffusion of thousands of ready-made house designs or plans. The majority of such designs leave much to be desired. Regional differences were great in the 17th and 18th centuries, and it is often difficult to determine whether a particular modern plan derives from Massachusetts (Sturbridge), the Middle Atlantic states, or Virginia (Williamsburg). Late Georgian high-style elements are often applied to a simple clapboard house with casement windows dating from the 1600s. Brick laid with an inappropriate mortar is often juxtaposed with cedar shakes and both are combined with fake stone facing to form what can only be described as an abortive mess.

If you wish to start from scratch and to build a new home that meets minimal historical standards, it would be best to consult a knowledgeable custom builder. Old skills have been relearned in workshops across North America; new materials can be handled and used in a way that is honest and convincing. And there are good ready-made plans which can be adapted to your particualr needs.

Duo Dickinson, Architect

Adding on to an old house is a much more difficult task than most people realize. The majority of additions are simply tacked on without any thought given to proportion and style. Better but more expensive options are either to design and build an add-on which matches the original building in all essential details or to enlarge a house by adding a modern but stylistically compatible unit. Duo Dickinson is a master of the latter approach.

The addition to the house illustrated is clearly modern but it is not out of harmony with the adjoining mansard roof building. Dickinson defines his firm's focus as being "expressive and sensitive additions and renovations of older homes." In this case and many others, there is no question but that he is right.

Dickinson has received several national and local awards. His firm is ready to act as a consultant or to serve as architect of record for projects of modest or large scale.

Duo Dickinson, Architect
70 Wall St.
Madison, CT 06443
(203) 245-0405

Historical Replications

The first step toward the building of a beautiful reproduction house is designing it. Historical Replications simplifies this crucial phase of the project by providing four portfolios of reproduction house plans. Each portfolio contains twenty to thirty line drawings and floor plans of different house styles, listing overall dimensions, ceiling heights for each floor, and square footage for each structure. Working drawings of any house can be ordered from the company. If you and your builder want to alter the design slightly, go ahead, but for major changes Historical Replications suggests that you send a sketch and describe what you'd like to adapt. The company will adjust the plans for you and make sure that your design will be safe. Custom plans can also be developed; send a sketch and information to the company, and you'll get an estimate of the time and cost of creating a suitable design.

The house shown here is a 2,522-square-foot Victorian structure with a dramatic foyer open all the way to the tower ceiling. It's from the company's original portfolio, which contains diverse houses, from an Acadian cottage to a reproduction of the Holly Springs, Mississippi, home of 19th-century senator General Cary Marshall. Other designs were inspired by a multi-gabled home in Norcross, Georgia and an 1842 parsonage in Madison, Georgia.

The Louisiana Collection contains homes with a Southern flavor that measure between 1,448 and 6,264 square feet. There is a heavy emphasis on French colonial and Greek Revival designs. The Classic Cottage portfolio features smaller houses measuring between 853 and 1,997 feet. A wide range of styles are represented, including Cape Cod, Georgian, Victorian, farmhouse, Greek Revival, English, French, and Acadian. Historical Replications' newest portfolio is called Colonial Heritage and contains Georgian, Federal, Williamsburg,

tion buildings—The Old Sturbridge Village Collection of House Designs. Sketches and floor plans of five residences are included in the catalogue for $6. A set of complete working drawings of any one of the houses is $150.

Illustrated is the Richardson House, originally located in Podunk, Mass., and now a part of the Old Sturbridge complex.

Russell Swinton Oatman also offers three other collections of period house drawings: "The Golden Age of Victorian Architecture," "The Cape Cod Collection of House Designs," and "The New England Collection of House Designs." Each catalogue is available for $5. The designs are based on actual historic buildings, slight alterations being made in each for purposes of modern construction and living needs.

In addition to its publications, the firm is also prepared to undertake a variety of restoration services. Considering the care given the plans for period buildings by the company, its offer to assist in other ways should be given serious consideration.

Russell Swinton Oatman Design
Associates, Inc.
132 Mirick Rd.
Princeton, MA 01541
(508) 464-2360

McKie Wing Roth

McKie Roth, Jr., began designing reproduction houses after discovering that, although he loved the look and feel of a two-hundred-year-old New England colonial, he did not want to hassle

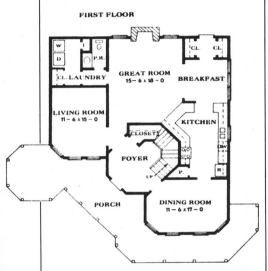

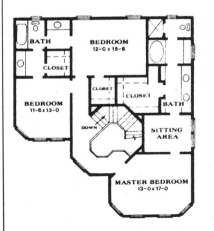

saltbox, Dutch, and Greek Revival house plans.

For further information, contact:

Historical Replications, Inc.
Box 13529
Jackson, MS 39236
(601) 981-8743

Lockhart Designs

William Lockhart's house plans are designed by him and are, for the most part, adaptations of colonial and early 19th-century buildings. They are pleasant, modest houses. Nearly all have one bedroom on the first floor and two on the second floor.

There are fifteen designs available and a customer can request a portfolio which includes a façade drawing and floor plans ($12) from which detailed blueprints ($75) can then be ordered.

Illustrated is a simple Southern Georgian colonial with a chimney at one end and a center hall and staircase.

W. S. Lockhart Designs
112 S. Warren St.
Timmonsville, SC 29161
(803) 346-3531

Russell Swinton Oatman Design

This firm has the distinction of producing the first museum-authorized catalogue of reproduc-

with properly repairing and restoring the property. He offers a collection of architectural plans for colonial houses in various sizes, buildings inspired by historic examples. These are not exact period copies but rather houses that can be built using today's materials and construction methods.

The Rhoda Wing House is one of the largest buildings for which

Roth provides plans. Design number S4-40, it is 3,170 square feet and has three and one-half baths and five bedrooms. The design is included in Folio II, the price of which is $15. A full set of building plans costs $150.

McKie Wing Roth, Jr., Associates
PO Box 130
Gardiner, ME 04345
(207) 582-3718

building, are not hidden away but honestly define the house, inside and out.

Riverbend supplies the timber-framed structure and stress-skin panel enclosure material; the building is then completed by an owner-builder or general contractor. Oak is the wood most often used for the framing. Other woods or even salvaged timbers, however, can be substituted.

General information package, $10.

Riverbend Timber Framing, Inc.
PO Box 26
Blissfield, MI 49228
(517) 486-4355

Riverbend Timber Framing

Riverbend houses are both contemporary and traditional—modern in appearance but old-fashioned in construction. And as it should be, the structural framing of the typical Riverbend house is expressed throughout. Mortise-and-tenon joinery is used, these joints being secured by the use of hardwood pegs.

Timber framing was first revived in New England in the 1970s and the technique has since been reborn in other areas of North America. Riverbend is dedicated to the design, development, and construction of this type of house or small commercial building. As shown, the structural members, just as in an early colonial

Sturbridge Studio

A portrait of a house in pen and ink is a popular way to capture its period charm. Something about a drawing evokes a more positive response than a simple photograph—as even real estate agents are now discovering. Sturbridge Studio specializes in house portraits.

Each Sturbridge Studio drawing is executed using a photograph supplied by the homeowner. This may be a black and white or color print or slide. The drawings are in

black ink on archival vellum paper. Each is finished with a bevel-edge mat in one of six colors, the customer making the choice. Cost for the smallest size drawing, 5 by 7, is $80; 11 by 14 is $125; and 20 by 24, $275.

Literature available.

Sturbridge Studio
114 E. Hill
Brimfield, MA 01010
(413) 245-3289

Schools and Study

Courses and workshops in traditional building methods, architectural styles, and the interior design of period buildings are very popular. These educational programs are especially useful to the do-it-yourselfer, but they are also instructive for anyone who is about to become involved in restoration or renovation work. Listed are only major, well-established summer programs. There are many other seminars, lectures, and adult education courses sponsored by preservation groups which are held from time to time throughout North America. The preservation organization in your area is likely to have information on similar programs.

Campbell Center

The Campbell Center's thirty-four workshops, ranging in length from two to five days, cover topics in historic preservation and conservation. Geared to professionals and interested students alike, the learning environment provided by the center enhances the quality of the overall experience. Whether a course is taught at the main campus or at one of the center's field sites, including such exciting locations as on-board a 19th-century whaling ship, you will always be taught by working professionals, experts in their particular fields.

Courses cover such diverse topics as "Wood Technology for Conservation and Restoration," "Light and Color Analysis for Conservators," and "Maritime Collection, Conservation, and Management."

Literature available.

Campbell Center
PO Box 66
Mt. Carroll, IL 61053
(815) 244-1173

Eastfield Village

Eastfield Village was established when Donald Carpentier moved his first building, a blacksmith's shop, into his father's east field over fifteen years ago. Now the village is both a living museum and a school for traditional trades and domestic arts.

With over twenty buildings and a study collection of thousands of architectural elements, participants in the five-day summer workshops are exposed to original documents dating from 1787-1840. They experience working with the tools and materials of the traditional trades taught. All instructors are well-respected in their individual fields and, while the emphasis of the courses is not on lectures, these craftsmen are always available to answer specific questions and assist with problems.

Courses include early 19th-century painting and graining, fireplace and bake-oven cooking, window restoration, and many more. While museum professionals from such prestigious institutions as Colonial Williamsburg and Monticello have attended these workshops, so have an equal number of interested private homeowners and handymen.

Heartwood's summer courses include a three-week house building course from the planning and design stages to framing and finishing, and a wide selection of one-week courses concentrating on the specific aspects of building design and construction. Topics for the shorter courses include contracting, carpentry, finish carpentry, timber framing, renovation, and masonry.

Heartwood's carpentry for women course, designed for those with little or no experience, is one of the most unique of all those offered. Taught by professional women contractors, it teaches self-sufficiency in home repair and remodeling. As is the case with all Heartwood courses, some classroom teaching and discussion is combined with practical application, working with both hand and power tools in the construction of a small building project.

The renovation course focuses on the planning, design, and construction of individual student projects. Students need to bring photos, plans, sketches, and measurements of any projects they may have in mind.

Heartwood's cabinetmaking course concentrates on the use of fine woodworking tools and materials, teaching, among other things, various joinery techniques. Enrollment is limited in this course, however, and some experience is necessary. All tools and other materials for the Heartwood courses are available at the school, and local accommodations can be arranged easily.

Literature available.

Heartwood
Johnson Rd.
Washington, MA 01235
(413) 623-6677

Preservation Associates

Preservation Associates has amassed enough knowledge in the field of preservation technology to publish four books and dozens of articles on the subject. Part of putting this knowledge into practice includes

Lodging is provided at the school, but students are on their own for meals.

Literature available, SASE.

Eastfield Village
Box 145, RD
East Nassau, NY 12062
(518) 766-2422

Heartwood

Heartwood offers a completely different way to vacation in the Berkshire hills. With Tanglewood, the summer home of the Boston Symphony, the Stockbridge Playhouse, the Jacob's Pillow Dance Festival, and the usual run of seasonal attractions available, a student can relax *and* learn to build or renovate a house.

conducting four college-level courses in construction methods and architectural history. Preservation Associates offers lectures and seminars and maintains a 12,000-item photographic library, which facilitates lectures, publications, or instruction series geared to many different areas.

Brochure available.

Preservation Associates
207 S. Potomac St.
Hagerstown, MD 21740
(301) 791-7880

Riverbend Timber Framing

What better way to learn a craft inside and out than to be apprenticed to a master of that specialty. Riverbend Timber Framing workshops are seven-day apprenticeships. Classes take place at actual building sites across the country. Students lay out the timbers, cut the joints, and raise the frame under the guidance of experienced craftsmen and instructors. This hands-on experience is augmented by instruction in timber-framing design and related issues, both through classroom teaching and assigned, related readings.

All students, experienced and inexperienced, young and old, are welcome. Riverbend projects have been completed from coast to coast in a wide range of styles and sizes.

Literature and newsletter available.

Riverbend Timber Framing, Inc.
PO Box 26
Blissfield, MI 49228
(517) 486-4355

Other Suppliers of Structural Products and Services

Consult List of Suppliers for addresses.

Architectural Salvage

Architectural Salvage Cooperative
Jerard Paul Jordan
Nostalgia
Spiess Antique Building Materials

Brick and Stone; Roofing Materials

Architectural Preservation Trust
Architectural Salvage Co.
Bergen Bluestone
Briar Hill Stone
The Brickyard
Colonial Brick
Delaware Quarries
Diamond K.
Great American Salvage Co.
Kane-Gonic Brick Co.
E. T. Moore, Jr.
Old Carolina Brick Co.
Pasvalco
Ramase
Structural Slate Co.
Tullibardine Enterprises
Vermont Marble Co.
Vintage Lumber

Ceilings

Architectural Antique Warehouse
Architectural Paneling
Architectural Salvage
Canal Co.
Old Jefferson Tile Co.
Remodelers' and Renovators' Supply
San Francisco Victoriana
Steptoe and Wife Antiques

Doors and Windows

Aged Woods
Architectural Antique Warehouse
Architectural Antiques Exchange
Architectural Salvage Co.
Art Directions
Canal Co.
Central Kentucky Millwork
Classic Architectural Specialties
Fireplace Mantel Shop
Whit Hanks
Iberia Millwork
Jerard Paul Jordan
M. J. May
Mountain Lumber
Nostalgia
Ohmega Salvage
Pelnik Wrecking
Silverton Victorian Mill Works
Spiess Antique Building Materials
United House Wrecking

Lumber

Central Kentucky Millwork
Vintage Lumber

Stairways

Architectural Salvage Co.
Classic Architectural Specialties
Fireplace Mantel Shop
Mountain Lumber
Sheppard Millwork

Consultants, Architects, and Contractors

American Building Restoration
Townsend Anderson
Artistic License
Carpenter and Smith Restorations
Allen Charles Hill
Historic Boulevard Services
Alvin Holm
William H. Parsons & Associates
Preservation Resource Group (PRG)
Rambusch
The Renovaton Source
S.P.N.E.A. Conservation Center
Skyline Engineers
Donald Stryker Restorations
Winans Construction

Reproduction Period Houses

Greatwood Log Homes
House Carpenters
Stephen P. Mack
Timberpeg, East

Schools and Study

Association for Preservation Technology
Clio Group
Day Studio-Workshop
National Preservation Institute
Preservation Associates
Preservation Partnership
Restorations Unlimited

2.

Architectural Decoration

The decorative architectural elements are those which serve no structural purpose but finish off the exterior framework of a building and its interior spaces as well. Of wood, plaster, metal, composition, and modern synthetics, these are the moldings, window and door casings, corbels and brackets, medallions and corner blocks. Properly fashioned, these elements endow a house with character. The line, the basic skeleton, is more fundamental, but we are more apt to notice only the way in which a building or room is dressed—the manner in which it is decorated.

Of all the elements, moldings are the most important. Cornice moldings appear both inside and outside a building. Shoe and base moldings may finish off lower walls. Window and door frames or casings are—in an older building—made up of one or more moldings. Elaborate door assemblies such as appear at the main entrance of a Georgian Colonial or Federal-style building are very complex constructions and moldings are their principal component.

The most beautiful old buildings are generally thought of as those which are the most elaborately turned out. The very term "old" as applied to architecture implies the use of the decorative element rather than the purely functional or "modern." In the 1980s we are being swept into a new wave of romanticism, of the decorative. Some abhor the move back in time to broken pediments and mindless gingerbread and prefer to label the movement escapist. Whatever its psychological dimensions, the new appreciation of the ornamental is to be welcomed if it brings with it a return to the same type of craftsmanship achieved during the late-19th century in the Arts and Crafts period. Unfortunately, much of the newly romantic is as tacky as the sleekly modern. One has to proceed cautiously across the commercial minefield of decorative objects, as the territory is full of "instant gratification." Packaged nostalgia—a bracket weighing as much as a soda cracker or a molding with the profile of a jagged tin can—is too readily available. Instead, turn back to the basics of good design and workmanship as outlined in these pages.

A selection of architectural antiques, including stained and leaded glass, from The Brass Knob, Washington, D.C.

Glass

Proper glass can be as important to the appearance of a period house as paint, moldings, or other trimmings. The differences between new plate glass and that used in the past are not readily noticeable by most people, but these can be considerable. Many homes have lost their old windows, transoms, or other glass panels. To replace them with modern plates of glass, however insulated they may be by double or triple glazing, can despoil a façade. This is especially true if the glass being replaced is stained, etched, or engraved.

Old window glass is not easy to obtain. A number of the restoration suppliers and consultants included in this chapter have a supply on hand from time to time. Reproduction panes can be obtained from a number of the glass workshops across the country.

Architectural Antiques West

Careful hand beveling and assembly, rigorous inspection, a chemical wash to finish the metal, and a final cleaning by hand give these glass windows the proper period look. Architectural Antiques West creates a number of transoms, sidelights, and panels in Victorian, Edwardian, and Art Nouveau styles. A dazzling display of diagonal lines forms a breathtaking window, available in two sizes: 36½" high by 21⅝" wide (model B-1) and 36½" high by 27⅝" wide (model B-2). A more sedate design makes the second window shown here a perfect accent for almost any Victorian room. It is sold in the same sizes as model W-1 and W-2.

Architectural Antiques West is a wholesaler only; however, its products are sold by distributors throughout the nation. To find the one nearest to you, contact:

Architectural Antiques West
3117 S. La Cienega Blvd.
Los Angeles, CA 90016
(213) 559-3019

Bendheim

For accurate renovation of colonial-era buildings, there's no substitute for handmade glass. Bendheim's "Restoration Glass" is mouth blown by fifth and sixth generation artisans in one of Europe's oldest glass blowing factories. The resulting glass with its slight distortions and imperfections is ideal for restoration work. It has been chosen for many of America's finest restorations including Old Sturbridge Village; Trinity Church in Newport, Rhode Island; The 1800 House in Nantucket; and Tryon Palace in New Bern, North Carolina. Illustrated is a window at the Vandalia State House in Illinois.

Bendheim's product comes in two sizes and thicknesses: full is about ⅛" thick and comes in sheets about 24" by 36"; light is about 3/32" thick and comes in sheets about 42" square. This product is now available in insulated glass units, too.

Literature available.

S. A. Bendheim Co. Inc.
122 Hudson St.
New York, NY
(800) 221-7379
(212) 226-6370 (NY)

Boulder Stained Glass Studios

The artists at Boulder Stained Glass Studios are competent in all types of decorative glasswork. Their many commissioned works include pieces which have been sandblasted or etched and those which employ leaded panels, beveled panels, painted, and stained embellishments. In addition, they are skilled at repairs and restoration work.

The company began in 1976 as a group of craftsmen dedicated to producing quality leaded glass panels and has since been involved in all aspects of decorative glass projects from the creation of custom artwork for entryways, skylights, sidelights, doors, and interior room dividers, to restoration of priceless antique lamps.

A partial list of the company's commissioned work includes leaded beveled glass entries for the Clairidge Hotel in Atlantic City; a leaded stained glass window for the Colorado senate chambers at the state capitol in Denver; and five leaded stained glass panels depicting the history of Englewood, Colorado, for a bank in that city.

Brochure available.

Boulder Stained Glass Studios
1920 Arapahoe Ave.
Boulder, CO 80302
(303) 449-9030

The Brass Knob

In Washington, DC, one of the best places to find architectural antiques is The Brass Knob. Turn-of-the-century items are featured, and the shop stocks a considerable amount of stained, leaded, beveled, and other types of decorative glass. Most items are one of a kind, so no catalogue is available, but correspondence is welcomed.

The Brass Knob
2311 18th St. N.W.
Washington, DC 20009
(202) 332-3370

Chatham Glass Co.

Hand-blown bullseye glass just like the type made during colonial days is produced today at Chatham Glass Co. This attractive, old-fashioned glass can be used decoratively or in place of existing panels to let light in, but retain privacy. Custom-made panels of any size will be created and delivery can take from one to four weeks after an order is placed, depending on what's in stock.

Brochure available.

Chatham Glass Co.
Box 522
N. Chatham, MA 02650
(508) 945-5547

Curran Glass & Mirror Co.

In the search for such specialized glasswork as an ornately beveled mirror to enhance a foyer or for decorative transom windows to adorn otherwise dreary office doors, Patrick Curran is the artist of choice. His beautiful work is highly esteemed in a variety of environments, from private homes to restaurants and bars to Tiffany's window displays.

Curran recently reproduced a set of seven matching transom windows for the United States treasury secretary's office in Washington, DC. The windows,

each 44½" long and 9" wide, are etched in the original pattern, c. 1860. For this project Curran chose his sandblasting technique because it ensures a crisp line. (Another method he employs, using acid to etch glass, results in softer lines and subtle details.) The borders on this work are in the Greek Revival style, exhibited by the smoothly flowing lines at each end and bound by a scallop design of variously shaped elongated teardrops.

Using original designs or reproducing patterns from a model, Curran achieves a broad range of effects by working with a variety of techniques, including glass bending, beveling, stenciling, etching, silvering, electroforming of metal on glass, and sculpting. He is also adept at restoring antique glasswork of all sorts. For Smith College Curran repaired an 1875 painted-glass seal, two feet in diameter, kiln firing some of the tiny pieces of colored glass as many as seven times to achieve a precise match. All of Curran's work is custom made.

Brochure, $1.

Curran Glass & Mirror Co.
30 N. Maple St.
Florence, MA 01060
(413) 584-5761

Ferguson's Cut Glass Works

A master glass cutter and beveler in the brilliant style, Cary Ferguson creates windows, entranceways, room dividers, and decorative mirrors that pierce the eye with their colors and clarity. This window, called "Perfection," is typical of his style. The four petals and center are elaborately cut, but the deft use of color wrestles with the intricate cutting for command of the viewer's attention. The interlocking bands are a deep, bright blue, interrupted at points by triangular or diamond-shaped slivers of clear and ruby-colored glass. The complete window is, quite simply, stunning.

Brochure available.

Ferguson's Cut Glass Works
4292 Pearl Rd.
Cleveland, OH 44109
(216) 459-2929

Glashaus Inc.

If the Art Deco style of decorating with solid glass blocks appeals to you, write to Glashaus Inc. for information about Weck glass blocks. These German-manufactured blocks come in a variety of shapes and sizes as well as several different textural designs. Blocks are either square, rectangular, or bullnosed for turning corners. Patterns filter light, distort it, or allow clear vision, but all designs are on the inside of the blocks. Block exteriors are smooth for easy cleaning.

To diffuse light, try the Aktis design, in which a crystal-like effect permits good light transmission. The Nubio distorts vision and permits privacy with random intersecting waves creating a marble-like appearance. Clarity, available in Cleartone or Goldtone, is a see-through block that, when stacked, provides a dramatic grid effect.

Brochures, $2.

Glashaus, Inc.
PO Box 517
Elk Grove, IL 60007
(312) 640-6910

Golden Age Glassworks

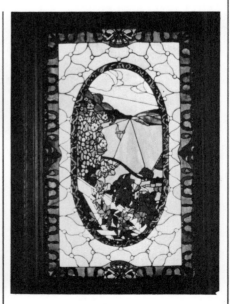

From the restoration of a 3½'-high by 4½'-wide window with a classical theme to the creation of a vivid yellow lampshade bordered with scarlet flowers and foliage in several shades of green, Barbara Arrindell displays skill and ingenuity. Working with verbal

58

hints, photographs, drawings, and her own artistry, she creates eye-pleasing panels like her "Victorian Cut Flowers," a detail of which is shown here. Measuring 24" high by 54" long, it features a bowl of deep-blue irises and gracefully intertwined yellow roses. Although she excels at re-creating many styles, Arrindell is at her best when tackling natural subjects—vines, trees, flowers, or entire pastoral scenes. She also manages Nottingham Gallery, which specializes in the sale of antique English, American, and Canadian windows.

Sets of slides or photographs, $2. each.

Golden Age Glassworks
339 Bellvale Rd.
Warwick, NY 10990
(914) 986-1487

The Kardell Studio Inc.

An active historic preservationist working in the field of 18th- and 19th-century architectural ornamentation, Ellen Kardell brings not only first-rate craftsmanship, but also original style to her work in leaded art glass. Her forte is creating new designs in period styles, and this she has done nationwide for hundreds of clients including the Smithsonian Institution, and various restaurants, homes, and churches.

Pictured is a detail of an intricately designed opalescent glass window depicting wisteria vines. The overall window size is 35" by 55".

It is made with handrolled American sheet glass in a blend of subtle pastel hues, primarily lavendars and greens. Also shown is an ornate panel designed in the

Renaissance Revival style. This piece features a variety of clear textured glass. It is 36" square. Both are original designs in historic period styles.

Catalogue, $3.50.

The Kardell Studio Inc.
904 Westminster Dr. N.W.
Washington, DC 20001
(202) 462-4433

Kraatz Russell

Kraatz Russell's hand-blown bullseye glass panes, shown, are appropriate for early American reproduction or restoration projects, but the unique character of this glass makes it suitable for more modern environments, too.

For the Boston Museum of Fine Arts, Kraatz Russell created a series of leaded diamond-pane casement windows for its reconstructed 1636 Fairbanks house, and the company welcomes work for today's architects, designers, and builders as well.

Leaded glass panels and decorative glass of all types for doors, transoms, sidelights, and windows are among the Kraatz Russell repertoire. Providing light and privacy, each panel design is developed in consultation with the client, taking into consideration such details as setting and color scheme. Once a design has been created, the glass is blown, shaped, cooled, and finally cut to size. Exterior panels are double-glazed for protection and insulation. Kraatz Russell craftsmen work with skilled cabinetmakers and can provide frames, sashes, and doors if necessary.

Pictured, too, is one of the company's decorative windows. Commissioned for the Indian River school building in 1987, this custom-designed hand-blown, leaded glass window is 36" in diameter. Executed in rose and clear crystal it complements the brick and granite structure beautifully.

Literature available.

Kraatz Russell Glass
Grist Mill Hill
RFD 1, Box 320C
Canaan, NH 03741
(603) 523-4289

Pompei & Company

Expert in all areas of fine art glass production, Joe and Ivy Pompei produce everything from leaded glass archtop windows and entry doors to stained glass business signs to Tiffany-style lamps. Their work is exclusively custom-made, and by maintaining this rule, they've been able to take on some very unusual assignments—a free-standing room divider in a bamboo and marsh flower design; windows in Victorian motifs; elegant mirrors decorated with leaded and beveled glass; and the

dogwood window, pictured.

Catalogue, $5.

Pompei & Company
454 High St.
West Medford, MA 02155
(617) 395-8867

J. Ring Glass Studio

Exquisite beveling and an elegant design distinguish these glass windows, created by J. Ring. The studio is skilled in the manufacture of such pieces, with the capacity to make bevels up to 1½" wide. Another specialty is the

reproduction of bent glass panels for lamps and windows; J. Ring is expert at restoring Handel and Tiffany lamps. The firm also resilvers mirrors, etches glass by both the abrasive and acid methods, constructs and restores stained and leaded glass windows, and glue-chips glass in featherlike patterns. No catalogue is available, as J. Ring does custom work almost exclusively.

J. Ring Glass Studio
2724 University Ave. S.E.
Minneapolis, MN 55414
(612) 379-0920

Sunflower Glass Studio

Karen and Geoff Caldwell's work speaks for itself. Their one-of-a-kind windows and panels testify to the couple's skill and artistry. Intricate beveling done in the studio, brilliant jewels, textured clear glass, and subtle use of colors give Sunflower's creations a dazzling elegance. The Caldwells also create lighting fixtures and will repair glass. Call for an appointment to visit the studio for a look at some unusually beautiful original pieces.

Sunflower Glass Studio
Box 99, RD 3
Sergeantsville, NJ 08557
(609) 397-1535

Ornamental Metalwork

Architectural iron is one of the most appealing products of the 19th century. This was the great age of cast iron. Today fountains, fences, gates, lawn sculptures of animals, window grilles for frieze windows, and roof cresting and finials are still objects of admiration. Antique cast iron can be found in some salvage yards and antique shops but it is growing more scarce each year. There are foundries that will reproduce old patterns or custom produce replacement parts. Don't forget, however, that a blacksmith may be able to help you out. His forge is a mini-foundry, although the smithy is likely to prefer wrought-iron objects to those which are cast. Among the sources of fine reproduction period metalwork are the firms that follow.

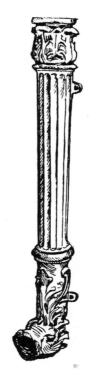

W. F. Norman Corp.

In addition to ceilings, roofs, and walls, the W. F. Norman Corp. specializes in the design and production of stamped sheet-metal ornaments and statuary.

The company offers exquisitely detailed moldings, rosettes, capitals, cornices, lintels, window hoods, finials, and weather vanes. Of the thirteen hundred catalogue selections available, most are worked in sheets of zinc, aluminum, bronze, and lead-coated copper. Other alloys are readily available on a custom basis. Custom work is done; designs can be based on antiques or original plans. An unparalleled degree of authenticity is available too, since the production techniques, and even some of the machinery, date back to the company's founding in 1892.

Pictured are two custom-designed copper roof finials. Each was pro-

duced using a combination of metal stamping and metal turning. Finial sizes usually range from 3' to 6'.

Brochure available.

W. F. Norman Corp.
Box 323
214-32 N. Cedar St.
Nevada, MO 64772-0323
(800) 641-4038
Missouri customers, call collect:
(417) 667-5552

Nostalgia

Savannah, Georgia's historic district provides a rich host of models for decorative designs. Among the fine features of the imposing Davenport House (built circa 1815) is a set of dolphin downspouts, a traditional metal spout with a gaping snout to let water run off from rooftops. In Nostalgia's successful attempt to copy this rare design, even the

pitting caused by rust is shown. The 8"-deep spout is 5" wide and 59" tall and is typical of Nostalgia's fine metalwork.

Catalogue, $2.50.

Nostalgia, Inc.
307 Stiles Ave.
Savannah, GA 31401
(912) 232-2324

Steptoe & Wife

Victorian-style cast-iron staircases are a specialty at Steptoe & Wife. These handsome alternatives to concrete are reproduced for use both inside and out. The Windsor balusters shown can be fitted into cast-iron staircase railings. The flowing scrollwork on these balusters is not only decorative, but also creates a tighter spacing than a straight baluster. They are

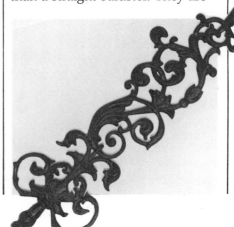

61

sold in Canada and the United States.

For other needs, Steptoe & Wife offers the Lawler line of decorative

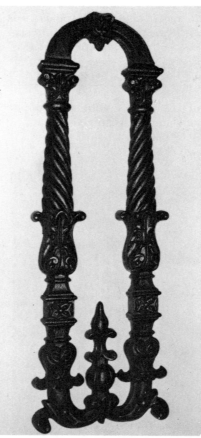

iron and aluminum castings. Three examples are shown. These pieces, available in Canada only, can be used to create decorative iron railed panels and fences.

They are also appropriate for gates, security grilles, newell posts, and can even be used to construct a gazebo.

Lawler Catalogue, $5 refundable with purchase.

Steptoe & Wife Catalogue, $3.

Steptoe & Wife Antiques Ltd.
322 Geary Ave.
Toronto, Ontario, Canada M6H 2C7
(416) 530-4200
(416) 530-4666 (FAX)

American Architectural Art

Call on American Architectural Art to fabricate simulated wood, stone, metal, masonry, or terra-cotta ornamentation. Using special compounds or either gypsum-reinforced, polymerized fiberglass (for interior use) or fiberglass-reinforced polyester (for exterior work), expert artists will execute any style or type of piece. In reproducing period work, American Architectural artists take a cast

from an existing ornamental piece if at all possible. Sculptures, urns, reliefs, cornices, ceilings, and capitals come from the hands of American Architectural Art's craftsmen. Sanding or spackling gives each piece an impeccable surface. The embellishments may be mounted with mortar, mechan-

Plaster, Composition, and Polymer Ornamentation

Most old house interiors are incomplete without a display of complementary moldings, ceiling ornaments, brackets, and other decorative elements. Happily, there are an increasing number of craftsmen extremely skilled in restoring and fabricating new plaster ornamentation. Many of the same imaginative craftsmen also work with compo, as the fibrous alternative to plaster of Paris is termed. Because of the high cost of such specialty work, new lightweight synthetic materials are also being used in place of plaster or composition materials. These are polymer-based products, and they are relatively easy to apply and to finish.
62 *Their use has spread even to the bastions of conservative old house restorers.*

ical fasteners, or construction adhesives.

Brochure available.

American Architectural Art Co.
PO Box 904
Adamstown, PA 19501

Architectural Masterworks

Exquisitely detailed, Architectural Masterworks's collection of period architectural components offers historical authenticity along with modern convenience. The company's finely cast designs, including cornice moldings, friezes, chair rails, doorways, pilasters, stair brackets, and much more, are molded directly from select plaster, clay, and wood originals and are formed from the company's Permacast material. With the density of white pine, this material allows for easy installation and is extremely durable both indoors and out.

The stately grace and fine detail of Architectural Masterworks's doorways are evidenced in this illustration. Each entranceway has several components, each of which is cast as a single element to avoid cracking and separation. Many of the components have been designed

to fit with each other, thereby offering numerous combinations of architecturally correct doorways. The Pineapple finial is one of two styles available for this entrance. It is 5⅛" wide, 9⅛" tall, and 3⅝" deep. The Rams Head pediment, with modillion blocks and rope detail, is one of three types offered. It is 73" wide, 22½" tall, and 5" deep. Below it, the plumed crossbar, one of two options, is 66" wide, 7¼" tall, and 1⅛" deep. Corinthian entrance pilasters complete this doorway and are available in various widths, each about 110" tall and from 2½" to 4¾" deep in the shaft and capital respectively.

The company's collection of stair brackets is especially pleasing. Six different patterns are available for either right- or left-facing stairs. Brackets range from 12¼" to 12¾" wide and from 6¾" to 7½" high. Projecting from ½" to 1¼", these stair brackets can be cut to size on the job to fit treads and risers. As is the case with all Architectural Masterworks's components, from doorways to moldings and rosettes, the brackets can be sawed, drilled, nailed, or mounted using an adhesive the company supplies. Each piece comes primed for later painting or finishing.

Also shown are two examples from Architectural Masterworks's broad selection of cornice

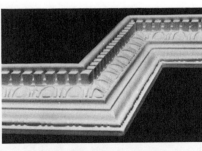

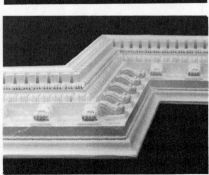

moldings, the Egg and Dart and Kensington designs. All moldings are designed to be installed with regular field carpenter tools.

Architectural Masterworks offers a complete design service, and provides detailed installation directions with each order.

Brochure available.

Architectural Masterworks
3502 Divine Ave.
Chattanooga, TN 37407
(615) 867-3630

Architectural Sculpture Ltd.

Architectural Sculpture Ltd. is a small shop of craftspeople and artists creating unique architectural plaster ornaments. Each piece is done in the company's New York City shop. The artists have compiled a catalogue of stock cast plaster architectural ornaments for interior use which includes lavishly decorated capitals, ceiling medallions, pedestals, brackets, cornices, and decorative plaques. In addition to their original designs, this company's artists enjoy taking on custom work. They have done restoration work, created new pieces based on drawings supplied by customers, and worked with clients to sculpt, cast, or create a new mold. Examples of Architectural Sculpture's commissions can be seen at the following New York City locations: The Waldorf-Astoria Hotel, Bergdorf-Goodman, Bloomingdale's, and The Parker Meridian Hotel.

Pictured are the Pegasus plaque, #420, measuring 30" square and

¾" thick; the Art overdoor plaque, #400, 17" by 34"; the Art Nouveau ceiling medallion, #132, 28" in diameter; and the Lavabo, #720, 16" wide by 7½" high with an 8½" projection.

Catalogue, $3.50

Architectural Sculpture Ltd.
242 Lafayette St.
New York, NY 10012
(212) 431-5873

Balmer Studios

The Balmer Architectural Art Studios is outstanding in the field for numerous reasons; in the area of longevity alone, the company has an impressive jump on the competition. Founded in 1835, Balmer has consistently produced the highest quality architectural and decorative art. Its talented artists and sculptors work in wood, clay, and compositions. Each Balmer architectural art product is copyrighted.

The company's catalogues, naturally, show thousands of beautifully crafted items from columns, pilasters, and brackets to niches, domes, panel moldings, and busts. Under the category of rosettes, for example, are pictured more than 250 different designs.

Whether restoring a building to its original glory, renovating to a period style, or creating an entirely new environment, Balmer's art ought to be considered.

Catalogues available.

The Balmer Architectural Art Studios
9 Codeco Court
Don Mills, Ontario, Canada
* M3A 1B6*
(416) 449-2155
(416) 449-3018 (FAX)

Decorators Supply Corporation

Decorators Supply offers a fine line of ornamental cast plaster and wood fiber items for exterior and interior use, and a group of composition capitals and brackets for interior use. The company has found that the demand for various period designs is increasing continually, and has therefore extended its already large line of ornaments. Decorators Supply's goods are illustrated in catalogues that are sent to customers on approval and payments are refunded if the books are returned in sixty days. Prices vary.

The Decorators Supply Corp.
3610-12 S. Morgan St.
Chicago, IL 60609
(312) 847-6300
(312) 847-6357 (FAX)

David Flaharty

DAVID FLAHARTY

David Flaharty creates his ornamental plaster sculpture in the manner of the old masters. From cornice moldings to medallions and more, not only does this artist create exquisitely detailed architectural ornamentation, but he does all his work in an authentic manner, custom sculpting and molding each different element and then casting and setting the finished pieces individually. In a dining room medallion like the one illustrated, for example, first the circular base plate is laid and then the real work begins. One by one each enrichment is carefully cast and attached either with plaster, as was done historically, or with more modern adhesives depending on the project.

Working from his own period designs or to architects' or decorators' specifications, Flaharty's plaster sculpting in American period styles is highly respected even by the most demanding. New York's Metropolitan Museum of Art recently used Flaharty's sculpted ornamentation to decorate its new American period rooms. For museum-quality artwork in your old house, Flaharty's sculpture exemplifies authenticity and excellence. All work is done on a custom basis.

Literature available.

David Flaharty
402 Magazine Rd., RD 2
Green Lane, PA 18054
(215) 234-8242

Focal Point

Focal Point's huge collection of architectural ornamentation is offered in two composite materials, Endure-all and Contour-all. Endure-all is tougher than wood or plaster and can be used indoors or out. It is easily applied and contains an effective fire retardant. Contour-all has all the same characteristics without being fire-retardant. In addition, it is flexible enough to be used on curved walls or stairwells. All Focal Point's ornamentation is primed either white for paint or beige for stain. The product accepts most finishes and can be

made to simulate most materials from wood to marble.

Focal Point's cornice moldings vary widely in size and design. Each is a finely detailed masterwork in its own right. Style 19210, the Eastlake, is 6″ deep and 5⅞″ high or 5⅜″ deep and 5¼″ high. The pattern itself repeats every 8¼″.

From the American 19th century collection, style 19220, the Pea Pod & Vine, repeats every 28⅝″, and it is 7⅝″ deep and 5¼″ high or 7⅛″ deep and 4¾″ high.

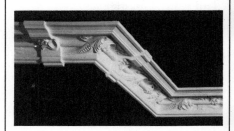

Style 16320 is one of several authorized by the Colonial Williamsburg Foundation. It is called the Governor's Palace. The pattern repeats every 1⅝″, and it is 7⅝″ high and 6⅜″ deep. All the company's cornice moldings are made in 10′ to 12′ lengths. When ordering, allow for waste. There is a 40′ minimum on each model ordered.

Other architectural ornamentation that Focal Point produces includes such items as ceiling medallions

and door, window, and wall pieces. Ceiling medallion 82345 is a reproduction from the Thomas/Arnett house, and is endorsed by the Victorian Society in America. It is 45″ long and 37¼″ wide and projects 3⅜″.

Item 97070 is one of the company's door, window, and wall pieces, the Régence. French in

style, it is designed to match the Régence cove cornice molding. It is 36″ wide, 14″ high, and ½″ deep.

Literature available

Focal Point Inc.
PO Box 93327
Atlanta, GA 30318
(800) 662-5550
(404) 351-0820 (GA and AK)

W. J. Hampton Plastering

Experts at repair and restoration of plaster ceilings and ornamentation, W. J. Hampton's craftsmen have worked on projects throughout the New York City metropolitan area. Numerous private homeowners can attest to the quality of Hampton's work, as can a wide variety of commercial clients. This firm has worked on Symphony Hall in Newark, the Stevens Institute of Technology in Hoboken, the Rodino Federal Building and Court House in Newark, and the Riotto Funeral Home in Jersey City. Hampton's artisans list such impressive historic landmarks as Grace Church Van Vorst and Old Bergen Church in Jersey City, among others, on their list of successfully completed projects.

A subsidiary of W. J. Hampton Plastering is Hampton Decor. This firm features a complete collection of pre-cast plaster ornamentation, including moldings, columns, plinths, pilasters, ceiling roses, and more, designed by the artists at Orac Decor. These items, designed in Great Britain, are imported directly from Belgium.

Literature available.

W. J. Hampton Plastering
30 Fisk St.
Jersey City, NJ 07305
(201) 433-9002

Broadway Market

Broadway Market's Palladia collection of three-dimensional architectural detail for indoors and out runs the gamut of decoration from dentil molding to Victorian style brackets. Products for various areas of the house are categorized in Broadway Market's catalogue. All items are made

from Molded Millwork, a high density polymer created to resist warping and rotting and to be impervious to insects. Arch surrounds, door and window trim, capitals, columns, and brackets are among the many items offered. Fine period design is

Oakleaf Reproductions

Recreating the warmth of old English settings, rich in wood paneling, ornamentation, and timbered ceilings, Oakleaf Reproductions manufactures high quality simulated wood products. All manner of architectural detailing are available: friezes, cornices, moldings, pillars, pilasters, and decorated panels. These display elaborate carvings as in the originals on which they have been modeled. Also available are rough-hewn looking beams, joists, and wall planking.

Brochure available.

Oakleaf Reproductions
Lucas G. Leone, Jr.
North American Agent
Stonewalls, Chester Springs, PA
  19425
(215) 827-9491

evidenced in these functional and durable elements.

Literature available.

Broadway Market MRA
79 Bridge St.
Brooklyn, NY 11201
(718) 643-0994

Barry Rose

Barry Rose creates masterful architectural detailing in terra cotta. For clients large and small he can provide complete design, production, and installation services, including sculpting original pieces, making molds, and supplying his designs for builders or other artists. Since 1973 Rose has completed many major commissions, including national historic restorations like those at the Denver Museum of Natural History and the Oxford Alexis Hotel to contemporary work for businesses around the country. This illustration shows an original detail sculpted in terra cotta as part of Rose's work to restore the Jonathan Flower House in Denver.

Barry Rose
1450 Logan
Denver, CO 80203
(303) 832-3250

Russell Restoration of Suffolk

Dean Russell and his co-workers start with bags of plaster, buckets of water, and some tools. From there, they carry out custom restoration work, handling jobs in which they remake walls, restore or create ornamental plasterwork on site, or custom cast or mold items in their shop. Skilled in the areas of historic restoration, the Russell crew includes among its clients the Orient Historical Society, the East Hampton Historical Society, the State of New York parks department, and the Falaise/Guggenheim Estate. Russell is also a consultant in the field for Fine Homebuilding magazine.

Russell Restoration of Suffolk
5550 Bergen Ave.
Mattituck, New York 11952
(516) 765-2481

San Francisco Victoriana

High quality and a large variety of designs are the hallmarks of San Francisco Victoriana, producers of some of the best architectural ornamentation around. The company's fiber-reinforced hand-cast plasterwork, like its excellent millwork, is displayed in a handy catalogue which gives a bit of history along with advice on selecting and installing its products. The four plaster ceiling centerpieces shown illustrate the fine detailing and accurate styling this company creates. Lotta, #301-11, is 25"; Lola, #301-13, is 26½"; Liberty Street, #301-15, is 28"; as is Queen Anne Lace large,

#301-16. In addition to the commonly found circular ceiling medallions, unusual shapes are produced, as are such items as capitals, cornices, and festoons.

San Francisco Victoriana
2245 Palou Ave.
San Francisco, CA 94124
(415) 648-0313

J.P. Weaver

The J.P. Weaver Company specializes in the design and manufacture of custom staff moldings and fine carving reproductions. From its collection of over 8,000 carvings, it can replicate any period in architectural history through Art Deco. Using a composition formula that has been a family secret since the 19th century, the company produces ornaments that are so sharp in reproduction that the most minute detail of the original is in clear relief. Every ornament is handmade. Designs are usually a combination of pieces to make a larger composite design. The average thickness of the ornaments varies from ¼" to ½" with some relief of 1". The sizes varies from ½" diameter to pieces that are 12" by 12". Weaver ornaments are pliable and self-bonding. When lightly steamed, they can be molded to curves and radiused arcs. The ornaments can be self-bonded to wood, drywall, mirror and metal, or any tight, dry, smooth surface. They can also be pre-painted, steamed, and installed on another color surface. Once installed, the oils evaporate and the ornaments take on a rock-like hardness and have a life span of 150 years. Having produced composition ornaments for countless movie palaces of the 1920s and '30s, and for Hearst's inimitable San Simeon castle, J.P.

Weaver knows all there is to know about composition ornamentation and its place in architectural history.

Brochure available.

J.P. Weaver
2301 W. Victory Blvd.
Burbank, CA 91506
(818) 841-5700

Applied Wood Ornamentation and Paneling

Such ornamental items as paneling, wainscoting, moldings, brackets, finials, columns, spindles, newel posts, and railings lie very much at the heart of period interior and exterior decoration. Depending on the style of your old house, at least several of these elements will come into play. Door and window casings, of course, are standard items in every old building; it is only in recent times that these openings have been left as unadorned holes in the wall. Such casings in old houses are usually comprised of a series of handsome moldings and panels. Moldings similarly make up and define paneled doors and may delineate ceilings from walls, and walls from floors. There are thousands of types of moldings and decorative ornaments that can be used in a period room or outside the house on a porch or to embellish entryways, windows, gables, and roof lines. Producers of period millwork are found everywhere in North America, and what they cannot supply from stock they will custom manufacture.

American Heirlooms, Inc.

American Heirlooms manufactures classic balusters from poplar in a single piece of wood without glued joints; or in laminated white pine with glued joints. Any wood is available, though, and the company's craftsmen specialize in oak. Styles include those suitable for staircases and balustrades (as shown). The company also makes newels with ball tops. A simple leaflet illustrating American Heirlooms' work is mailed free of charge upon request. A more elaborate brochure is planned for the coming year.

Brochure available.

American Heirlooms, Inc.
Rt. 2, Box 347 A
Bean Station, TN 37708

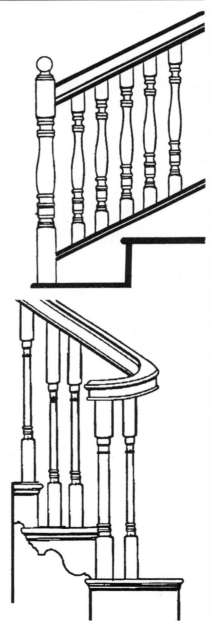

American Heritage Shutters

Adding shutters to an interior is a quick way to give a room depth and warmth; adding them on the exterior or replacing existing outside shutters is sure to dress up any home. Unlike other window treatments, shutters can be a permanent architectural improvement that increases the value of your property.

Manufactured primarily from Western pine, American Heritage Shutters are custom-made to fit any dimension and are created in a range of designs: full panel styles, louver styles, even arched windows can be fitted with shutters. The company also offers a number of color and material options, and provides custom finishing and expert installation.

Literature available.

American Heritage Shutters, Inc.
2549 Lamar Ave.
Memphis, TN 38114
(901) 743-2800

Anthony Wood Products

Victorian gingerbread or carpenter's lace, as it is sometimes known, is an engagingly styled form of architectural detail suitable for more than just Victorian houses. The numerous gingerbread items offered by Anthony Wood Products can lead to imaginative designs all around the house. Brackets like the five illustrated can enhance entryways in kitchens, dining areas, between living room and hallway, and, of course, porches. The culmination of most gingerbread-trimmed houses is a gable unit. Two of the many fine such units Anthony makes are shown. Fan brackets placed on the porch or screen door often correlate with the gable unit. Creating a welcoming entrance above any door is easily done with an Anthony header, one of which is shown.

All Anthony Wood Products are made individually, as the originals were. Mass-production is not practiced. Each item is made from premium "C" grade ponderosa pine and clear heart redwood.

Architectural Components

Do you need assistance in bringing a period room to life? Architectural Components will help you to design a raised-panel wall that suits the room and your taste. Then the firm will construct the paneling, typically of $^{15}/_{16}$"-thick clear kiln-dried eastern white pine, but sometimes of cherry, poplar, oak, or another type of hardwood. Mortise and tenon

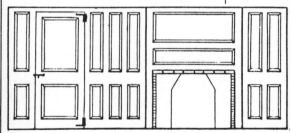

joinery is used exclusively, and the surfaces are hand-planed. Featheredge or beaded wainscoting is also available.

Brochure, $3.

Architectural Components
Box 249
Leverett, MA 01054
(413) 367-9441

Barewood Inc.

Barewood is a custom woodworking shop specializing in hard-to-find items and the production of goods for architectural preservation and restoration projects. The

Designs are accurate reproductions of patterns used in the past or are modeled after antiques.

A new service at Anthony is its custom reproduction department that can duplicate missing or deteriorated gingerbread. For those restoring buildings to historic standards, Anthony can help, too.

Catalogue, $2.

Anthony Wood Products
PO Box 1081
Hillsboro, TX 76645
(817) 582-7225

69

company operates from a 14,000-square-foot workshop in the Redhook section of Brooklyn, New York. The craftsmen at Barewood are equipped to handle special jobs, following blueprints or specifications with care. Among their areas of expertise are doors and sashes, custom moldings, staircase parts, mantels, wainscotting, paneling, and decorative woodcarving. Barewood has produced custom work for Trinity Church and the Vivian Beaumont Theatre, both in New York City, among others.

Brochure available.

Barewood Inc.
106 Ferris St.
Brooklyn, NY 11231
(718) 875-9037

Bay-Waveland Woodworks

Victorian gingerbread from Bay-Waveland is delightfully crafted and suitable for both interior and exterior use. So, even if your house exterior can't accommodate the fanciful curves and scrollwork, perhaps a bookshelf in the living room could. Fretwork, too, can be used for interior decoration. Bay-Waveland also manufactures a handsome Victorian-style porch bench, several custom-carved mantels, and does other custom woodwork.

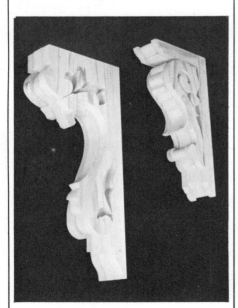

| Brochure, $1.

Bay-Waveland Woodworks
Rt. 4, Box 548
Bay St. Louis, MS 39520
(601) 467-6126

Beech River Mill Company

Whether adding finishing touches to a house or an office, the Beech River Mill Company is capable of meeting the design requirements with its cutsom-made louvered and paneled shutters and doors. Using machinery first employed in the Victorian era for shutter making, the Beech River Mill Company follows the time-honored processes that turned out some of the best millwork for nearly one hundred years. Because of the job-specific woodworking equipment, Beech River Mill can produce any louvered or

Bendix Mouldings

Both variety and quality make Bendix an outstanding supplier of wood ornamentation and moldings. The company makes and sells almost fifty types of ornaments and rosettes, over fifty styles of carved wood moldings, six dentil moldings, three scalloped untextured moldings, eight overlays made of flexible birch plywood and backed with glue, and thirty-nine embossed moldings, plus various beaded, rope, bolection, and crown moldings. They are sold in random lengths of 3' to 15', with most pieces ranging from 6' to 10' in

paneled item requested. In addition to those already mentioned, the company makes cabinet doors, folding doors, room dividers, and louvered vents. Most products are made from clear dry pine, but the company also works with cherry, mahogany, cyprus, oak, and ash.

Pictured is an interior raised-panel shutter, IP200. The finished product is ¾" thick, has 1⅜" stiles, a 1¾" top rail, 2⅛" bottom rail, and a 1¾" cross rail. This style provides extra insulation when properly installed. For shorter versions, the cross rail is not necessary. Other options for this type of interior shutter are flat panels, and rabbeted and beaded center closure.

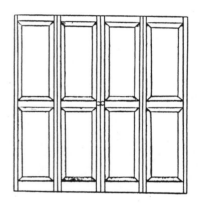

Catalogue available.

Beech River Mill Co.
Old Route 16
Centre Ossipee, NH 03814
(603) 539-2636

length. The beaded styles are sold only in lengths of 2½' and 3'. Samples of the moldings and carvings are available.

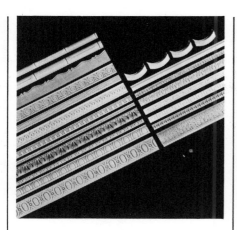

Catalogue, $2.

Bendix Mouldings, Inc.
235 Pegasus Ave.
Northvale, NJ 07647
(800) 526-0240
(201) 767-8888 (NJ)

Carlisle Restoration Lumber

The materials for pine or oak paneling are available at Carlisle Restoration Lumber, which sells boards that are perfect for the purpose. Square-edged 14″- to 21″-wide pine and 5″- to 10″-wide oak are kept in stock, as is 8″- to 12″-wide ship-lapped pine. Carol and Dale Carlisle provide instructions for installing and caring for their paneling.

Literature available.

Carlisle Restoration Lumber
Rte. 123
Stoddard, NH 03464
(603) 446-3937

Chadsworth Incorporated

Chadsworth brings back to life the architectural grandeur of classic Greek and Roman columns. Care-fully detailed in every respect, Chadsworth columns are true to the specifications set down in 1563 by the Italian Renaissance master architect Giacomo Barozzi da Vignola, who formulated guidelines for the use of these ancient supports. Additionally, Chadsworth produces columns in the Doric, contemporary, and Art Deco styles and custom-designs others from sketches, photographs, or architect's drawings.

All interior and exterior columns are constructed of either redwood, pine, poplar, oak, teak, or mahogany, but other special lumber can be used, too. Columns range from 6″ to 36″ in diameter with heights up to 40′. Among the many custom creations by Chadsworth are columns for the MGM studios at Walt Disney World's Epcot Center, the new IBM Tower in New York, and the United States embassy in Cairo, Egypt.

Pictured are Tuscan, Roman Doric, and Temple of the Winds columns.

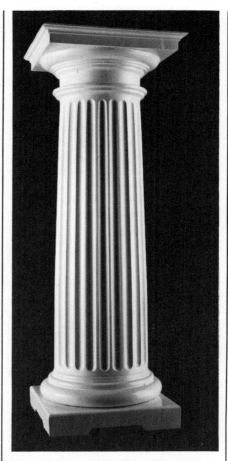

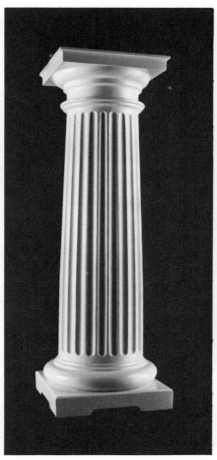

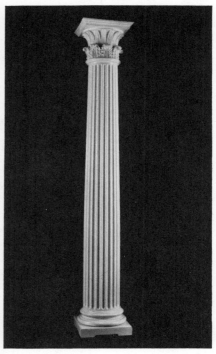

Catalogue, $2.

Chadsworth, Inc.
PO Box 53268
Atlanta, GA 30355
(404) 876-5410

Coco Millwork & Supply Co.

From custom cabinets, mantels, brackets, window frames, and sashes to full-scale moldings up to 5″ thick and 8″ wide, Coco Millwork does it all. This fifty-year-old company offers a fine selection of stock moldings including those pictured, available generally in poplar and cypress; some are also stocked in red oak and ash. Coco grinds its own knives to create its moldings. Sometimes the machinery can be altered to create a new molding or to copy an antique. Custom orders are a specialty.

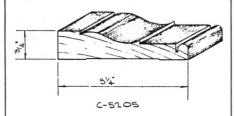

C-5205

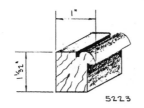

5223

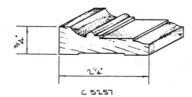

C 5257

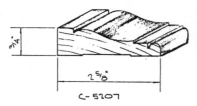

C-5207

A catalogue showing the many stock moldings is mailed free of charge upon request. An expanded technical catalogue appropriate for architects is available for $25.

Coco Millwork & Supply Co., Inc.
19151 Highland Rd., PO Box 2601
Baton Rouge, LA 70821-2601
(504) 291-0950

Craftsman Lumber

The toughest part of Craftsman Lumber's restoration and reproduction projects is finding the wide boards of white pine, so plentiful when colonists built their homes. Knotty white pine, kiln dried to a moisture content between 6% and 8%—as dry as is feasible, without promoting cracking—can be planed in various ways to yield excellent wood paneling. Edges are generally featheredged, ship-lapped, or tongued and grooved, with molding or beading as options.

Craftsman Lumber
R.R. 1, Box 65
Ashby, MA 01431
(617) 386-7550

Crawford's Old House Store

Protecting a corner of a wall may not seem an important task, but once a new paint or paper job begins to show the wear it gets in normal use, you'll see why Crawford's protective molding is so valuable. This simple, but decorative wood molding is easily applied, and can be painted to coordinate with the rest of the room.

Crawford's also offers a variety of goods from other manufacturers from hardware to lighting fixtures.

Brochures available.

Crawford's Old House Store
550 Elizabeth St.
Waukesha, WI 53186
(800) 556-7878
(414) 542-0685 (WI)

Cumberland Woodcraft

Cumberland offers a full line of Victorian-style woodwork designed to put the finishing touches on your house. Although the company also makes exterior ornaments, it is their line of interior items that merits special notice. It includes bead board paneling, carved column capitals, bar rail moldings, ceiling treat-

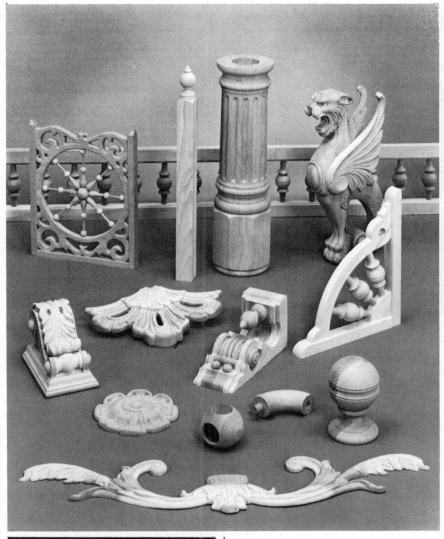

ments, screens, and partitions. The photographs show a few of Cumberland's many solid-oak and poplar interior brackets, corbels,

carvings, elaborate moldings, and fretwork grilles. All of the company's wood ornaments are made from high-quality hardwoods.

Catalogue, $3.75.

Cumberland Woodcraft Co., Inc.
Drawer 609
Carlisle, PA 17013
(717) 243-0063

Custom Millwork, Inc.

Custom projects, no matter how unusual or demanding, are ably undertaken by the fine craftsmen at Custom Millwork. Pictured is a recently completed solid mahogany library for a private residence in Washington, DC. This work shows the caliber of Custom Millwork's expertise. Special casework, custom wood windows, and reproduction of wood items

for historic buildings are among the company's specialties. But all manner of architectural woodworking from ornamentation to furniture making is undertaken by this company.

Literature available.

Custom Millwork, Inc.
PO Box 562
Berryville, VA 22611
(703) 955-4988

Devenco Products

Devenco's wooden Venetian blinds replicate the look of 18th century window coverings. This window treatment adds not only the warmth of fine woods to a room, but also an uncommon touch to the decor. Devenco blinds are custom made, and are finished in a natural wood tone or painted in one of several colors. Complementary colored tape is used when the blinds are assembled. Devenco's wooden Venetian blinds are constructed to last a lifetime with minimal maintenance.

In keeping with tradition, Devenco also offers authentically styled raised panel shutters. Another type, plantation shutters, revived from the old South, have 2½"-wide louvers, permitting a great deal of light and an unobstructed view of the outside. They can be made to size for all sorts of win-

Shown are the 1¾" diameter, 1¼" diameter, and 1" diameter. Also manufactured are ¾" and ⅜".

Driwood offers a custom design service for those who would like assistance in selecting appropriate moldings and other architectural ornamentation for their homes.

Catalogues, $6 credited toward first purchase upon request.

Driwood Moulding Company
PO Box 1729
Florence, SC 29503-1729
(803) 669-2478

Franklin County Millwork

Reproduction of 18th- and 19th-century architectural millwork is the specialty of the craftsmen at Franklin County Millwork. Working from measured drawings and actual examples, the company produces a line of interior and exterior doors, small-pane window sashes, plank window frames, and a variety of moldings. These items are stocked, but custom orders are also accepted. Franklin County Millwork has custom manufactured pediment entrances, raised paneled walls, paneled shutters, cabinets, moldings, and more.

The breadth of work undertaken by these woodworkers is tremendous. They reproduce historic period entryways from the simplest box frame with transom to the most elaborate broken pediment using time-honored methods of joinery and construction.

dows, including arched windows and fanlights.

Literature available.

Devenco Products, Inc.
PO Box 700, Dept. OHC
Decatur, GA 30031
(404) 378-4597

Driwood Moulding Company

Period moldings and millwork are produced by Driwood in a method which makes them at once im-

pervious to chipping and cracking and also reasonably priced. All the company's architecturally correct items are machine-embossed from hardwoods and in some cases in combination with wood fibers. They achieve the same looks as hand-carved items, but are considerably less expensive. Moldings kept in stock are made from Appalachian poplar, but other hardwoods can be used, including walnut, oak, mahogany, and cherry. All are ready for paint or stain.

The rope molding shown is a recent introduction. Available in five sizes and in varying lengths, this design makes an interesting accent in a room of any period.

Because of the care taken with each job, museum quality reproductions are guaranteed. The company's woodworkers will travel anywhere in the continental United States to handle a job, and they will set up millwork on-site.

Franklin County Millwork
PO Box 30
St. Clair, MO 63077
(314) 927-5770

Gazebo & Porchworks

Gazebo & Porchworks offers several types of wood trims in addition to its line of outdoor swings and structures. The selection includes a variety of shoes, fillets, and oak or hemlock rails. The rails are sold in increments of 2' with a maximum length of 16'. Two styles of gable trims are available; one has spindles and fanciful curves, and the other features a stylized sunburst design. Sturdy corbels ranging in thickness from 3" to 5" are also sold; an example measuring 23½" high by 5" wide by 9" deep is shown.

Catalogue, $2.

Gazebo & Porchworks
728 9th Ave. S.W.
Puyallup, WA 98371-6744
(206) 848-0502

Iberia Millwork

Practical, versatile, and expressive of many moods, shutters have wide and justified appeal. From standard components, fabricated to custom sizes, Iberia Millwork's shutters grace numerous restoration projects. Solid wood rails and warp-resistant laminated stiles of first growth heart redwood form Iberia's exterior shutters. Interior shutters come in stain-grade white cypress and Ponderosa pine or paint-grade yellow poplar. Custom rolling slat shutters are Iberia's specialty, but the firm can furnish fixed louver, panel bottom, and round- or angle-topped shutters, as well. Iberia recommends using its $^{15}/_{16}$"-thick shutters when possible; $1^{1}/_{16}$" and unusually thick shutters are also available. Other items from Iberia include cabinets, French doors, and various types of custom millwork.

Brochure available.

Iberia Millwork
500 Jane St.
New Iberia, LA 70560
(318) 365-5644

Humberstone Woodworking

A fine line of colonial posts and columns and related architectural woodwork is manufactured by Humberstone. Exterior porch columns as tall as 20' are made in a variety of styles and are available plain or fluted. Turned porch posts and square porch posts, colonial door entrances, cupolas, and several styles of louvered shutters are also offered.

Brochure available.

Humberstone Woodworking
PO Box 104
Georgetown, Ontario, Canada
*   L7G 4T1*
(416) 877-6757

Mark A. Knudsen

Mark A. Knudsen works for exacting customers "who know what they *won't* settle for." A quarter of a century's experience with hand tools and machinery renders Knudsen expert in hand-turning spindles or posts with up to 16" diameters and lengths of 14'. Using a German tracer lathe, the artist can machine-turn 50" pieces with 12" diameters. Another lathe produces ornamental or spiraling turnings for vases or lamp bases. If you're still not convinced, write for Knudsen's references!

Brochure available.

Mark A. Knudsen
1100 E. County Line Rd.
Des Moines, IA 50320
(515) 285-6112

Mad River Woodworks

Ornamental woodwork is a specialty at Mad River. The company carries almost everything you'd need, from lacy brackets and corbels to sawn or turned balusters to the gingerbread running trims shown, which measure 5" high by 96" long by ¾" thick. Six graceful styles of spandrels are also available and are hand-assembled. The length of the woodwork depends only on your

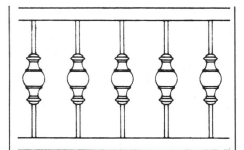

specifications; model SS-100, shown here, is 12″ high and 1½″ deep.

Another Mad River product is one which we applaud wholehearted-ly. Metal gutters can be unsightly, but well-built, attractive wooden gutters can be next to impossible to find. Fortunately, however, Mad River makes a pleasant-looking and useful redwood gutter which comes in random 8′ to 20′ lengths and measures 3½″ high and 3½″ deep.

Catalogue, $2.50.

Mad River Woodworks
Box 163
Arcata, CA 95521
(707) 826-0629

New England Woodturners

From chess pieces to columns, balusters to bedposts, corner blocks to finials, New England Woodturners is a complete wood-turning service. All turnings are hand sanded in both directions and suitable for paint or stain. An overwhelming demand for a pro-duction series baluster that is traditionally styled has inspired New England Woodturners to create its Signature Series balusters. These graceful balusters are offered in five different styles. The company's customizing capa-bilities make the balusters suitable for any project. Standard lengths are 32″, 34″, and 36″, but any baluster up to 54″ can be turned. Customers can choose from a variety of hard, soft, and exotic woods.

Literature available.

New England Woodturners
75 Daggett St., PO Box 7242
New Haven, CT 06519
(203) 776-1880

Maurer & Shepherd Joyners

Few reproduction room elements are more convincing than wood paneling. Its presence adds a richness that nothing else can. Maurer & Shepherd's wood paneling, with its lovingly hand-planed surfaces, is no exception to the rule. Like all of the company's wood products, it is custom-made entirely by hand. Maurer & Shepherd is also known for its fine interior and exterior doors, mantels, flooring, shutters, and windows.

Brochure available.

Maurer & Shepherd Joyners Inc.
122 Naubuc Ave.
Glastonbury, CT 06033
(203) 633-2383

Old World Moulding & Finishing

Hardwoods are used to create the numerous moldings and trims produced by the artisans at Old World Moulding. Ornamental items tailored to complement period decors in the French Provencial, Victorian, Tudor, Moorish, Georgian, Spanish, and early American styles are the company's specialties. Old World has its own patented system for modular fabrication of complete interiors which keeps the price of such elaborate treatments low. The company has created entire rooms—cabinetry, mantels, paneling, trim, and various moldings—to individual items such as doors in the Louis XVI mode for a suburban foyer, a wainscoted stairway for another home, and carved panels over a bar in a restaurant.

Catalogue, $2.

Old World Moulding & Finishing Co., Inc.
115 Allen Blvd.
Farmingdale, NY 11735
(516) 293-1789

Ornamental Mouldings Limited

Ornamental makes wood moldings for the do-it-yourselfer. This company's precut detailed embossed wood moldings are designed for those who wish to create an antique look in a house that is devoid of moldings. The products come ready for painting or staining, and with four-step installation instructions that should make it easy to add character to a plain room.

Shown are four of the numerous styles of ceiling cornices and chair rail moldings produced by Ornaental Mouldings. Each is available in oak or poplar. All moldings are available in 86" and 42" lengths.

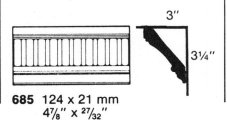

685 124 x 21 mm
4⅞" x ²⁷⁄₃₂"

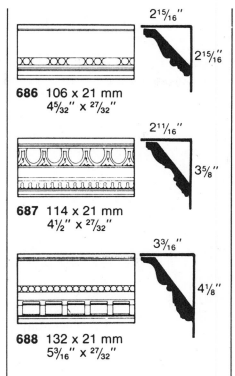

686 106 x 21 mm
4⁵⁄₃₂" x ²⁷⁄₃₂"

687 114 x 21 mm
4½" x ²⁷⁄₃₂"

688 132 x 21 mm
5³⁄₁₆" x ²⁷⁄₃₂"

Brochure available.

Ornamental Mouldings Ltd.
PO Box 336
Warterloo, Ontario, Canada N2J 4A4
(519) 884-4080
(519) 884-9692 (FAX)

Pagliacco Turning and Milling

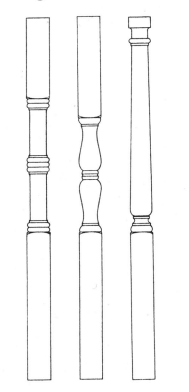

Faithful to old designs and equipped with modern methods, Pagliacco manufactures sturdy wood decorations from dried California redwood. Although other species are used occasionally, the company prefers redwood for its strength and resistance to decay and termite infestation. Pagliacco's porch posts are especially attractive. Reproduced from drawings in catalogues issued between 1870 and the early 20th century, they come in twenty-one styles, 6" and 8" widths, and three standard heights—8', 9', and 10'. Those illustrated here have the proportions of 9' posts. Larger sizes can be made on request. The posts accept rails between 36" and 42" high and coordinate well with Pagliacco's equally fine balusters and newel posts. Shipped sanded and ready for finishing, they should be primed and painted with oil-base products. If your selection will be bearing an unusual amount of weight, the company recommends that it fashion your order from Douglas fir.

The firm also makes redwood columns, available in five shaft styles with turned wood or a choice of eight composition capitals. The two shown here, the Doric capital

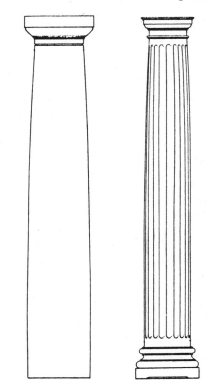

and Attic base combination and the Greek Doric style, are each manufactured in twelve standard sizes. Diameters at the shaft bottom range from 8″ to 30″, and height is determined by your specifications. The shaft may be fluted or plain, and four shapes are available: full, half, three-quarter for corners, and two-thirds for placement against walls. Pagliacco takes a good deal of care to ensure that its columns are authentic in proportion and accurate in architectural detail.

Catalogue, $6.

Pagliacco Turning and Milling
Box 225
Woodacre, CA 94973
(415) 488-4333

Perkins Architectural Millwork

Mindful of authentically creating period styles in American houses and of the historic heritage of this country that is found in its architecture, Perkins Architectural Millwork strives to produce accurate products for its customers. "Millwork is the essential part (of a home) that creates the atmosphere and prime relationship between the architectural details and furnishings," says Kenneth Perkins. The company, therefore, uses the services of an experienced architectural consultant in helping plan its work, when homeowners desire. Perkins does all manner of woodworking. Among the sought-after items it manufactures are 7″ crown molding, 5″ window and door trim, and a large variety of traditional moldings.

Catalogue and videos available.

Perkins Architectural Millwork
Rt. 5, Box 264-W
Longview, TX 75601
(214) 663-3036

Perkowitz Window Fashions

For almost 90 years Perkowitz has manufactured shutters and shades in a variety of styles and sizes. It's surprising to see just how many different shutters can be created by combining elements from some of the basic styles. Fabric frames can be paired above louvered panels or below them, louvered panels can be placed above or below solid panels, and, of course, louvered panels can be custom made to suit any room's windows. There are double-hung louvers and fabric frames with arch tops and plain tops. Wooden shutters are available finished or unfinished.

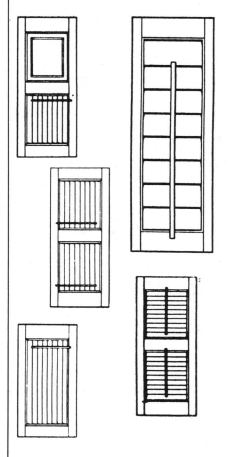

Brochures available.

Perkowitz Window Fashions
136 Green Bay Rd.
Wilmette, IL 60091-3375
(312) 251-7700

The Renovation Source, Inc.

As its name declares, The Renovation Source is a storehouse of items any home renovator would find exciting. The business stocks a great selection of salvaged architectural materials culled from a variety of buildings. These one-of-a-kind goods are supplemented by the company's offerings of reproduction products.

Illustrated are six solid oak spandrels, which come fully assembled and unfinished, ready for painting or staining at home. The beading and dowels on each are made from solid hardwood. Fretwork is ¾″ thick and is set in frames 1⅛″ thick by ¾″ wide. Item #1084 drops 18″ from the ceiling, and its center drop is 10″. Stock lengths of this model are 3′, 4′, 5′, and 6′. Number 1275 has an 18″ ceiling drop, an 11¾″ center drop, and is also available in lengths 3′, 4′, 5′, and 6′. Model 1278 has a 22″ ceiling drop, a 15¾″ center drop, and is available in 4′, 5′, and 6′ lengths. Model 1176 has a 22″ ceiling drop, with a 16″ center drop, and it is available in lengths of 3′, 4′, 5′, and 6′. Number 1076, with a heart-shaped motif in its center, has an 18″ ceiling drop, a 12″ center drop, and comes in stock lengths of 3′, 4′, 5′, and 6′. Number 875 drops 18″ from the ceiling, but has a center drop of 18½″. It is available in stock lengths of 4′, 5′, and 6′.

The Renovation Source catalogues include other millwork, and plumbing and hardware fixtures.

Catalogues, $2.

The Renovation Source, Inc.
3512-14 North Southport
Chicago, IL 60657
(312) 327-1250

Restoration Supply

A tremendous breadth of decorative accessories modeled after antiques is offered by Restoration Supply in its Classic Re-Creations catalogue. This collection of items ranging from cabinet posts to leafy sprigs is made from wood fibers crafted with fine detail to appear as the originals. Every item in this group is finished, ready to apply in a one-step application. These pieces are excellent for repair or enhancement of antiques. Most products in the catalogue are shown in full size.

Catalogue, hardware and trim, $2. Furniture pamphlet, 50¢.

Restoration Supply
Box 253
Hawesville, KY 42348
(502) 927-8494

Sheppard Millwork

Grinding their own knives and executing their turnings by hand, the staff at Sheppard Millwork produces a wide variety of high-quality ornamental woodwork. The company's stock includes two styles of sturdy shutters (models S-158 and S-159); a 1⁹⁄₁₆"-tall,

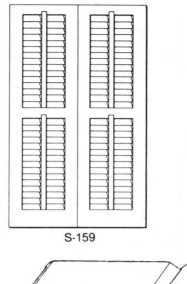

S-159

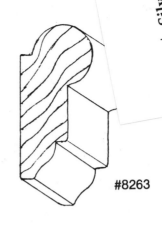

#8263

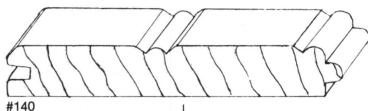

#140

gently-curving picture mold (model 8263); an unusual beaded ceiling mold (model 140); and an ornate cornice mold formed by the combination of three individual moldings. The complete selection of trims incorporates dentil moldings, casings, baseboards, a fireplace mold, stops, plinth blocks, rosettes, handrails, and a bar rail as well. In addition, Sheppard can match existing moldings or create new ones from drawings.

Brochure available.

Sheppard Millwork, Inc.
21020 70th Ave. W.
Edmonds, WA 98020
(206) 771-4645
(206) 672-1622 (FAX)

Shuttercraft

Solid pine shutters trim a colonial or Victorian home in style. Thin, plastic copies don't compare, and they boast no lasting advantage, either. Correctly sealed wooden shutters from Shuttercraft will last as long as your house, and the firm's naturally ventilating wood shutters won't encourage rot in the wooden siding they cover. Galvanized yoke pins are similarly durable. Use hinges for moveable shutters, or install shutters as a fixed decorative accent. Large shutters may also be ordered as door panels with a center rail at doorknob level.

Brochure available.

Shuttercraft
282 Stepstone Hill Rd.
Guilford, CT 06437
(203) 453-1973

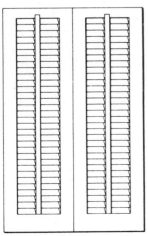

S-158

Silverton Victorian Mill Works

At Silverton, George Crane replicates turn-of-the-century moldings and millwork. This historical line of over 350 moldings, headblocks, baseblocks, casings, wainscoting, and baseboard is available in a standard stock of premium-grade pine and oak. Redwood, mahogany, and other exotic woods are offered on a custom basis. Because of the variety of millwork offered, the old-house devotee can plan the woodwork of his home around a wide array of Victorian styles. A catalogue is available which illustrates the various moldings offered as well as over forty detailed construction drawings showing the typical uses. Illustrated here is just a sampling of Silverton's stock: repeating ornaments, plate rails, moldings, corner blocks, posts, and exterior window trim. The firm's advanced equipment and modern facilities are also shown.

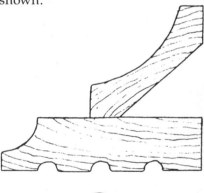

Catalogue, $4.

Silverton Victorian Mill Works
PO Box 2987-OCE
Durango, CO 81302
(303) 259-5915

Somerset Door & Column Company

Somerset's columns for interior or exterior use add a classical elegance to any decor. If, however, columns are too imposing for your purposes, the company also makes a complete line of pilasters and square columns. Decorative rather than structurally necessary, these are available in a variety of shapes and sizes.

They come straight or tapered, fluted or plain, with ornamental capitals and more.

Custom orders and designs are welcomed. You provide the diameter, dimensions of returns, and all the other measurements necessary. You may also choose from several woods, including clear Northern white pine, clear heart redwood, Pennsylvania sound knotty white pine, and poplar.

Brochure available.

Somerset Door & Column Co.
Box 328
Somerset, PA 15501
(800) 242-7916
(800) 242-7915 (PA)

States Industries

A relatively inexpensive way to achieve the period look of a warm wooded interior is to use States Industries' beaded-pattern panels. Reproducing the time-honored ceiling bead patterned lumber often found in old houses on soffits, ceilings, wainscots, and on full walls, States has employed a three-ply construction with a knot-free veneer face. Panels are ¼" thick by 4' by 8', prefinished or unfinished in natural oak, or finished in peach, oatmeal, oyster, or pewter. Also available are coordinated chair rail moldings.

Literature available.

States Industries, Inc.
29545 Enid Rd. E., PO Box 7037
Eugene, OR 97401
(800) 537-0419

Victorian Warehouse

Elegant items for your home. That's the motto on the cover of Victorian Warehouse's inclusive catalogue. This business carries all manner of goods for the Victorian home, and most are certainly useful in a house of any period. The catalogue includes a selection of wood ornaments, moldings,

and trim.

Catalogue, $3.50.

Victorian Warehouse
190 Grace St.
Auburn, CA 05603
(916) 823-0374

Vintage Wood Works

Almost every location in a Victorian house can benefit from Vintage's products. Indoors, use ornate shelves in a variety of sizes to hold books, dishes, and whatnots; the company will manufacture almost all of them in any length you desire. An enormous selection of ¾"-thick brackets can be used in many locations. Heavier 1½"-thick brackets are available for exterior use.

Thick corbels decorate the outside of the house, turning ordinary corners into festive spaces. They

add a look of permanence and substance where thinner trims would look flimsy. None of Vintage's corbels are less than 3" thick. The roof can be adorned with ¾" running trim. The design at the bottom left of the photograph, called Fleur, stands 3½" high and is shipped in 48'-long sections.

Doorways, foyers, and the spaces between built-in cabinets can be enhanced by the addition of spandrels. Simple ball-and-dowel versions are available, as well as the scrolled designs illustrated and a few with turned spindles instead of balls. Vintage will manufacture them in any length to the nearest ¹⁄₁₆". Wood grilles can serve the same purposes and are sold in two styles: the large, elaborate Queen Victoria and the smaller, daintier Shell. The Queen Victoria is 19⅛" high and comes in 47⅝'-

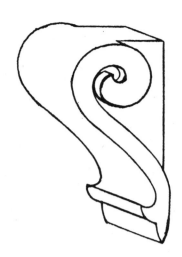

long and 60″-long sizes; the Shell is 10¼′ high by 18¾″ long. Both are ¾″ thick with 1½″-thick frames.

While you're trimming your house with gingerbread, don't forget gable decorations. Model 42-140, called Old Lace, has 38″-long sides and is available in any standard roof pitch. For the ambitious, there's a design called the Flying Circle Gable. Measuring 72″ long at the bottom and made only for a square roof pitch, it takes some skill to install.

Catalogue, $2.

Vintage Wood Works
513 S. Adams, #1276
Fredericksburg, TX 78624
(512) 997-9513

For dramatic entranceways, Vintage makes striking arches. The Sun Ray measures 26″ high by 62″ wide by 1½″ thick and consists of two brackets interrupted by a 2″ by 2″ drop. Headers can enliven doors and windows; model 110 is 6½″ high, 24″ wide, and ¾″ thick.

The Woodworkers' Store

All the classic molding designs are available at The Woodworkers' Store. Specialty moldings include panel and bamboo styles and half-round or full-round poplar rope patterns in five sizes. French Provincial-style trim in oak, birch, or walnut adds an elegant touch to doors, walls, and cabinets. The Woodworkers' Store also carries several types of carved and embossed hardwood moldings, perfect for frames, furniture, paneling, fireplaces, or walls. They apply easily with brads and glue.

You can shop at one of the company's retail stores in San Diego, Minneapolis, Seattle, Denver, Boston, or Columbus, Ohio, or write for more information about ordering products by mail.

Catalogue, $1.

The Woodworkers' Store
21801 Industrial Blvd.
Rogers, MN 55374
(612) 428-4101

3/4″ x 24″ x 6½″

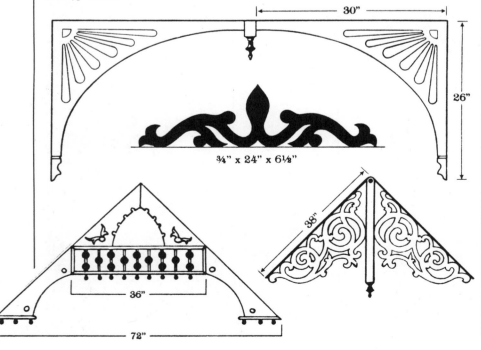

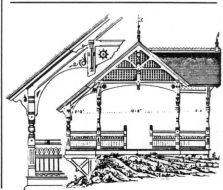

Cabinetry

Finding a craftsman who can execute traditional cabinetry such as bookcases, cupboards, chimney breasts and mantels, and room ends is not as difficult as it used to be. Ten or fifteen years ago, one nearly had to kidnap an old-fashioned carpenter from a rest home. Some of these octogenarians, however, passed down their skills to a new generation of woodworkers, and these artisans have inspired yet others. They are found in nearly every North American town and village, working quietly in their shops on furniture and millwork, and reproducing one-of-a-kind traditional cabinetry pieces. Included here are also suppliers of materials for do-it-yourself projects. For further leads to professionals who can produce cabinetwork for you, consult chapter 9 on furniture, chapter 4 on hardware and heating and cooking for suppliers of mantels, and the preceding section of this chapter on applied wood ornamentation and paneling.

Marion H. Campbell

Reproductions and restorations of fine antique woodwork are no problem for Marion H. Campbell. Shown below is an elaborate paneled room end; at right is a built-in corner cabinet, one of a pair designed to match the room's woodwork. Campbell is also an exceptional furniture maker.

Brochure, 50¢.

Inquiries may be addressed to:

Marion H. Campbell
39 Wall St.
Bethlehem, PA 18018
(215) 865-3292

To visit the workshop or to call during business hours, contact Campbell at:

Barber and Plymouth Sts.
Bath, PA 18014 (215) 837-7775

The Fireplace Mantel Shop

Finding cabinetry to match your house's style is made easier with The Fireplace Mantel Shop's three cabinet designs. Each can be modified by the addition of reeded or fluted pilasters, an arched top, raised-panel doors on the upper portion, a plaster shell, or, as in this case, Chippendale-style glass doors. The basic unit, D-501, is shown on the next page. It is open on the top with two raised panel doors at the bottom. These doors may be either ¾" or 1⅛" thick and may be lipped or flush. One stationary sugar pine shelf rests behind the doors.

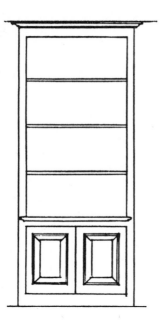

Two heights, 96" and 108", are available; the 96" cabinet is fitted with three sturdy ¾"-thick sugar pine shelves which may be adjustable or stationary. The 108" cabinet comes with four shelves. Both sizes are 36" wide and have an interior depth of 11¼". The sides and backs may be built of plywood or of solid wood; sugar pine is standard, but a host of hardwoods are available as well, including poplar, red oak, cherry, and walnut.

Catalogue, $2.75.

The Fireplace Mantel Shop, Inc.
4217 Howard Ave.
Kensington, MD 20895
(301) 564-1550

Tile Ornamentation

Don't despair if you've just made your first trip to a ceramic tile supplier and discovered that everything on display is either speckled or tinted in a sickly pastel. Unless you are a complete defeatist, you will be ready to search further for tile that is truly attractive and fitting for an old house interior. In chapter 5 some of the leading suppliers of handsome floor tiles are described. Many of these same firms produce decorative tiles which can be used effectively for fireplace surrounds, hearths, kitchen and pantry counters, and as splashboards.

Designs in Tile

In the late-Victorian period, when the aim of the Aesthetic Movement was "to surround the home and everyday life with objects of true beauty," the use of decorated tiles was an easy and relatively inexpensive way to introduce art into the home without seeming frivolous. Design in Tile, contemporary producers of custom hand-decorated tiles and murals, was inspired by the philosophy and art of the Aesthetic Movement. The firm's goal, superbly realized, is the revival of art tile—fine art rendered on ceramic tile and, by extension, the creation of a strikingly and expertly integrated environment employing art tile.

Each tile created by Designs in Tile is individually decorated by hand, using only the finest ceramic materials. All work is fired to a high temperature, making each tile extremely durable

and causing the colors to vary slightly in shade from tile to tile and lot to lot. Such color variation is a desired and inherent characteristic of all handcrafted ceramic products and clearly distinguishes the firm's work from the dull uniformity of machine-made tile.

Designs in Tile offers stock designs in historic styles ranging from Victorian transfer tiles in the Anglo-Japanese style to Art Nouveau tiles and even Art Deco tiles. (Illustrated are Victorian transfer tiles in the Gothic Revival style and tiles from the Arts and Crafts collection.) In addition, traditional and contemporary designs—from country motifs to children's patterns—are also available. If Design in Tile's wide range of stock murals, border, and field tiles do not suit your needs, the firm will customize designs for you or reproduce patterns and colors from any wallpaper, fabric, or original piece of art.

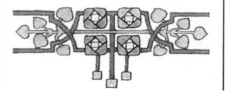

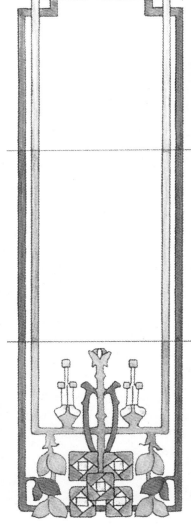

Catalogue, $3.

Designs in Tile
Box 4983
Foster City, CA 94404
(415) 571-7122

Moravian Pottery & Tile Works

Determined to do more than merely regret the loss of Pennsylvania-German pottery methods, Henry Chapman Mercer (1856-1930) first apprenticed himself to a potter and then built the Moravian Pottery & Tile Works in about 1900. Mercer focused on tiles and mosaics, inventing some designs and culling others from the British Museum and from European castles and abbeys.

Decorative tiles like this 4" by 4" horse can highlight hearths, tabletops, and counters. Others can be used on stands, trivets, and hangers. Multi-tile mosaics, originally for floors, can set off tables and walls equally well. Mercer designed most of these mosaics, centering on themes of history, nature, and the arts and crafts tradition. Colors for these handsome tiles include buff blue, gold rust, beard brown, and cream on red, among many others. Finishes include smoked red, gray, and black; brick red, ranging from dark to light; half-glazed, with a brick red surface and recessed coloring; and several others.

Catalogue, $4.

Moravian Pottery & Tile Works
Swamp Rd.
Doylestown, PA 18901
(215) 345-6722

Rye Tiles

Rye Tiles is a limited production factory catering specifically to customers who want specialized attention for tiling projects with an emphasis on color, design, and quality. Because the method of manufacture gives each job a specific shading plus depth of color, it is important to order sufficient tiles to complete a job. If you run short and need to reorder, there is a risk of having a different shade effect in another batch of tiles.

Numerous designs for walls and floors are offered by this company. In addition to overall patterns, hand painted mural panels and many border designs are created. Shown are just twelve designs from the company's vast offerings.

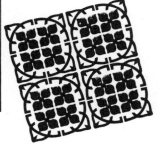

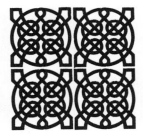
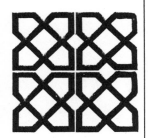

changes in the appearance of the pattern, from the classic optical illusion of steps or cubes to six-pointed stars surrounded by diamonds.

In addition to offering other standard tile designs in geometric patterns, Saxe-Patterson produces a number of other ceramics products including light fixtures and basins.

Literature available.

Saxe-Patterson
Taos Clay Products, Inc.
Box 15, Camino de la Merced
Taos, NM 87571
(505) 758-9513

Helen Williams

Nowhere in this country can you find a larger collection of antique Dutch wall tiles than at Helen William's shop. The 5"-square Delft tiles date from 1600 to 1850, and genuine examples display their authenticity at a glance since they show the tin-glazed finish known as "faience." Early tiles are multicolored, but Delft shows shades of blue and brown. The tile pictured here, portraying Mary, Joseph, and Jesus traveling to Jerusalem, represents innumerable Bible tiles that taught Bible stories to children as they gazed at colorful walls and fireplaces.

Literature available.

Rye Tiles
Ceramic Consultants Ltd.
Wishward, Rye, Sussex, England
*   TN31 7DH*
(079) 722-3038

Saxe-Patterson

Saxe-Patterson creates ceramic tiles in designs ranging from those in use for thousands of years to others achieved only through computer science. The possibilities are endless. The designers and craftspeople at this company will invent new shapes, patterns, and color schemes if the varied stock patterns don't fit the customer's needs. Tile sizes range from 1½" to 6" square.

The Baby's Blocks design shown is composed of diamonds in various colors. Perfect for entry areas or as a decorative border, proper color emphasis can create dramatic

Other designs available from Helen Williams include sea animals, flower vases, soldiers, shepherds, mythological animals, ships, and windmills. Williams also offers more recent English Liverpool and Spanish transfer

tiles, as well as a limited selection of Minton and Art Nouveau pieces.

Send a SASE when requesting a brochure.

Helen Williams/Rare Tiles
12643 Hortense St.
Studio City, CA 91604
(818) 761-2756

Other Suppliers of Architectural Decoration

Consult List of Suppliers for addresses.

Glass

Architectural Antique Warehouse
Architectural Antiques Exchange
Architectural Salvage
Art Directions
Blenko Glass
Canal Co.
Glass Arts
Governor's Antiques
Great American Salvage
Great Panes Glassworks
North Fields Restorations
Nostalgia
Ohmega Salvage
Pelnik Wrecking
Sunflower Glass Studio
Tullibardine Enterprises
United House Wrecking
Vintage Wood Works
Williams Art Glass Studios

Ornamental Metalwork

Architectural Antiques Exchange
Architectural Iron
Architectural Salvage
Governor's Antiques
Irreplaceable Artifacts
Ohmega Salvage
Schwartz's Forge and Metalworks
Stewart Manufacturing
United House Wrecking

Plaster, Composition, and Polymer Ornamentation

American Wood Column
Classic Architectural Specialties
Fypon
Nostalgia
Old Wagon Factory
Pagliacco Turning and Milling
Steptoe and Wife Antiques
Victorian Collectibles

Applied Wood Ornamentation

Aged Woods
Architectural Antique Warehouse
Architectural Antiques Exchange
Architectural Salvage
Art Directions
Artistry in Veneers
Central Kentucky Millwork

Classic Architectural Specialties
Fireplace Mantel Shop
Governor's Antiques
Great American Salvage
Pete Holly
Joinery Co.
Kenmore Industries
Mountain Lumber
North Fields Restorations
Pelnik Wrecking
Remodelers' and Renovators' Supply
San Francisco Victoriana
Sunshine Architectural Woodworks
Tullibardine Enterprises
Frederick Wilbur
Woodworkers Store

Cabinetry

Aged Woods
Alexandria Wood Joinery
Dovetail Woodworking
Joinery Co.
Smith Woodworks and Design

Tile Ornamentation

American Olean Tile
Laura Ashley
Canal Co.
New York Marble Works
Victorian Collectibles

3.
Lighting

Lighting is one of the most subtle and complex dimensions of an effective period interior. Yet, with the flick of a switch and little or no understanding of the electrical processes involved, even the most amateur home craftsman can radically transform a room in appearance. The science of artificial lighting has so evolved in recent years that it is possible to achieve almost any effect. Bulbs of many types are readily available; the fixtures themselves are made in thousands of varieties. Antique lighting devices are not difficult to find, and there are many skilled professionals who can retool them for modern use.

The desired lighting result determines the degree to which an interior need be specially wired or equipped. If the aim is to bathe a room and its furnishings in the type and level of illumination typical in the gaslight era, for example, it would be necessary to use special bulbs that burn softly. Gas fixtures simply did not throw as much direct or as bright a light as do today's electrical fixtures. The intensity of the light was also affected by the type of device used. Many Victorian gas fixtures are fitted with heavy globes that serve as protective heat shields and also diffuse the light. A Victorian parlor is a room of light and shadow with pools of soft illumination.

Properly lighting a colonial dining room or sitting room is no more difficult today than lighting the Victorian parlor. Again, almost any effect can be achieved—whether using real beeswax candles or their imitation in flickering electric form. Unless a room is intended only for antiquarian purposes, however, it will be necessary to moderate the enthusiasm for a period look. Most colonial households did not and could not make use of an extensive collection of brightly illuminated fixtures. Even candles were expensive to burn. The level and extent of artificial illumination, then, was limited to work and reading places. This is a limitation with which most people today cannot live. Consequently, it is sensible and acceptable to modify colonial-period lighting systems just as Victorian systems have been altered. By using devices that are authentic in form, at least appearance can be approximated.

Of the many suppliers presented in the following pages, each has his special interest. Some craftsmen are renowned for their reproduction chandeliers or sconces; others limit their business to the electrification of antique fixtures; a few highlight such accessories as crystal pendants, shades, globes, and bulbs. Investing in period fixtures can be an expensive proposition. Shop around and ask questions regarding materials, ease of installation, and authenticity of design. If properly selected, these fixtures will add to the value of any home and should last at least a lifetime.

A selection of antique lighting devices from The Brass Knob, Washington, D.C.

Antique Lighting Devices

A reproduction fixture is rarely as appealing as one that is antique. The number of craftsmen who enjoy working with authentic pieces, rendering them practical for modern use, is quite amazing, and these accomplished tinkerers are found practically everywhere. Most antique fixtures can be electrified without destroying their basic lines. Caution should be used, however, when buying an antique from a dealer in architectural salvage. Prices are high for even 20th-century pieces, and the mixing and matching of parts is not uncommon. If possible, the buyer should show the intended purchase to a lighting craftsman and get an opinion as to its antiquity and assurance as to the cost and ease of electrification. Some old-house purists, of course, use antique fixtures as they were originally intended—and this is fine, if effective illumination is not of primary concern.

Authentic Lighting

With a huge in-house workshop where all the company's work is accomplished, Authentic Lighting will restore, repair, rewire, or refinish any gas or electric lighting fixture. The company also offers a broad range of already restored gas, early electric, and Art Deco fixtures. If the right sconce, table lamp, or other fixture is not available, simply furnish the plans, drawings, or photos of any piece, and Authentic Lighting will reproduce it. In addition, Authentic Lighting polishes and lacquers all types of brass work and does plating in silver, gold, chrome, nickel, and pewter.

No catalogue is available, but photos will be sent upon request.

Authentic Lighting
558 Grand Ave.
Englewood, NJ 07631
(201) 568-7429

The Brass Knob

Antique lighting fixtures like this elaborate cut-glass chandelier are among The Brass Knob's specialties. Emphasizing Victorian pieces, but featuring many other styles as well, including Art Nouveau and Art Deco, The Brass Knob warehouses an exclusive collection of architectural antiques. Much of the company's stock is one of a kind, so the selection is ever changing. No catalogue can keep up with the stock's turnover, but written inquiries are welcome. Visits to The Brass Knob's shop are recommended.

The Brass Knob
2311 18th St. N.W.
Washington D.C. 20009
(202) 332-3370

Century House Antiques

Marilyn and Hal McKnight call Century House an "antique lamp emporium." Their motto is: "If we do not have it, it's not available." Included in the inventory are table, floor, carriage, wall, miniature, and finger lamps; sconces, chandeliers, and Gone With the Wind fixtures. In age, lights range from candle-burning to early electric.

Shades are another specialty, and there are thousands on hand. Century House will also reproduce cut and pierced, stenciled, candlewick, and country fabric shades, and the McKnights will paint shades to match bases.

The McKnights are well equipped to provide such antique replacement parts as shades, tripods, burners, chimneys, smoke bells, and parts for Aladdin lamps.

The shop is open Monday through Saturday (closed Thursday) from 10:00 A.M. to 5:00 P.M. Any prospective customer traveling a distance is advised to call for an appointment. Mail orders are, of course, invited.

Flier available, SASE.

Century House Antiques
46785 Rte. 18 West
Wellington, OH 44090
(216) 647-4092

City Lights

Restoring and selling antique lighting fixtures dating from 1850 to 1920 are the sole occupations of the workmen at City Lights. The repair and restoration process is long and complicated and involves several chemical baths, polishing, and wiring of fixtures. The end result is well worth the wait. Dealing primarily in solid brass fixtures, City Lights's stock of one-of-a-kind lighting devices is ever changing and includes every type of fixture from sconces to chandeliers to pool table lights.

This simple gas sconce, circa 1880, is a typical wall light of its time. In order to electrify it, however, City Lights added a 5" backplate. Otherwise, this model looks exactly as it did over a century ago. The etched-glass shade is from City Lights's large collection of an-

tique shades. The company also makes reproduction shades in hard-to-find period designs, but these are the only reproductions in which City Lights will deal. With its straight arm, the sconce extends 11″ from the wall and is 7″ high.

Since City Lights's inventory is always changing, no catalogue is available for ordering purposes. Photographs of items currently in stock will be sent on request.

Literature available.

City Lights
2226 Massachusetts Ave.
Cambridge, MA 02140
(617) 547-1490

Greg's Antique Lighting

Each restored lighting fixture in stock at Greg's is unique. Dating from 1850 to the early 1920s, almost all the styles are American and range from early Victorian to Anglo-Japanese (Eastlake) to Arts and Crafts. The company deals in all types of fixtures that were available during that time period: chandeliers, table and floor lamps, sconces, among many others.

The eight-arm brass chandelier is designed to use both gas and electricity. Four of the arms are for gas fixtures and four for electric. The chandelier could be adapted for all-electric or all-gas use if required. The fixture is American and dates to 1895.

The twelve-arm brass chandelier shown is a gas fixture, c. 1875. The company's ever-changing inventory makes catalogues impossible, but specific requests yield prompt response with photographs. Greg's has the largest stock of antique lighting fixtures on the West Coast, and a visit to the company's warehouse is recommended.

Literature available.

Greg's Antique Lighting
12005 Wilshire Blvd.
Los Angeles, CA 90025
(213) 478-5475

Half Moon Antiques

Lee and Lynne Roberts display their unusual antique fixtures at shows throughout the Northeast and offer such smaller fixtures as sconces and ceiling lights to mail-order customers. Half Moon's specialties are restored chandeliers, ceiling lights, and sconces from the period 1880-1930. All the fixtures are supplied with antique etched- or pressed-glass shades.

Illustrated is a chandelier supplied by the firm for a 1902 house restoration in Glen Ridge, New Jersey. Its high quality is typical of the original fixtures to be found at Half Moon Antiques.

Half Moon Antiques
PO Box 141
Fair Haven, NJ 07701
(201) 219-0027

Illustrious Lighting

If you're in the market for period lighting fixtures, Illustrious Lighting is one source that should certainly be contacted. All types of lighting fixtures are handled by this company, both "as-is" and thoroughly restored. More than 350 chandeliers and gasoliers dating from 1860-1940 are offered, both in European and American styles.

In addition, Illustrious Lighting also fashions an exhaustive line of Victorian and Craftsman reproduction fixtures and period furniture to match. Since the company is affiliated with Artistic License, a San Francisco artists guild, top-quality restoration and reproduction work is guaranteed.

No catalogue is available, but if room descriptions, measurements, and other specifics are sent, the company will supply an appropriate response by mail. Photos are sent, too, for a small fee.

Illustrious Lighting
1925 Fillmore St.
San Francisco, CA 94115
(415) 922-3133

John Kruesel

John Kruesel is an antiques dealer and auctioneer who specializes in unusual antique lighting fixtures. Discovering and buying worthwhile antique fixtures is only a small part of what Kruesel accomplishes. His workmen then restore each piece to museum-quality condition. Resale of these finely restored fixtures takes little effort. Most of the pieces are immediately acquired by individuals wishing to refurnish their homes, with authentic lighting devices in original, good-as-new condition. Kruesel's list of happily satisfied clients goes on and on.

Literature available.

John Kruesel's General Merchandise
22 Third St. SW
Rochester, MN 55902
(507) 289-8049

Watertower Pines

Judy and Jim Oppert work out of a 120-year-old carriage house, a building that is about the same age as many of the antique fixtures they repair and restore. The stock changes frequently, and there is always a good selection of chandeliers, wall sconces, table lamps, and floor lamps on hand. Watertower Pines offers electrified and nonelectrified fixtures. In addition, the Opperts will polish, lacquer, rewire, and otherwise renew any fixture. The owners will also paint and recover shades.

One important consideration to keep in mind is summed up in their literature: "Any fixture purchased at our shop may be returned in good condition and 'traded up.'" This is a useful op-

tion for the old house owner who wishes to improve a lighting collection over a period of time.

The shop is open daily, but if a visit is planned, it is best to call for an appointment.

Free brochure.

Watertower Pines
Rte. 1 South, PO Box 1067
Kennebunk, ME 04043
(207) 985-6868

Chandeliers

The chandelier is the aristocrat of lighting fixtures. It serves to mass light in a dramatic fashion and is appropriately used in many situations. The most common use of a chandelier is in a dining room or main entry hall. Even a three-branch chandelier, however, requires adequate space in which to hang and to be viewed. If a room is small or cluttered, a hanging lamp or light might be a more aesthetic choice. If the ceiling is low, a chandelier must be carefully positioned and sized proportionately.

The variety of chandeliers of a period design made today is almost endless. Those presented in the following listings are by no means all-inclusive, but they are representative of the kind of craftsmanship that is within the reach of practically everyone who lives in North America. The most popular designs are those that glitter and gleam. These may not, however, be suitable for many houses of a more humble ancestry. Not every home should aspire to the elegance of The Breakers in Newport or Tara of popular fiction. A simple wrought-iron fixture with candleholders may often be a more appropriate choice.

Ball and Ball

Simple hand-forged iron chandeliers that are fitted with brass cups are made in three styles by Ball and Ball. These are the type of fixtures appropriate for many plain but handsome colonial homes. They do not dazzle the eye but, rather, testify to sturdy, tasteful workmanship.

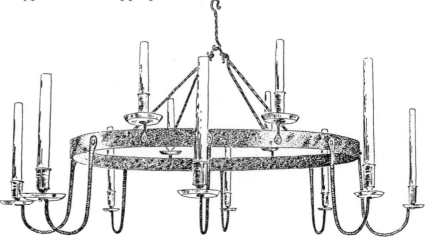

These W-series chandeliers are not based on antique models but are similar to fixtures found in country-style homes of the past. They would also be appropriate for rural colonial churches and other period public buildings. The models range from a three-arm candle-burning type to a twelve-arm oval with electric wax candles.

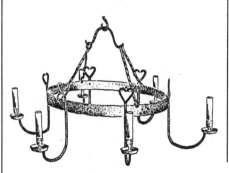

Complete catalogue, $5.

Ball and Ball
463 W. Lincoln Highway
Exton, PA 19341
(215) 363-7330
(215) 363-7639 FAX

Brass Light Gallery

Anyone searching for honest, well-made early 20th-century lighting reproductions should consider Brass Light's offerings. The firm has two basic collections: the Goldenrod and the Continental. All the models are of solid brass.

Santa-Barbara, shown here, is in-

cluded in the Continental line and is available in either two- or four-arm models. The shades can be fitted either up or down and are of ruffled 7″ prismatic glass (as il-lustrated), white opal bell, or emerald green French case glass. The fixture measures 26″ wide by 35″ long.

Brochure available, $3.

Brass Light Gallery
719 S. 5th St.
Milwaukee, WI 53204
(414) 383-0675

City Lights

City Lights deals only in fully-restored and electrified antique lighting fixtures. The company's rococo four-light gas fixture, model G-3, is one of the most or-nate models currently offered.

This chandelier, circa 1850, looks exceptionally fine with the double-etched glass shades. The fixture is 32″ wide and the minimum length is 36″.

The six-arm electric chandelier is another highly decorated example of the company's work. Including the etched-glass shades, the width is 30″ and the minimum length is 42″.

If fully-restored brass lighting fix-tures dating from 1850 to 1920 are of special interest, City Lights' col-lection should be investigated. Photographs of current stock will be sent upon request.

Literature available.

City Lights
2226 Massachusetts Ave.
Cambridge, MA 02140
(617) 547-1490

Experi-Metals

When it comes to ornate work in brass and bronze, Frank Boesel is certainly the man to call. He is presently creating hardware for the restoration of the Wisconsin State Capitol in Madison and re-cently completed reproduction work in the Tennessee State Cap-itol in Nashville.

Illustrated is one of three brass chandeliers reproduced for the Tennessee project. This fixture has fifteen arms and measures 6½′ by 7′.

93

Boesel has no literature available but will be glad to answer inquiries regarding custom work.

Experi-Metals
524 W. Greenfield Ave.
Milwaukee, WI 53204
(414) 384-2167

Historic Hardware

Simple but elegant country-style lighting fixtures, hardware, and decorative accessories are the forte of this New England firm. Quality and authenticity are guaranteed by owners John and Julia DeWaal. Lighting fixtures available include post and wall lanterns, chandeliers, sconces, and foyer lights. Many of the pieces are made of hand-forged iron.

The Basket Twist chandelier is one of the most imaginative early

Gates Moore

Early American lighting fixture designs are the focus of Gates Moore and have been for fifty years. All the fixtures' parts, wood and metal, are shaped by hand as the originals were, but unlike the originals, these reproductions can be electrified so that no modern components, in most cases, will be visible.

Whether dining by candlelight or electric light, Gates Moore's chandeliers are excellent additions to any dining room's decor. They can serve equally well as foundation pieces for a completely new look. The five-arm chandelier is

one of several beautiful designs. With metal arms and a turned-wood center, its diameter is 11", and it is 7" high. This design also comes with eight arms. The chandelier with the leaves in the center comes with eight to ten arms. It is fashioned completely of metal and is either 32" or 48" in diameter. The height is always 16",

and the finished product can be painted in any of Moore's custom-blended colors.

Catalogue, $2.

Gates Moore
River Rd., Silvermine RD 3
Norwalk, CT 06850
(203) 847-3231

lighting forms. It is hung from a hook. The weaving of the iron creates an especially graceful appearance as the six arms flow from this interwoven centerpiece. The chandelier has a 24″ span and is 16″ high.

Catalogue, $2.

Historic Hardware Ltd.
PO Box 1327
North Hampton, NH 03862
(603) 964-2280

(showroom)
821 Lafayette Rd.
Hampton, NH 03842
(603) 926-8315

Historic Housefitters

Dining in the warm glow of candlelight is always a treat. Historic Housefitters offers finely crafted, hand-forged iron chandeliers. Traditionally styled, this fixture has a twisted center shaft with four burnished-brass candle cups held in place by delicately formed

iron arms. It is 29″ high and 17″ wide. If candle glow is too subtle, electrified fixtures by Housefitters blend the charm of antique styling

with the modern amenities of the light bulb. Hand- and machine-forged iron and brass fixtures and hardware are the company's specialty. Custom hand-forging is also done.

Hurley Patentee Lighting

Handcrafted lighting fixtures modeled after museum pieces and items in private collections comprise the attractive offerings from Hurley Patentee. Each is a faithful copy of an outstanding 17th- or 18th-century fixture; many have been electrified and use fifteen-watt candle bulbs set in sleeves made to resemble aged, dripped candles. The effect is authentic, the mood colonial—with the modern twist of adequate light.

The Colonial Dignity chandelier has six tubular arms radiating

The Meetinghouse chandelier is yet more graceful, with thirteen gently curved arms of iron. Its turned and carved center is made from antique wood.

Hurley Patentee chandeliers are supplied with complete ceiling canopies and two feet of chain, but more chain can be requested.

Catalogue, $3.

Historic Housefitters Co.
Dept. 5
Farm to Market Rd.
Brewster, NY 10509
(914) 278-2427

from a hand-turned wooden center post. Its upright look derives from the symmetrically curved arms.

Catalogue, $3.

Hurley Patentee Lighting
Hurley Patentee Manor
RD 7, Box 98A
Kingston, NY 12401
(914) 331-5414

Metropolitan Lighting

Metropolitan's Vintage collection of chandeliers and ceiling lights spans most major periods in the history of lighting design. European styles from Louis Quatorze to Empire to Art Deco are all represented in Metropolitan's carefully handworked ornamentation and precisely reproduced patterns.

The three-armed Louis Quinze chandelier is an excellent example of the exquisite detail achieved by Metropolitan's craftsmen. Cast of bronze, this chandelier has an antique gold finish. It is 18" in diameter and 19" high.

The four-armed, eight-candle Empire chandelier is cast of bronze

with a doré gold finish. An especially attractive chandelier because of its alabaster bowl shade, this model is 30" in diameter and 48" tall.

Another Empire chandelier has six arms, cut and frosted bowl-shaped glass shades, and a single frosted-glass globe. It is cast of bronze with an antique gold finish and is 33" in diameter and 46" in height. Metropolitan's lighting fixtures speak for themselves and must be seen to be appreciated.

Literature available.

Metropolitan Lighting Fixture Co., Inc.
315 E. 62nd St.
New York, NY 10021
(212) 838-2425

Rejuvenation Lamp & Fixture

The Overlook is a superb example of Rejuvenation's range of late 19th- and early 20th-century lighting fixtures. Simply designed with gracefully curving geometric lines, this chandelier is fashioned of solid brass, polished and lacquered, and measures 18" in diameter, with a minimum height of 26". A huge selection of authentic shade designs is available to achieve the perfect look with every fixture. Shades are etched, frosted, colored, pressed, or handblown, depending on the style. All the company's gas

shades have 4" fitters, while the electric models have 2¼" fitters. Custom fixture designs, which can be based on photographs or drawings, are also manufactured by Rejuvenation.

Brochure, $3.

Rejuvenation Lamp & Fixture
901 N. Skidmore
Portland, OR 97217
(503) 249-0774

Roy Electric

Roy Electric adapts and reproduces antique gas lighting fixtures for modern use. The company's careful workmanship is nowhere better demonstrated than in its line of chandeliers, which ranges from outrageously ornate styles to relatively conservative models. If Roy Electric does not stock what is needed, the designers will plan a fixture from photos, drawings, or even a verbal description.

Fashioned of solid brass, the three-arm gas chandelier is one of the more restrained models available. With tubing that is roped, reeded, or plain, this style is perfect for any dining room or entryway. It is 31" wide and a minimum of 27" tall.

The fancier two-arm model, also of solid brass, with an intricately gilded centerpiece, is 32″ wide and a minimum of 24″ in height.

A wide selection of glass shades and diffusers is offered by Roy Electric so that many different looks are possible for each fixture. The company offers a free design service and welcomes all sorts of custom work.

Literature available.

Roy Electric Co., Inc.
1054 Coney Island Ave.
Brooklyn, NY 11230
(718) 434-7002

William Spencer

Among other magnificent colonial reproduction lighting fixtures, William Spencer offers a grandly scaled chandelier called the Governor's Hill. Available with twelve, fifteen, twenty-one, or thirty-five arms, in one, two, or three tiers, these chandeliers are crafted of solid brass, sand cast, and specially spun. The twelve-arm Governor's Hill is 48″ tall and 42″ in diameter. Intricately designed but not excessively ornamented, these chandeliers, and all of Spencer's fixtures, are available with a polished brass, antique

brass, or pewter finish. With clear hand-blown glass as a standard, Spencer also has a number of special designs that can be hand cut into the shades as an option. The company has worked in many private homes, but it has also built an excellent reputation with businesses. Although William Spencer's inventory is remarkable, custom designs and orders are more than welcome, and quotes are provided by phone.

Literature available.

William Spencer
Creek Rd.
Rancocas Woods, NJ 08060
(609) 235-1830

Victorian Lightcrafters

The Stansfield family began restoring and selling Victorian lighting fixtures in 1971. In 1979, their company, Victorian Lightcrafters, expanded and began making its own reproduction fixtures, basing its designs on original models. All of the company's products are soldered and assembled by hand, using the same techniques as those used more than a century ago. Victorian Lightcrafters' lights are formed of solid brass, and all the components are cast, spun, or stamped. Various finishes are available.

Although the customer can choose the type of tubing, length, number of arms, type of finish, and more for many fixtures, a large collection of standard

models is also available. The eight-arm gas-style chandelier is an excellent example. Its width is 32″. The minimum length is 29″, maximum length is 67″, and the shade fitter is 4″.

Victorian Lightcrafters' workmen wire all lights for electrical use. There are numerous shade styles and sizes from which to choose, too. An attractive style for the eight-arm gas chandelier is the milky white, opalescent swirl design, 5″ high and 7″ wide.

Catalogue available.

Victorian Lightcrafters, Ltd.
PO Box 350
Slate Hill, NY 10973
(914) 355-1300

Victorian Reproduction Lighting

Victorian Reproduction Lighting offers a large collection of reproduction brass electric and gas fixtures dating from the late 1800s to the 1920s. The company's craftsmen carefully hand pour and machine all the brass castings, and the individual body parts are hand spun from the company's own wooden forms. Each piece is hand soldered to the next, and the final fixture is then highly polished and given a protective coat of lacquer.

Whether your interest lies in a simple, unadorned, three-arm gas chandelier or in a highly ornate, twelve-arm electric-gas combination model, Victorian Reproduction Lighting will invariably have what is needed. Custom orders are undertaken on the basis of drawings or photographs.

Catalogue available.

Victorian Reproduction Lighting Co.
PO Box 579
Minneapolis, MN 55458
(612) 338-3636

Hanging and Ceiling Fixtures

This type of fixture is coming back in popularity. Often used instead of a chandelier, a ceiling or hanging fixture takes up less space and commands less visual attention. Especially well-suited to a hall, it is a device that can be mounted directly on the ceiling or suspended from it at any level. Lanterns, which can also be used in this manner, are included in a separate section. Almost every major supplier of period fixtures includes several models of hanging and ceiling lights in its repertory—from hand-blown glass pendants to swirling Art Deco spheres.

Art Directions

Art Directions includes the Camelot fixture in its Original Cast collection. The strong horizontal frame and wide domed shade create a distinctive impression and mood. It is an attractive design and is well-constructed of polished brass. Only one of several lighting fixtures and accessories offered in Art Directions' Original Cast collection, the Camelot comes with a choice of four shades in three different sizes, making the overall fixture height 28¼″, 30¾″, or 32½″. Shades can be white acrylic or colored art glass. Art Directions' hanging and ceiling lights are made of brass, copper, aluminum, or a combination of these metals. Most hang by chain link, but other hanging options include one solid bar or a series of ornately decorated smaller bars linked together.

Literature available.

Art Directions
6120 Delmar Blvd.
St. Louis, MO 63112
(314) 863-1895

Classic Illumination

It would be hard to find a better source for reproduction Art Deco lighting fixtures than Classic Illumination. All orders are made to the specifications of the customer, including finish, shade, and overall height (including stem). Four of the firm's most popular hanging fixtures are shown here. Each makes use of the company's solid brass stem model #1930-1. The designs, of opal glass blown from original molds, are, from left to right: Pointed Deco (14PD), Pointed Deco with Black Lines (14PDL), Small Deco (9SD), and Large Deco (16LD).

Both Pointed shades have a 6″ fitter, a diameter of 14″, and a height of 8″. The small Deco shade has a 4″ fitter and measures 8½″ in diameter by 9″ high; the larger model comes with a 6″ fitter and is 10″ in diameter by 16″ high.

Brass is used for all the stems and fittings and can usually be finished in several different ways. A fixture can even have a combination of finishes. The Deco stem fixtures are offered in solid brass polished to a high luster, polished with a clear lacquer coating, lightly darkened by a treatment of acid and then lacquered, or chromium plated. This last finish is the most expensive but is also appropriate for lights that date to 1930.

The Deco fixtures by no means exhaust Classic's repertory of hanging lights. There are also models that date to the early 1900s and the late 1930s.

Illustrated catalogue, $3.

Classic Illumination, Inc.
2743 Ninth St.
Berkeley, CA 94710
(415) 849-1842

Cumberland General Store

Cumberland offers a Victorian hanging lamp which stands out for its period design and practicality. It is cast of solid iron and is 31" high. The fixture is fitted with an opal font, shade, and smoke bell. Offered electrified, it may be converted to kerosene by simply replacing the bulb socket with a burner and wick. Used as an electric lamp, the fixture must hang at a given height, but if converted to kerosene and freed of its wiring, it can be raised and lowered.

Catalogue, $3.

Cumberland General Store
Rte. 3
Crossville, TN 38555
(800) 334-4640
(615) 484-8481 (TN)

Decorum

Decorum specializes in lighting, hardware, furniture, and plumbing—a wide spectrum for any old house supplier. The lighting fixtures are all made to order and include brass and glass pool table and kitchen lights as well as sconces, several chandeliers, a telescoping table or architect's lamp, and three or four floor lamp models. The pool table or kitchen lights may be made up with two or three 8" holophane shades.

When ordering a light, the customer is asked to include a sketch of required dimensions—overall height, width, and depth. Decorum will then contact the prospective buyer with questions regarding globe type and color. Finally, a sketch and price quote is provided.

Brochure available upon request.

Decorum
235-237 Commercial St.
Portland, ME 04101
(207) 775-3346

Gates Moore

Gates Moore has been making lighting fixtures by hand since 1938. Dealing specifically in early American lighting designs, the company molds each part, whether it is wood or metal, and then paints the finished piece with custom-mixed paints.

Moore's hanging and ceiling lights are excellent additions to period rooms, but they are also excellent decorative devices when standing alone in a hallway or stairwell. The hanging light with the star-design chimney is 5" deep, 5" wide, and 16" high, and is constructed entirely of metal. It is also available with six sides.

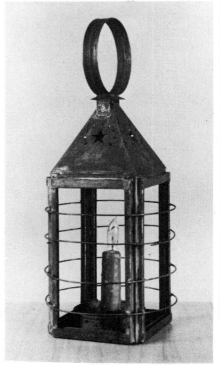

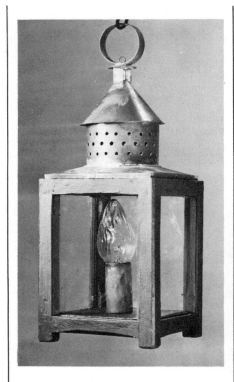

Another hanging lantern design, with a circular, grooved chimney, has a metal top and wood sides. The bulb on this model can be installed either on the top or the bottom. This fixture is 6″ wide, 6″ deep, and 16″ high. All Moore's ceiling and hanging lights come supplied with matching ceiling canopy, hook, and handmade chain, and each is ready for immediate installation.

Catalogue, $2.

Gates Moore
River Rd., Silvermine RD 3
Norwalk, CT 06850
(203) 847-3231

Metropolitan Lighting

Each lighting fixture in Metropolitan's Vintage collection of ceiling lights is not only modeled on original European designs but also imported from Europe. In order to reproduce these designs as precisely as possible, the various pieces for each lighting fixture are manufactured in the same European factories and cast from the same molds as the originals. Reflected in these fixtures are the elegant styles and unique tastes of such periods as Louis Quatorze, Louis Quinze, Louis

Seize, Hollandaise, Empire, and Art Deco. Metropolitan's work characteristically includes sand casting, hand-chased ornamentation, 24k gold plating, and lost-wax casting.

The Country French lantern, with its swirling ornamentation and engaging shape, is made of cast bronze with cut, frosted, and opal glass shades. It is 22″ in diameter and 42″ high.

Literature available.

Metropolitan Lighting Fixture Co.,
Inc.
315 E. 62nd St.
New York, NY 10021
(212) 838-2425

Rejuvenation Lamp & Fixture

Specializing in turn-of-the-century lighting fixtures of all types and designs, but concentrating in Arts and Crafts and Victorian fixtures and accessories, Rejuvenation Lamp & Fixture forms all its pieces from solid brass. This brass may be polished, brushed, or given an antique finish. Polished nickel, polished copper, and japanned copper are also available as finishes, with or without lacquer.

An excellent example of the attractive simplicity of Rejuvenation's Arts and Crafts ceiling lights is the Alameda hanging light. This single fixture is available with a standard caramel-colored, textured art glass shade, but pink, blue, green, and cream art glass are also offered.

The company's exterior porch light is a Victorian model and is 8″ wide and 12″ high, including the shade. This model will accept any of Rejuvenation's hand-blown colored and decorated glass shades or diffusers.

The Ainsworth hanging light is a single-pole Mission fixture. It is 6″ wide and to be in proportion must hang at least 14″. Like all Rejuvenation's fixtures, it is appropriate for interior or exterior mounting.

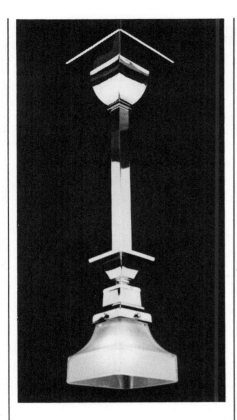

Catalogue, $3.

Rejuvenation Lamp & Fixture
901 N. Skidmore
Portland, OR 97217
(503) 249-0774

Roy Electric

Roy Electric began as specialists in the restoration and modernization of antique lighting fixtures in New York City brownstones, town-houses, and other old buildings. The company's current collection of reproduction lighting fixtures is based on that restoration and preservation experience and on careful research into a means of inexpensively producing quality lighting devices in antique styles.

All of Roy Electric's work is in solid, polished brass with lac-quered or unlacquered finishes. The company's selection of hang-ing lights is remarkable for its diversity of shape, style, and size. The single-stem hanging light is 10¾″ wide and a minimum of 12″ tall. The three-stem model is 11½″ wide and a minimum of 24″ tall. All of Roy Electric's hanging fix-tures come with a choice of plain,

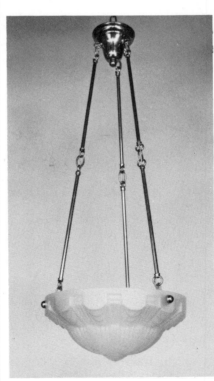

reeded, or roped tubing, and the type of shade must also be speci-fied from among a huge selection of clear, opaque, etched, and colored-glass styles.

Particularly appealing to those who wish to add elegant architec-tural detailing to a room without

risking excessive ornamentation is Roy Electric's collection of ceiling lights. All the metal fittings are cast of solid, polished brass with lacquered or unlacquered finishes. The glass is pressed, etched, and frosted, although other shade op-tions are available with most of the company's fixtures.

The hanging fixture with the ribbed-brass canopy and finial and the etched floral-patterned

diffuser is 7½″ wide and a minimum of 10″ high. The ceiling light with the brass finial and the flush diffuser is 10″ wide and a minimum of 9½″ high. The other two flush ceiling fixtures are 11½″

wide and a minimum of 7½″ tall and 10″ wide and a minimum of 9½″ tall. Roy Electric welcomes custom orders and offers a free design service for those who need help creating unique fixtures.

Literature available.

Roy Electric Co., Inc.
1054 Coney Island Ave.
Brooklyn, NY 11230
(718) 434-7002

St. Louis Antique Lighting

Whether the game is bumper pool or billiards, St. Louis Antique Lighting's selection of pool table lights will fit most specifications. Hanging 36" from the ceiling, these light fixtures are solid brass, polished and lacquered or unlacquered. Nickel plating is an option with all fixtures. At 36" wide and 32" deep, this four-arm pool

table light is the largest model in stock. The shade fitter is 2¼", so a variety of the company's shade styles will fit it. Custom projects are welcome.

Catalogue available.

St. Louis Antique Lighting Co.
801 N. Skinker
St. Louis, MO 63130
(314) 863-1414

William Spencer

From the same designs that were used when the company was first founded in 1897, William Spencer reproduces colonial brass lighting fixtures for private homes and big businesses alike. Sand cast, these fixtures come with hand-blown clear glass or with one of Spencer's own hand-cut glass designs. The De Cou Pond three-light ceiling fixture, with its large bowl-shaped shade, is 13" wide and 22" high. There are a number of similar styles in a range of sizes also available, and each of them is of the highest quality. Spencer's polished-brass finish is the most popular, but antique brass and

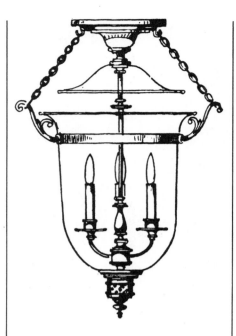

pewter finishes are also available. William Spencer welcomes custom orders.

Catalogue available.

William Spencer
Creek Rd.
Rancocas Woods, NJ 08060
(609) 235-1830

Sconces

Although placement can be difficult sometimes because of wiring restrictions, a wall sconce is an effective means of subtly lighting a space. Frequently used in pairs, this type of fixture is especially useful in a hallway where other fixtures are impractical. The sconce is also a good aesthetic choice for a dining room where the main light source is a chandelier or hanging lamp, and additional light is needed around the perimeter. The light from a sconce travels either up to the ceiling or down to the floor. A sconce is not practical for reading or work spaces. It is important not only to determine how far a sconce will project from the wall but also to carefully measure the space in which it will be used.

Ball and Ball

Renowned for its fine reproduction hardware, Ball and Ball is also a good source, if somewhat limited, for reproduction lighting fixtures. The firm has produced chandeliers for Independence Hall as well as smaller, more commonplace fixtures. In addition to chandeliers, Ball and Ball's repertory includes sconces, hanging lights, lanterns, and candlestands.

The W165 series of brass sconces is unique. Each fixture consists of a narrow backplate that holds a smoke bell and, of course, an arm, cup, and shade. Some of the models are candle burning; others are electrified. They range in size from 23" to 26" tall.

Complete catalogue, $5.

Ball and Ball
463 W. Lincoln Highway
Exton, PA 19341
(215) 363-7330
FAX (215) 363-7639

Brass Light Gallery

This sturdy and functional reproduction sconce is from Brass Light's Goldenrod collection of American Mission/Prairie school lighting. It would do as nicely in an early 20th-century home as it would in a public building of the same period design. Called the Sherman Park, it can be mounted up or down. Its dimensions are 9" high, 13" wide, and 7¾" deep.

Brass Light also offers a single-light wall sconce, the Evanston, of similar design, as well as the Evanston II, an up-and-down double sconce.

All the fixtures are made of solid brass and can be finished in one of three ways: polished brass, antique brass, or nickel chrome.

Brochure available, $3.

Brass Light Gallery
719 S. 5th St.
Milwaukee, WI 53204
(414) 383-0675

Catalogue, $2.

A. J. P. Coppersmith & Co.
20 Industrial Pkwy.
Woburn, MA 01801
(800) 545-1776
(617) 932-3700 (MA)

Josiah R. Coppersmythe

Early American lighting fixtures are the sole concentration of the craftsmen at Josiah R. Coppersmythe. Cut, formed, soldered, and finished by hand, each light is individually made of solid brass or copper. There is a choice of four finishes: natural, antique, verde, or pewter. Shown is one of the sconces from the vast collection offered by Coppersmythe. Its pewter finish is achieved by applying colored and rubbed galvanized steel to the solid base metal.

A. J. P. Coppersmith

Sconces served a very specific purpose when they were originally conceived: to furnish a more diffused light source than regular reading or sewing lanterns. Among Coppersmith's collection of colonial lighting fixtures and decorative accessories is a large collection of sconces for candles as well as electric lights.

The Farmer's sconce, particularly effective because of its two light sources, is 11" high and 8" wide, although other sizes are available. Coppersmith's round, mirrored sconce is adapted from a colonial design that used mud and bits of glass to form an effective reflector. The company today fashions the

reflectors for these models from more than one hundred small bits of mirror. At 10½" high and 7¾" wide, these mirrored sconces provide the charming glow of flickering candlelight. All Coppersmith's lighting fixtures are available in a variety of finishes.

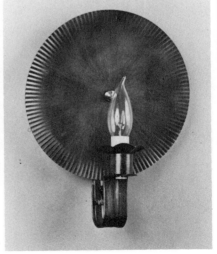

Any fixture can be modified. Coppersmythe will also undertake custom work.

Catalogue, $2.

Josiah R. Coppersmythe
80 Stiles Rd.
Boylston, MA 01505
(508) 869-2769

Federal Street Lighthouse

Working with a variety of craftsmen, the Federal Street Lighthouse has developed a selection of unusual reproduction lighting fixtures. Fashioned in brass, copper, tin, and iron, these fixtures include sconces, chandeliers, lanterns, and more. The Pineapple sconce, offered for use with

candles or electric bulbs, comes either 18" high and 6¾" wide or 16" high and 5" wide. It is made of copper with a clear or verdis finish.

Catalogue, $3.

Federal Street Lighthouse
38 Market Sq.
Newburyport, MA 01950
(617) 462-6333

Historic Housefitters Co.

A varied collection of hand-forged iron lighting fixtures is offered by Historic Housefitters, a company that also specializes in brass fixtures and machine-forged iron items. The electric wall lamp shown is a simple piece somewhat reminiscent of an eighteenth-century model but electrified for modern use. The cord is neatly hidden behind the wall bracket. This hand-forged iron fixture measures 12" high and 9½" deep; the shade is not included.

For a more authentic colonial look, the heart sconce is a graceful sweep of hand-forged

iron, ending in a burnished-brass candle cup. The soft glow of candlelight is reflected in the cutout heart on the wall bracket. This fixture measures 8" high by 5" deep, enough room to keep the candle's heat clear of wallpaper and paint.

Catalogue, $3.

Historic Housefitters Co.
Dept. 5
Farm to Market Rd.
Brewster, NY 10509
(914) 278-2427

Hurley Patentee Lighting

Since the first edition of *The Old House Catalogue* in 1976, the sconces reproduced from colonial originals by Hurley Patentee Lighting have been highlighted for their fidelity to history and their general excellence. The sheer variety of colonial fixtures offered makes the Hurley catalogue a browser's delight.

Aptly named the Majestic Mirror sconce, this five-sided, mirrored, tin wall fixture creates the illusion of many lights with a single bulb. This is just one of numerous *new*

fixtures handcrafted by Hurley, specialists in accurately reproduced 17th- and 18th-century lighting devices. The Majestic Mirror measures 25" high, 11½" wide, and 7½" deep. All the more than forty sconces produced by Hurley Patentee are modeled after antiques currently in museums or private collections. Other sconce designs use crimped or hammered tin, polished brass, or wood. Sconce designs in the primitive style feature candles but are also available electrified and can be fitted for wall connections if requested.

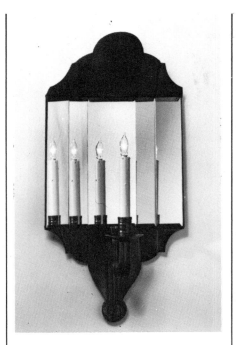

Catalogue, $3.

Hurley Patentee Lighting
Hurley Patentee Manor
RD 7, Box 98A
Kingston, NY 12401
(914) 331-5414

Price Glover

Price Glover preserves the fine details of select 18th- and 19th-century English brass lighting fixtures through precise casting and careful hand finishing. In addition, all glass shades are hand blown in several authentic patterns. The firm's three-arm sconce

is an exact reproduction of a Regency original. The stamped backplate is mounted on a large, hand-carved, shell-shaped teak backplate, and the shades are etched in Price Glover's flower pattern.

The Georgian brass sconce, c. 1730, is designed for an unshaded candle. The S-scrolled arm, mounted on a simple, smoothly turned backplate, culminates in a tulip-shaped candle socket. It is 5″ high, 4″ wide, and 10″ deep.

Price Glover's single sconce, with its hand-blown plain-glass shade, is reproduced from a style that was commonly exported during the late 18th and early 19th centuries to the eastern parts of the British Empire. It is 17″ high, 6″ wide, and 11″ deep.

All of Price Glover's lighting fixtures are designed for use with candles, but electric wiring may be requested. All fixtures may also be lacquered by special order.

Brochure available.

Price Glover, Inc.
817½ Madison Ave.
New York, NY 10021
(212) 772-1740

Rejuvenation Lamp & Fixture

Arts and Crafts lighting fixtures make up Rejuvenation's Craftsman collection of reproductions. Restorers of such prestigious projects as the Old Executive Office building in Washington, D. C. and the Pennsylvania and Texas state capitol buildings have used this company's fixtures.

The Craftsman collection is especially suited for houses of the late 19th and early 20th centuries.

Made in the same way as the originals, Rejuvenation's replicas are crafted of solid brass. Each may be finished as polished brass, antique brass, brushed brass, polished nickel, polished copper, or japanned copper. A variety of colored and textured art-glass shades is also available with most designs.

The Manzanita, a single Mission-style wall sconce, is an excellent

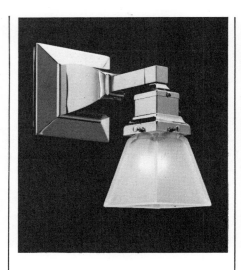

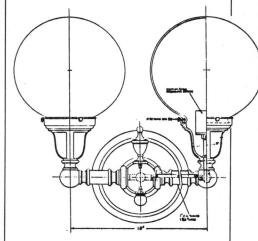

example from the company's Arts and Crafts collection. Available with a choice of shades, the projection depth is 10", height 9", and width 6". All Rejuvenation's catalogue designs are easily modified on a custom basis, and the company will also fashion lamps and other fixtures from a customer's own specifications.

Catalogue, $3.

Rejuvenation Lamp & Fixture
901 N. Skidmore
Portland, OR 87217
(503) 249-0774

Roy Electric

Restoring, modernizing, and reproducing antique lighting fixtures have been Roy Electric's triple focus for more than twenty years. Working only in solid brass, this company has an exhaustive inventory, but it is possible to have plans drawn up should a custom fixture be desired. The fine ornamental detail that Roy Electric's craftsmen achieve is demonstrated in the company's selection of sconces.

The sconce highlighted by the angel front piece is 13" high, 7" wide, and extends 10" from the wall. The model with the child at the front is 12" tall, 7" wide, and extends 9½". Although there is a huge selection of glass shades from which to choose, two particularly pleasing designs are the colored, dotted, hand-blown shade on the former sconce and the frosted, acid-etched shade on the latter.

Literature available.

Roy Electric Co., Inc.
1054 Coney Island Ave.
Brooklyn, NY 11230
(718) 434-7002

St. Louis Antique Lighting

Offering a variety of antique reproduction lighting fixtures and shades, St. Louis Antique Lighting remains rooted in the business with which it first started. Custom restoration and reproduction of antique lighting fixtures and designs is the oldest and foremost concern of this firm.

Offering both a consultation-design service and a production service, this company was recently hired to plan and design the lighting fixture restorations in the Minnesota State Capitol building. Later, St. Louis Antique Lighting

was awarded the production contract and began making its own designs. Exact reproductions of existing fixtures, these sconces are cast of brass, but the company also casts in plaster, bronze, and polyester.

Literature available.

St. Louis Antique Lighting Co.
801 N. Skinker
St. Louis, MO 63130
(314) 863-1414

Saxe-Patterson

With the Ziggurat line of reinforced porcelain sconces, Saxe-Patterson has propelled ceramics from playing merely a background role in architectural decorating to a more noticeable part in a room's decor. Ceramic tiles and basins are still part of Saxe-Patterson's work, but much more alluring are the straight lines, sharp angles, and curved three-dimensionality of these sconces. The porcelain's

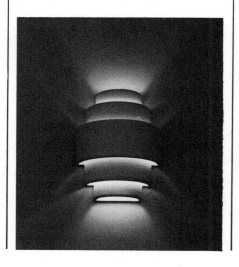

natural surface is suitable for painting at home, but the sconces are available in ten fire-matte colors, including alabaster, buckskin, twilight blue, and mauve, and the finished texture may be either smooth or stucco. The double Ziggurat, with its five tiers, is one of ten variations on the same basic style. It is available in two sizes: 14" high by 10½" wide by 5½" deep, weighing ten pounds; 18¼" high by 13" wide by 7" deep, weighing fifteen pounds. Each style comes with a plexiglass lens device for exterior mounting. Saxe-Patterson always welcomes custom orders, too.

Literature available.

Saxe-Patterson
Taos Clay Products, Inc.
Box 15, Camino de la Merced
Taos, NM 87571
(505) 758-9513

Victorian Lightcrafters

Using only stamped, spun, or cast solid brass, Victorian Lightcrafters creates period lighting fixtures that have served in such diverse settings as the White House, Wheeler Opera House in Aspen, Colorado, and a saloon in Alaska. Every lighting device the company stocks is a reproduction of an antique or was modeled after an illustration found in the company's extensive library of antique lighting catalogues. Fixtures are soldered and assembled by hand and finished in one of three ways: polished, polished and lacquered, antiqued and lacquered.

Two small, carefully detailed electric sconces are models W-660 and W-975. Each is 5" wide and 8" deep. The former is 9" high, and the latter is 11" high. Each has a 2¼" shade fitter. A beautiful selection of pressed, etched, and colored glass shades in many shapes and sizes is offered to coordinate with any fixture.

Catalogue available.

Victorian Lightcrafters, Ltd.
PO Box 350
Slate Hill, NY 10973
(914) 355-1300

Table and Floor Lamps

Table and floor lamps are the principal kinds of fixtures used in homes today. Attempting to find a lamp of this type suitable for an old house interior can be quite a challenge. Ginger jars, pottery jugs, and metal candlestick lamps are standbys among table lamps. The wrought-iron floor lamp used for reading, with us since the early 1900s, is a popular choice. There is nothing wrong with any of these selections, as uninspired as they may be. Good lighting craftsmen, however, can provide many other options. The conversion of a kerosene- or oil-burning lamp is one such alternative. Another option is to choose an antique or reproduction reading lamp of an early electric design.

Ball and Ball

Candlestands were used in the 18th century for reading or such activities as sewing, writing, or mending. Made in either floor or table size, they could be adjusted in height to bring the light where needed. Ball and Ball makes excellent reproductions of these practical fixtures.

The company has five models of candlestands with brass or iron trim, double or single armed. Four are floor-standing models, and one is a table stand. Tastefully simple in appearance, the stands are made for use as candle-burning fixtures, but any one of them may be electrified.

Complete catalogue, $5.

Ball and Ball
463 W. Lincoln Highway
Exton, PA 19341
(215) 363-7330
FAX (215) 363-7639

Brasslight

Brasslight's original lighting fixture designs are produced beginning with a 12' length of solid brass tubing. Cut, cleaned, and then bent by hand, the tubing is

fashioned to the desired shape. All decorative pieces, bodies, and other ornamentation are then attached to the basic shape and hand soldered for strength. Finally, each piece is polished and lacquered, or simply polished and left to darken naturally with time.

The Main Street table lamp, at 24½" tall, with its smooth curves and simple beauty, is perfect for a desk or side table. Although the shade shown is the standard for this style, other designs may be easily substituted.

Catalogue, $3.

Brasslight, Inc.
90 Main St.
Nyack, NY 10960
(914) 353-0567

Cumberland General Store

Very ornate lamps were made in the Victorian era only by craftsmen at the height of their careers. Cumberland's selection of brass and glass table lamps reflects that tradition. The bases of each come with either a polished antique brass finish or a heavy antique bronze finish. The glass shades are acid etched and complete the period image. Available either 18" or 19" high, these fixtures come with two pull-chain light switches, making them convenient to use as well as pleasing to view.

Catalogue, $3.

Cumberland General Store
Rte. 3
Crossville, TN 38555
(800) 334-4640
(615) 484-8481 (TN)

Federal Street Lighthouse

Table lamps with a period appearance are featured in Federal Street's collection of reproduction fixtures. The lamps are made of brass and can be left unlacquered or given a pewter or gun-metal finish.

The two lamps shown are the two-arm model ATL2, which is 18" tall and 13" wide, and the

three-arm ATL3, also 18" high but with a 12½" width.

Federal Street is noted as well for its many models of sconces, post lanterns, chandeliers, and hanging lights. And if shades are a special need, the firm offers custom-designed and hand-cut shades by Kit Cornell in various attractive color combinations.

Cornell's work gives an otherwise ordinary lighting fixture a personalized, unique flavor. The polished and lacquered brass table lamp is a standard turned-metal style. It is 18" high and 4"

wide. The shade is trimmed with velvet soutache in wine, moss green, navy, dusty blue, rust, or beige combinations.

Catalogue, $3.

Federal Street Lighthouse
38 Market Sq.
Newburyport, MA 01950
(617) 462-6333

Lehman Hardware & Appliances

Lehman is a true country store serving the Amish and Mennonite communities of Ohio. Through an annual direct mail catalogue, however, Lehman reaches a nationwide audience. The products offered are sensible, inexpensive, and unabashedly old-fashioned. Included among the many thousands of items are non-electric lamps and accessories.

All of the lamps are oil burning. The Paul Revere wall lamp, 1⅝"

high, can be used on a table or hung on a wall. It has a reflector and is available in three finishes — polished brass, antique pewter, or antique bronze. The Mary Ann leaded crystal lamp is made in Austria. The chimney is etched, and the base is of lead crystal. The lamp measures 12″ high.

Lehman is also noted for its extensive collection of Aladdin mantel lamps, produced since the turn of the century. Aladdin has recently reintroduced the Rayo oil lamps, which use a round wick that provides a larger flame and a brighter light than ordinary oil-burning fixtures. The Rayo lamps are available in four models.

Catalogue, $2.

Lehman Hardware & Appliances, Inc.
PO Box 41, 4799 Kidron Rd.
Kidron, OH 44636
(216) 857-5441

Renaissance Marketing

Renaissance Marketing's Lily collection offers exact reproductions of Louis Comfort Tiffany's Art Nouveau lighting fixture designs. In addition, a number of lamp models using the same Tiffany motif are available to suit today's needs. The lost-wax cast-bronze edition of Tiffany's twelve-arm table lamp is the most famous design in the collection. At 21″ high, this lamp is finished with a verde patina in order to obtain the green-brown coloring for a natural look. The lamp is finished with hand-blown, Favrile silver-luster art-glass shades and is signed, numbered, and accompanied by a certificate of authenticity. Renaissance carries a range of lighting fixtures in this same style, including chandeliers, table lamps, tray lamps, and hanging lamps.

Literature available.

Renaissance Marketing, Inc.
PO Box 360
Lake Orion, MI 48035
(313) 693-1109

Victorian Reproduction Lighting

Victorian Reproduction Lighting's extensive collection is a testament to tasteful imitation. Faithful as these fixtures are to the originals, these solid-brass reproductions do not sacrifice modern convenience.

Reproduction Victorian table lamps are designed for use either as electric or gas fixtures and incorporate twisted, fluted columns, detailed castings, a wide variety of finials, and a broad selection of reproduced period glass shades. Some of these models are movable, too, enabling the source of light to be positioned as necessary.

The company also offers a number of reproduction floor lamps. Detailed scrollwork adorns most of the sturdy pedestal bases, while fluted brass shafting is relieved by faux marble and faux bois ornamentation. A wide assortment of reproduction shades —including colored, etched, and pressed glass and a number of decorated cloth varieties—is also available.

A number of brass finishes, including highly polished and antique, are offered. The company will also make custom reproductions based on drawings or photographs.

Catalogue, $4.

Victorian Reproduction Lighting Co.
PO Box 579
Minneapolis, MN 55458
(612) 338-3636

Lanterns

Ever since Longfellow immortalized Paul Revere's ride and the lantern placed in the steeple of North Church, the lantern has been a particularly homey American symbol. This simple type of lighting device was widely used in colonial America and continued in popularity during the 1800s. At a time when fixed systems of illumination were unknown, a portable lantern was the handiest of all lighting devices. Used indoors and out, upstairs and downstairs, a lantern was available for every possible daily purpose. Today, a lantern is almost always fixed in position—as a hanging or wall fixture or as a post lamp. There is no reason, however, why a lantern cannot also be used as a portable fixture. Fitted with a battery, its utility is greatly enhanced. Included in the following listings are a number of models that can be electrified or left as candle-burning devices. Lanterns appropriate for outdoor use are included in the next section of this chapter.

A. J. P. Coppersmith

As railroads spread across the United States in the mid- and late-19th century, so did the various styles of the Dietz globe lantern. The larger lanterns were commonly used at railroad stations, while the smaller models were favored by conductors who carried the lamps from large wire bails designed to encircle the arm, thereby leaving both hands free. This lantern is offered by Coppersmith, in its wall-mounted form—25″ high, 12″ wide, and 14″ deep—or as a post lamp or a hanging lantern.

oppersmith also has a wide range of simpler lanterns from which to choose. The company's barn lantern demonstrates the excellent craftsmanship and straightforward beauty of these lighting fixtures. The barn lantern with reflector and wooden handle, is 19" tall, 9" wide, and 9½" deep.

All Coppersmith's fixtures are fashioned of solid copper or brass. They may be finished in antique copper, antique brass, lead-coated copper, terne metal, or verdigris.

Catalogue, $2.

A. J. P. Coppersmith & Co.
20 Industrial Pkwy.
Woburn, MA 01801
(800) 545-1776
(617) 932-3700 (MA)

Josiah R. Coppersmythe

A Coppersmythe light is unique because each is cut, formed, and soldered completely by hand. Offered in many sizes and styles, these fixtures come in antique, verde, pewter, or natural finishes. A natural finish is achieved by polishing the fixture, but not lacquering it, so that natural aging occurs. Clear seedy glass is standard on most models, but amber seedy is available, too.

As with most Coppersmythe designs, the Waltham-style fixture is available as a wall-bracket, hanging, or post-mounted fixture

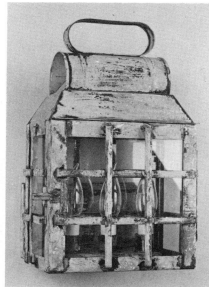

with a 3" opening for the post. Shown as both a bracketed lantern and a hanging fixture, the Waltham-style lantern is made of solid copper and has a verde finish. Any of Coppersmythe's catalogue models may be modified, and the craftsmen there will also produce lights of the customer's own design.

Catalogue, $2.

Josiah R. Coppersmythe
80 Stiles Rd.
Boylston, MA 01505
(508) 869-2769

Hurley Patentee Lighting

Lanterns were a staple in 18th- and 19th-century homes. Stephen and Carolyn Waligurski have taken great care to reproduce only the finest examples of these two-hundred-year-old lighting devices in their accurately handcrafted Hurley Patentee collection. In a Hurley lantern, metal is aged to resemble old tin, and all fixtures are reproduced in the exact size of the antique used as the model. Modifications will be done upon request, however.

The simple John Brown's lantern is 15½" high from base to handle top and 8½" wide. It is 4" deep and has a curved back with a mounting piece. A sliding glass panel enables access to the three lights.

A bit fancier is the pierced-tin English lantern with two lights. It

measures 12½" high, 6" wide, and 5½" deep. Again, a sliding glass panel provides access to the lights, and the fixture is ready for wall mounting.

The wood and glass lantern features wood corner posts extending through the top and bottom plates. Shown with three lights, this lantern also comes with two, or a single light. The fixture is 15" high, 7½" wide and deep. A 12"-high version is also available. Chains and canopies for these items are sold separately. While all electric fixtures include either beeswax or white dripped, waxed candlesleeves, bulbs must be ordered separately.

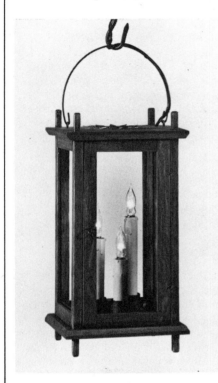

Catalogue, $3.

Hurley Patentee Lighting
Hurley Patentee Manor
RD 7, Box 98A
Kingston, NY 12401
(914) 331-5414

The Washington Copper Works

Serge Miller is proud of his handmade reproductions, and for good reason. Each is made of 24-gauge copper and carries the Underwriters Laboratories label. Hinges

are hand wrought and wires are unobtrusively enclosed in copper conduits. Miller is shown with a one-of-a-kind commission made for a restaurant in Westport, Connecticut.

Along more practical lines for the homeowner is the Forge light. Available in small (15" wide by 29" high) and large (18½" wide by 36" high) models, it is equipped with a down light and six (small) or twelve (large) candle bulbs.

Two small lanterns are what Miller calls "wall lights": Darcy's Teahouse (left) and Bourbon Street (right). The former measures 6" square by 9" high; the latter, 4¼" wide by 4¾" deep by 9" high.

The Craftsman is another new offering from Miller. Also a wall light, it is inspired by the style established by Gustave Stickley. The fixture measures 5" square at the roof, has a 4½" square main body, is 7" deep, and has a body height of 8".

All the wall lights can be used indoors or out. The Forge light may be weatherproofed for outdoor use.

Miller recommends two finishes for the heavy-gauge copper: untreated or stained. "In its natural state," he explains, "the copper is less expensive and will age naturally, taking on the esteemed beautiful brown, green, and gray hues called verdigris."

The Washington Copper Works handles many orders through the mail. If you plan to visit the workshop in northwest Connecticut, it is best to call for an appointment.

Catalogue, $3. (refundable with order)

The Washington Copper Works
Washington, CT 06793
(203) 868-7637 (workshop)
(203) 868-7527 (residence)

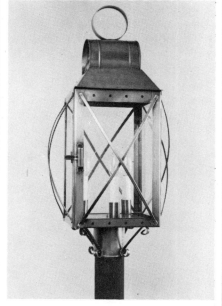

Outdoor Lighting Fixtures

The post lantern has become a ubiquitous symbol in suburban America. Its use is certainly preferable to the high-intensity street lamp. The colonial-style lantern, however, does not exhaust the possibilities of outdoor lighting and is, in fact, a fixture inappropriate for many homes built after the mid-1800s. Outdoor fixtures used during the gaslit years of the late 1800s are very different in style. So, too, are those of the early electric age. And there is no reason why modern-style lighting devices should not be used outdoors as long as the post or standard is screened from view.

Brass Light Gallery

Distinctively designed to blend with any Craftsman or Prairie school interior or facade of the early 1900s, the Craftsman lantern with an Evanston bracket is practical and stylish. The model shown is made for indoor use,

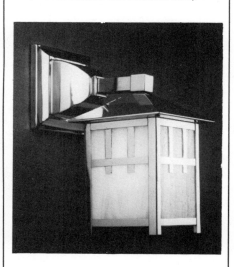

but could also be mounted outdoors. The fixture measures 5½″ wide, 10″ high, and 8″ deep. There are four choices of glass for the

shade: gold/white, green/ivory, white/opal, or clear.

Similar to the Craftsman is the Stamford. The lantern or shade has slanted rather than straight sides. It is given a verdigris copper finish. This fixture is primarily for exterior use.

Brochure available, $3.

Brass Light Gallery
719 S. 5th St.
Milwaukee, WI 53204
(414) 383-0675

Josiah R. Coppersmythe

No two Coppersmythe lighting fixtures are exactly alike. Each is cut, formed, soldered, and finished by hand in the manner of early American craftsmen. Only solid brass and copper are used to fashion these lights, although a variety of finishes are available, including pewter, natural or antique, and verde, which gives the green color of copper exposed to the elements. Model 102 is named the Haverhill and is made as a wall bracket, post (shown), or

hanging light. Posts are not included. With each model, in addition to a choice of finishes, you may also select clear or amber seedy glass. Any lighting fixture may be modified, and estimates will be provided for custom designs.

Catalogue, $2.

Josiah R. Coppersmythe
80 Stiles Rd.
Boylston, MA 01505
(508) 869-2769

Gates Moore

The craftsmen at Gates Moore work primarily in brass, copper, and tin when forming their lighting fixtures. While the designs and production methods are early American, the final product may be finished for use with candles or electric lights. All the parts are cut, bent, and crimped with simple hand tools. No modern fittings can be seen, and soldered joints are left exposed as they were in the originals.

All Moore's outdoor fixtures are made of copper and can be oxidized or painted flat black. The simplicity of the post lantern, with its double chimney, and the more decorative lantern with the eagle finial are particularly pleasing. The post lantern is 31″ high, 16¼″ wide, and 16¼″ deep; the eagle lantern is 28½″ high, 16¾″ wide, and 16¾″ deep.

Catalogue, $2.

Gates Moore
River Rd., Silvermine RD 3
Norwalk, CT 06850
(203) 847-3231

Historic Housefitters

While most of its fixtures and accessories are crafted of brass, hand-forged iron, or machine-forged iron, Historic Housefitters's exterior lighting fixtures are formed of solid copper for long-lasting use. Exposure to the elements will naturally darken the finish of the firm's period-style wall and post lanterns to a rich satin brown color. Illustrated is the Wolfeboro post light. Highlighted by its gracefully refined finial, this lamp is 23" high and 12" wide. Each Historic Housefitters post lantern comes with a standard 3" post collar and is carefully hand soldered. All catalogue items are kept in stock for immediate availability. The company also custom hand forges iron fixtures and accessories.

Catalogue, $3.

Historic Housefitters Co.
Dept. 5
Farm to Market Rd.
Brewster, NY 10509
(914) 278-2427

Nostalgia

Nostalgia is one of the South's foremost architectural antiques specialists. The firm is also noted for reproduction pieces. Nostalgia's wide range of reproduction lamps and lanterns is highlighted by its outdoor lighting fixtures. Pictured are two post lanterns—the Pall Mall, 50⅜" high and 31½" wide, and the Paddington, 38½" high and 15½" wide. These fixtures are made of copper with brass and stainless-steel fittings (the crown on the Paddington is brass, too). Each can be finished with polish and lacquer, left natural, or etched and sprayed a black satin matte. The columns for these post lanterns must be ordered separately and are usually crafted of aluminum, a metal combining strength and light weight. Cast iron, however, may be substituted. Lamp posts are supplied with black or red primer.

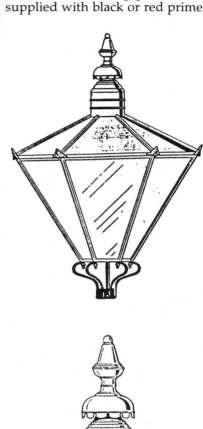

Catalogue, $2.50

Nostalgia, Inc.
307 Stiles Ave.
Savannah, GA 31401
(912) 232-2324

Supplies and Services

Many lighting outlets offer a good selection of basic supplies, including wire, switches, and plates. Some will even display a selective collection of glass shades. For such special needs as heavy shades and globes—and not those so flimsily produced in Taiwan—various types of bulbs, and replacement parts, contact one of the suppliers in the following listing. Remember, too, that some of the antique lighting dealers may be able to help you find needed parts.

Bradford Consultants

In an age of plastic Christmas trees and excessive commercial holiday hype, Bradford's old-fashioned, blown-glass figural Christmas light bulbs are a refreshing sight. Each set of bulbs, not to be confused with the plastic bulb covers of today, comes as a string of fifteen figures with one spare. These bulbs are 120 volt and completely safe, and up to three strings may be linked. Bradford Consultants also makes two styles of gaslight mantels for both indoor and outdoor lights. One is inverted and the other stands upright.

Literature available.

Bradford Consultants
PO Box 4020
Alameda, CA 94501
(415) 523-1968

Classic Accents

Recaptured in Classic Accents' collection of push-button light switches is the romantic styling associated with great Victorian homes as they entered the age of electricity. The solid brass switch, weighing nearly half a pound, is cast in a single elegant plate. Its design is reproduced from a Victorian home near Detroit. The classic wreath pattern is polished by hand and lacquered or given an antique finish for a more subdued look. Classic Accents also fashions brass-plated hooks, picture lights, and hand-painted plating.

Literature available.

Classic Accents, Inc.
Dept. L, PO Box 1181
Southgate, MI 48195
(313) 282-5525

Crystal Mountain Prisms

Rather than discard antique lighting fixtures or reproductions simply because some parts are worn or missing, think about first attempting to restore them. Some necessary parts might be found at the local hardware store, while others may take a little more hunting. Hardest of all to find for restoring Victorian lighting fixtures are cut-glass prisms, pendants, drops, and other types of cut-glass decoration that adorned so many of the lighting fixtures of that age. Offered in all shapes, sizes, and colors, Crystal Mountain Prisms' sole occupation is crafting these ornamental details.

The company's selection includes prisms, pendalogues, balls, pendants, drops, chains, and much more cut-glass ornamentation. The U-drop clear crystal glass pendants range in size from 2" to 6", and the colors include clear, amber, aurora, and ruby. Crystal Mountain's pendalogues are either 1½" or 2" long, and the colors include clear, blue, aurora, ruby, and amethyst.

Literature available.

Crystal Mountain Prisms
PO Box 31
Westfield, NY 14787
(716) 326-3676

Elcanco

For electric fixtures that look like the original candle-powered lighting devices of old, Elcanco's Starlite candles and Candlewick light bulbs can simulate the appearance of candlelight. The Starlite electric wax candles are fashioned in a manner similar to real candles, with each hand dripped to give the true effect of a burning candle. Made of beeswax in either an ivory or gold color, the Starlite candle is wired for a six-volt adapter.

The ultimate for the wax-candle effect, however, is Elcanco's Candlewick bulb, designed especially for the Starlite candle. Radiating a soft, flamelike glow of only three watts, even up close it is difficult to distinguish between this bulb and a real candle. With a life expectancy of five thousand hours and an adapter provided, the Elcanco Starlite candles and Candlewick bulbs together add the final touch to any colonial lighting fixture, antique or reproduction.

Brochure, $1.

Elcanco, Inc.
Beharrell St.
Concord, MA 01742
(508) 369-7609

Kyp-Go

The only manufacturer of carbon-filament bulbs left in the United States, Kyp-Go has offered these old-style incandescent bulbs for more than twenty years. First developed by Thomas Edison and Sir Joseph Swan in the late 1870s and further improved in the last years of the 19th century, these bulbs emit a soft, warm, mellow glow absent in modern bulbs. Exceptionally attractive with the etched-glass shades used with most early fixtures, Kyp-Go's bulb is perfect for turn-of-the-century lighting fixtures of all types.

Literature available.

Kyp-Go, Inc.
PO Box 247, 20 N. 17th St.
St Charles, IL 60174
(312) 584-8181

Littlewood & Maue

Craig Littlewood and J. Craig Maue offer slide lectures and demonstrations of 19th-century lighting fixtures as part of their business. Their specialty, however, is the restoration and conservation of antique lighting devices. Also available from Littlewood & Maue is a research and location service for antique lighting and a custom reproduction service. For restoration and preservation, the company uses only museum-quality materials and authentically produced period finishes. All electrification is accomplished in such a manner that antique fixtures are not disturbed, and modern conservation methods are employed to properly preserve the historic value of each object.

For the company's custom reproductions, only molds made from original 19th-century parts are used for brass castings, and all the designs are fully replicated from original patterns and details.

Littlewood & Maue also produces custom-made glass-shade reproductions. Many hand-blown, molded, frosted, etched, and painted-glass patterns are stocked,

but almost any globe or pattern can be reproduced by special arrangement. The variety of the firm's custom shades equals the large number of historic lighting devices for which it can supply fittings. The virtuosity of Littlewood & Maue can only be hinted at in the accompanying illustrations.

The company's Vintage solar lamp globe, c. 1840, with its smooth curves and careful detailing, has a 6" base. The Swag solar lamp globe, c. 1840, with its wavy

chimney, also has a 6" base. The Trumpet-shaped, and vase-shaped Argand globes are for English and American Argand lamps, c. 1820. The Princess Feather gas globe, c. 1840, is only for period gas fixtures. Other patterns in this style are also available.

Literature available.

Littlewood & Maue
  Museum Quality Restorations
PO Box 402
Palmyra, NJ 08065
(609) 829-4615

Old Lamplighter Shop

Located in The Musical Museum, with its collection of restored pump organs, nickelodeons, grind organs, and other musical antiques, the Old Lamplighter antique workshop focuses on the repair and restoration of antique lighting fixtures and parts. Founded in 1948, this company will custom paint china lamps and lampshades to match existing patterns or parts, a service not easily found elsewhere. While copying an existing pattern first-hand ensures the most accurate reproduction, photos are often adequate. In addition, if an exact match is not required, the Old Lamplighter Shop can choose a similar antique shade pattern from its huge collection of decorated china shades. Antiques of all kinds are appraised by this company, and estimates on custom work are readily obtained.

Literature available.

Old Lamplighter Shop
The Musical Museum
Deansboro, NY 13328
(315) 841-8774

Roy Electric

Among Roy Electric's huge collection of reproduced lighting fixtures and accessories is an enormous stock of reproduction glass shades in over a hundred different styles. Designed for normal-size gas and electric fixtures, with some also for larger pendants and hanging lights, these shades come as acid etched, ribbed, pressed, swirled, dotted, frosted, colored, or clear blown glass. Fitter sizes for standard electric fixtures are 2¼" or 3¼"; those for gas are 3¼" or 4". Shades for unusually large fixtures vary in fitter size as well as in overall dimensions, and there is again a broad choice available. For any lighting fixture or accessory needs, Roy Electric is well worth contacting.

Literature available.

Roy Electric Co., Inc.
1054 Coney Island Ave.
Brooklyn, NY 11230
(718) 434-7002

St. Louis Antique Lighting

Although St. Louis Antique Lighting's primary concerns are with custom reproduction and restoration of antique lighting fixtures, the company also stocks reproduction fixture and shades. Imported from France, the shades vary in style from simply shaped colored-glass shades to more flamboyant, molded, and etched models, and are offered for gas or electric fixtures with either 2¼" or 4" fitters. Exceptionally attractive with St. Louis's own fixtures, these shades will coordinate well with other antique or reproduction lighting devices. St. Louis Antique Lighting also offers a design and consultation service.

Literature available.

St. Louis Antique Lighting Co.
801 N. Skinker
St. Louis, MO 63130
(314) 863-1414

Other Suppliers of Lighting

Consult List of Suppliers for addresses.

Antique Lighting Devices

Architectural Antique Warehouse
Architectural Reclamation
Architectural Salvage
The Bank
E. Cohen's Architectural Heritage
Gaslight Time Antiques
Governor's Antiques
Whit Hanks
Irreplaceable Artifacts
Roy Electric
United House Wrecking
The Wrecking Bar
Yankee Craftsmen

Chandeliers

Antique Hardware Store
Architectural Antiques Exchange
Art Directions
Authentic Designs
Authentic Lighting
Robert Bourdon, The Smithy
Brasslight
Classic Illumination
A. J. P. Coppersmith
Federal Street Lighthouse
Heritage Lanterns
Hippo Hardware and Trading
King's Chandelier
M-H Lamp & Fan Co.
Nowell's
Period Furniture Hardware
Period Lighting Fixtures
Price Glover

Hanging and Ceiling Fixtures

Antique Hardware Store
Brass Light Gallery
Brasslight, Inc.
A. J. P. Coppersmith
Federal Street Lighthouse
M-H Lamp & Fan
Period Furniture Hardware
Price Glover
Silver Dollar Trading
Victorian Lightcrafters
Washington Copper Works

Sconces

Antique Hardware Store
Authentic Designs
Robert Bourdon, The Smithy
Brass Knob
Brasslight, Inc.
City Lights
Classic Illumination
Heritage Lanterns
Hippo Hardware and Trading
King's Chandelier
M-H Lamp & Fan
Nowell's

Silver Dollar Trading
Washington Copper Works

Table and Floor Lamps

Baldwin Hardware
Robert Bourdon, The Smithy
Hurley Patentee
King's Chandelier
M-H Lamp & Fan
Nowell's
Period Furniture Hardware
Price Glover
Silver Dollar Trading
Victorian Lightcrafters

Lanterns

Federal Street Lighthouse
Heritage Lanterns
Metropolitan Lighting Fixtures
Period Furniture Hardware
Period Lighting Fixtures
Sunflower Glass Studio
E. G. Washburne

Outdoor Lighting Fixtures

A. J. P. Coppersmith
Federal Street Lighthouse
Heritage Lanterns
Old Wagon Factory
Period Furniture Hardware
Period Lighting Fixtures
Silver Dollar Trading
E. G. Washburne
Washington Copper Works

Supplies and Services

Brass Light Gallery
Burdoch Silk Lampshade
Federal Street Lighthouse
Paxton Hardware
Victorian Lightcrafters

4.

Hardware, Heating and Cooking

It is difficult not to love hardware—yes, really love it. You may not share our enthusiasm for bits and pieces, tools, and various kinds of devices that make things work. But we know there are millions of others like us "out there" who are similarly passionate about visiting old-fashioned hardware stores, or perusing the latest copy of a colorful mail-order hardware catalogue. There is, perhaps, a bit of the tinkerer in each of us. We want to know what makes something tick, to put it together and to take it apart again. At the same time, there is an aesthetically appealing element about such useful mechanical objects. And nowhere is this more the case than in the old house field.

The typical restored house is a gold mine of locks, latches and bolts, pulls, and various kinds of utensils and gadgets. In a time before everything was machine-stamped or sealed with a synthetic, it was necessary to fashion many objects by hand out of the most durable and affordable material available—iron, tin, and brass being most common. Today there are many metalsmiths who will create new hardware with the same artistry as the old. The demand for quality period hardware is great, and increasing numbers of young men and women have taken up the old crafts of black-smithing, tinsmithing, and fine metal working.

Related to bath and kitchen hardware are fixtures such as sinks, tubs, basins, and toilets. Some antique models can be recycled; others are so pitted with age that they are best junked. Manufacturers of new fixtures have been quick to recognize the market for old-fashioned designs, and there is a good supply of these available.

Not everyone is interested in using an old-fashioned stove for cooking or heating, but, for those who are, both antique and new models are offered by specialty dealers described in the following pages. Models range from the classic Waterford wood cooking range, still manufactured in Ireland, to refurbished parlor heaters.

The closest most old-house owners are likely to get to an old-fashioned source of heat is a working fireplace. Almost every house built before the turn of the century includes at least one fireplace. It is difficult to deny the aesthetic and psychological appeal of such an architectural feature. Framed with an attractive mantel, a fireplace gives a room character.

Handmade custom cire perdu hardware by Cirecast, San Francisco, California.

Antique Hardware

The pace at which old architectural America is being ripped down has increased rapidly. New building often means the loss of the old, even if it is only a barn or a decayed tenement. Wreckers, unlike those of the recent past, however, no longer scatter everything to the wind. More and more individuals are rushing in to save building materials and ornamentation before they are reduced to dust. It is not only valiant to do so; it is economically advantageous. The number of architectural antiques emporiums across North America is increasing—and they are having no problem in disposing of such items as old bricks, mantels, hardware, flooring, windows, and doors. These outlets are valuable sources of supply when the need arises. And the need—and the stock, of course—include choice bits of antique hardware and ancient plumbing fixtures. Remember, however, that stock constantly changes. The objects inventoried in such stores and warehouses are largely one-of-a-kind.

The Antique Hardware Store

All manner of old and reproduction fittings from shower heads and faucets, sinks and toilets, to lock sets and hinges are stocked at this small shop chock-full of supplies for the home renovator and the creative homeowner. Customers searching for specific items to match or replicate antiques can write shop owner Tim Judge about their needs. He enjoys finding sought-after pieces. Judge carries a large assortment of antique clawfoot tubs in "bathtub alley" next to the hardware shop. He sells only tubs with the inside porcelain in excellent condition, and advises against buying tubs with resurfaced interiors, because he doesn't believe any of the methods available are permanent cures for worn porcelain. Tub exteriors can be rough, though, because they are easily cleaned with a wire brush and sand-blaster, Judge says.

Catalogue, $3.

The Antique Hardware Store
43 Bridge Street
Frenchtown, NJ 08825
(800) 422-9982
(201) 996-4040 (NJ)

The Brass Knob

Antique doorknobs are not easy to come by, especially of the quality offered by The Brass Knob. Specializing in brass hardware and lighting fixtures, this architectural salvage company exhibits many fine architectural antiques in its vast collection of period artifacts such as doors, columns, glass, and mantels. Concentrating on Victorian detail, the company's collection features many different styles, including Art Deco and Art Nouveau. Although no catalogue is available of its ever-changing inventory, The Brass Knob is glad to respond to any inquiry. Visits are recommended.

The Brass Knob
2311 18th St. N.W.
Washington, DC 20009
(202) 332-3370

Monroe Coldren & Son's Antiques

Specializing in unique authentic pieces may preclude a catalogue, but it hasn't stopped Monroe Coldren & Son's from becoming one of the world's largest suppliers of original antique hardware. The firm will see you through all hardware requirements for any project. It skillfully repairs and restores antique pieces crafted from brass, copper, and iron, and if no antique from the extensive inventory of 18th- and 19th-century hardware suits your purpose, Monroe Coldren & Son's will create a reproduction to your specifications.

No catalogue is available, but customers can write or call with specific inquiries.

Monroe Coldren & Son's Antiques and Restorations
723 E. Virginia Ave.
West Chester, PA 19380
(215) 692-5651

Howard Kaplan Antiques

Calling itself an antiques department store, Howard Kaplan's carries a variety of architectural elements. "We specialize in the extraordinary and the unique," say this firm's owners. Among the numerous household items found in the store are etched glass doors and balcony railings.

In Kaplan's Bath Shop, both period items and reproductions are offered. China pedestal sinks, high and low tank syphon bowl water closets, bidets, racks, shelves, dressing tables, and shaving mirrors are always in stock.

Catalogue available for bathroom items only, $2.

Howard Kaplan Antiques
827 Broadway
New York, NY 10003
(212) 674-1000

Roy Electric

Under layers of colored coatings or old nickel and chrome plating,

Roy Electric knows there are exquisite antique solid-brass bath fixtures to be had. The firm will provide beautifully restored ball and claw tubs, pedestal sinks, and more unusual plumbing items. Roy Electric polishes, lacquers, and epoxy bakes them, or the firm will ship them "as is" for the hardworking do-it-yourselfer.

As Roy Electric has expanded the range of its business, it has begun to fabricate solid brass to outfit antique plumbing fixtures. For example, large oval, round, or rectangular shower curtain rings are now available. Accessories include everything from shelves and hampers to toothbrush holders. Roy Electric will strip and refinish customers' antique finds, and nickel or chrome plating is available as well.

Catalogue, $5.

Roy Electric Co., Inc.
1054 Coney Island Ave.
Brooklyn, NY 11230
(718) 339-6311 or
(718) 761-7905

Vintage Plumbing

Vintage Plumbing has amassed a huge library of appropriate manufacturing catalogues to guide its fine restoration work on rare, decorative turn-of-the-century bath fixtures. Inquire about the specifics and you'll receive color

photographs and full descriptions of particular items including antique clawfoot tubs, pedestal lavatories, showers, pull chain toilets, and brass accessories.

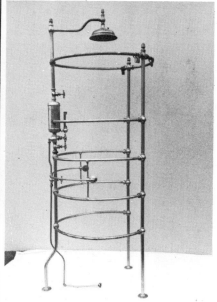

Brochure available.

Vintage Plumbing and Sanitary Specialties
9645 Sylvia Ave.
Northridge, CA 91324
(818) 772-6353

Wooden Nickel Antiques

Elegant bathroom furnishings, such as the porcelain pedestal sink and clawfoot tub illustrated, can be found at Wooden Nickel Antiques. While the company's offerings cover the broad category of architectural antiques, a specialty is "fancy" Victorian furnish-

ings. Wooden Nickel also buys such items. Send a photo and description to:

121

Wooden Nickel Antiques
1400-1414 Central Pkwy.
Cincinnati, OH 45210
(513) 241-2985

Architectural Hardware

At the beginning of the 19th century the term "hardware" meant chiefly mechanics' tools and builders' hardware, but it soon came to mean all small metal articles used in the construction of houses or for household purposes, tools of mechanics' trades, furnishing goods for kitchen and dining room service, tin plate, sheet iron, nails, screws, fence wire, etc. By the beginning of the 20th century it was not uncommon for a large hardware house to have in its catalogues nearly 100,000 kinds and sizes of articles. Given the quantity and variety of hardware hand made and mass produced in America, it's no wonder that most old houses still have original pieces intact. Guard and preserve these artifacts from the past, but, if you need to seek replacement parts, collect some of the excellent catalogues of reproduction pieces that follow. We haven't counted, but we think that you'll come close to the quantity available at the turn of the century.

A-Ball

Is there a damaged or missing heating grate in your old house? If so, A-Ball can replace it with one of eight stock styles or custom cast one from your original. The grates are aluminum reproductions of Victorian pieces; choices include the curving, spiky design of model GG108 and the more

geometric pattern of model GG104. Model GG108 is 13½" long and 10¾" wide; GG104 measures 16" by 16". A-Ball's grates can also be used as imaginative boot scrapers, table tops, plant stands, trivets, or wall

decorations. A-Ball carries an extensive line of hardware and plumbing supplies.

Catalogue available.

A-Ball Plumbing Supply
1703 W. Burnside
Portland, OR 97209
(503) 228-0026

Acorn Manufacturing Co., Inc.

Hardware can do more than simply hold a building together. With the huge selection of designs available, almost any impression can be achieved by today's decorator. Acorn Manufacturing Co. offers period patterns ranging from French to Spanish to American colonial.

On the door illustrated are Acorn's Warwick doorstraps. Modeled in a period English style, these straps are normally forged as rough iron, purposely duplicating the uneven weathered surface often found on European ironwork.

For an early American look, Acorn hardware is also available forged as smooth iron. All Acorn products come with a wide selection of finishes: relieved iron, dull black, colonial white, antique copper, antique brass, and antique pewter. Maintaining its surface and finish permanently, Acorn ironwork need never be polished or otherwise touched up.

Catalogue, $5.

Acorn Manufacturing Co., Inc.
PO Box 31, School St.
Mansfield, MA 02048
(800) 835-0121
(508) 339-4500 (MA)
(508) 339-2977 (MA)

Architectural Iron Co.

Tired of propping windows open with boards, bricks, or books? Although Architectural Iron specializes in manufacturing magnificent decorative and functional ironwork, this company had you in mind when it began mass producing 1½- and 2-pound window weights. Originally part of many old house windows, these weights are often missing or broken today. They are, however, easily replaceable. Each is made

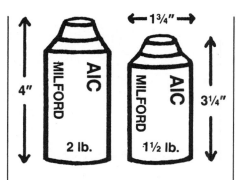

of cast iron and is designed for easy installation. The weights fit snugly over each other or stack onto most other types already in place so that the proper balance can always be found.

Catalogue available.

Architectural Iron Co.
PO Box 126, Schocopee Rd.
Milford, PA 18337
(717) 296-7722
(212) 243-2664

Arden Forge

Peter A. Renzetti's Arden Forge, established in 1970, is notable both for its collection of antique hardware and for its highly accurate reproductions. Renzetti works in wrought iron, cast iron, steel, copper, lead, tin, pewter, zinc, and wood using anvil, forge, and assorted power and hand tools and machining equipment. Arden Forge is often chosen to do restoration and reproduction projects for museums and historical socie-

ties. Hardware from the Victorian period is an Arden specialty, although the company does just about everything from making nails by hand to restoring and appraising antiques. No catalogue is available, but calls and letters are welcome. Renzetti can reproduce any piece in Albert H. Sonn's *Early American Hardware*—just specify plate and page numbers—but if you'd like something custom made, he will be glad to accommodate you. The photographs here illustrate a small portion of Arden Forge's vast selection.

The Arden Forge
301 Brinton's Bridge Rd.
West Chester, PA 19382
(215) 399-1350

Ball & Ball

Ball & Ball employs forty craftsmen who carefully reproduce thousands of antique hardware items. The company's 108-page catalogue is a treasure chest of photographs and elaborate illustrations of the fifteen hundred stock items Ball & Ball carries. A small percentage of those are made by other manufacturers, and this is carefully noted in the catalogue. Ball & Ball will copy or repair any hardware piece, and will take on other custom work.

The high style decorative cast hinge, item V53, is modeled directly after an original. Available in either brass or bronze, with a loose pin and threaded finials, it is 4½″ by 4½″.

The cast iron vertical lock, V6, is a true copy of one of the most widely used original locks from the 1840-1870 period. Overall size is 3⅛″ wide, 4¼″ high, 2⅜″ backset to the spindle hole. Available in either a right hand or left hand model, the lock comes without a knob.

Ball & Ball showrooms and museums are housed in several attractive buildings. The museum comprises a collection of originals spanning a fifty year period, and is open during weekdays.

Catalogue, $5.

Ball & Ball
463 W. Lincoln Highway
Exton, PA 19341
(215) 363-7330
(215) 363-7639 (FAX)

Circast

Finish hardware in the Victorian house was a very important element of design. Highly decorative items were produced in great quantity. Parts with matching decorative patterns were manufactured for use throughout a building to create a cohesive decorative mood.

Circast reproduces original historic hardware pieces that were designed and patented between 1870 and 1885. The Columbia pattern, patented in 1882 by the Reading Hardware Co., is a highly detailed design of swirls and columns. Brocade, patented in 1882 by the P & F Corbin Co., is a more delicate design with a floral motif. Ekado, patented in 1885 by the Sargent Lock Co., features a tiny floral pattern set into diamond-shaped sections. The

Lilly pattern has been attributed to the Sargent Co. also, and is thought to have been patented before 1880. In this intriguing design, each piece of hardware is sectioned into a variety of differently shaped compartments and a stylized lilly, an angular shape, or some other design element is placed within each compartment.

All Cirecast hardware is handmade using the lost wax casting process which produces an item of superb detail. In addition to selling these lines, the company caters to architects and designers throughout the United States by offering help in specifying, locating, and reproducing authentic builders' hardware as well as designing and manufacturing custom pieces.

Catalogue, $2.25

Cirecast
380 7th St.
San Francisco, CA 94103
(415) 863-8319

18th Century Hardware

Reproduction hardware in the William and Mary, Chippendale, Hepplewhite, and various Victorian styles is made by foundrymen at 18th Century Hardware using the same methods employed more than a hundred years ago. Molten metal is poured into sand molds to produce the explicit detail of this company's hardware.

Most brass hardware is given a satin finish, but an antique finish or polished finish are other options. Brass items include cabinet pulls, handles, escutcheons, and knobs. Black forged iron hardware is also produced by this company. Hinges, handles, latches, and shutter dogs are made by a combination of hand and machine forging, which keeps the prices low.

Customers with questions about which hardware best suits particular antique pieces can write the company. Special orders for original designs or duplications of antiques are accepted.

Catalogue, $3.

18th Century Hardware
131 E. Third St.
Derry, PA 15627
(412) 694-2708

Gainsborough Hardware

Classically styled door and cabinet hardware and coordinated accessories by Gainsborough are designed with wear-resistant finishes to withstand the test of time.

Solid brass door knobs and pushplates are coated with a protective finish warranted for five years against the tarnishing effects of natural body oils and salt air. Porcelain knobs, pushplates, and switchplates are glazed smooth. A variety of designs are available in matched sets or as coordinating pieces. Porcelain patterns include florals, solid white and almond, and a striking ebony. Gainsborough's Stoneline offers an earthenware look; the Timberline knobs and accessories are crafted of wood and acquire a rich patina with repeated use.

Brochure.

Gainsborough Hardware Industries, Inc.
PO Box 569
Chesterfield, MO 63017
(314) 532-8466

Historic Hardware

The items offered by Historic Hardware are among the finest in reproduction hardware. Pieces carried by this company evidence faithfulness to period designs and an understanding of how each was used in the past.

The Norfolk thumblatch set shown came into popularity around 1800 and continued in use well into the 20th century. Norfolk latches were among the first hardware items machine-made. The Suffolk thumblatch predates the use of machinery. Hand forged iron Suffolk latchsets came into popularity in the early 1700s. Historic Hardware offers three of the most popular Suffolk styles in accurate hand forged reproductions. Shown is the arrowhead style. The more sophisticated Hadlyme latch is an exact copy of a latch found on a Federal period house in Hadlyme, Connecticut.

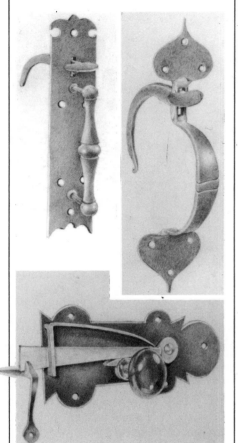

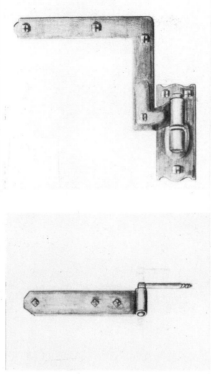

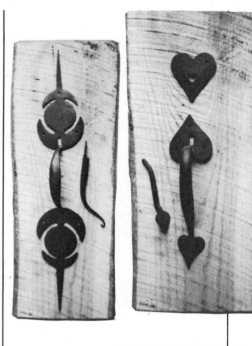

Catalogue, $2.

Historic Hardware Ltd.
PO Box 1327, 76 Post Rd.
North Hampton, NH 03862
(603) 964-2280

Historic Housefitters Co.

Does your house look tired and worn even after a fresh coat of paint? Only gravity is to blame, for gravity affects shutters, making them sag and give your home a sleepy, careworn appearance. This problem can be solved easily with Historic Housefitters' shutter hinges, made of machine-forged iron with matte black finish. The Connecticut model is simple and strong with a two-piece hinge and a screw pintel. It is 4"

long. The sturdy New York style acts both as a corner bracket and a hinge. It is 4¼" high and 5" wide, and the mounting plate is 3⅛" high and 1⅛" wide.

Catalogue, $3.

Historic Housefitters Co.
Farm to Market Rd.
Brewster, NY 10509
(914) 278-2427

Kayne & Son

Kayne & Son takes pride in keeping costs low enough to let its customers ignore die-cast or flimsy steel stampings in favor of cast brass and bronze or hand-forged iron hardware. The authentic colonial styles offered are taken from antique models, and rare pieces make Kayne & Son a treasure cache for the most demanding old house enthusiast. Selections in-

125

clude a weighty, rugged Dutch-door quadrant to secure upper and lower doors. Slender points, crescents, and circles adorn matching thumb-latch handles and thumb pieces. A heart-shaped keyhole cover is crafted of hand-forged iron. The firm found its inspiration for an unusual bean shutter dog in Charleston, South Carolina's, historic district. Early designs include leather-thonged locks and hand-wrought nails to secure window sash and a hand-forged iron or brass door knocker shaped like a musical note.

Catalogue available.

Kayne & Son
76 Daniel Ridge Rd.
Candler, NC 28715
(704) 667-8868

Brian F. Leo

Brian Leo has created his own catalogue of hardware replications drawn from antique patterns. He also enjoys customizing the pieces he makes to fit into modern homes. "I can produce composites or 'hybrids' to meet a customer's desire to have a unique product," he comments. "It seems I'm constantly making dimensional changes, metal changes, often I change the center line distances in escutcheon plates to position knobs and lock cylinders for modern mortise locksets." If the designs already available in his files are still not what a customer desires, Leo will create original items or reproduce existing antiques even if they're damaged or broken.

Leo has supplied custom-made hardware for many restoration projects nationwide including the National Park Service, the state capitol of Florida, and the Universty of Minnesota.

Catalogue available.

Brian F. Leo
7532 Columbus Ave. S.
Richfield, MN 55423
(612) 861-1473

M. J. Mullane Co.

Slate roofs have been popular in the United States since the mid-1700s. They are still prized for their good looks and durability. But in wintertime, slate roofs need a little extra protection to prevent sudden ice or snow slides that can hurt people and property below.

Snow guards staggered across a roof handle this job neatly. Cast in bronze for enduring wear, M. J. Mullane's snow guards replicate two classic versions of 18th and 19th century designs. The standard guard is T-shaped and was popular in the late 19th century; the eagle head is similar to guards installed on townhouses, estates, and government buildings in the 18th and 19th centuries.

The guards are easy to install and do not require removal of slates. Instead, using a special tool or two flat bars, adjoining slates are raised and the guard is slid into place between them until it hooks fast. To test whether the guard is firmly attached, the installer pulls it until the hook can be felt engaging the head of the slate. To be effective, snow guards must be installed in sufficient quantity, about twenty to twenty-five per one hundred square feet of roof area.

Mullane's snow guards can be installed on copper, metal, shingle, and shake roofs, too, by other methods. The company is also known for its custom metal fabrications for the restoration trade.

Brochure available.

M. J. Mullane Co.
PO Box 108, 17 Mason St.
Hudson, MA 01749
(508) 568-0597

Omnia Industries

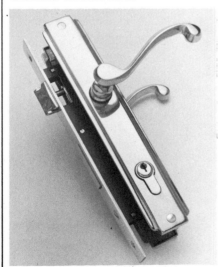

It's usually easy to find hardware for the front door, but what if your house has French doors,

patio doors, or other doors with narrow stiles? Omnia Industries makes a variety of hardware for such doors, including the narrow stile backset mortise lock shown here. Standing 6¾" tall and trimmed in solid polished lacquered brass, it is available with a double profile cylinder or with the turnpiece on the inside. A selection of nine lever handles, four backplate styles, and four finishes—polished brass, polished chrome plated, satin chrome plated, or shaded bronze plated—makes it versatile enough to suit almost any door. Omnia also makes solid brass Cremone

bolts for French doors. One of the firm's finest models (2057/CR) comes with two rods, five guides, and two strike plates. It is distinguished by an oval knob with a classical foliage design and beaded rim and by guides shaped like columns interrupted by wreaths. Omnia sells only to distributors, but will inform consumers of the dealer nearest them.

Omnia Industries
5 Cliffside Dr., Box 330
Cedar Grove, NJ 07009
(201) 239-7272

Samuel B. Sadtler & Co.

Replacing an old lock with this attractive polished cast brass lock from Sadtler & Co. will brighten up any doorway. The lock is 5¾" by 3⅜" by ¾" with a ¾" by 3⅜" by ¾" keeper. The set comes com-

plete with two brass keys, six set screws, and a door hardware set: two 2" polished brass knobs, spindle, rosette, escutcheon and set nails. For a more utilitarian look, choose the flat black steel lock. It is 6" by 4" by 1" with a 1" by 4" by 1" keeper. The set comes complete with two keys, five set screws and the same door hardware set as for the brass lock.

Brochure available.

Samuel B. Sadtler & Co.
340 S. Fourth St.
Philadelphia, PA 19106
(215) 923-3714

Urfic, Inc.

Urfic's collection of hardware includes a handsome selection of solid brass door knockers. The lion is available in two sizes: 7¾" high by 5" wide with a 2" projection; and 6½" high by 4" wide with a 1¼" projection. The drop ring knocker is a bit smaller at 4¾" high by 4½" wide with a 1½" projection. The familiar colonial style is 6" high by 3" wide and has a ¾" projection.

Catalogue available.

Urfic, Inc.
1000 South Broadway
Salem, OH 44460
(216) 332-9500

Windy Hill Forge

The snowstorm that leaves your pitched-roof period home looking like a Currier and Ives winter print can spell trouble for weighted-down rain gutters and for the roof itself. Windy Hill Forge offers fanciful snow irons shaped like fans, leaves, acorns, eagles, or flowers. Steel bolts, brackets, and castings accompany all irons. Among Windy Hill Forge's other hardware selections, take note of twenty-one different kinds of decorative cast-iron brackets. A few simple hacksaw cuts will convert many of these designs to the scale that best suits the shelving in your home. A col-

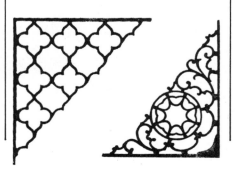

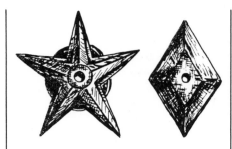

lection of cast-iron washers shaped like diamonds, flowers, or stars (ranging from 7" to 14") is one of the most exceptional offerings from the firm. These are the decorative structural devices seen on the brick walls of old multi-story buildings that prevented the walls from bulging and spreading. They can also be ordered in brass or aluminum for indoor use on through bolts.

Brochures

Windy Hill Forge
3824 Schroeder Ave.
Perry Hall, MD 21128-9783
(301) 256-5890

Woodbury Blacksmith

If you live in a 17th- or 18th-century house and insist on the historical authenticity of all replacement hardware, then you require work hand-forged at the fire by Woodbury Blacksmith & Forge Co. Thumb latches, spring latches, strap and side hinges; H, HL, and butterfly hinges; bar latches and rat-tail hinges; bolts, hasps, and hooks; shutter dogs and Norfolk latches—all have been ordered from the Woodbury

blacksmiths for impressive restoration projects throughout North America. Since the designs for each of these hardware types are representative of the differing styles favored in particular colonial regions, you can select with certainty the styles of hardware that are indigenous to the location of your house. Woodbury hardware is not die-stamped, cast, nor reworked commercial hardware. It is hand forged and faithfully copied from good originals. While the smiths prefer to forge from pure wrought iron, shortness of supply requires occasional substitution of soft steel. Shown here is a ram's horn side hinge, typical of Woodbury's stock output. The firm is more than willing to accept custom jobs and will work from excavated artifacts, drawings, or original hardware.

Catalogue, $2.

Woodbury Blacksmith & Forge Co.
Box 268
Woodbury, CT 06798
(203) 263-5737

Household Hardware

The old house can greatly profit from attention to details. This does not mean we must slavishly attend to every particular in order to wipe out all traces of modernity. Such a task, aside from its great difficulty and cost, is quite impractical, especially in the selection of common household hardware. But by careful choice, many traditional objects can be put to proper use to enhance the period decor and enrich the experience of the user. If the prospect of standardized household hardware depresses you, then the high quality of the selections that follow will illustrate how some history-minded manufacturers are pursuing the quest for excellence and helping to dispel the gloom of contemporary mediocrity.

Ball & Ball

W. Whitman Ball's father founded this family-run company in 1931 to bring quality reproductions to the antiques trade. The first catalogue featured thirty-four items. Now, more than fifty years later, Ball & Ball employs forty-five craftsmen producing an inventory of more than one thousand items. Ball & Ball's very informative catalogue tells a little of the history of each hardware style made, and carefully explains how to order items to replace missing or damaged pieces.

The D series Hepplewhite oval pulls are stamped from thin sheet brass in hardened steel dies as the originals were. They are available in a bright polished finish or an antique finish. The many designs in this series include floral, leaf, eagle, horn of plenty, and concentric ovals.

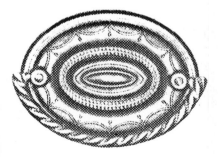

The E series Rosette pulls have cast bails. Available in a number of popular styles ranging from William and Mary to Chippendale and Hepplewhite, the designs include beaded edges, rope edges, and leafy sprays. Ball & Ball's Victorian collection is on the rise, as patterns new to the company are introduced regularly. Now available are decorative hinges, doorknobs, cupboard catches, and a variety of handles and pulls.

Catalogue, $5.

Ball & Ball
463 W. Lincoln Highway
Exton, PA 19341
(215) 363-7330
(215) 363-7639 (FAX)

A Carolina Craftsman

A Carolina Craftsman offers an extensive collection of authentic hardware and accessories accurately created in the styles of the past. Solid brass cast dresser pulls for use with "American oak" furniture from the period 1890 to 1910 are individually made in tiny mold boxes, just as they were made one hundred years ago. The result of this laborious method is thin, lightweight pieces of elegant hardware with fine detail. The more angular Eastlake hardware for American furniture made during the period 1870 to 1880 enables owners of this style to restore their antiques with appropriate hardware.

The company also offers hand-carved gingerbread made from native American oak to replace broken or missing pieces from antique furniture. Each item is carved in solid oak.

Ice box collectors can find replacements for lifts, latches, and even nameplates in the Carolina Craftsman catalogue. Most are available in polished brass or nickel plate finish.

Catalogue, $2 refunded with first order.

A Carolina Craftsman
975 Avocado St.
Anaheim, CA 92805
(714) 776-7877

Conant Custom Brass

Nothing is more aggravating than trying to sweep that last bit of dust out of the corners on stairs or floors. You never quite feel that you've gotten it all. Conant Custom Brass presents an old solution that for some reason has been forgotten in recent years—the dust corner. Introduced in the 1890s, dust corners quickly evolved from wood to brass. They save time and give an ordinary

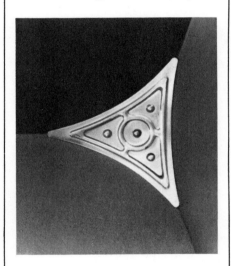

staircase a period look. Conant's solid brass corners come with an embossed surface (smooth surface on request). A minimum of ten corners must be ordered. They come with round-headed brass nails and a special steel punch for easy installation. Conant sells other types of brass hardware as well.

Literature on dust corners available.

Conant Custom Brass
270 Pine St.
Burlington, VT 05402
(802) 658-4482

Faneuil Furniture Hardware

With 143 pages of pulls and pushplates, hinges and handles, knobs and knockers, Faneuil Furniture Hardware's catalogue is a browser's delight. Hardware styles represented include Chippendale, Hepplewhite, oriental, and a variety of Victorian styles. Most hardware is crafted in brass, solid cast brass, wrought brass, and brass plated steel. The company also offers a selection of accessories like finials, ornamental hardware, trivets, gift items, and unusual shower curtain rod escutcheons.

Catalogue, $3.

Faneuil Furniture Hardware
163 Main St.
Salem, NH 03079
(603) 898-7733

Historic Housefitters

Historic Housefitters is outstanding among producers of authentically replicated hardware. The company's collection is vast, covering most areas of the house. Half of the work done by Historic Housefitters' craftsmen is executed in brass, and the rest is in hand- or machine-forged iron, allowing two price ranges of iron goods. The hand-forged ironwork is much like that produced by 18th and 19th century American blacksmiths. While faithful replications are made, the company has branched out, too, offering some contemporary designs which bridge modern and traditional tastes.

The complete thumblatch set includes a simple trim set (shown) with a plain latch bar, drive staple, and drive catch. The thumb-operated handle for this set is available in four different styles.

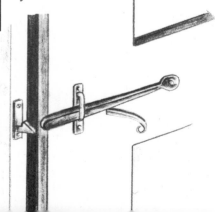

The closet latch shown includes a "coiled rat-tail" latch bar with a screw mounted staple and a drive-style catch. This basic colonial door knocker is gracefully curved. It measures 7½" high by 1" wide. Combining decoration and utility, the solid brass kickplate will protect the base of any door. It is available in four sizes: 6" by 30", 6" by 34", 8" by 30", and 8" by 34".

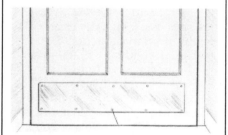

The polished brass door knocker in the bell style measures 9" high and 6" wide. A wooden door knob like the Oakleigh is a luxury. Made of a warm, honey-colored solid oak, it can be matched with cabinet knobs for any room.

Catalogue, $3.

Historic Housefitters Co.
Dept. 5
Farm to Market Rd.
Brewster, NY 10509
(914) 278-2427

Bath and Kitchen Hardware

The fixtures and fittings found in the kitchen and bath are those which are usually the first to go in any renovation. Careful thought, however, should be given to the replacement of sinks, tubs, and toilets. In many cases, it is possible to refinish these antique pieces. If that proves impossible, they can be replaced with fixtures that are at least old-fashioned in appearance. Specialty plumbing and salvage houses around the country regularly supply reconditioned and reproduction fixtures. Similarly, these dealers can supply reproduction old-style fittings such as faucet sets that can be substituted for the hopelessly corroded antique.

A-Ball

It's good, simple design and first-rate quality that have made A-Ball an *Old House Catalogue* favorite. Those elements are apparent in this cast-iron porcelain pedestal sink (model ER1011). The lines are pleasing, and it's a strong, durable piece. It's drilled for a 12" widespread faucet and measures 30" high by 24" wide by 20" deep. Another example is this solid oak high-tank toilet with a white china bowl. The hardware for it is available in brass or chrome, and each part can be ordered separately.

However, it's more than fine reproduction that makes A-Ball special; it's also the company's efforts to solve problems that occur frequently in the restoration of old houses. This exposed mixing faucet (BL2), popular in the 1930s and subsequently forgotten, is just one of A-Ball's solutions for old pedestal sinks that cannot be adapted for widespread faucets. Its gooseneck spout is 12" high, and its width is adjustable and can measure from 5½" to 14" between the handle centers. Brass or porcelain spoke-style handles are available, and lever handles can be substituted (model BL3). Choose the finish you prefer— polished brass or chrome-plated brass. For more information, write to A-Ball.

Catalogue available.

A-Ball Plumbing Supply
1703 W. Burnside
Portland, OR 97209
(503) 228-0026

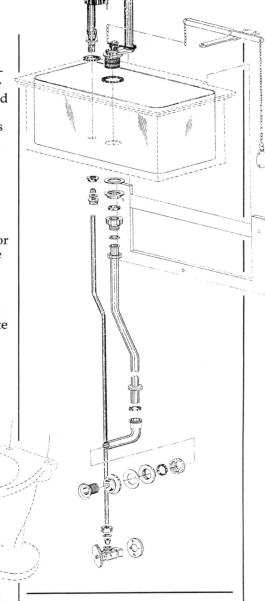

Antique Baths & Kitchens

S. Chris Rheinschild began designing and manufacturing fixtures while restoring his own Victorian home because he was dissatisfied with the quality of the antiques then available. He now offers a catalogue of his own authentically styled bath and kitchen fixtures, plus a selection of equally appropriate items from other manufacturers.

The Richmond pedestal basin has straightforward classic lines and is suitable for any Victorian bathroom. Manufactured in Europe, it is made from porcelain and finished with a white glaze. Its dimensions are 32" high by 26" wide, and it measures 19½" from front to back.

131

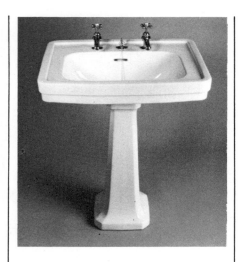

The copper kitchen sink is Rheinschild's own design. Modeled after antiques saved from homes built in the early 1900s, this elegant sink combines grace and utility. It is constructed of the same heavy gauge copper and quality hardwood as the originals. It is made to be mounted underneath the counter top. The single-basin sink measures 19" by 27" by 7"; the basin is 6" deep. A larger, double-basin model is also made.

The Victorian drinking fountain is another of Rheinschild's own designs. Perfect for an old-fashioned garden or yard, it is made of cast iron, polished brass, and stainless steel. The pedestal is cast from molds used during the Victorian era. The fountain measures 32" to the rim, and the base is 10" square.

Catalogue, $1.

Antique Baths & Kitchens
2220 Carlton Way
Santa Barbara, CA 93109
(805) 962-8598

Besco

Expert in restoration, Besco has filled its Boston showroom with antique plumbing supplies and re-surfaced porcelain, and makes faucets and fittings to order. Besco

stocks many fine reproductions and can custom-copy fixtures, as well. Solid brass (polished or satin finish), porcelain, or fluted china basins are also available.

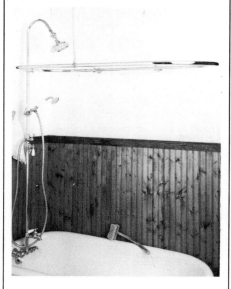

Besco participates in a collector's network and can often accommodate orders for unusual items.

Besco Plumbing
729 Atlantic Ave.
Boston, MA 02111
(617) 423-4535

Brass Finial

The Brass Finial offers all kinds of period reproduction hardware, from a brass Chippendale pull or a porcelain cabinet knob to a clawfoot tub. Shown here is the company's reproduction of a turn-of-the-century pedestal sink, the Berkeley model, composed of vitreous china. As the company's name implies, most of its fixtures are made of polished brass, left unlacquered to achieve an attractive patina over time. Chrome finish is available, if you prefer.

Catalogue, $1.

The Brass Finial
2408 Riverton Rd.
Cinnaminson, NJ 08077
(609) 786-9337

The Broadway Collection

If you want to combine the beauty of the past with the efficiency of the present, The Broadway Collection offers twelve complete lines of bathroom hardware that blend well with period furnishings. Each line contains almost everything the well-equipped period bathroom might need—faucets, handles, levers, shower heads, pedestal lavatories, towel bars, robe hooks, soap dishes, shower rods, and drains. All the metal is solid brass and is available in several finishes—polished unlacquered, coated, or electro-plated.

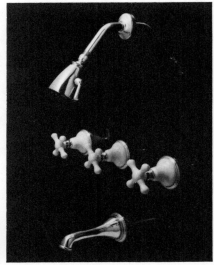

Model 19844-3 is a three-valve tub and shower set from Broadway's Colony White Suite. "HOT" and "COLD" lettering is available on the porcelain handles. The faucet is 5½" deep, and the centers of the outside valves are 8" apart. Brass fittings for Colony White hardware are available polished with clear lacquer, coated in a slightly darker finish that Broadway calls French bronze, or electroplated with pewter or polished chrome.

If you prefer all-metal fixtures to combinations of brass and porcelain, the Old Dominion Suite may suit your taste. Model 19230 is a faucet set available in polished unlacquered or polished lacquered brass, French bronze, or pewter on polished chrome electroplating. It is about 5" deep, with a maximum distance of 20" between the handle centers. All handles in this suite are lever style.

One of Broadway's finest lines is the Edwardian Suite. Model 19770 is a graceful gooseneck faucet that stands 11¾" tall with two spoke handles whose centers can be mounted a maximum of 20"

apart. The handles are topped by small white insets which bear the letters "H" and "C". Broadway's Edwardian fixtures range from the very simple—a smooth white pedestal lavatory (model 10070-3)—to the very complex—the exposed tub and hand shower wall mount (model 19797). The latter extends about 5" from the wall and features two spoke style handles whose centers are 8"

apart, a porcelain lever, and an elegant hand-held shower head resting in a delicate cradle. All of the Edwardian Suite fixtures are available in polished unlacquered or polished lacquered brass or electroplated with pewter or polished chrome.

Catalogue available.

The Broadway Collection
250 N. Troost
Olathe, KS 66061
(800) 255-6365
(913) 782-6244 (KS)
(800) 468-1219 (Canada)

The Chicago Faucet Co.

The Chicago Faucet Co. manufactures a tremendous range of bath and kitchen fixtures. Many items the company now produces approximate period styles and are recommended for their quality and authentic look to home renovators. Among these are a series of gooseneck spouts for tubs and sinks; brass lavatory sets with porcelain or wood-trimmed handles; and brass towel bars mounted on wooden wall plates.

The products are sold through retail stores, but a catalogue and listing of local distributors is available through Chicago Faucet's main office.

The Chicago Faucet Co.
2100 S. Nuclear Drive
Des Plaines, IL 60018
(312) 694-4400

Cumberland General Store

Right next to the carbide lamp-cap in Cumberland General Store's all-inclusive catalogue, are the turn-of-the-century bath fixtures and kitchen accessories. Made from solid brass, solid oak, and fine porcelain, the company's collection features toilets, drains, faucets, and more.

The Cumberland bath tub, model 8247, is made of galvanized steel with a natural, silver-gray finish. With golden oak cradle legs 2¼" thick, this tub comes with cutouts for standard tub faucets, waste, and drain flow. The overall dimensions are 21¾" high and 59½" long. The width at the top of the rim is 27".

A less common tub today is the hip bath, model 17002. Once the rage in Europe, this style quickly became popular in America for its refined styling. With arm and soap rests, the hip bath was designed to give complete arm and back support. Cumberland's hip bath is 30" high and 31" wide and is completely galvanized inside and out.

The Cumberland pump, 3682, completes the country kitchen. Made of cast iron, it is 15" high and can be used inside or out for both hot and cold running water. This hand pump will not interfere with other faucets. The pump comes completely assembled and can be installed in less than an hour.

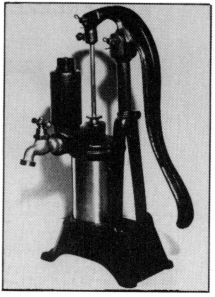

Catalogue, $3.

Cumberland General Store
Route 3
Crossville, TN 38555
(800) 334-4640
(615) 484-8481 (TN)

Historic Housefitters Co.

Virtually indestructable and yet aesthetically pleasing, forged iron has been preferred for centuries by the makers of often-used items from huge stoves to the smallest hooks and latches. In the 18th and 19th centuries, the decorative beauty of brass was integral to the functionality of iron for fancy home hardware. Historic Housefitters' craftsmen create useful and decorative items from brass and iron.

Pictured is the firm's pot rack, made of hand-forged iron. Decorated with leaves at either end, this large bowed rack has six removable hooks and is 26½" long and 6½" deep. Also shown are Historic Housefitters' kitchen and bath towel ring designs. Three-and-a-half inches or 4¾" in diameter and 7½" or 9½" long, these rings fit anywhere. Historic Housefitters' brass robe hook is another attractive piece, and with a 3" diameter, it mounts easily on the bathroom door or wall.

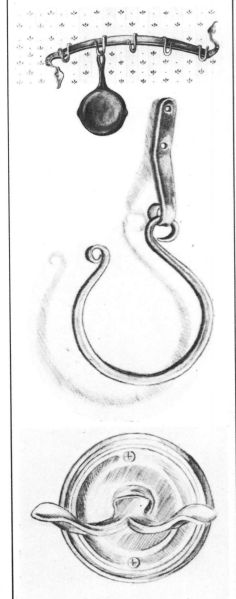

All hand-forged iron is left finished as it came from the forge. The machine-forged iron is given a baked-on, matte black finish, and brass work is polished and lacquered.

Catalogue, $3.
Historic Housefitters Co.
Dept. 5
Farm to Market Rd.
Brewster, NY 10509
(914) 278-2427

Kohler

Kohler has long been known as a producer of durable kitchen and bath hardware. In response to the demand from home renovators and those looking to incorporate old-fashioned charm into modern homes, Kohler has introduced a line of fixtures modeled after antiques. The Antique Water-Guard

kitchen faucet shown combines a clean design with a gracefully curved spout. It is available in polished brass, polished and brushed chrome, or polished and brushed gold. The six-pronged handles shown can have colored china or onyx inserts or can be replaced by lever handles.

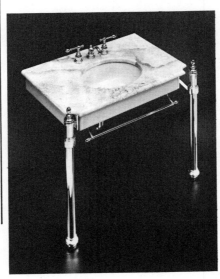

Kohler's console sink features lavatory legs and a towel bar, and can be complemented by any of the company's faucet sets. This elegant piece features a marbled top, and legs and towel bar of polished brass and chrome in the IV Georges Brass styling. The basin is vitreous china. This sink

is one of a collection of dramatic console tables suited to lavish bathrooms, powder rooms, or dressing rooms.

For a period-styled bathroom, Kohler offers its Vintage high tank toilet reminiscent of the Victorian originals. The pull-chain toilet features a high tank in either vitreous china or oak lined with plastic. A matching oak seat and cover are also available. The chain and piping come in either polished chrome or a polished gold finish.

A newly added service at Kohler is the company's Color Coordinates, a system for matching pieces and colors from Kohler's vast collection of fixtures with other items needed for the bathroom. The customer selects a set of color choices with secondary accent colors to match, and

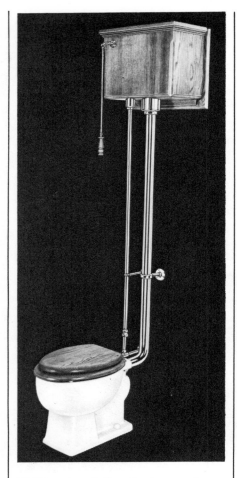

Kohler then helps find manufacturers of paints, papers, tiles, or whatever the customer needs to coordinate the decor.

Brochures available.

Kohler Co.
Kohler, WI 53044
(414) 457-4441

Olde Virginia Restoration

For the person thinking of refinishing an old porcelain tub, Olde Virginia Restoration has created a kit and detailed instructions to take the mystery out of this skill. The company offers kits for restoration and refinishing of tile, formica, appliances, wood, and terra cotta as well. Many old house owners will find at least some of these materials in need of touch-up on their property.

Concise written or video instructions are available for all the company's kits. The porcelain basin refinishing kit helps restore a worn out bathroom or kitchen

sink and can also be used on a worn porcelain Hoosier cabinet top. Olde Virginia's GLAZ-COATE 5-step system is used for this work, which the company says should take from three to four hours from start to finish.

Catalogue, $3.

Olde Virginia Restoration
PO Box 3305
Portsmouth, VA 23701
(804) 397-0948

Perma Ceram

In just one day, the people from Perma Ceram can resurface old and worn porcelain bathroom fixtures with the company's Porcelaincote process. It's less costly than replacing old fixtures, and can retain antiques with a fresh look. The process uses a chemical coating specially designed for bathroom use, and it's made to resist peeling, fading, cracking, and discoloring.

Brochure available.

Perma Ceram Enterprises, Inc.
65 Smithtown Blvd.
Smithtown, NY 11787
(800) 645-5039
(516) 724-1205

St. Thomas

Finely crafted porcelain basins and pedestal sinks are manufactured by St. Thomas and available through local dealers. Basin styles include a variety of oval shapes with fluted edges.

Brochure available.

St. Thomas Creations Inc.
79-25 Denbrook Rd. Suite D
San Diego, CA 92126
(619) 530-1940

Saxe Patterson

Clay from Taos, New Mexico is formed into stunning ceramic art by the craftsmen at Saxe Patterson. Self-rimming basins are available in round (18" outside diameter, 15" inside diameter) or oval (15" by 19" outside diameter, 12" by 16" inside diameter) styles.

Hand-finished vitreous porcelain, fired at white-hot temperatures, receives a coating of glaze at 2350° Fahrenheit. Saxe Patterson creates its own glazes, glossy and matte—many including local ingredients

—for a distinctive and durable formula. Glaze samples are available for varying charges, refundable with large orders.

Brochure available.

Saxe Patterson
Box 15
Salazar Rd.
Taos, NM 87571
(505) 758-9513

Sink Factory

When self-taught potter Michael Stringer could discover no manufacturers of Victorian sinks to suit him, he retired to his garage, mixed up a ceramic recipe that worked, and began casting,

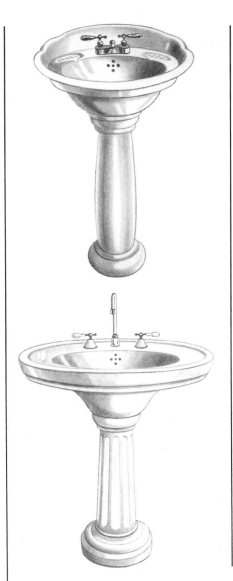

firing, and glazing. Pedestal lavatories offered by his Sink Factory include the Bentley, the Berkeley, the Whitney, and the Yardley. Vanity basins come in several sizes and shapes; vanity

tops, in four sizes of a round style, three ovals, a scallop shape, a shallow kidney design, or the angular Wellington.

Catalogue, $3.

The Sink Factory
2140 San Pablo Ave.
Berkeley, CA 94702
(415) 540-8193

but need to install a shower head, Steptoe suggests its Converto Shower. It comes complete with curtain rod and supports, can be assembled quickly by even a duffer, and won't ruin the period effect you are striving for. All Steptoe hardware is available in chrome-plated or polished brass finish.

Brochures available.

Steptoe & Wife
322 Geary Ave.
Toronto, Ont., Canada M6H 2C7
(416) 530-4200

Sunrise Specialty

Sunrise Specialty manufactures high quality reproduction Victorian bath fixtures in the same materials as the originals: solid oak, vitreous china, and solid brass. The cast-iron clawfoot tub is 6'2" long with a solid oak rim, and stands on four sturdy cast-iron brass plated legs. The vitreous china toilet features a fluted base to match the authentically styled pedestal sink base. To complete the Victorian bathroom, Sunrise offers brass shower fittings, porcelain and brass faucets, and even an appropriate bathroom ceiling fixture.

Catalogue available.

Sunrise Specialty
2204 San Pablo Ave.
Berkeley, CA 94702
(415) 845-4751

Vermont Soapstone

Soapstone sinks are in a class by themselves. Prized for their natural beauty, these custom-made items are handmade to your specifications by the craftsmen at Vermont Soapstone, a small family-run business. The sinks are suitable for bath, kitchen, and greenhouse, and can be made with or without a drainboard and backsplash.

Brochure available.

Vermont Soapstone Co.
PO Box 168, Stoughton Pond Rd.
Perkinsville, VT 05151-0168
(802) 263-5404

Steptoe & Wife

Specializing in the manufacture and distribution of quality architectural restoration products, Steptoe & Wife offers porcelain-handled brass faucets and basin cocks, ceramic and brass shower

heads, reproduction pedestal sinks, and many other bathroom fixtures for period homes. If you have an old clawfoot tub that is perfect for a long, leisurely soak,

Watercolors

Imported directly from Great Britain and available only through Watercolors is the complete line of Regal luxury antique style bathroom and kitchen fittings. Shown is the Regal "antique" bath and shower mixer, a deck-mounted bath filler with hand-held shower. Made of solid brass, it is available finished in chrome, gold plate, or an antique-looking finish—a gold alloy plate with the look of worn brass, but requiring no maintenance. Other hardware in this collection are fittings for wash basins, showers, and bidets, with optional pop-up drains or the traditional chain and plug type.

Newly added in 1988 is the Colore series of fittings characterized by a maintenance-free finish. This finish is tarnish-resistant and extremely durable, and it needs no polishing to

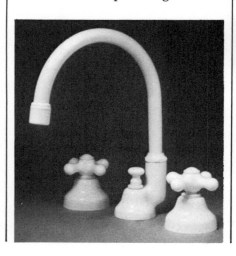

keep its original appearance. Shown is the Colore gooseneck faucet, fashioned of solid brass and finished in baked white enamel. Other finishes include black, red, yellow, beige, and brown baked enamel, and polished chrome. Obviously manufactured for contemporary use, the Colore series is evocative of early twentieth century design. Although these products are available only through architects and interior designers, Watercolors will furnish information about its fittings by mail.

Watercolors, Inc.
Garrison-on-Hudson, NY 10524
(914) 424-3327

Stoves and Supplies

The choice of wood as an alternative fuel source in recent years has rescued many an old cast-iron monster from the junkyard. But before you buy one of these originals, beware. While an antique can be equally as warming as a reproduction, make sure that it has been expertly refurbished. A stove that isn't airtight can be just as great a fuel thief as that oil burner down in the basement, and a hundred times as dangerous.

Many companies have capitalized on the recent demand for wood-burning stoves by mass-producing reproductions in record numbers. It's therefore easy to find one; what's difficult is to locate one that's handsome as well as utilitarian. The manufacturers listed in the following section have not sacrificed style for the sake of utility or profit: they offer many attractive models, some based on 19th-century originals, in a variety of sizes and styles to suit every need.

Barnstable Stove Shop

Located in a restored horse barn once used for cranberry processing, Barnstable Stove Shop displays more than 300 antique kitchen ranges and parlor stoves. Each stove is completely sandblasted and rebuilt; all seams are cemented and spray painted. Doug Pacheco, owner of Barnstable, guarantees the quality of

his nickel plating and foundry work. His selection of period stoves includes Mica Baseburners made from 1880 to 1920, turn-of-the-century Glenwoods, and Crawfords made by Walker and

Pratt Co. beginning in the 1850s. If you have a prize behemoth that needs refurbishing, Barnstable will do it for you, or will trade it in on a model more suitable for your needs.

Brochure, $1.

Barnstable Stove Shop
Rt. 149, Box 472
West Barnstable, MA 02668
(508) 362-9913

Country Comfort Stove Works

Country Comfort Stove Works specializes in buying, selling, and restoring antique wood and coal stoves, but to look at this company's work you would think its forte to be the production of originals. Before each stove is ready to be resold, it is completely dismantled, sandblasted, reassembled with fresh bolts and sealer, and given a rebuilt firebox and new nickel-plated trim. Country Comfort is so confident in the quality of its work that a lifetime money-back guarantee is included with each finished product.

The Art Bay State is one of the most ornate kitchen ranges that Country Comfort offers. Highly decorative, this stove is a pleasing addition to any kitchen. Less fancy but equally attractive kitchen ranges are available in addition to a full spectrum of parlor

stoves. Since Country Comfort Stove Works is buying and selling stoves constantly, its stock is permanently in flux. While a specific model may not be available at a particular time, chances are that a similar model is usually at hand.

Stoves may be picked up at the shop or shipped anywhere in the U.S.

Brochure, $2.

Country Comfort Stove Works
Union Rd.
Wales, MA 01081
(413) 245-7396

Cumberland General Store

For those who want to do more than recreate a look, the Cumberland General Store offers wood- and coal-burning cooking ranges. Now it is once again possible to cook just like Grandma did.

Elmira Stove & Fireplace

Elmira Stove and Fireplace continues the tradition begun by the Oval company in 1906. Elmira offers state-of-the-art airtight wood heating stoves, fireplace inserts, and an attractive line of charming wood/coal/electric cooking stoves. Pictured is the Elmira model 5000, a combination wood and electric cooking stove. Obviously suitable for any kitchen, its features include a large ash pan for convenient ash removal; stainless steel firebox; durable cast-iron cooking surface; an oven broiler; and an overhead storage cabinet with a

In designs that have withstood the test of time, stoves like the Old Reliable cooking range, 4700-A, are created for looking good and cooking well. Damper and draft control allow for maintenance of the proper cooking temperature. Constructed of heavy cast-iron, the stove measures 65″ high and 21¼″ wide. The oven itself is 15″ by 14″ by 11″.

Catalogue, $3.

Cumberland General Store
Route 3
Crossville, TN 38555
(800) 334-4640
(615) 484-8481 (TN)

built-in exhaust fan. The oven is electric only.

These durable, attractive stoves carry with them a history of warmth, security and old-fashioned quality. A smaller combination model, the Sweetheart, is also available for those with limited space. Recently introduced is the all-electric cookstove for those who want to create the "warm" atmosphere, but retain the modern convenience of electricity. The company plans to market a gas range in early 1989.

Catalogue available.

Elmira Stove & Fireplace
145 Northfield Dr.
Waterloo, Ontario, Canada 2NL 5J3
(519) 747-5443
(519) 747-5444 (FAX)

Good Time Stove Co.

For people who appreciate the workmanship of the past, antique heating and cooking stoves rank among the finest examples of the merging of art and utility. Good Time Stove Co. has gathered a collection of antique stoves fully restored to their original elegance and efficiency. Each stove is guaranteed to add warmth and

character and enhance any home, comments stove black Richard Richardson. As well-versed in the subject of restoring and using antique stoves as anyone in the field, Richardson takes a personal interest in locating the right stove for each of his customers. Many people correspond with him until they find the perfect stove. Richardson keeps a file of options,

measurements, and price ranges customers desire. Because stock changes constantly, Good Time's brochure can only show models commonly available. A visit to the showroom might be helpful.

Brochure available.

Good Time Stove Co.
PO Box 306, Rt. 112
Goshen, MA 01032-0306
(413) 268-3677

Lehman Hardware

While many people know Waterford, Ireland, as the home of the world's finest crystal, few know of the superbly built wood stoves produced there. The Waterford Foundry has been producing stoves in Ireland almost since the time of the American Revolution, and Lehman is offering them now in the United States.

The Waterford Leprechaun is forged in a time-honored design that is compact and versatile. A built-in after-burner automatically engages as the door closes to boost efficiency. With poured-in-place refractory-lined bottom and double-thick cast-iron side and back walls, this model is extremely durable for its small size, 25⅛" high, 15" wide, and 25" deep. The glass door with the decorative sunburst window frame is well complemented by the glow of the flames from within.

Catalogue, $2.

140

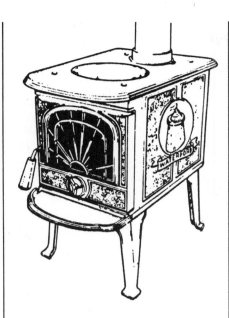

Lehman Hardware
PO Box 41
4779 Kidron Rd.
Kidron, OH 44636
(216) 857-5441

Lunenburg Foundry

The art of keeping warm is no secret to residents of Nova Scotia. Since 1891 the Lunenburg Foundry has been manufacturing cast-iron stoves at its Nova Scotia factory. The Bluenose, an airtight wood-burning stove, is a small, simple, and handsome model with side panels emblazoned with the famous schooner Bluenose. It is 27" long by 20" wide and 26½" high. Its features include a cast-iron baffle, sensitive draft control, effective primary and secondary combustion, and a cooking lid. The Campfire model is a coal- or wood-burning stove, 24" high by 23" wide and 23" deep. It can be cooked on, broiled in, and is both a fireplace and a heater.

For those looking for durability and rugged charm, Lunenburg Foundry shouldn't be overlooked.

Brochure available.

Lunenburg Foundry & Engineering Ltd.
PO Box 1240, 53 Falkland St.
Lunenburg, Nova Scotia, Canada
* B0J 2C0*
(902) 634-8827
(902) 455-2461
(902) 634-8886 (FAX)

Portland Stove

Portland Stove's Queen Atlantic is billed as the reigning majesty of household ranges. This reproduction of the 1906 model is indeed sturdy, reliable, and stately. Constructed completely of cast iron with no steel alloys or sheet metal parts, its thick walls assure uniform cooking. The Queen Atlantic is available in either wood- or coal-burning models. Extra long and deep fireboxes accommodate

lasting nickel plated ornamentation. The Queen Atlantic measures 32¼" to the range top, another 30" from range to the back of the main top, and is 57" long. The roomy oven is 19¾" deep, 18¼" wide, and 11" high.

Portland Stove also manufactures a smaller Princess Atlantic cook stove, Franklin stoves, pot bellies, and box stoves.

long burning loads and infrequent ash cleanouts. And a lot of cooking can be done on the six-lid top. An elevated warming oven and high shelf are options to make the Queen Atlantic even more useful. The stove is decorated with long-

Literature, $2.

Portland Stove Company
PO Box 377, Fickett Rd.
N. Pownal, ME 04069
(207) 688-2254
(207) 775-6424

Wendall's Wood Stoves

Restored pre-1935 wood- and coal-burning stoves and ranges are the stock in trade at Wendall's. All stoves are dismantled, cleaned, repaired, and sealed before they enter the showroom floor for sale. The selection of attractive, effi-

cient stoves varies, so no catalogue is available. Wendall's does produce a flyer, updated frequently, featuring photographs of current stock. This gives a hint of the many brands and styles the shop carries. Stoves can be crated and shipped anywhere in the United States.

styles. All the work is carried out in England by skilled craftsmen who painstakingly hand carve each mantelpiece, so essentially no two mantels are exactly alike. In addition to the extensive range of designs offered from the Hallidays catalogue, custom carving is done.

The Checkendon is a dignified style of the Georgian era with fluted frieze and jambs. Another

Mantels

If you're fortunate enough to have one or more working fireplaces, good period mantels will be of interest to you. Every fireplace should be properly "framed," in much the same way you would set off a treasured painting. The companies listed in the following section can supply antique and reproduction mantels in a variety of styles, materials, and sizes to meet every need and to suit every period decor. Other suppliers can be found in Chapter 1, Structural Products and Services.

The Brass Knob

The decorative antique mantel pictured is only one of the many beautifully preserved items in The Brass Knob's extensive collection of architectural antiques and salvaged period items. This ar-

chitectural salvage company specializes in turn-of-the-century brass hardware and lighting fixtures, but also deals in ironwork, columns, glass, doors, plumbing fixtures, and much more. Most items are from the Victorian era, but Art Deco and Art Nouveau styles are also stocked. Since most of The Brass Knob's items are one-of-a-kind decorative pieces, no catalogue is available. Visits to the shop are recommended, but written inquiries are welcome.

Brill and Walker Associates, Inc.

Brill and Walker is the exclusive American importer and distributor for Hallidays of England. This firm specializes in hand carving wood mantelpieces in the Georgian and Regency

Georgian mantelpiece, the Honey-suckle has finely carved anthemion and urns. From the mid-Georgian period, the Garford is done in the William Kent style with a carved shell flanked by husk swags. The classic Grosvenor is an imposing mantel in an Adam style with carved urn and swags on Ionic columns.

Catalogue, $3.

Brill and Walker Associates, Inc.
PO Box 731, OHC
Sparta, NJ 07871-0731
(201) 729-8876

Marion H. Campbell

A builder and designer of American period furniture and architectural woodwork, Campbell has a thorough appreciation for and understanding of the styles in which he works. Paneled fireplace walls are one of his specialties. Campbell uses authentic joinery techniques, appropriate moldings, turnings, and carvings, and hand applies the proper finishes to his work. Shown is a detail of a Federal mantel Campbell created.

Brochure available.

Workshop
Barber and Plymouth Sts.
Bath, PA 18104
(215) 837-7775

Mailing Address
39 Wall St.
Bethlehem, PA 18018
(215) 865-3292

Decorators Supply Corporation

A selection of wooden mantels with applied composition ornaments is offered by Decorators Supply. Each mantel is custom made to fit a customer's fireplace. No items are kept in stock, but shipments are usually made in about four weeks after an order has been placed.

The first two mantels, 15712 and 15729 with fluted columns, are colonial in style. Mantel 15701, with its graceful curves, is French in style. The company also produces cast ornamental plaster items, capitals and brackets, and fiber carvings. A separate catalogue is available for each grouping.

Catalogues, $2 each.

Decorators Supply Corporation
3610-12 S. Morgan St.
Chicago, IL 60609-1586
(312) 847-6300

Fireplace Mantel Shop

For more than thirty-five years The Fireplace Mantel Shop has specialized in manufacturing architectural woodwork, including moldings, panels, valances, staircases, and more than a dozen styles of decorative mantels. One of its most flexible mantel designs, the Multee, can be used with either a flush fireplace or a projected facing and is available in a choice of three styles: with bed molding, bed and dentil molding, or bed and dentil molding finished with an oval casing. The Chestertown features a bull-nose shelf; the Metropolitan, squared-off columns and handsome vertical detail; and the Shipwright, a gracefully curved breast board and delicate proportions. Each mantel can be ordered in custom sizes to fit your exact specifications, and each is crafted of kiln-dried pine, sanded but left unfinished so that you can add your own decorative paint or stain.

Brochures available.

The Fireplace Mantel Shop, Inc.
4217 Howard Ave.
Kensington, MD 20895
(301) 564-1550

Heritage Mantels

When new items are cast from molds made directly from the original antiques, they can truly be called authentic. That's the method used by Heritage Mantels to create its finely detailed reproductions. The company's craftsmen use a marble composition made from pulverized marble that has been pre-blended with mineral fillers and fused together with a binding agent. The resulting product when cast in the mold creates mantels virtually indistinguishable from the originals. Among the marble colors available are limestone, beige perlato, rouge royal, and forest green. Illustrated are, from top to bottom,

#300 Italian Renaisssance, #112
Louis XIV, #128 Louis XV,
#105 Louis XV.

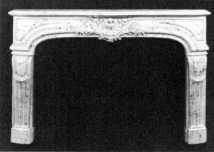

Catalogue, $3.

Heritage Mantels, Inc.
PO Box 240
Southport, CT 06490
(203) 335-0552

Maizefield Mantels

"Maizefield," a magnificent 18th century mansion in Dutchess County, New York, with eight different styles of mantels, is the inspiration behind Maizefield Mantels. Experts in designing and constructing beautiful mantels and mantelshelves, Maizefield's craftsmen create custom pieces and also work with a wide range of standard designs. From reproduced traditional models with hand-planed moldings and carved ornamentation, to more contemporary work with exotic woods, metals, and neon, Maizefield does it all. Shown is the Montgomery mantel, with a shelf depth of 8½", a breastboard height of 1'11", and a leg width of 10¾". Also pictured is the Van Ness mantel, with a 10" shelf depth, a 1'2" breastboard height, and a 9" leg width. Each mantel's overall dimensions depend on the size of the fireplace

opening. Also available is a selection of Victorian mantels, complete with over-mantel shelving, beveled mirrors, and highly figured burls and inlays.
Maizefield Mantels has a standard line of mantelshelves as well, and the company creates custom staircases and does custom woodwork of all kinds.

Normally, Maizefield's mantels and mantelshelves are formed of kiln-dried alder. Some of the moldings may be hemlock and some of the structural parts Douglas fir. Other woods used include red oak, black walnut, and cherry. Glue and nails are used for joining all the separate pieces. If a mantel will be painted, Maizefield will supply it pre-primed. Unpainted mantels come with a coat of clear sealer. Various other options on Maizefield products include secret panels, embossed moldings, cast ornamentation, inlays, and exotic woods and finishes.

Catalogue, $3.

Maizefield Mantels
PO Box 336
Port Townsend, WA 98368
(206) 385-6789

Nostalgia

Careful reproductions of architectural antiques primarily in historical Southern styles are the exclusive pursuit of Nostalgia. Located in Savannah, the belle of the old South, this company's collection of antique-style mantels is particularly interesting. These mantels are reproduced as the original European imports were, of cast stone, but they are also available in oak, mahogany, and pine to accommodate modern needs. Illustrated is the Marlborough plaster surround carved with a classic acanthus leaf design in deep relief. The standard size is 50" wide, 4¾" deep, and 34" high, but special dimensions are accommodated.

Catalogue, $2.50.
Nostalgia, Inc.
307 Stiles Ave.
Savannah, GA 31401
(800) 874-0015
(912) 232-2324 (GA)

Fireplace Accessories

If you've just taken possession of the old house of your dreams and are about to purchase the first accessories for a fireplace, you'll probably want to begin with andirons, tools, and a screen. There are hundreds of styles and sizes to choose from: some of the best and most attractive are described in the following listings. After you've taken care of those necessities, you might consider additional pieces. How about a wood box? Or a swinging crane from which to hang a copper pot? Or a cast-iron fireback? Any of these pieces, if selected with an eye to design and workmanship, can increase your enjoyment of the fireplace for years to come.

Country Iron Foundry

Firebacks serve several purposes. They protect the rear wall of a fireplace, radiate heat, make an attractive backdrop in the fireplace, and dress up the fireplace when it's not in use. Firebacks were sturdy symbols of a good home during the American colonial days. Made in cast iron, they were also a medium for artistry.

The Country Iron Foundry produces a fine selection of hand-made cast-iron firebacks from molds taken directly from antique originals. Stove plates, used in the same way as firebacks, were taken from broken European and Scandanavian five- and six-plate stoves. The Country Iron Foundry also offers a group of reproduction stove plates modeled after the originals.

The Pineapple and Urn fireback is an exact replica of a French piece dating from about 1750. The pineapple, a symbol of hospitality, is a prevalent decorative accent in Georgian English and colonial American architecture. This fireback measures 24" wide, 28" high, and ¾" thick.

The Lady-on-Horseback fireback also dates from about 1750 in France. The graceful shape and subject make this plate suitable for an average-sized fireplace in a house of any period. It is 20" wide, 25" high, and ½" thick.

The Three Goddesses fireback is a more formal piece taken from an original found in New Jersey and similar to an English fireback now in the Rochester Museum, England, dated 1697. The English version identifies the three as Pallas, Juno, and Venus. This piece is 16" wide, 25" high at the center, and more than ½" thick.

Catalogue, $2.

The Country Iron Foundry
Box 600-OHC
Paoli, PA 19301
(215) 296-7122

Historic Housefitters Co.

To fill the dark, dreary void in a fireplace in summer or to highlight the warm glow of a crackling fire in winter, Historic Housefitters offers a collection of handsome and practical andirons. Specializing in hand- and machine-forged iron hardware, Historic Housefitters' craftsmen have chosen brass for the refined Hampton andirons, shown. The log rests are made of iron for extra durability. Carefully formed, each piece of the set is hand-polished and protected with heat-resistant lacquer to insure a long-lasting and beautifully finished product. Historic Housefitters also does custom hand-forged ironwork.

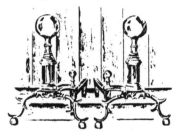

Catalogue, $3.

Historic Housefitters Co.
Dept. 5
Farm to Market Rd.
Brewster, NY 10509
(914) 278-2427

Lemee's Fireplace Equipment

The Lemee family has compiled a catalogue of fireplace accessories ranging from fire screens to chestnut roasters. There's a brass wood box decorated with scenes of an English courtyard; a flame-proof hearth rug; a cast-iron grate for shallow fireplaces; and a broiler stand for indoor fireplace cooking. The owl andirons il-

lustrated are perched on tree limbs. Their glass eyes glow with the fire's warmth.

Catalogue, $2.

Lemee's Fireplace Equipment
815 Bedford St.
Bridgewater, MA 02324
(508) 697-2672

Pennsylvania Firebacks

First introduced in late-15th-century Europe, the fireback quickly became popular because of its heat-saving design and later, its decorative qualities. Pennsylvania Firebacks offers nine different original designs by J. Del Conner, each molded of durable cast-iron. Shown are the American Eagle and the Field of Stars, the latter designed to be installed either horizontally or vertically. The Field of Stars is available in standard 21½" by 18" size or in a more flexible 14" by 21½" model so that several can be

combined to fit a variety of fireplace sizes. You may wish to mount the fireback with strong steel anchors and bolts (available from the company), or merely to prop it at the back of the hearth.

Pennsylvania Firebacks also offers hand-painted fireboards designed by Carol Nagel.

Catalogue, $2. (refundable with purchase)
Brochure, 10¢.

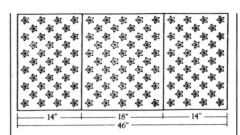

Pennsylvania Firebacks, Inc.
308 Elm Ave.
North Wales, PA 19454
(215) 699-0805

Tools

Even if you are not a do-it-yourself craftsman in need of tools and special building and cabinetry supplies, you will find the catalogues of the major suppliers an unending delight. These publications range from the very simple offerings of the specialty toolmaker who supplies only one particular type of instrument to the glorious color publications of suppliers of thousands of items from all over the earth. Undoubtedly, even if you are all thumbs, you will discover something that you must have because it is not only handy to have around the house but is, in itself, a work of art.

Garrett Wade

Garrett Wade's color Woodworking Tools catalogue is so artfully put together it makes even a humble screwdriver look glamorous. In addition to photographs of the many and various tools in this 208-page book, line drawings show how tools work, how to use them properly, and how to detect signs of wear. Helpful hints, too, make this catalogue more than a sales list. Everything for woodworking from drill bits to house plans is included. Active customers also receive catalogue updates in quarterly newsletters.

Woodworking Tools Catalogue, $4.

Garrett Wade Co.
161 Ave. of the Americas
New York, NY 10013
(800) 221-2942 (credit card orders)
(212) 807-1757 (NY)

Mechanick's Workbench

You've seen wonderful displays of furniture made just the way colonial craftsmen did—but what happened to the tools those craftsmen used? The Mechanick's Workbench has preserved them—everything from an Archimedean

drill to an invoice from Quackenbush, Townsend, & Co. Many of the tools are completely intact and in splendid condition. An eel spear, every delicate prong whole, is just one of the firm's novel prizes. An 1865 edition of a carpenter's and joiner's handbook and a carved bone pump drill suitable for a museum display show the hard-won quality and variety at the Mechanick's Workbench.

The Mechanick's Workbench has an ongoing research project chronicling New England planemakers of the 18th century. The firm has plotted out estimates of apprenticeship periods, marriages, and relatives who were planemakers as well. A Foster's patent turn-table iron smooth plane is a star example in the tool collection. Its use varies with the adjustable angle of iron to body. The single production run of this model, means that a scant number of these tools, dated January 29, 1907, remain. Pick up—and don't put down—a catalogue from the Mechanick's Workbench.

Catalogue available, $10.

The Mechanick's Workbench
Box 668, Front St.

Marion, MA 02738
(617) 748-1680

Other Suppliers of Hardware, Heating and Cooking

Consult List of Suppliers for addresses.

Antique Hardware

Architectural Antiques
Canal Co.
Ohmega Salvage
Vintage Plumbing

Architectural Hardware

Antique Hardware Store
Architectural Antique Warehouse
Baldwin Hardware
Blaine Window Hardware
Robert Bourdon, The Smithy
Cassidy Brothers Forge
Classic Architectural Specialties
Elephant Hill Ironworks
Federal Street Lighthouse
Ohmega Salvage
Old Wagon Factory
Period Furniture Hardware
Remodelers' and Renovators' Supply
Tremont Nail Co.
Willimasburg Blacksmiths
Woodworkers Store

Household Hardware

Antique Hardware Store
Architectural Antique Warehouse
Bona Decorative Hardware
Robert Bourdon, The Smithy
Classic Accents
Classic Architectural Specialties
Country Loft
Hurley Patentee
Period Furniture Hardware
Remodelers' and Renovators' Supply
Williamsburg Blacksmiths

Bath and Kitchen Hardware

Acorn Manufacturing
Antique Hardware Store
Architectural Antique Warehouse
Baldwin
Robert Bourdon, The Smithy
Classic Architectural Specialties
D. E. A./Bathroom Machineries
DeWeese Woodworking
Governor's Antiques

Hippo Hardware and Trading
Lehman Hardware
Ohmega Salvage
Omnia Industries
Pelnik Wrecking
Remodelers' and Renovators' Supply
Tennessee Tub
United House Wrecking
Wrecking Bar

Stoves and Supplies

Aetna
Bona Decorative Hardware
Robert Bourdon, The Smithy
Bryant Stove Works
Hearth Realities
Kayne & Son
Nostalgia
Period Furniture Hardware
Schwartz's Forge and Metalworks
Helen Williams

Mantels

Architectural Antique Warehouse
Architectural Antiques Exchange
Bay Waveland Woodworks
Marion H. Campbell
Central Kentucky Millwork
Classic Architectural Specialties
E. Cohen's Architectural Heritage
Dalton-Gorman
Decorator's Supply
Governor's Antiques
Great American Salvage
Whit Hanks
The Joinery
Jerard Paul Jordan
Ohmega Salvage
Pelnik Wrecking
Sheppard Millwork
Somerset Door and Column
Wrecking Bar

Tools

Arden Forge
Frog Tool
Lehman Hardware
Preservation Resource Group (PRG)
Woodworkers Store

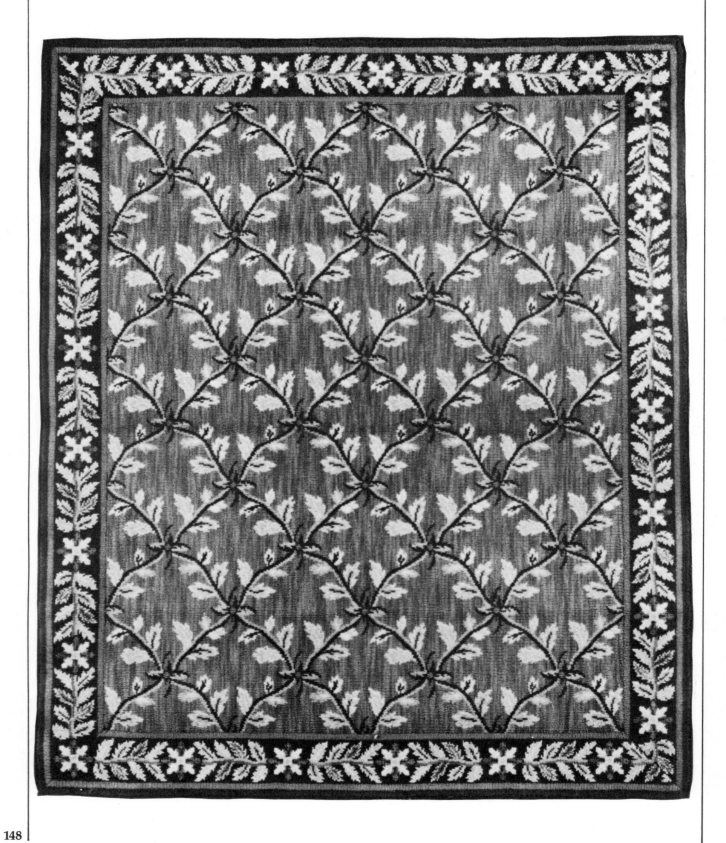

5.

Floors and Floor Coverings

Only a few years ago it would have been impossible to recommend more than a handful of manufacturers of reproduction rugs and carpets appropriate for period interiors. The best suggestion at the time was to seek out suppliers of reasonably priced oriental carpets—new or old. Flat-weave kilims were then bargains as were early 20th-century weaves. Prices on these "antique" floor coverings have risen greatly, but at the same time the supply of reproduction rugs and carpeting has almost caught up with demand. This is due in large part to the requests of historic house museum curators and restoration architects and designers. Old-fashioned designs have returned to the collections of many major carpeting manufacturers, and documents and paintings that record past styles in floor coverings as well as remnants of antique materials are being used to re-create Jacquard, Brussels, and Wilton weaves both here and abroad.

A demand for less expensive formal floor coverings such as floorcloths—used widely in the 18th and 19th centuries—has also grown tremendously. There are dozens of craftsmen producing these designs on canvas. Some of the best of these artisans are included in the following pages. So, too, are the makers of cotton area rugs and runners. It is no longer necessary to depend solely on suppliers of hooked rugs, although these remain an appropriate alternative for many interiors.

The flooring industry has also undergone major changes. Random-width designs in pine are now offered by most major manufacturers. Traditional parquet designs in oak and other fine woods have made a comeback as well. Marble, slate, and ceramic tile in imaginative patterns and colors are now real choices for kitchens, bathrooms, and hallways. Properly maintained, any of the quality wood, stone, and ceramic flooring materials can last for generations.

The Clichy carpet made in France for Stark Carpet Corporation, New York City.

Flooring Materials

Many home centers and lumberyards now offer a wide selection of flooring materials appropriate for an old or period-design house. It is not the material itself but how it is manufactured that is important and, in the matter of wood and ceramic tile, how it is designed. No one seeking an authentic look need consider fake nail holes, badly printed vinyl, or a polyurethane finish. Rather, look for thickness of material—whether wood, stone, vinyl, or ceramic—and the fineness of the pattern or design. If it is impossible to find traditional and substantial designs then refer to the following suppliers who specialize in providing quality materials.

American Olean

American Olean's extensive collection of ceramic tile spans all shapes, sizes, colors, and designs. Limitless effects are possible with such a huge variety of basic components.

For 2"-square tile that is versatile and attractive, one of the company's recommended options is the Satinglo line, glazed for walls and unglazed for flooring. Scratch resistant and stainproof, this tile is available in thirty-two colors, including neutrals, pale pastels, mid-tone greens, and blues. This tile may be used outdoors as well as indoors.

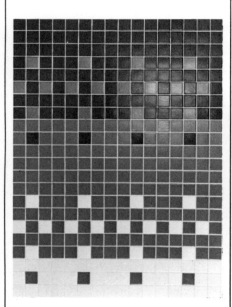

American Olean's Distinctions glazed ceramic floor tile is durable and attractive but, most important, inexpensive. Offered in 8" or 12" squares, this tile provides excellent traction and is offered in fresh greens and blues, as well as

rose, taupe, and other shades. Floor patterns combining light and dark shades of the same color are recommended.

For a more rugged look there is the Quarry Mesa Grande tile. In 8" squares, stain protection is combined with durability. This textured-surface tile comes in four colors—sunrise, gray flash, ember flash, and sand flash.

A completely different look and feel is achieved with American Olean's Border and Pattern tiles. Providing a more varied and colorful appearance, the company has patterns for any setting. Most

of these patterns use combinations of a choice of three colors, and they come in 12" by 24" sheets. Custom designs can also be ordered.

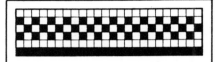

SB-1104

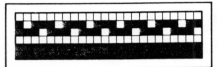

SB-1105

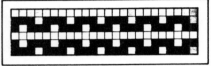

SB-1106

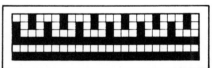

SB-1107

SB-1111

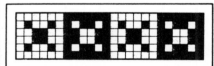

SB-1112

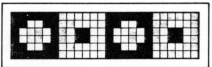

SB-1113

SB-1114

Literature available.

American Olean Tile Co.
1000 Cannon Ave., Box 271
Lansdale, PA 19446
(215) 855-1111

Carlisle

Many old houses still have original pine flooring and paneling so attractive to old-house enthusiasts. To achieve that look in any house, Carlisle Restoration Lumber offers timber newly milled in the antique style. In various widths, 8' to 16' lengths, and the original ⅞" to 1" thicknesses—rather than the ¾" of today's flooring and paneling—Carlisle mills wide pine, ship-lapped pine, wide oak, and Southern yellow pine boards. The company will ship anywhere in the country, and it also offers a design and consultation service on the East Coast from Maine to Maryland.

Brochure available.

Carlisle Restoration Lumber
Rte. 123
Stoddard, NH 03464
(603) 446-3937

Craftsman Lumber

In colonial America the rule among builders was to use the widest possible timbers for flooring and paneling. Sometimes these boards measured up to 40" wide, but for the most part the largest straight tree trunks (over 24" wide) were reserved for the ships of the king's navy. Craftsman Lumber offers kiln-dried boards for flooring or paneling from 12" to 32" wide in Eastern white pine, clear pine, and clear red oak (4" to 16" wide) for the highest-quality restoration work. Lengths vary from 8' to 16'. Allow for 20 to 30 percent waste when ordering.

Victorian wainscoting is available milled from clear pine and clear oak, ⅝" thick and 3¼" wide.

Craftsman Lumber also does custom milling for molding of any size or shape. Woods available include poplar, oak, pine, walnut, cherry, maple, and a variety of other hardwoods.

Catalogue, $1.

Craftsman Lumber Co.
PO Box 222
Groton, MA 01450
(508) 448-6336

Goodwin Lumber

Goodwin Lumber is primarily a dealer in flooring and paneling, but the company will also mill beams, posts, and boards in any dimensions up to 22' in length. Southern long-leaf yellow heart pine, felled over one hundred years ago, is the main timber, but much work is done in red cypress as well. All the logs are sawed, kiln dried, planed, and finished at the company's mills, although cypress can be left out to weather to a natural silver-gray color. Goodwin Lumber also offers exotic rosemary (or curly) heart pine for trim, as well as old-growth heart cypress and pecky heart cypress.

Goodwin Lumber Co.
Rte. 2, Box 119-AA
Micanopy, FL 32667
(904) 373-WOOD

Kentucky Wood Floors

Carrying on a rich European legacy of excellent flooring design and craftsmanship, woodworkers in early America took advantage of the country's wealth of timber and created some of the finest wood flooring ever seen. Kentucky Wood Floors continues this tradition, fashioning flooring for such prestigious settings as the Oval Office and East Room of the White House, the Metropolitan Museum of Art, and the Smithsonian Institution.

Although the company has a collection of standard patterns, custom designs are welcome, and an in-house consultation service is offered. Regardless of the pattern chosen, the customer must decide on the woods to be used, among them oak, ash, cherry, African padauk, and Brazilian purpleheart.

The company's Brittany pattern, a cross within a diamond within a square, is especially appealing in quartered oak. Prefinished or unfinished, each panel is 28" square and ¾" thick.

Kentucky Wood Floors offers unfinished plank and strip flooring, too. Solid plank is available in any

species, in random or specified widths. Each piece is tongued and grooved for nail-down installation, and edges may be beveled or squared. Plugs of matching wood, contrasting wood, or brass are available.

Unfinished parquet flooring is similar to the unfinished plank and strip flooring. It is an affordable way to install parquet flooring in large areas. A number of patterns are available. Once pieces have been glued down, on-site sanding and finishing complete the job.

For all the company's flooring, optional surface and finish treatments include beveled edges, a wire-brush texture, hand-distressed texture, or prefinishing with sealer. Matching architectural millwork is also offered, such as quarter-round, baseboard, nosing, and reducer strips.

Literature, $2.

Kentucky Wood Floors
4200 Reservoir Ave.
Louisville, KY 40213
(502) 451-6024

Maurer & Shepherd

Working entirely by hand and on a custom-order basis, Maurer & Shepherd's talented workmen restore and reproduce 17th- and 18th-century joinery. Pegged mortise and tenon construction is used on all projects. Along with wide Eastern white pine hand-planed flooring, Maurer & Shepherd will produce almost any item from any type of wood. The company's work includes moldings, architectural ornamentation, doors and entryways, mantels, windows, shutters, and more. As the company's order form invites: "Challenge us."

Brochure available.

Maurer & Shepherd Joyners, Inc.
122 Naubuc Ave.
Glastonbury, CT 06033
(203) 633-2383

Mid-State Tile

Ceramic tiles of all shapes, sizes, colors, and decorative designs have been Mid-State's forte for more than thirty years.

With an embossed grid pattern creating the illusion of many facets on the bright or matte glazed surface of the tile, the company's Graphics collection offers

almost unlimited decorative possibilities. Available in ten colors, the tiles are 4⅜" square. Many trim shapes are available as well.

Mid-State's La Jolla tile is offered in 12" squares and comes in three colors. The two-tone frame edges allow a varied play of patterns.

Literature available.

Mid-State Tile Co.
PO Box 1777
Lexington, NC 27292
(704) 249-3931

Moravian Pottery

When Henry Chapman Mercer founded the Moravian Pottery and Tile Works in 1900, he did so to preserve a Pennsylvania-German art form threatened with extinction. Revitalization of Mercer's original facilities allows Moravian's craftsmen to produce tiles today much as they were produced by Mercer himself. All the tiles are hand crafted and finished with glazes mixed at the tile works according to formulas that duplicate the original colors. Each is then fired in one of the original brick coal-firing kilns. As a result of the primitive methods of production, no two Moravian tiles are exactly alike.

Quarry tile patterns range from 2" to 4" square. An assortment of other comparably scaled shapes is also made, and a variety of borders and decorative tiles enable customers to create repeating patterns or scenes. Needless to say, the designs on all the tiles and borders are unique to Moravian, as is the overall look of the finished product.

Literature, $4.

Moravian Pottery and Tile Works
Swamp Rd.
Doylestown, PA 18901
(215) 345-6722

Rye Tiles

Rye Tiles offers a massive selection of decorative designs from florals to both simple and complex geometric patterns. Each 6"-square tile is hand-painted. Rye Tiles offers a choice of 110 colors, and thereby almost infinite combinations can be put together. The tiles themselves are either of Rye or Bristol white-glazed ceramic clay, and they are decorated using 18th-century techniques.

Although the company's floral wall and floor tiles are beautiful, as is the wide range of border

styles, the collection of geometric designs is in a class by itself. Two extremely ornate patterns are the Victoriana, with its incredible detail completely filling the tile face; and the Rococo, also intricately detailed but with a circular open space at the center of each of the tile quarters.

More simply patterned is the Blazer design, with its twice-outlined quarters, once with a heavy line and again with a light one. The handkerchief pattern is also more open, with three bars of equal width surrounding each quarter, overlapping at the corners.

Since all the tiles are hand produced, colors are subject to variation from batch to batch. Be sure to order enough pieces to complete a single project, for a second order might not match exactly.

Literature available.

Rye Tiles
The Old Brewery
Wishward, Rye TN31 7DH
England
(0797) 223038

Tiresias

Heart pine once flourished in the U. S. over a 100,000-square-mile area on the eastern and southeastern coast from Virginia to Texas. Milled from trees standing up to 170' tall, and ranging in age from 150 to 400 years, heart pine was prized by Americans and Europeans for building everything from wharves to houses, ships, and railroad cars. The keel of the warship USS *Constitution* was made of a single heart pine timber.

Today, however, heart pine is a rarity. Most of the existing stands are protected by the government and cannot be lumbered. A preexisting supply is available from Tiresias through the process of recycling. Select stock is milled by Tiresias for flooring, paneling, and other custom projects. The quality and good looks that have made heart pine so valuable over time have made Tiresias' product an attractive option for builders and preservationists alike.

Tiresias mills flooring and paneling in three basic patterns—tongue and groove, V-joint, and shiplap. Board lengths run from 8' to 16', and the color ranges from light honey to dark reddish-brown. Boards are planed on both sides, and the wood grain is dense.

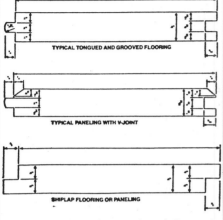

TYPICAL TONGUED AND GROOVED FLOORING

TYPICAL PANELING WITH V-JOINT

SHIPLAP FLOORING OR PANELING

Brochure, wood samples, $10.

Tiresias, Inc.
PO Box 1864
Orangeburg, SC 29116
(803) 534-8478

Vermont Cobble Slate

Having spent hundreds of millions of years forming and decades weathering to achieve their unique texture, color, and markings, Vermont Cobble Slate's hand-cut slate tiles serve a variety of purposes. They provide flooring, hearth and mantel pieces, and tiling for baths, kitchens, and other wall and counter surfaces. Tiles are easy to install and have the additional benefit of being a natural insulator. They come in black, green, purple, gray, and a rare red. If darker colors are needed, simply apply a sealer.

Literature available.

Vermont Cobble Slate
Smid, Inc.
Sudbury, VT 05733
(802) 247-8809

Floor Coverings

Floorcloths and cotton rugs of a simple linear design are frequently found in country stores and boutiques. Popularized in home decorating magazines, both types of rugs are currently produced by many craftsmen. As with most other enterprises, only some of the products are adequately produced. It is always a struggle for a true artisan to maintain quality standards once demand grows for his work. The firms and individuals described in the following listings have proven their worth for some time and—along with such major manufacturers of rugs and carpets as Schumacher, Stark, and Patterson, Flynn & Martin—offer handsome choices for the thoughtful old house owner.

AMS Imports

The patterns for AMS Imports' new Röllakan rugs were created by Swedish artists for an effect at once old and new. Each is hand-woven in India to the artist's specifications, crafted of 100-percent mothproofed wool yarns, and finished with hand-knotted fringes. Some rugs have the designer's initials woven into the pattern itself. Available in a number of different designs, these reversible floor coverings include such colors as bold blues, browns and greens, natural tones, and pastels. Since some of the yarns are hand spun and all the rugs are handwoven, colors may vary from carpet to carpet.

The rugs come in three sizes: 4'7" by 6'7", 5'7" by 7'11", and 6'7" by 9'10".

Literature available.

AMS Imports
23 Ash Ln.
Amherst, MA 01002
(800) 648-1816
(413) 253-2644 (MA)

J. R. Burrows

Imported directly from England, Burrows' carpets display handsome and documented designs of special interest to old house enthusiasts and curators of historic house museums. These Wilton and Brussels weaves incorporate designs from the Regency and Federal periods through the Victorian and Edwardian eras.

The same techniques used to weave these designs in the 1800s are still used by Burrows' suppliers today. To capture intricate details, a narrow-gauge loom is used to produce a pile count of almost 100 tufts per square inch. (The industry standard today is 64 per square inch.) The tightness of the weave increases the resiliency of the carpeting and it also permits finer line weights in patterns. Carpets woven in this manner are available only in 27"-wide strips. This is fine if the strips are intended to be used a runners; if not, they must be sewn together by a qualified installer on-site.

Carpet borders are produced in the same manner, but are 18" wide. Because of size restrictions, borders traditionally have been woven separately from what is termed the "body" of the carpet. This need not be a drawback, however, since Burrows produces a matching border where necessary.

An 80 percent worsted wool-20 percent nylon blend is the only one used. Each carpet is woven to order in its original color scheme; custom colorations, however, are frequently substituted. The designs illustrated are excellent examples of the breadth and depth that Burrows has to offer.

Pattern 12/6840 dates to 1878. It is an Anglo-Japanese design with a matching border that completes the overall floral motif.

William Morris created the next design, Lily and Tulip, 04/7899, c. 1875. Its lush and imaginative interplay of pattern is in keeping with the output of Morris and the other designers in his company.

Burrows' pattern 26/6971 is made as a carpet body and a border. Dated to 1875, the design lends itself to strong coloration, an emphasis that Victorian decorators were not reluctant to indulge.

More refined and reserved, carpet body and border 17/6990 is suitable for many mid-19th century interiors. The repeating geometric pattern could also be used in of-

fices as well as homes. The design is said to date from 1870.

Peacock is the obvious name for pattern 14/693. It is made as both a body and border carpet. The design is reminiscent of the work of Louis Comfort Tiffany and Associated Artists, the famous decorating firm active in the 1870s and 80s.

The clear, crisp lines of pattern 15/6941 attest to the precision and skill of early 19th-century weavers. This neoclassical design dates from 1815 and is most appropriate for Federal and early Greek Revival interiors.

Pattern 14/6987 swirls with rococo embellishments. The bright bouquets of roses are imaginatively highlighted. It dates to 1822 in England and could have been used in the United States well into the mid-century.

Burrows will be glad to advise on the availability of these patterns and others. The firm will also supply information on installation and qualified installers.

Literature available.

J. R. Burrows Co.
PO Box 148,Cathedral Station
Boston, MA 02118
(617) 451-1982

Family Heir-Loom Weavers

In the early part of the 19th century, Joseph-Marie Jacquard developed an apparatus that, when mounted on a hand loom, enabled weavers to create pictorial designs more easily and rapidly. The country-style carpets produced, however, fell out of fashion at about the end of the century and have only recently been reintroduced by such artisans as Family Heir-Loom Weavers.

Using pre-Civil War patterns, the company began to weave ingrain carpet, a flat-woven floor covering presenting patterns and colors that are reversible. Practical, colorful, and durable, this carpeting is initially woven in 36″ strips that are later cut and sewn together by hand. Intricately detailed designs, like those in the full carpet shown, are the result of this process.

Family Heir-Loom Weavers was recently commissioned by the National Park Service to produce three ingrain carpets for the Abraham Lincoln Homestead in Springfield, Illinois. The detail of the carpet with the geometric and floral design is from a floor-covering pattern used in two rooms of this house.

The company also makes runners for stairs and hallways in the same patterns and by the same methods as the carpeting.

Literature, $1.

Family Heir-Loom Weavers
RD 3, Box 59E
Red Lion, PA 17356
(717) 246-2431

Floorcloths Incorporated

In 18th-century America rugs and carpets were far too expensive even for many of the rich and powerful. An inventory dating to 1729 for the estate of William Burnet, royal governor of New York and New Jersey, lists two

"chequered canvases to lay under the table." Such floorcloths continued in use until the late 19th century.

Each design at Floorcloths Incorporated is based on documented 18th- and 19th-century patterns found in museum archives or period paintings. In addition, the firm has a custom-design service for anyone needing such assistance.

Lozenge, like many of the decorative patterns of the 18th century, attempts to imitate a costlier material, in this case expensive floors of marble. It is available with 6", 8", or 10" lozenges and custom colors.

Ephraim Starr is taken from an 1802 painting by an artist of the same name. The original colors are brown and cream, but Floorcloths will re-create this design in any combination of two or three others.

Offered in any four-color combination, Brewster is taken from a painting, c. 1800, by an artist named John Brewster.

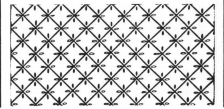

Alex Weatherstone, century floorcloth p was so fond of the (pattern that he usec trade card. Floorclo porated offers this p in any combination c

Literature available.

Floorcloths Incorporated
920 Edgewater Rd.
Severna Park, MD 21146
(301) 544-0858

Folkheart

Surrounded by Vermont's beautiful Green Mountains, Folkheart's artisans hand weave rag rugs in the Amish style, using 100 percent preshrunk cotton or 100 percent wool. Plaid or hand stenciled, these floorcoveings are durable and long lasting.

The Amish plaid rug is custom colored, and is available in 2' or 3' widths and in any length. Folkheart's specialty is larger rugs,

155

...m colored and sized, and the company's artists will execute custom-order stencil designs. All the firm's rugs are machine washable.

Brochure, $1.

Folkheart Rag Rugs
18 Main St.
Bristol, VT 05443
(802) 453-4101

Good and Company

Nancy and Philip Cayford cut their own heavy cotton duck canvas, treat it, and hand-stencil each floorcloth design individually. Standard colors include soldier blue, brick red, light green, and gray. Other colors and a variety of sizes can be custom ordered. The floorcloths require little care and serve well as small area rugs, runners, and room-size rugs.

The company's Crewel design is appropriate for small area rugs or runners. Larger rugs can be stenciled with a central design surrounded by the Crewel border, if desired.

The Diamonds pattern is excellent for a wall-to-wall floorcloth, as in a bedroom. Imitating more expensive marble flooring was the original purpose of this design.

The Cheshire and Philip designs are popular for large area rugs and runners. The finely detailed floral designs are colored to match

the border strips unless otherwise requested. With custom designs a specialty, Good and Company has worked for a variety of museums and historical societies, including Old Sturbridge Village and the Abraham Lincoln Homestead in Springfield, Illinois.

Catalogue, $2.

Good and Co., Floorclothmakers
Salzburg Sq., Rt. 101
Amherst, NH 03031
(603) 672-0490

Pat Hornafius

Pennsylvania-German women began making colorful hooked rugs in the 1800s, but the craft flourished only when burlap bags replaced hand-woven tow bags on the farm after the Civil War. Left-over burlap bags provided the base for each rug. Designs were hand-drawn on the burlap and then scrap materials were hooked through this base.

Pat Hornafius has been hand hooking rugs in this old manner since 1976. Hand-dyed ¼" wool

strips are worked into a base of Scottish burlap and finished with a binding of rug yarn and dyed-to-match rug tape. These rugs are custom colored and sized.

Having sold rugs to shops and museums, including the Museum of American Folk Art, and to private customers, Hornafius has several designs in production at any one time. These designs are in constant flux, however, so no catalogue is available. She will also produce custom designs.

Literature, SASE.

Pat Hornafius
Lancaster County Folk Art
113 Meadowbrook Ln.
Elizabethtown, PA 17022
(717) 367-7706

Import Specialists

Import Specialists offers goods ranging from rugs to placemats, pillows, and baskets. One of its most visually appealing lines of floor coverings is based on designs and patterns drawn from the Museum of American Folk Art's collection and archives. All these rugs, and the matching pillows, are handwoven of 100 percent cotton, hand stenciled, and hand printed.

The Lincoln Logs rug and pillow feature a colorful, plainly

geometrical pattern highlighting a soft background color and border stripe. Rug sizes are 2' by 3', 4' by 6', and 6' by 9'.

The Texas Star rug and pillow pattern is equally geometric and colorful, but the background colors are bolder and usually somewhat darker. Contrast is the rule with this pattern. This style of rug comes in the same sizes as the others in the Museum of American Folk Art collection.

Other rugs in Import Specialists' inventory include soft dhurries, denim rag rugs, twill rag rugs, rope rugs, and other brightly colored rag rugs in various patterns and color combinations. Contact Import Specialists' main office for the nearest retail outlet.

Literature available.

Import Specialists, Inc.
82 Wall St.
New York, NY 10005-3688
(800) 334-4044
(212) 709-9633 (NY)

K & D Supply

Braided rugs by Capel, and available through K & D, are created to look exactly like those used by America's early settlers. Frontier cabins were hurriedly built, and the floors became seamed and cracked. The settlers needed coverings as protection from cold and uncomfortable floors. Braided rugs provided this protection; they also livened up an otherwise drab atmosphere.

These early rugs were woven from strips of various leftover fabrics or worn-out clothing. Capel spins its own yarns, then dyes, weaves, braids, and sews each rug at its North Carolina factory, as it has

since 1917. The final rug is hand-crafted by one person, whose signature appears on the rug. All rugs are reversible.

Ovals are among the most popular of several shapes offered, with solid bands of color or multicolored braids created in tones ranging from subtle to bold. Rectangular flat-woven rugs done in a basket-weave pattern of variegated colors are also appropriate for country and colonial decors.

Literature, $2, refunded with first order.

K & D Supply Company
2717 High Ridge Rd.
Charlotte, NC 28226
(704) 846-4345

Olde Virginea Floorcloth

Olde Virginea Floorcloth makes floor coverings as they were made some two hundred years ago. Each is handcrafted of heavyweight canvas, hand stenciled with oil paints in authentic colonial colors, signed, dated, and then finished with a low-luster varnish for a durable and easily cleaned surface.

Pictured is the company's Dutch Colonial design, common in homes of the period. Stenciled

with a 1' by 1' alternating black and white square pattern, this style is available with any two colors, either plain or marbled, as shown. The overall size is 6' wide and 10' long, but all other sizes are also offered. Olde Virginea Floorcloth has a wide selection of designs and colors, including old pewter, brick, bronze, ming, redcoat red, and many more. Custom designs and color matching are possible; fringing is optional.

All floorcloths over 10' wide are seamed. One variation of the standard cloth is the company's hearthcloth. This semicircular covering, hand stenciled, is an attractive way to protect any carpet or wooden flooring around a fireplace.

Literature available.

Olde Virginea Floorcloth & Trading Co.
PO Box 3305
Portsmouth, VA 23701
(804) 397-0948

Patterson, Flynn & Martin

Patterson, Flynn & Martin's craftsmen are experts at restoring and reproducing period carpets. The firm has had experience working for museums as well as private customers, and an excellently crafted final product is a certainty.

Reproduced from a Scotch ingrain carpet in the Victoria and Albert Museum in London, a mid-19th-century pattern, number 1815/

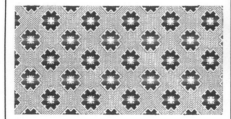

7384, is made of geometric shapes forming stripes on a filigree background. Woven in a 27" Wilton weave, this floor covering may only be orderd with custom coloring.

Pattern 1817/7386 is reproduced from a carpet originally found in the home of Sir Walter Scott, Ab-

botsford House. This English Brussels carpet design dates to the early 19th century. It is well covered with large sprays of leaf and flower, planted to show sixteen different colors. Offered only in custom colors, this carpet is a 27" Wilton weave.

Pattern 1832/7393 is also an English Brussels carpet. From Haddow House, in Aberdeenshire, England, this mid-19th-century design features quatrefoil shapes linked diagonally by a trellis. Custom colored, this floor covering is a 27" Wilton weave.

Literature available.

Patterson, Flynn & Martin
950 Third Ave.
New York, NY 10022
(212) 751-6414

Pemaquid

For decorating or re-creating a colonial or country home, floorcloths are very useful. As attractive as any flooring or floor cover-

ing produced today, these cloths are durable and long lasting. Most are patterned after period originals, but for more contemporary styles, too, Pemaquid should be considered. Each cloth is made of heavy cotton canvas, treated, painted, stenciled, and varnished by hand. Rubber backing can be applied for extra cushioning and to prevent skidding. All the company's work is hemmed to lay flat, and any length is possible with a maximum width of 9'. Custom designs and color schemes are welcome.

Brochure, $2.

Pemaquid Floorcloths
Round Pond, ME 04564
(207) 529-5633

Schumacher

Art Moderne architecture and interior design alike are well illustrated in the styling and design of New York's Radio City Music Hall, opened in 1932. From Radio City's and Schumacher's own archives, the company has developed a collection of fabrics and floor coverings imitating and reproducing many of these styles.

Musical Instruments is the original floor covering design used in the Music Hall's grand foyer. A Wilton weave of 100-percent wool, this rug is available in 6' by 9', 9' by 12', or 12' by 15' sizes. Designed in 1931, the pattern has been recolored for contemporary applications in shades including peach, rose, mauve, and more.

From another Schumacher collection, the Hyde Park series, comes the Calla Lillies design. Imported from Madeira, each carpet is made of 100-percent wool and is worked in handmade needlepoint (petit point). A wide range of standard colors is available. Special colors may be ordered as well.

The Brazilian design, Versailles, is from the company's Casa Bella collection. This handmade needle-point carpet is 100-percent wool and comes sized to order. Colors include multicolored pastels with a soft-blue border and a cream field.

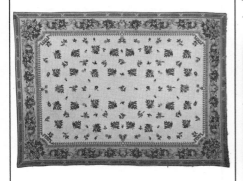

Literature available.

F. Schumacher & Co.
79 Madison Ave.
New York, NY 10016
(212) 213-7900

Stark

Among Stark Carpet's large selection of variously sized, colored, and styled carpets and floor coverings, the 100-percent wool Wilton carpets stand out because of their stately, elegant design and high-quality craftsmanship.

The company's Lozenge Directoire, with its floral diamond pattern silhouetted by delicate beading, is made just as are all the carpets in this collection—in Brussels loop or of cut-pile construction with matching borders. All are also offered in custom colors and sizes.

The simple detail in the repetitive floral pattern, Petit Carnation, brightens any room without being overbearing.

One of the more ornate patterns is the French Design. Rich in appearance and texture, this carpet might have come straight from a Paris salon.

The Clichy carpet, made in France, combines a delicate vine pattern with antique colorations of salmon and pale blue. It is available in stock widths of 3'3".

Stark's Reubens carpet features an overall pattern of linking bows in a diamond design overlaying a background of smaller diamonds. Stocked in light green on white, it, too, comes custom colored and sized.

The floral pattern, Large Medallion, is as intricate as the French designs, but it is more organized, with a logical, geometric unifying scheme. Recommended colors are dark and medium blue with three different shades of gray.

Literature available.

Stark Carpet Corp.
979 Third Ave.
New York, NY 10022
(212) 752-9000

Flooring and fireplace detail, Pusey House, Chatham vicinity, Pennsylvania. Photograph by Ned Goode, Historic American Buildings Survey.

Other Suppliers of Floors and Floor Coverings

Consult List of Suppliers for addresses.

Flooring

Aged Woods
Architectural Preservation Trust
Architectural Reclamation
Laura Ashley
Canal Co.
Central Kentucky Millwork
Conklin's Authentic Antique
    Barnwood
Victor Cushwa & Sons
Diamond K.
Glen-Gery
Whit Hanks
Heart-Wood
Joinery Co.
Jerard Paul Jordan
Mr. Slate
E. T. Moore, Jr., Co.
Mountain Lumber
New York Marble Works
North Fields Restorations
Ramase
Rising & Nelson
Robinson Lumber
Saxe Patterson
Tullibardine Enterprises
Vintage Lumber
The Woods Co.

Floor Coverings

Canal Co.
Good & Co.
Linoleum City
Partridge Replicatons
Scalamandré
Schumacher
Victorian Collectibles

6.

Paints and Papers

Painting a building, inside and out, remains the most common way to transform its appearance. Certain combinations are thought to be traditional for a period building. Mustard and barn red, for example, have become so frequently used for 18th-century-style houses that we have accepted these colors as traditional whether they are or not. Recent evidence suggests that the colonists usually painted only barns red and used many colors other than mustard for their houses. Regardless of what the textbooks tell us, however, paint is a sensible and economical way of cleaning up the past.

While a new coat of paint will renew a building in the eye of the beholder, it may, in fact, be injurious. The build-up of layers prevents the original surface—whether of masonry or of wood—from releasing moisture that naturally accumulates in the building material. Proper preparation of a surface that is to be painted, especially the exterior, will cut down on this problem. Sometimes it is helpful to use an oil-base paint rather than a latex formula. Oil nourishes wood or clay products and bonds more effectively. However, oil should not be used over old layers of latex paint.

Papers are enjoying a new popularity, as they should. They can dramatically change an interior space. There are all types of papers—for ceilings, cornices, that lower area of the wall below a chair rail known as the dado, and, of course, for whole wall panels. Paper borders can also be used around doors and windows and along a chair rail. There was a time when wallpaper was used with great abandon. Under the layers of paint inside your old house may be one or two of paper as well: commercially printed papers were cheaper than paints until ready-mix formulas were introduced in the late 1800s.

Room size and amount of natural light will determine to a large extent how wallpaper is used. There is no reason why two or even three designs—complementary, of course—can't be employed in the same space. You will be better off staying with papers that are not pre-pasted or coated with a synthetic finish. There are papers of this type that are perfectly suitable for period rooms—and a few are included in the following pages—but, in general, the appearance of uncoated papers is superior and their installation not that much more difficult. In fact, some people find them easier than applying the pre-pasted kind. Trying to reposition a paper that already has an adhesive coating can be a frustrating experience, especially when the material stretches.

A dining room finished with coordinated papers in the Neo-Grec style, c. 1887, by Bradbury & Bradbury Wallpapers, Benicia, California. Photograph by Ron Mitchell.

Paints

Use of carefully coordinated shades for Victorian and colonial façades—rather than deadly white—has increased each year, and more major paint firms are addressing themselves to the needs of the majority of American buildings that date from these two historical periods. There are smaller paint companies that have put together carefully conceived period paint collections. These are also listed following. The reader, however, is further advised to consider the use of custom-mixed colors. There is almost always at least one paint merchant in any area who enjoys the challenge of matching one shade to another. It costs more, of course, to have this done, but if you plan to live with the color for at least a few years, it should be done right.

Allentown Paint

America's oldest ready-mix paint company, Allentown Paint was established in 1855. The company's Pennsylvania-Dutch paints are still produced with the same attention and in the same colors as the originals were in 1867. More than fifty bright, cheerful colors are available, including myrtle green, sky blue, copper brown, and old ivory. This line includes an exterior paint with a linseed-oil base, remarkable for its permeability, excellent spreading rate, color retention, and mildew resistance.

For trim, shutters, porches, arbors, lawn furniture, and masonite siding, Allentown manufactures an alkyd paint with a linseed-oil base for easy spreading. Eight colors include maroon, green, and bright red. Other Pennsylvania-Dutch paint and finishing products include an indoor-outdoor enamel, roofing paints, and latex interior and exterior paints. For more information, contact the company's home office.

Allentown Paint Manufacturing Co., Inc.
Box 597, E. Allen & N. Graham Sts.
Allentown, PA 18105
(215) 433-4273

Antique Color Supply

Milk paints—no, they aren't for making chocolate or strawberry drinks—are nontoxic, free of harmful ingredients. They also provide the only authentic medium with which to paint reproduction woodwork from trim to house and barn façades.

Milk paint's rough texture, flat finish, and superb hardening qualities give any surface an antique look that will survive decades of use. The paint comes in a powdered form ready to be mixed with water. Powder sizes include 1-, 6-, 12-, and 48-ounce packages, and colors include barn red, soldier blue, mustard, bayberry, Lexington green, pumpkin, oyster white, and pitch black. Mixing various colors creates possibilities limited only by your imagination. The painted surface requires no finish, but stain or oil may be applied if desired. Special treatments include drying with a heating gun or hair dryer for an antique, cracked look or sanding the painted surface for a distressed look.

Brochure available, SASE.

Antique Color Supply, Inc.
PO Box 1668
Lunenburg, MA 01462
(508) 582-6426

Bradbury & Bradbury

Bradbury's specialty is Victorian wallpapers and enrichments. The company has recently expanded its offerings to include a selection of related products that are unusual or hard to find. The company's Chromatone gold paint, EMP-005, has been admired by all who have used it for its lasting brilliance and easy application. A substitute for gold leaf, it is perfect for picture molding, stenciling, and hand-painted embellishments. It also coordinates with the gold used on Bradbury's papers.

Catalogue, $8.

Bradbury & Bradbury Wallpapers
PO Box 155-D
Benicia, CA 94510
(707) 746-1900

Cabot Stains

Solid-color stains by Cabot provide an oil-base finish with tremendous hiding power and deep color penetration. They are perfect for a variety of applications. Water repellent, weather resistant, crack and peel proof, these stains can be used on shingles, shakes, siding, and masonry surfaces of all kinds. They are easily applied over previously stained, sealed, or painted surfaces. Colors include spruce blue, Cordovan brown, dune gray, barn red, and more. You can even use these stains on pre-primed metal.

Cabot stains are available throughout North America. Contact Cabot's home offices to locate a supplier nearby.

Samuel Cabot, Inc.
1 Union St.
Boston, MA 02108
(617) 723-7740

California Paints

Beautiful historic Newport, Rhode Isand, is best known for the Gilded Age summer homes of the Vanderbilts and their peers. There is more to Newport than The Breakers, however. The town has been popular with Americans since the early 17th century. Like all seaports in the colonial days, Newport was known for its brightly colored buildings. These same bright colonial colors are reproduced by California Paints in the company's Historic Newport Colors collection of exterior house paints in three finishes: 100 percent acrylic latex flat, 100 percent acrylic latex satin gloss, and alkyd-oil-base gloss.

More than thirty standard colors are available. These colors range from Vernon yellow to Brenton blue, Dudley gray, walnut room brown, and Hunter House dark green.

Literature available. California Paints are distributed only in the Northeast. Call for further information and local retailers.

California Paints
California Products Corporation
169 Waverly St.
Cambridge, MA 02139
(800) 225-1141
(800) 842-1161 (MA)

Chromatic

Professional decorative painters use Chromatic colors worldwide, but few people know that these superb paints are available for any do-it-yourself decorator. Chromatic's Japan Colors exhibit excellent adhesion to wood, metal, and paper.

These paints are appropriate for furniture, picture frames, floors, walls, metalwork, signs, and much more. They are, in addition, ideal for a variety of such decorative painting techniques as graining, tole work, stenciling, antiquing, glazing, staining, lettering, and striping. Use them to tint flat paints, as well, where control of luster is desired.

The paints are offered in thirty-one colors ranging from Prussian blue to Venetian red, raw umber, American vermillion, and more.

Chromatic paints are available nationally. Write or call for further information.

Chromatic Paint Corp.
PO Box 690
Stony Point, NY 10980
(800) 431-7001
(914) 947-3210 (NY)

Cook & Dunn

Cook & Dunn's Historic Colors collection is composed of shades that can be found in actual restorations dating back to the 18th century. The selection includes the subtler hues of the colonial era as well as brighter and distinctive Victorian colors. Among the shades are Eastlake yellow, patriot blue, commons green, Cape russet, Darby plum, and a host of others.

All colors come in a variety of interior and exterior finishes designed to decorate and protect. Interior finishes include flat, semigloss, and gloss enamel in either a latex or an alkyd (oil) base. Exterior finishes include house paint, trim, and floor enamels with either latex or alkyd bases.

If you have trouble locating a suplier near you, or if you have any other questions, call Cook & Dunn for further information.

Cook & Dunn Paint Corp.
Box 117
Newark, NJ 07101
(201) 589-5580

Finnaren & Haley

Finnaren & Haley offers two historical paint collections to meet the old house lover's needs and tastes. In the Authentic Colors of Historical Philadelphia collection, the company joined forces with the National Park Service to research and scientifically analyze the original colors of several landmark buildings in the city. This work resulted in the selection of thirty-one colors, ten of which are authenticated; the rest, although unauthenticated, are generally believed to have been used.

Paints are offered in formulas for interiors and exteriors with alkyd oil or acrylic water bases. Colors include Germantown green, Belmont blue, Supreme Court yellow, Fort Mifflin brown, to name a few. One of the most interesting colors—Liberty gray—was used in the Assembly Room of Independence Hall at the time of the adoption of the Declaration of Independence.

Finnaren & Haley also makes a line of paints specifically for Victorian homes. It features sixteen period interior and exterior colors in addition to a number of trim and floor finishes. Included are such hues as mauve (Cape May), sea green (Van Ness), purple (Knob Hill), and muted orange (Cannery). These and other colors are representative of those used on the East and West Coasts.

For more information, or to locate a dealer nearby, contact the firm's home offices.

Finnaren & Haley, Inc.
2320 Haverford Rd.
Ardmore, PA 19003
(215) 649-5000

Glidden

Glidden's historic colors collection—The American Color Legacy—is particularly strong in the subdued, weathered tones common to early buildings of the West and Southwest. These are smooth pastels, pale golds, and neutral grays of the Spanish colonial, Pueblo, and Mission styles.

Glidden offers these exterior colors in a number of finishes: flat latex, satin latex-eggshell, gloss latex, high-gloss oil base, and a special flat latex developed specifically for stucco and other types of masonry.

These paints and finishes should be available locally, but suppliers can be easily located by contacting the company.

The Glidden Co.
925 Euclid Ave.
Cleveland, OH 44115
(216) 344-8000

Martin-Senour

The Colonial Williamsburg Foundation has authorized only one company—Martin-Senour—to reproduce the paint colors used in the historic Virginia city. These paints combine traditional beauty with modern science and are available in three types: interior flat latex, interior satin gloss latex enamel, and exterior satin gloss latex.

Interior colors range from Raleigh Tavern dark green to Palace Chambers light yellow, with more than eighty-three shades from which to choose. Market Square Tavern shell to Burdett's Ordinary black-green are just two of the variety of exterior colors available. These exterior paints are excellent for wood, metal, masonry, and siding. All the company's paints are blister, peel, fade, chip, and mildew resistant. Martin-Senour also simulates colonial whitewash in an alkyd flat paint. It is a superb addition to period interiors, blending perfectly with stone, brick, or wood.

Contact the company for a nearby dealer.

The Martin-Senour Co.
1370 Ontario Ave. NW
Cleveland, OH 44113
(216) 566-3140

Benjamin Moore

Whether a house is an 18th- or 19th-century original building or a colonial reproduction, Moore's Historical Color collection is useful. Paints for interiors and exteriors are offered in a variety of finishes and a complete range of colors. The latex and enamel exterior paints come in thirty-six standard period hues ranging from Greenfield pumpkin to Narragansett green and Van Buren brown.

Moore's interior latex and enamel paints are appropriate for plaster, wallboard, wood, metal, and, sometimes, masonry. They are available in forty-eight period colors, including Blair gold, Waterbury green, and Mayflower red. Additional colors may be selected from the more than one thousand choices in the Moor-O-Matic II Color System.

For further information or to locate a dealer near you, contact:

Benjamin Moore & Co.
51 Chestnut Ridge Rd.
Montvale, NJ 07645
(201) 573-9600

Muralo

Muralo's Restoration Colors collection offers the home preservationist and the professional restoration expert interior and exterior paints specifically designed for period homes. The offerings include the deep chocolate of Athenaeum brown, various natural-tone grays and tans, discreet greens, and subdued blues, in addition to traditional shades of white, black and colonial red.

These paints are distributed nationwide, but to locate a specific supplier contact Muralo's home office.

The Muralo Co., Inc.
148 E. 5th Ave.
Bayonne, NJ 07002
(201) 437-0770

The Old Fashioned Milk Paint Company

Imagine living in the 18th century and using curdled milk to paint your cottage. Old Fashioned Milk Paints are still made as they have always been—the natural way. The company uses no chemicals, preservatives, or petroleum-based products. Once dried the paint is inert and thus safe.

The paint comes in powdered form and is easily mixed and applied. Watch out, though, because once applied it will take an enthusiastic sanding to remove it. Colors include such favorites as barn red, mustard, bayberry, and soldier blue.

Catalogue, $1.

The Old Fashioned Milk Paint Co.
PO Box 222
Groton, MA 01450
(508) 448-6336

Olympic

Staining protects new woodwork from mildew, aging, rotting, and cracking, and it can also help give weather-damaged wood a healthier, more attractive look. Preparation of the wood surface is a key ingredient in either case, with sanding and brushing usually required before staining can begin.

Whether you want the texture and grain of the original wood to show through or want to deepen the color and still let the texture of the wood be seen, Olympic has the stain to suit your needs. Semitransparent oil stains add subtle coloring to complement the wood grain and texture, while the company's latex and oil solid stains camouflage discolored woods. The semitransparent and solid-color stains together offer more than sixty colors.

Olympic dealers can help with all stain and finishing needs, or one may contact the company directly.

Olympic Stain
2233 112th Ave. NE
Bellevue, WA 98004
(800) 426-6306

Ox-Line

Ox-Line has designed oil-base and latex paints in a huge range of colors for all kinds of old houses. There are even suggested appropriate color combinations for that often difficult task of choosing house colors. A Puritan Stone body with Kentucky green shutters, soft white trim, and black doors is a possibility for a Victorian house, for example.

For wood shakes, clapboards, shingles, and all masonry surfaces, Ox-Line's acrylic latex paint offers good protection and good looks. Sixteen colors are available with a flat finish and twelve with a mid-gloss finish.

Ox-Line's Heritage collection also features a line of alkyd linseed oil exterior paints in satin and gloss finishes. Eleven gloss-finish colors and nine satin-finish colors are offered. For a colonial house, a Miami gray body with deep charcoal shutters, white trim, and Colony red doors is suggested. These paints are found primarily in the Northeast. Write or call for information on local suppliers.

Ox-Line Paints
California Products Corp.
169 Waverly St.
Cambridge, MA 02139
(800) 225-1141
(800) 842-1161 (MA)

Pittsburgh Paints

Historic Colors paints and finishes by Pittsburgh are being used nationwide for restored houses. The company manufactures authentic colors in a variety of paint types for any use imaginable. For interiors there is Manor Hall latex eggshell flat enamel, Wallhide latex flat wall paint, and Satinhide alkyd or latex low-luster enamels. For exteriors choose among the Sun-Proof latex house, oil house and trim, acrylic semigloss house and trim, or Pitt-Cryl acrylic paints. Avalable for interior and exterior use are several enamels.

Colors include such historical hues as Dodge City tan, Kentucky bluegrass, and Newport brown. There are more than fifty to choose from.

Brochures include helpful color samples and suggested combinations. For the nearest supplier contact Pittsburgh Paints.

Pittsburgh Paints
One PPG Plaza
Pittsburgh, PA 15272
(412) 434-2400

Pratt & Lambert

Pratt & Lambert is the exclusive licensee of a collection of paints— Early American Colours—documented by the Edison Institute's Henry Ford Museum and Greenfield Village. The hues are drawn from historic building interiors and exteriors, furniture, fabrics, and other antique documents. The shades run from light tan Gallery flower to bright Cotswold rose to a very dark Webster green. There are thirty-six shades from which to choose, and all are available in oil or latex finishes for interiors and exteriors.

Pratt & Lambert also offers three hundred calibrated shades of solid rustic stains in latex or alkyd.

Pratt & Lambert's products are distributed nationally. Contact the company for further information or help in locating a local supplier.

Pratt & Lambert Paints
PO Box 22, Dept. GV
Buffalo, NY 14240
(716) 873-6000

QRB Industries

When it comes time to remove paint—a task eventually faced by every old house owner—the products of QRB may come in handy. The Hacks, owners of the firm, have been cabinetmakers for generations. They know the importance of properly removing old paint so that the material underneath is not damaged.

QRB paint remover is a non-caustic solution containing no acids. Created for use on furniture, the solution can also be used effectively on woodwork. A liquid remover is much easier to use on carvings and moldings than other types of solvents.

The product is designed to remove varnish, paint, baked-on enamel, lacquers, acrylics, most milk paints, and even that bane of modern times, polyurethane. The remover does not raise the grain of a wood; therefore, the cleaned surface usually will not require sanding.

QRB Industries also offers two types of translucent non-grain-raising stains.

For further information, contact the firm.

Literature available, SASE.

QRB Industries
3139 N. U.S. 31
Niles, MI 49120

Tsigonia

Tsigonia's alkyd high-gloss super-enamel paints are intended for interiors and exteriors alike. Ideal for wood, metal, or concrete, these industrial-strength paints not only last long, but are also perfectly safe to use.

Architectural high-gloss enamel colors include a lively vermillion, lush royal blue, and a more subdued sand drift tan. There are twelve standard colors all together.

The twelve urethane-fortified alkyd enamel colors include a soft colonial blue, stately walnut brown, and a lighter chestnut brown.

Industrial-strength paints and finishes without a hard industrial appearance are Tsigonia's specialty. For surfaces that are subject to harsh weathering or other abuse, use of an industrial paint may be the solution. Write or call for the name of a nearby supplier.

Tsigonia Paints & Varnishes
568 W. 184th St.
New York, NY 10033
(212) 568-4430

Decorative Painting

Painters who undertake special ornamental work, most of whom are also stencil artists, are becoming easier to find. Their talents are especially called for in the restoration of highly decorative Victorian-style buildings that employ a wide variety of ornamental devices and colorful effects. We are learning also that the colonial period of our history was not quite as somber and monochromatic as had once been thought. Careful research has uncovered evidence that various types of finishes were used on woodwork and walls, and that many of them were false or imitation treatments meant to suggest marble, a fine hardwood, or even plaster.

If you are considering stencil decoration, study the various alternatives carefully. Stenciling has become all the rage and, unfortunately, artists of little or no ability are on the loose. Stenciling, like any other artistic technique, should be executed only by those who have mastered its method. Its use should also be limited. Once begun, the temptation to apply designs nearly everywhere is hard to resist.

Included in this category for the first time are suppliers of quality stenciling materials and teachers of ornamental painting. These are expecially useful sources for the do-it-yourself practitioner.

Architectural Color

Jill Pilaroscia's firm, Architectural Color, offers a unique consulting service for private homeowners and commercial clients. What makes her services like no one else's is her guiding philosophy that color itself should be seen as an actual architectural element and not simply as one of several qualities that any one architectural element possesses.

After considering photos and other available documents, as well as the client's own suggestions, Pilaroscia and her associates create two different color schemes from which a customer can choose. The selections are a reflection of the total architectural character of a building and its site.

An excellent example of a completed interior scheme is the main hall of the San Mateo County Courthouse. Examples of exterior schemes are shown in a San Francisco private residence and the Phillips Building in downtown San Francisco.

Pilaroscia supplies a color board, a list of detailed specifications,

and a diagram with each proposed scheme. The firm also offers a color rendering service for those who want to see the proposed scheme fully illustrated or those who simply wish to have an attractive, professional rendering of their home or other building for posterity.

Literature available.

Jill Pilaroscia
Architectural Color
220 Eureka St.
San Francisco, CA 94114
(415) 861-8086

ARJ Associates

Having studied the field of decorative art and design in England and Iran, Ali Reza Jahedi now makes his home in Boston. The work of ARJ Associates is displayed throughout the Boston area, in New York City, and in Philadelphia.

Skilled in highly specialized restoration techniques, Jahedi also designs and executes original work. Stenciling, gilding, glazing, mural painting, and tiling are among the means he employs for new as well as restoration projects.

Although some residential work is done, the firm's specialty is interior public spaces. One such recent project was the restoration of St. Paul's Cathedral in downtown

Boston. Jahedi is shown at work applying the finishing touches to an archway. Other Boston-area projects that he has completed include the old Middlesex County Courthouse and the Copley Plaza Hotel.

ARJ Associates, Inc.
310 Washington St.
Brighton, MA 02135
(617) 783-0467

Artistic License

In the 1880s William Morris and Walter Crane joined with other English artisans to form an exhibition society fostering the fledgling Victorian Arts and Crafts movement. In the 1980s Victorian revival artists in the San Francisco area have likewise banded together to promote this same aesthetic. They call themselves Artistic License.

Guild members share the same goal of reproducing the great styles of the past for the enjoyment of people in the present. Since many of the Victorian decorative arts involved various painting techniques and styles, it is natural that Artistic License has among its craftspeople a number of highly respected specialty painters and others in closely related fields.

George Zaffel's specialty is ornamental painting and stenciling, while Bob Buckter is the guild's expert color consultant. Robert Dufort concentrates his skills on painting and refinishing; Joni Monich's business is decorative refinishing. Bruce Nelson is a painting restoration expert, and Paul Duchsherer is the architectural and decorative arts historian for the group.

All told, one-third of the artisans

at Artistic License are involved in decorative painting or a closely allied field. They are available for projects in and outside the San Francisco area.

Literature available.

Artistic License in San Francisco
1489 McAllister St.
San Francisco, CA 94119
(415) 922-5219

Biltmore, Campbell, Smith Restorations

The American branch of a famed English restoration firm, Biltmore, Campbell, Smith has been in existence since 1982. In the last six years it has completed some of the most important painting restoration projects in North America, including the rotunda of the Pennsylvania State Capitol; the Damascus Church in Lumpkin, Georgia; Flagler College, St. Augustine, Florida; and the Atlanta-Biltmore Hotel in Atlanta, Georgia. In each project, the firm cleaned and expertly restored such valuable artwork as murals, ceiling paintings, and wall decorations.

Although the restoration of paintings is its forte, the group of artists and technicians is also skilled in more basic decorative techniques as graining, marbling, stenciling, and gilding. The group's work is always on display at the Biltmore Estate in Asheville, North Carolina, headquarters for the firm. It is here that an apprenticeship program for aspiring restoration craftsmen is also conducted.

Biltmore, Campbell, Smith
*   Restorations, Inc.*
One Biltmore Plaza
Asheville, NC 28803
(704) 274-1776

Larry Boyce & Associates

Boyce & Associates is a San Francisco-based group of highly respected, well-trained artists offering the skills and experience necessary for creating, executing, and restoring decorative finishes. They are masters of a wide assortment of decorative techniques—stenciling, trompe l'oeil, faux finishes (marbling, graining, and antiquing), glazing, stippling, gilding, striping, polychroming, and mural painting. Moreover, this firm can display its skills on any surface, including floors, walls, ceilings, molding, fabrics, furniture, papers, and other types of objects.

The company's work is not limited to the San Francisco area. Recently Boyce & Associates completed restoration work in the office of the vice president of the United States in Washington's landmark Executive Office Building.

The hall illustrated is located in Beverly Hills, California. Designed and executed by Boyce & Associates, this project features intricate stenciling with polychrome glazing.

The second illustration shows a stenciled and gilded ceiling in San Francisco.

Literature available.

Larry Boyce & Associates, Inc.
PO Box 421507
San Francisco, CA 94142-1507
(415) 923-1366

John Canning

A superior craftsman with a feel for the authentic, John Canning excels at characteristically Victorian decoration. Born and trained in Scotland, he has practiced his trade in America for a number of years and is well known for his work at Yale University's Battell Chapel, the Connecticut State Capitol in Hartford, and other Connecticut institutions.

There is hardly a decorative technique—stenciling, stria, mottling, stippling, crosshatching, gilding, trompe l'oeil, graining—which is not within his grasp.

John Canning
132 Meeker Rd.
Southington, CT 06489
(203) 621-2188

The Color People

With questions like "What are your thoughts on colors?" and "What impression do you want your building to make?" James Martin of Color People begins to formulate a paint color scheme tailored to a customer's preferences. All the services are provided through the mail and rely on the client supplying photographs of the building as well as completing the questionnaire.

At the same time, Color People's designs take into account a building's architectural history and its locale. James Martin, called by the *Denver Post* his city's "Color Wizard," is particularly interested in the restoration and preservation of Victorian houses.

Literature available.

The Color People
1546 Williams St.
Denver, CO 80218
(303) 388-8686

The Day Studio-Workshop

Founded by JoAnne Day in 1975 in San Francisco, the studio-workshop is among the best known in North America today. Working from coast to coast, the staff is able to undertake restoration and new design projects.

Craftsmen at the Day Studio-Workshop know their art well enough to teach it to others. Two-day seminars for professionals and nonprofessionals are held each year in San Francisco and New York. At these are discussed glaze formulas, color mixing, tools and supplies, as well as basic business techniques for the new decorative painter. Fully demonstrated are wall glazing and painted finishes, including graded shading, provincial distressing, trompe l'oeil, pickling, and silk and linen finishes.

For further information, contact:

Day Studio-Workshop, Inc.
1504 Bryant St.
San Francisco, CA 94103
(415) 626-9300

EverGreene Painting Studios

The rare material is unavailable. Or it's fragile. Or it won't last. These reasons, as well as economy, promote the use of skillfully painted faux finishes. Lapis lazuli and limestone, malachite and marble, tortoiseshell, precious wood, and more have been mirrored in paint for centuries. With such clients as the Guerlain department at Bergdorf-Goodman and the U.S. government, Ever-Greene has built a deservedly high reputation.

EverGreene champions such decorative techniques as stippling, polychroming, fresco secco, stria, color washing, gilding, scagliola, and antiquing.

Brochure available.

EverGreene Painting Studios
365 W. 36th St.
New York, NY 10018
(212) 239-1322

Lynn Goodpasture

Anyone who has stopped at the Plaza Hotel or the 21 Club in New York City or visited the Martin Van Buren historic site in Kinderhook, New York, has probably enjoyed the decorative artistry of Lynn Goodpasture. Her wide range of skills includes gold leafing, stenciling, and marbling, and she works on any type of surface—walls, ceilings, floors, furniture, screens, floorcloths, carved wood, and glass.

The illustration shows a detail of a glass wall design for the Pickwick Hotel in Birmingham, Alabama. It is entitled "Sunflowers and Fiddleheads" and was created by sandblasting the glass.

Goodpasture is always ready to travel on the job, and she has extensive restoration and design experience as an independent contractor for architects, designers, and private homeowners.

For more information, contact the artist.

Lynn Goodpasture
42 W. 17th St.
New York, NY 10011
(212) 645-5334

Grammar of Ornament

During its ten years of existence, Grammar of Ornament has achieved impressive restoration work at many sites in the Rocky Mountain region, including the U.S. Mint and the Museum of Western Art, both in Denver; the Wheeler Opera House in Aspen, Colorado; and the Grant-Kohrs Ranch in Montana. The partners in the firm—Ken Miller and Larry Jones—have an understanding of period ornamentation, how it was applied and how it can be properly restored.

The execution of decorative finishes is the primary focus of the firm's work, but also offered are site and finish analysis, documentation, research, drawings, full-scale color renderings, and samples.

Marbling, stenciling, gilding, glazing, and graining are offered for projects of almost any size and of any period design.

The Grammar of Ornament, Inc.
2626 Curtis St.
Denver, CO 80205
(303) 295-2431

Merilyn Markham

Markham is known throughout New England for her stylish creation and execution of decorative finishes and stenciled designs. Interior ornamental painting for homeowners and businesses is her specialty. Working her magic

on floors, furniture, and walls, Markham custom designs and cuts her own stencils and uses oil paints to create any tone and effect desired.

This stenciled tree is so crisply and cleanly executed that it looks like a Japanese artist of ages past had fashioned it for a prince's palace. In fact, it blooms in a small hallway outside a Boston penthouse.

Look at the rich, refined setting that the glazed wall and stenciled border create in this Boston office. Such workmanship has built a solid reputation for this artist.

Merilyn Markham is more than happy to travel on assignment.

Information available.

Merilyn M. Markham
90 Main St.
Andover, MA 01810
(508) 475-4931

Matthew Mosca

Authenticity should be Matthew Mosca's middle name. He is a consultant in the field of historic paint research and restoration. An acclaimed scholar in his field, he worked with the National Trust for Historic Preservation on developing a methodology for the analysis and restoration of architectural finishes. The work was based on constituent identification employing microscopy, ultraviolet exposure, microchemical testing, and various other means of examination. Now he applies his knowledge and experience commercially as a consultant.

Mosca's clients have included, among others, the Metropolitan Museum of Art, the Smithsonian Institution, the U.S. Treasury Department, and the U.S. State Department. His complete program of research includes exposure of original finishes, collection of sample material for dating and testing, examination of these materials by polarized light microscopy, chemical analysis and testing, reconstruction of the historic finishes using accurate pigments and media, and, finally, a summary report detailing all findings.

Mosca's most important project was the work he did at George Washington's Mount Vernon estate. His study resulted in the complete restoration of the interior decoration. Mosca's portion of the project involved a comprehensive finish analysis and supervision of the interior restoration painting in which virtually all of the finishes were applied with brushes made according to 18th-century standards. The same materials and pigments as originally used were applied wherever allowed by law.

Literature available.

Matthew John Mosca
2513 Queen Anne Rd.
Baltimore, MD 21216
(301) 466-5325

Edward K. Perry Co.

Few decorating firms have more experience in restoration work than the Perry Co. Boston-based, the company is noted for its expertise in the field of colonial-period building restoration. One of its projects involved the famous Paul Revere House in Boston's North End. The exterior of the building was restained and the interior woodwork refinished. Wallpaper was also repainted. The original restoration of the building was completed in 1908 by the grandfather of the firm's current president.

The company researches and tests its materials continuously to ensure that they are appropriate and effective for the job. In addition to projects involving painting and refinishing, the firm is also noted for its trompe l'oeil work, oil and water glazing, graining, mural painting, marbling, and stenciling. Work on new structures is also undertaken by Perry.

Edward K. Perry Co.
322 Newbury St.
Boston, MA 02115
(617) 536-7873

Stencilsmith

Karl Smith uses his professional name—Stencilsmith—more and more as time goes on and his work becomes more widely known. Painted finishes and decorative painting of all kinds are his forte, including stenciling, gilding, antiquing, glazing, trompe l'oeil, graining, marbling, and murals. Smith will work in any style or motif on any interior surface, as well as on furniture, window and lamp shades, floorcloths, and more.

Stenciling is definitely Smith's technique of choice. All his designs are custom created and cut in his studio. The colorful ornamentation on the stairway illustrated, for example, would offer an interesting dimension to any setting.

The flower and feather design on the window shade adds a fanciful touch to this otherwise plain window dressing.

The elegant still-life fireboard illustration is perfect for any room with a fireplace. The fireboard can also be used as a freestanding low screen.

Stencilsmith welcomes all inquiries, and estimates are available.

Literature offered.

Stencilsmith
71 Main St.
Cold Spring, NY 10156
(914) 265-9561

Tromploy

Fooling the eye is what the artists at Tromploy do best. Founded in 1981, this firm is a cooperative of fine artists who have mastered the art of decorative painting, especially trompe l'oeil. They apply age-old techniques with contemporary wit and sensibility. Whether a customer wants to enlarge a small room, conceal an architectural flaw, embellish a plain area, or otherwise personalize an interior, this firm is guaranteed to have an artist with the skills required. In addition to trompe l'oeil, the artists execute interior and exterior murals, illusionary ceilings, faux marble, faux bois, marquetry, and much more.

A faux marble treatment of paneled walls perfectly matches the real marble of the floor in one interior created by Tromploy.

A narrow space can be opened up with an illusionary mural like the one illustrated. The closet door has become an open door with a vista of a Scottish castle and grazing sheep. The family cat can't decide whether to leave the scene or not.

Tromploy also offers workshops to teach the techniques and processes that the firm has perfected. Four are offered: materials and glazes, faux bois and marquetry, faux marble and inlay, and trompe l'oeil and mural painting. All inquiries are welcome.

Brochure available.

Tromploy Inc.
400 Lafayette St.
New York, NY 10003
(212) 420-1639

Carolyn Warrender

Carolyn Warrender's interest in stenciling led her to begin an English mail-order stencil kit business. It has grown into a large-scale retail and wholesale supply enterprise. Her selection of merchandise includes more than 140 precut, reusable stencils; specially designed fast-drying paints; and carefully constructed brushes.

Warrender's Architextures stencil collection is made up of twenty designs gathered from sources all over England. The patterns are taken primarily from neoclassical moldings, some of which include bows, tassels, and cords. The designs are intended to substitute for more expensive wood or plaster moldings.

The Utopia stencil border, AT-UT1, is 5¾" wide by 10" long. It can be used in place of a picture rail.

The Castille border, AT-CT2, is one of the smallest patterns offered in this collection and is 1½" wide and 1½" long.

The Arcadia pattern, AT-AC1, has a definite neoclassical flair. It is 4½" wide and 1¼" long.

The Maypole Double stencil, AT-MPD2, is 1⅛" wide and 4⅛" long. This is an excellent pattern to take the place of a stair or chair rail.

These designs are only a small sampling of Warrender's imaginative offerings. For any do-it-yourself stenciler, this is a collection worth exploring.

Catalogue, $7.

Carolyn Warrender
91-93 Lower Sloane St.
London SW1W 8DA, England
01-730-0728

Waterman Works

Scott Waterman draws.on the works of the Etruscans, classical Greeks, and Renaissance artists as well as the motifs of the Arts and Crafts movement, postimpressionists, and abstract artists in creating his individual works. Working on all manner of interior surfaces, the traditional decorative painting techniques Waterman utilizes include trompe l'oeil, marbling, stenciling, glazing, graining, gilding, and leafing. He will also execute murals.

An excellent example of his work is located in the Biltmore Hotel of Atlanta, Georgia. He designed and executed a trompe l'oeil mural that effectively doubles the apparent length of the Gothic arched hallway in the hotel's lobby.

Stenciling, effective use of faux finishes, trompe l'oeil, and glazing are all combined in a second interior inspired by neoclassical sources. Waterman's glazing effects are built from many layers and create surfaces at once subtle and luminous.

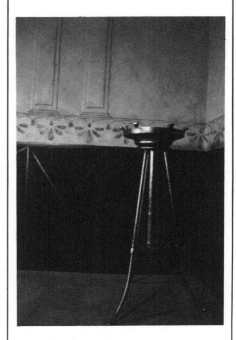

Waterman is a knowledgeable, skilled, and experienced artist worthy of the attention of private homeowners and commercial clients. Although most of his work is done in the Atlanta area, he will travel on the job.

Literature, $5.

Waterman Works
266B Oxford Pl., NE
Atlanta, GA 30307
(404) 373-9438

Papers

Ever since wallpaper could be inexpensively produced in continuous rolls by high-speed printing presses in the mid-19th century, papers have found numerous practical and decorative uses in the home. Today's homeowner will find papers similarly useful and ornamental. Available in various finishes and textures, modern papers are generally easier to hang and to keep clean than the old-fashioned variety. There are hundreds of well-documented reproduction designs from the 18th and 19th centuries to choose from, as well as thousands of adaptations and interpretations of traditional florals, stripes, and geometrics. Slowly but steadily, the old practice of using two or three papers in a room is once again gaining favor. Wallpaper borders can be effectively used to create cornice and frieze designs; other papers are appropriate for use on the ceilings or as wall panels. Special embossed and textured Victorian papers such as Lincrusta Walton and Anaglypta are being produced once again and are especially appropriate and attractive substitutes for wainscoting in hallways and dining rooms.

Bassett & Vollum

Using more than sixteen different silkscreens for some papers, Bassett & Vollum reproduces a large variety of antique patterns from European and American originals.

The company's Venetian Point wallcovering is a versatile design sold in three-panel units. These units can be used continuously around a room or as individual

panels either within a frame or cut out, highlighting any of the various elements from the complete design. Panels are printed 20″ wide and 8′ high, but the paper can be trimmed at the top and bottom for a low ceiling. Colorways include gray silk and gold, desert holly and white, antique satin and celadon, white and putty, celadon and white, and white and marigold.

Bassett & Vollum also offers ten superb period border patterns including five one-color print bandings and five multicolor designs, two of which have more than fourteen hues. The one-color print bandings include, in order of appearance, Athenium, 3¼″ deep with a 3¾″ repeat; Rosettes, 1½″ deep with a 3¾″ repeat; Rose & Key, 2⅛″ deep with a 6¾″ repeat; Little Acorns, 1¾″ deep with a 2″ repeat; and Acorns, 3½″ deep with a 4″ repeat.

Bassett & Vollum can custom color any of its papers, and the company welcomes special orders of other kinds, too.

Literature available.

Bassett & Vollum Inc.
217 N. Main St.
Galena, IL 61036
(815) 777-2460

Louis W. Bowen

Large-scale English florals, decorative early American borders, and special stone and marbleized stylings are among the patterns in Bowen's Volume 25 collection of wallcoverings. All these patterns feature brilliant colorings as well as some softer, more contemporary color combinations.

Country Vine displays brightly colored buds and spring flowers placed along winding vines. Accompanying Country Vine is a loosely woven cane pattern called Trellis Fantasy.

Heavy blossoms of roses are interspersed with rosebuds and chrysanthemums in the Old English Rose pattern. The companion fabric, Special Combed Effect, is a heavy textural pattern that picks up the coloring from the main wallcovering.

Dentelle and Dentelle border offer an appealing combination of old-fashioned and contemporary design. The seemingly freehand style of the overall floral motif on a honeycomb background gives the pattern a stark, modern feeling. When the same design is incorporated into soft intertwining lace, however, it takes on the look of an antique.

The colorful swirls of Bowen's Unmatched Marbleized Bookends pick up a popular period pattern. The multicolor treatment adds to the paper's timeless appeal.

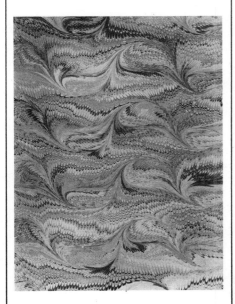

In addition to the Volume 25 collection, Bowen offers hand-painted wallcoverings imported from China along with contemporary, European, and Oriental scenics. A full breadth of

patterns—including textures, trompe l'oeil configurations, large-scale florals, small overall prints, and geometric florals—rounds out the firm's offerings.

Bowen has showrooms in New York, Los Angeles, San Francisco, Chicago, and Boston; for more information, contact:

Louis W. Bowen, Inc.
950 Third Ave.
New York, NY 10022
(212) 751-4470

Bradbury & Bradbury

In his Benicia, California, studio, Bruce Bradbury and his associates produce some of the best late 19th-century reproduction papers available in North America or Europe. These historic wall and ceiling coverings and coordinated elements are organized into a number of collections, including the William Morris, Neo-Grec, Anglo-Japanese, Woodland, and Aesthetic Movement. In turn, each collection is subdivided into an almost endless number of paper patterns, accents, designs, and coordinating pieces. Bradbury's modular approach to wallcoverings allows for the use of easily interchangeable elements so that almost any setting can be created or re-created down to the most minute detail.

The company's Neo-Grec collection is based on the work of the English architects George and Maurice Ashdown Audsley during the 1880s. Several elements are featured in the ceiling plan illustrated. Decorative blocks containing allegories of each of the four elements, two of which are shown (IGT and ZPT) are each 18" square. The corner fans (NGT) are each 24" square. Starting from the outside and working inward, the border and filler patterns featured

are the Neo-Grec fret border (NGB), 8½" wide, and matching corner blocks (NGC), 8" square. The wave border, next (WVB), is 3" wide, and the Star Trellis Enrichment (STE) is made in 27" strips. The Laurel border (LRB) and matching blocks are 3" wide, and the innermost design is the Neo-Grec dado (NGD) trimmed from the standard 27"-wide strips.

The Neo-Grec roomset photograph, above, and drawing, below, show another combination of the individual elements in this collection. The Neo-Grec dado is seen in full at the bottom. The Anthemion wallpaper (AFW) combines wonderfully with the Neo-Grec frieze (NGF), either 14" or 18" high at the top. Corner fans, decorative blocks, and a number of other papers and borders are on the ceiling.

Seen in another view is Star Trellis Enrichment (STE). Colorways for this and the other elements of this set are in primary shades of terra cotta, cream, jasper green, dove blue, and ashes of roses.

William Morris's love of nature found full expression in the wallpapers and fabrics he designed in the mid- to late 19th century. Bradbury fully captures this spirit with the Morris collection.

Acanthus border (ACB) is 9" wide. It forms a narrow frieze above a wall fill area of Marigold paper (MAW). A 1"-wide Chevron

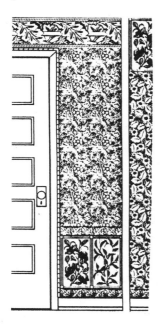

border (CVB) outlines the narrow doorframe, and Pomegranate panels (PGP), trimmed to 17", are banded by Leaf border (LEB), 3" wide, to form the dado. The room's overall height is 8'. Color

schemes for the entire collection are organized around ashes of roses, dove blue, terra cotta, indigo, and aesthetic green.

The Fenway collection features natural designs popular from the 1870s through the 1890s. Fens, or marshes, serve as the inspiration for this original Bradbury collection.

This room features the company's Serpentine wallcovering (SPW); Iris frieze (IRF), 27" wide; Raindrop enrichment (RDE); Spiral corner blocks (SPT), 6" square; Gossamer ceiling paper (GSC); and the 4"-wide Moth borders.

Shown in detail is the Iris frieze. Without the borders it is 18" wide. The upper border is 6" wide, and the lower border is 3" wide. Colorways for the Fenway collection include eucalyptus, aesthetic green, indigo, and ashes of roses.

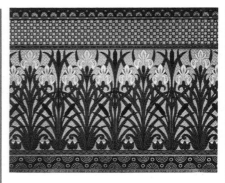

Historically accurate, the company's Aesthetic Movement collection is named for a style that emerged in the late 19th century. One possibility for decorating a

room in this style is shown in the drawing of the 8'-tall wall. The upper border, 6" wide, is trimmed from Emilita's frieze (EMF). The central wall filler features the richly textured Cherry Blossom paper (CBW), and the dado is

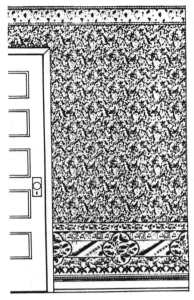

formed from Emelita's frieze, 25" high when used with all its borders, placed just above the narrow baseboard. Colorways for this collection focus on burgundy, aesthetic green, terra cotta, and eucalyptus.

Bradbury & Bradbury's Woodland collection features the designs of William Morris and Walter Crane. Morris's exquisite florals are perfectly complemented by Crane's whimsical animal designs.

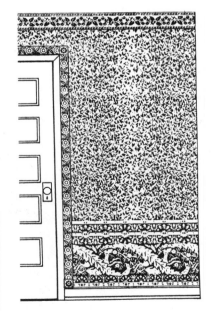

A drawing of an 8'-high wall shows the Rose border (ROB), 6" wide, used as a narrow frieze, while Crab Apple paper (CAW) is the central wallcovering. The narrow doorframe is enhanced by the

Aster border (ASB), 3" wide, and Aster corner blocks (AST), 3" square. The Deer and Rabbit frieze (DRF), 24" wide, is set on the narrow baseboard as a dado. Its matching border, 6" wide, is used as the top rail and is offered separately as Woodland border (WOB). Colorways center around eucalyptus, aesthetic green, ashes of roses, and terra cotta.

By dividing his many collections into their individual components, Bruce Bradbury allows endless design and decorative possibilities. Having so much to choose from, however, can also lead to a splitting headache for the amateur or do-it-yourself decorator. The company has anticipated this problem and has formed a department of professional designers who will work with the customer to tailor hundreds of options to his or her specific needs and desires. These specialists will provide a complete room design plan with specifications, and the cost will be credited toward the first wallpaper purchase from Bradbury.

Catalogue, $8.

Bradbury & Bradbury Wallpapers
PO Box 155
Benicia, CA 94159
(707) 746-1900

Brunschwig & Fils

At least three major decorative arts museums in America have licensed Brunschwig to reproduce their period wallpaper patterns: the Cooper-Hewitt Museum, the Museum of Early Southern Decorative Arts, and the Winterthur Museum. Documented papers from sources such as these, as well as a number of other period and contemporary collections, have made this company one of America's most respected paper manufacturers. Dedication to beauty and authenticity is the company's hallmark.

From the Winterthur Museum collection comes the Hare and Hound border. Adapted from the embroidered bed hangings in the museum's Patuxent room, this delightful pattern is now available

as a vinyl wallcovering. Brunschwig offers this charming bit of scenic folk art in the original greens and golds as well as blue and russet. The pattern repeats every 23½".

From the company's Cooper-Hewitt Museum collection comes the Marieko paper. This Anglo-Japanese design derives from late 19th-century French or English woodblock prints. Colorways for today's tastes are based on garnet, teal, gray-green, shell, aubergine, and stone gray. The pattern repeats every 23½".

For more information or to locate a dealer near you, contact the company's main offices.

Brunschwig & Fils
75 Virginia Rd.
North White Plains, NY 10603
(914) 684-5800

J. R. Burrows

Burrows replicates wallpaper designs drawn largely from the English Arts and Crafts movement. The company's designs, however, put less emphasis on the repeating geometry of the English designs by William Morris and his followers. Rather, following the aesthetic of such designers as Aldam Heaton, active in London during the 1880s and 90s, Burrows papers emphasize large-scale patterns with repeats that are less pronounced. All Burrows' colorways are faithful to the original documents.

Most of the company's papers are hand printed in England using traditional techniques of hand blocking the patterns and hand brushing the grounds. Several of the later 19th-century patterns are also offered as hand-screen-printed papers made in America.

Illustrated in a house in Newton, Massachusetts, is the Heaton pattern, named for the designer. A design with a 42"-square half-drop repeat, it is made up of two widths of paper marked pattern A and pattern B. Both must be used to complete the design. Roll sizes of each pattern are 21" by 7 yards. Heaton is printed in three documentary colors on a colored ground.

Burrows papers are available through trade showrooms or by special order from the firm. The company also offers a fine selection of period carpet and fabric designs.

Literature available.

J. R. Burrows & Co.
PO Box 418, Cathedral Station
Boston, MA 02118
(617) 451-1982

Carefree Wallcoverings

A hallmark of Carefree's Jay Yang Interiors collection is the simulation of a warp-printing technique used in France during the 1700s. This printing method integrates patterns, locking one part of a design into the next. The collection's large-scale florals appropriate for many high-style colonial interiors, are graceful and elegant whether arrayed in sprays, on vines, or singly. Other motifs include a wide variety of stripes, latticeworks, bows, and an imperial-sized paisley design.

The elegant florals of the company's Chardon wallcovering are shown on the front wall and stairway. In the back room is Carefree's Salerno wallcovering, from this same collection. Colorations include ebony, mandarin, teal, plum, Venetian pink, wisteria, silver frost, pale aqua, cotton candy, and more. The ninety-two wallcoverings in this collection are gravure printed, prepasted, scrubbable, and peelable. All styles are pretrimmed and stain resistant. Forty-eight complementary fabrics are also offered, printed on 100 percent cotton.

For more information or to locate a dealer near you, contact:

Carefree Wallcoverings
23645 Mercantile Rd.
Cleveland, OH 44122
(216) 464-3700

Crown

When Frederick Walton invented Lincrusta, which has a composition similar to linoleum, in 1877, he created a product that allowed the average Victorian homeowner to use durable, attractive, and relatively inexpensive embossed wallcoverings for the first time. The lower or dado section of a wall in a front hall, library, or dining room was often given some special treatment in the homes of the wealthy. The material used might be oak paneling, carved woodwork, plasterwork, metalwork, or embossed cordovan leather. Lincrusta was not only reasonably priced, but it was even more durable than the other, more expensive, materials.

Twenty decorative patterns have been revived by Crown Decorative Products of England in recent years. These are widely distributed in North America and are available as friezes, borders, and dado and wallpapers. Beautifully formed, Lincrusta is waterproof and perfect for high-traffic areas. It has been used in many outstanding restoration projects and can be painted—using an oil-base paint—to fit in with any decorating scheme.

Anaglypta is another compound developed ten years later—in 1887. It is available in several different forms. There are more than twenty patterns available in this material. Design RD: 125 features a traditional pattern of repeating large-scale medallions.

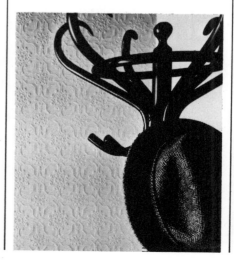

Crown has recently introduced two versions of vinyl Anaglypta—"luxury" and "fine." These papers are especially easy to clean and are suited to areas of high humidity.

A closely related wallcovering is Crown's Supaglypta, providing the same qualities as Anaglypta but with a deeper pattern relief. It is also known as Anaglypta SupraDurable. Cotton fibers are added to give the material extra strength. Design RD: 655 will transform a wall or ceiling with its interlocking medallions and grilles repeating every 10½".

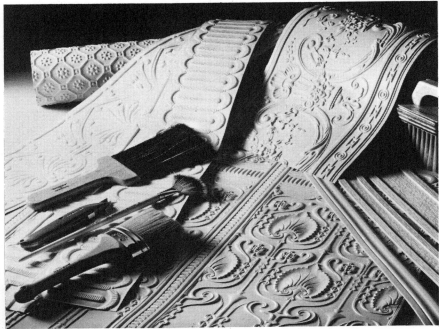

Embossed border papers called Pelmets form yet another category. These feature a variety of classical designs that can be used on their own or with a cornice. They are not as sturdy as the other Crown materials, but they need not be since they are used in out-of-the-way places.

Although all these relief wallcoverings are offered only in white, each can be painted according to the needs of any setting. A good heavy-duty vinyl clay-based paste is advised for hanging all the materials except the heavier Lincrusta. Crown suggests that anyone using its premier material seek the advice of his or her paper dealer in choosing the right adhesive.

Grouped here is a further selection of this family of wallcoverings. Byzantine (top left) is a classic Lincrusta wallcovering. Shown at left are Pelmet borders. The ornate Empire frieze (top right) is a sophisticated and state-ly pattern, while the slender Lincrusta borders (right) are highly recommended for chair rails that may have to endure some wear and tear. The handsome Lincrusta Edwardian dado (center) is stylish and very durable. It makes a perfect wainscot in halls or stairways.

For more information concerning Crown products, contact a quality paints and wallpapers dealer near you or contact one of the principal distributors in North America, Bentley Brothers.

Bentley Brothers
918 Baxter Ave.
Louisville, KY 40204
(800) 824-4777
(502) 589-2939 (KY)

Elizabeth Day

Elizabeth Day is a wallpaper designer and printer with the skill and experience to match the best of her kind from any era. Her specialty is hand-printed floral wallpaper borders, each of which has a strong period character. Seven standard patterns are offered in a variety of widths.

Among her designs (from top to bottom) are Oriental, Hawthorne, Poppy, and Daisy. Colors available include slate, sage, apricot, and burgundy.

Day will also accept commissions to design and print borders, papers, and fabrics to a customer's specifications. Day lives and works in England, but will ship her work anywhere.

Brochure available.

Elizabeth Day
Pippins
Town Row
Rotherfield, East Sussex TN6 3HU
England
089285 3112

Greeff

Each year Greeff expands its collection of late 18th-, 19th-, and early 20th-century wallpapers and fabrics. One of the company's most renowned collections is drawn from the Shelburne Museum. A variety of American period designs and brightly colored florals replicate documentary papers and fabrics in this New England museum's collection.

The room illustrated features Greeff's Chloe wallcovering and Chloe border. Both are derived from a 19th-century oilcloth. The paper comes in 27"-wide strips with multicolored floral prints over a background of dark blue, cream, or yellow. The border colorways coordinate with the paper, and these include slate and gold on ivory, seafoam and blue on white, slate and gold on white, light blue and cranberry on white.

For more information, or for help in locating a dealer, contact Greeff at:

Greeff Fabrics, Inc.
150 Midland Ave.
Port Chester, NY 10573
(914) 939-6200

Katzenbach & Warren

Katzenbach & Warren is now a part of the C & A Wallcoverings family. Founded in 1929 by William Katzenbach and Phelps Warren, the company is well known for its collection of designs from Colonial Williamsburg. These are being continued under the C & A umbrella with a second volume of the Williamsburg Small Prints collection.

Illustrated are the Savannah Floral (back wall), Savannah (side wall) wallpapers, the Savannah border, and a complementary fabric. These are all from the Katzenbach Classics collection and are available in four colorways: pineapple ice background with rose flowers, ecru background and peach flowers, vanilla background and violet flowers, and pearl gray background with lavender flowers.

Katzenbach's standard triple rolls are 27" wide and five yards long. The eighty-eight papers and twenty-four borders in the Classics collection are rotary screen printed, pretrimmed, strippable, washable, and vinyl coated.

The Katzenbach papers are marketed by C & A and distributed by Kinney Wallcoverings. They are available in many paint stores and home centers. If you have difficulty locating the line, contact:

C & A Wallcoverings
23645 Mercantile Rd.
Cleveland, OH 44122
(216) 464-3700

Milbrook Wallcoverings

Inspiration for Milbrook's 79 sidewalls, 31 borders, and 37 cor-relating fabrics in the company's Metropolitan Museum of Art collection comes from widely varying cultures and artifacts—a Kashmir shawl, an 18th-century Chinese silk, an Indian bedcovering, and a Japanese folding screen, for example.

Dramatic florals with a definite period character are used in this room. Calcutta Chintz (top), companion Calcutta Stripe (bottom), and Calcutta Chintz border include in their designs floral and paisley combinations, marbled stripes, and a classic textural flamestitch. Colorways include deep raisin, peach, mahogany, ruby, mocha, navy, tea rose, lilac, and many more.

All Milbrook's wallcoverings are prepasted, scrubbable, and strippable. For more information, or to locate a dealer, contact the company's home office.

Milbrook Wallcoverings
23645 Mercantile Rd.
Cleveland, OH 44122
(216) 464-3700

Sanderson

Morris and Company's hand-blocked wallpaper prints had already been famous for more than a century when Sanderson acquired the original blocks from which they were first produced. Sanderson, an English firm, still uses these same blocks when printing its limited-edition papers. At the same time, the firm also produces less expensive silkscreen prints that are accurate in every respect. The patterns shown here are produced in both manners.

Foliage was designed by J. H. Dearle and is offered in three colorways, including the original

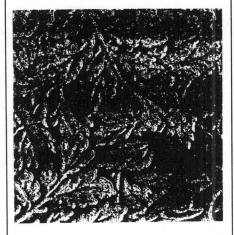

celadon-forest green-honey ivory. The other combinations are beige-stone and oyster-pink.

The fanciful, highly detailed Indian pattern is a William Morris

original inspired by painted or embroidered furnishings. Colorways include bronze and pink, various blues and greens, bronze, peacock, and cardinal red.

William Morris's own Acorn is one of his simplest and most popular.

Colorways include yellow ochre, silver gray, warm gray, coral, and green.

Blackberry is among the most colorful prints that Sanderson offers. It originated with Morris's company and was designed by J. H. Dearle. The original colorway is coral-forest green-honey on ivory, but yellow-olive-gray and bronze-gray-blue are also available.

Sanderson's Morris papers—whether block or screen printed—come in twenty patterns and sixty-two colorways. The firm also offers a number of matching or coordinating fabrics and borders.

Contact the company at its New York location for more information.

Arthur Sanderson & Sons
979 Third Ave., Suite 403
New York, NY 10022
(212) 319-7220

Schumacher

Nineteenth-century reproduction wallpapers and fabrics have always been Schumacher's specialty. The firm has hundreds of paper and border patterns, including American, English, and French designs. Recently, Schumacher has taken a giant step into the 20th century with its Radio City Music Hall collection. The patterns reproduce designs found in the architecture and decoration of the famous 1930s Rockefeller Center complex in New York City.

The Rockettes border, 503900, is a vinyl top-coated wallcovering

adapted from a bas-relief under the hall's marquee. It is 27" wide and comes in platinum or brass.

This same border is used with the Music Hall Marble design, series 503790. Colorways for the paper include malachite, forest, topaz, and other jewel tones and natural hues.

Orchestra, 503840, is an exhuberant design of repeating curves, a favored motif of the Art

Deco style. Colorways are attractive combinations using ruby, teal, golden brown, evergreen, and several other appropriate period colors.

For information on these papers and more traditional selections, contact a local dealer of Schumacher papers. If one is not nearby, contact the company for assistance.

F. Schumacher & Co.
979 Third Ave.
New York, NY 10022
(212) 415-3942

Flexi-Wall Systems

Flexi-Wall's Plaster-in-a-Roll is specifically designed for problem walls when standard types of wall coverings won't suffice. While it can be used by itself and is available in three weaves and fifty colors, Plaster-in-a-Roll is especially recommended as a liner paper. (Traditionally, linen is used to line difficult walls.) Plaster-in-a-Roll will also hide irregularities on any wall and form a smooth surface for the application of a decorative paper or paint.

Plaster-in-a-Roll is available in 48"-wide rolls of forty square yards. It is installed like any other wallcovering, but it is advisable to use Flexi-Wall's special adhesive.

Contact the company for more information.

Flexi-Wall Systems
PO Box 88
Liberty, SC 29657
(803) 855-0500

182

Richard E. Thibaut

Thibaut and the National Preservation Institute of Alexandria, Virginia, have teamed up to create the Historic Homes of America collection of wallpaper, border, and fabric designs. These designs are based on historic documents from some of America's most famous landmark homes, including Oak Hill, President James Monroe's estate in Aldie, Virginia; Eleutherian Mills, the ancestral home of the du Pont family in Wilmington, Delaware; and Tudor Place, built in Washington, D.C., by the granddaughter of President George Washington.

The reproduction papers and fabrics in this collection are drawn from all periods of American history and from all architectural styles. Colorways include those documented and more contemporary combinations for today's tastes.

Phelps Ashlar is an important design for those looking to restore an early Victorian interior or for those interested in a trompe l'oeil effect. The original paper hangs in the Captain Arah Phelps house in North Colebrook, Connecticut. Gold on ecru were the original colors, but three other combinations are available.

The Japonais paper and border patterns come from the Harry Packer mansion in Jim Thorpe, Pennsylvania. Its colorways in-

clude metallic silver, dusty blue, and mauve.

The Ostrich Plume border was originally used in Locust Thicket, a home located in Lynchburg, Virginia. Colorways include metallic gold, burgundy swag, and gray plumage.

The Rockwood wallpaper and fabric are excellent examples of the Gothic Revival style. This gracious fruit and leaf design was drawn from a canopy fabric at the Rockwood Museum in Wilmington, Delaware. The original document colors are rose-grape on a cream background. Three other color combinations are available.

The Boxwood border from The Jethro Brown House in Yancyville, North Carolina, draws the eye upward to the elegant ceiling line of this gracious room. The design is a harmonious combination of wonderfully drawn birds, flowers, and scrollwork. The original document colors for the border are a dramatic blue and gold combination on a cream background. Its companion paper is called Caswell. It is a harmonizing pattern with a metallic print. Border colorways also include teal, gold, and green. The paper is available in three additional colorways.

Thibaut's Historic Homes of America collection is only one of many that the company offers. It encompasses four borders in sixteen colorways, twenty-three papers in ninety-five colorways, and ten fabrics in forty colorways. All the borders and papers are prepasted, strippable, and vinyl coated. Contact the company for more information.

Richard E. Thibaut, Inc.
706 S. 21st St.
Irvington, NJ 07111
(201) 399-7888

Van Luit

One of the many sources of inspiration for Van Luit paper and fabric patterns is the Henry Francis du Pont Winterthur Museum. Several Van Luit paper collections feature documentary patterns and colors adapted from objects in this museum's vast collections.

Amberleigh is from the company's third edition Winterthur collection of documentary papers. The design features alternating stripes of floral sprays and medallions and is typical of patterns used by furniture makers during the 1820s. The original design was printed in yellow madder. Amberleigh is also offered in combined brick-loden-azure, oyster-terra cotta-juniper, jade-rose-toast, and navy-tobacco-brick. The Amberleigh border paper features the medallions in a stripe.

In 1810 arborescent patterns in short repeats were being printed

in brilliant yellows, blues, and greens. Van Luit's Zenobia paper typifies these patterns. The original fabric was block printed in England in 1812. Colorways include celadon-ivory-pearl, pineapple-rose-olive, beige-lavender-taupe, camel-peach-pewter, and brick-carmel-gold.

Evoking a Chinese design popular in Europe in the 18th century, the company's Boca Grande is a large-scale pattern of peonies, flowering branches, and long-tailed birds. It replicates a block-printed fabric dating to England of the 1780s. Colorways include emerald-amethyst-brown, celery-melon-straw, rust-blue-wine, tan-gray-orange, and blue-red-brown. On a smaller scale in coordinated colors, Winter Pear (on the foreground wall)

serves as a companion paper. The Boca Grande border is designed to complement this group of fabrics and papers.

Gouveneur Damask is a perfect example of a mid-18th-century French textile. Its large symmetrical pattern of various floral designs is typical of this period. It is offered in color combinations of smoke pearl-antique gold, buff-sauterne, coral-sand, dove-pewter, and jade-teal. The paper is 27" wide.

There are dozens of documentary designs from which to choose in the Van Luit Winterthur collection. Suitable adaptations of historic designs are to be found in Van Luit's other collections.

The company has showrooms throughout the Northeast. For further information, contact:

Albert Van Luit & Co.
200 Garden City Plaza
Garden City, NY 11530
(516) 741-9440

Victorian Collectibles

Victorian Collectibles' Brillon collection of wallpaper patterns encompasses 1,379 different designs dating from the late 19th to the early 20th century. Comprised of designs by American artists, this exquisitely detailed collection may be viewed at New York's Cooper-Hewitt Museum; some are also displayed at the Victoria and Albert Museum in London. Stored on over 4,500 rolls, the original papers had limited or no exposure to daylight for years, and they have since been deacidified and coated to preserve their detail and original coloring.

The Brillon wallpapers are reproduced from the originals using modern silkscreening techniques. Pictured are Dayle, shown on the wall and ceiling to the right of the room divider, and Fortino, used on the wall and ceiling in the second photograph. Fortino is characterized by a slim, delicately intertwined leaf design, while Dayle is a more striking floral motif. Each is available in

several original or contemporary colorways.

Victorian Collectibles also offers ceramic tiles, fabrics, hand-woven rugs, stenciled floorcloths, plaster moldings, and French lace in patterns to complement the company's papers.

Catalogue, $3.

Victorian Collectibles, Ltd.
845 E. Glenbrook Rd.
Milwaukee, WI 53217
(414) 352-6910

Painted murals from the Parke House, Parkesburg, Pennsylvania. Photograph by Ned Goode, Historic American Buildings Survey.

184

Other Suppliers of Paints and Papers

Consult List of Suppliers for addresses.

Paints

Laura Ashley
Dutch Boy
Fuller-O'Brien

Decorative Painting

Architectural Resources Group
Bob Buckter
George Studios
Judith Hendershot
Koeppel/Freedman Studios
Oehrlein and Associates
Preservation Partnership
Robson Worldwide Graining
San Francisco Color Service
Victorian Collectibles
Wiggins Brothers
Wick York

Papers

Laura Ashley
Bentley Brothers
Nina Campbell
Clarence House/Cole and Son
Cowtan and Tout
A. L. Diament
Anna French
Hill and Knowles
Lee Joffa
San Francisco Victoriana
Steptoe and Wife Antiques
Warner
Waverly

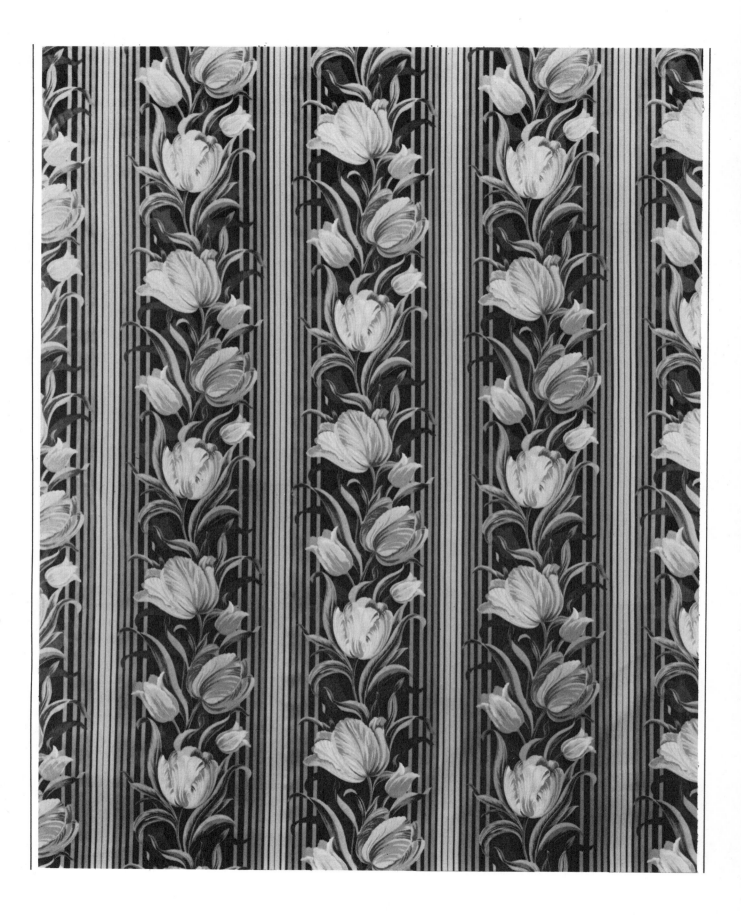

7.

Fabrics

Ever since the advent of machine-printed textiles in the early 1800s, it has been possible to drape and cover up almost any object or element in a room at a reasonable cost. Before that time, fabrics at the window were minimal and the primary use of expensive material was in bed hangings. Gradually, throughout the 19th century, more and more fabric was employed. No one is known as a draper today, but those who knew how to arrange fabric artfully around a chair or at a window were as important a century ago as painters and other decorators are in the 1980s. Historians are continually researching early uses of fabric. When we think we know it all, there is yet another new discovery—about the use of muslin, for example, or unbleached cotton. The manufacture of reproduction designs continues to grow each year. Many of these materials were prepared originally for a particular house restoration and may be available now only on a custom-order basis. Other reproductions, however, are part of the regular stock of the fabric manufacturers and merchants. Included in this category are many of the museum collections, such as those carrying the Sturbridge Village or Williamsburg designation. There are also "adaptations" of traditional designs which may be perfectly suitable for period decorating. To adapt a design is usually to make it somewhat less complex in coloration or detail so as to lower the cost of its production. In addition, many designs that were originally woven are now adapted as prints.

The following pages comprise a swatch book of reproduction fabrics and suitable adaptations. Unfortunately, it is not possible to present these designs in color. It is also impossible to represent all the different kinds of materials that are available. But, within the limits of reason and taste, a home renovator should have no problem selecting appropriate materials, given the wide range of price, style, and quality available but only hinted at in the present chapter.

A cotton fabric, Deco Tulips, from
F. Schumacher & Co.'s Radio City
Music Hall Collection, New York City.

Alexandra's Textile

Founded in response to an increasing interest in traditional country styles nationwide, Alexandra's Textile provides reproduction patterns and originally designed weaves in a rainbow of color combinations. Hand dyed and hand loomed, these homespuns are fashioned of 100 percent cotton in several weights for many purposes. Lightweight plaids, heavier commercial-weight checked patterns, woolen weaves,

and the company's mattress ticking are just a few of Alexandra's attractive and affordable homespuns. Also offered are reproduction coverlets and blankets fashioned from the company's weaves. Order by the yard, but remember to allow for six to eight percent shrinkage.

Brochure available.

Alexandra's Textile
5606 State Rt. 37
Delaware, OH 43015
(614) 369-1817

Amazon Drygoods

Closeouts and special-order fabrics augment Amazon Drygoods' selection of stocked and always-available yard goods. Most of the fabric is printed on 100 percent cotton, but dacron, rayon, and acetate, the highest-quality silk substitute, are also used alone and in combination. Weights range from very heavy to extremely light; strip widths vary from 35" to 54", depending on the pattern. Fabrics may be purchased by the yard or half-yard.

Amazon will quote on hard-to-find fabrics; various types are available at any given time. Most fabrics come in more than twenty colors or color combinations, while slipper satin comes in ninety-five.

Be sure to preshrink all fabrics before use. A color-matching service is available for those who wish it. Look into the company's sewing notions and findings, also, for the selection is almost as great as it is in textiles.

Catalogue, $2.

Amazon Drygoods
2218 E. 11th St.
Davenport, IA 52803
(319) 322-6800

Beachwood Wallcoverings

The designs in Beachwood's Legends collection of fabrics and papers emphasize classical elegance and luxury. Patterns feature intricate florals, geometrics, and tailored flamestitch designs.

The Juneau fabric and matching wallcovering are highlighted by a butterfly-and-floral design. The fabric is offered in colorways ranging from soft pastels—cream, seafoam, and pearl gray—to deeper hues of peach, mauve, chocolate, jade, and many more.

The Legends collection offers thirty-four fabrics with seventy-eight correlating paper and twenty-eight border designs. All fabrics are 100 percent cotton and Scotchgard protected.

Literature available.

Beachwood Wallcoverings
23645 Mercantile Rd.
Cleveland, OH 44122
(216) 464-3700

Nancy Borden

Textile furnishings based on 18th- and 19th-century designs are Nancy Borden's specialty. Such furnishings include curtains, upholstery, slipcovers, floor coverings, domestic linens, and bed hangings. Serving as a consultant and producer of textiles, she can guide you in the historic styles and usage of such period furnishings. Borden's completed custom work attests to the huge amount of research, construction, and finishing time that is invested in each project. Borden also offers on-site consultation.

The 18th-century tab curtains are from Borden's Farmhouse collection and may be custom-proportioned for any window. This style is available plain, with small checks, or with large checks. Colors are white, indigo blue, mustard, apple red, and many more. Measurements should be included when ordering.

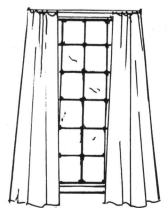

Literature and swatches available.

Nancy Borden Period Textile
*   Furnishings*
PO Box 4381 OH
Portsmouth, NH 03801
(603) 436-4284

Carol Brown

For more than sixty years Carol Brown has been operating a one-of-a-kind shop out of her house in Putney, Vermont. She deals in unusual and interesting natural fiber fabrics from around the world, including cottons, woolens, linens, and silks. Special textiles available are Welsh and Irish tweeds, Liberty and Pima cottons, Madras plaids, and Japanese prints. Materials are offered by the yard or in panels. Samples are available on request.

Brochure, SASE.

Carol Brown
PO Box C-100
Putney, VT 05346
(802) 387-5875

Brunschwig & Fils

Brunschwig & Fils's fine materials include cottons, silks, wools, linens, and even horsehair. Always a stickler for authenticity, this firm has gathered and reproduced period patterns from the Winterthur Museum, the Museum of Early Southern Decorative Arts, and many other leading collections.

One of Brunschwig's best-known textiles is the 52"-wide Laurel silk damask of bouquets enclosed by garlands of leaves and fur. This late 18th-century design is perfect for upholstery or draperies and is used for chair seats and window hangings in the White Hall dining room, a period setting re-created by the Museum of Early Southern Decorative Arts. The original colors are white against bronze; the design is also available in six other combinations.

From Brunschwig's Winterthur Museum collection comes Montmorenci Moiréd Stripe, an adaptation of a silk moiré fabric used on a Federal sofa in the museum's Library Hall. The original colors of this 66 percent cotton-34 percent Bemberg Italian-manufactured textile are pink and green. In addition there is a subtle white on white, blue and white, yellow and white, pink and blue, yellow and coral, and beige and white. The stripe is supplied in 50" widths.

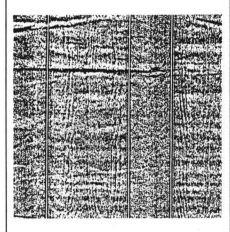

In order to meet the needs of a young or not-so-young customer with good taste and a limited budget, Brunschwig introduced the Bis collection. These are 100 percent cotton prints. Anastasia combines a paisley and a stripe pattern appropriate for many late-Victorian interiors. There are three different multicolor combinations in the 52"-wide fabric. Altogether there are nine lively prints in the collection, including five glazed chintzes.

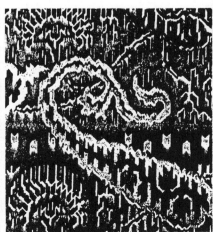

To view Brunschwig & Fils fabrics, consult an interior designer or try the home decoration department of better department stores. Contact the firm for more information.

Brunschwig & Fils
75 Virginia Rd.
North White Plains, NY 10603-0905
(914) 684-5800

J. R. Burrows

Burrows' carpet, textile, and wallpapers bring the 19th century back to life in many historical museums and private homes. The firm's selection of English carpets is illustrated in chapter 5. Of no less interest is Burrows' line of Nottingham lace produced in Scotland.

This lace is available in various lengths and as window panels. The Neo-Grec design illustrated was first shown at the 1876 Centennial Exposition in Philadelphia. The design incorporates neoclassical and Gothic elements in a typically eclectic Victorian manner. Panel lengths range from 72" to 144" and are produced in a 60" width.

Literature available.

J. R. Burrows & Co.
PO Box 148, Cathedral Station
Boston, MA 02118
(617) 451-1982

Carter Canopies

Hand-tied fishnet canopies are the heart and soul of Carter Canopies. Offered in a number of different patterns and woven of 100 percent cotton double four-ply yarn, pre-shrunk and hand washable, each white or natural canopy is custom made. Designs include Single Diamond, Lover's Knot, Margaret Winston, Large Scallop, and Straight Edge.

The Double Diamond pattern is available in matching canopy and bedspread for twin, double, queen-, or king-size beds. Each of the company's canopies can be hung on a variety of frames, depending on how it is sized when ordering.

Brochure available.

Carter Canopies
Rt. 2, Box 270G
PO Box 808
Troutman, NC 28166-0808
(704) 528-4071

Colonial Weavers

Handweaving is an art form that has lasted through the ages. The patterned fabrics produced are often beautiful as well as durable. Colonial Weavers specializes in handwoven coverlets, placemats, tablecloths, and other useful items in traditional patterns. The coverlets are woven on looms 45″ to 60″ wide and require 900 or more warp ends to produce the proper width. Each loom is threaded for only one pattern, a day's work, but colors are easily changed. The coverlet panels are then sewn carefully together so that the final fabric is the right size.

Illustrated are examples of the two types of weaves executed by Colonial Weavers. The Queen Anne's Lace pattern, lighter in tone and characterized by alternately interlocking diamonds and circles, is worked in the colonial overshot weave which is nonreversible, showing floats of wool yarn that form the pattern. This design is most attractive when done in two colors.

The second pattern is a variation of the Virginia Beauty and is a summer and winter weave, reversible with one side light for summer and the other dark for winter. This is a denser weave than the overshot and requires a more complicated loom.

All fabrics are woven with a combination of wool and cotton, usually with one color and white but sometimes with two or three colors. Various standard patterns are available; custom reproductions also can be arranged. Colors, too, can be designed to the individual's specifications, often by matching an existing fabric or room color.

Catalogue, $2.

Colonial Weavers
Box 16
Phippsburg Center, ME 04562
(207) 389-2033

Laura Copenhaver

This company has been operated by the Copenhaver family for three generations ever since it was founded by Laura Lu Copenhaver in 1916. Still dedicated to preserving the mountain crafts of Virginia and West Virginia, Copenhaver uses only authentic colors, patterns, materials, and finishes. The coverlets, canopies, furniture, quilts, and rugs—the company's staples—are still produced by individual craftsmen.

Curtains are offered in natural or white cotton muslin in several standard sizes or to custom specifications. Each natural honeycomb curtain features jabots and swag styling finished with a 5″ hand-tied peacock tail fringe. The curtain is sized to fit a standard 48″-wide window.

The muslin curtains with valance feature either a 3″ or a 5″ peacock tail fringe. Each of the two curtain panels is 46″ wide and 82″ long. The valance and matching tie-backs are optional.

Also shown is one of the company's canopy ruffles. It is 12″

wide, including 5″ of the peacock tail fringe. It is shirred to a band so that it can be tacked to a frame easily. The ruffle comes with or without a canopy top. Ruffles and tops are available only in custom sizes.

Brochure, $2.

Laura Copenhaver Industries, Inc.
PO Box 149
Marion, VA 24354
(800) 227-6797
(703) 783-4663 (VA)

Especially Lace

When considering window treatments be sure not to miss Especially Lace's Heritage Lace Curtain collection. For privacy without eliminating light, lace is the perfect decorating option, a fact well known in Victorian times.

The lace is fashioned with a number of different techniques and in an assortment of materials. The company's color catalogue includes more than thirty pages of material for windows, doors, beds, and tables. The many designs cover everything from snowflakes to country cottages, flowers, animals, fruit, and even abstract designs.

Macramé ring lace is one-third cotton and two-thirds polyester.

The Victoria macramé design, 2203, is one of the most intricate. It comes in an écru shade and is 16″ long.

Wild Rose, 2222, a sophisticated pattern, is also available in écru and is 21″ long.

Easily identifiable, the Pineapple design, 94095, is one of the longest of all the macramé laces. It is 24″ long and comes only in écru.

The Snowflake lace, 37086, is a country knit lace, 100 percent polyester. It is available in 12″ or 24″ lengths and is off-white.

Floral Fantasy, 2271, is a Jacquard lace. It comes in 12″, 24″, and 60″ lengths and is white. It, too, is 100 percent polyester.

All laces come in custom widths. When measuring, however, be sure to allow for the proper fullness. Doubling of the window width is recommended for most laces.

Catalogue, $1.

Especially Lace
202 Fifth St.
West Des Moines, IA 50265
(515) 277-8778

Family Heir-Loom Weavers

An almost lost art has been revived at Family Heir-Loom. The artists there are once again weaving on a Jacquard loom just as was done more than 150 years ago. The materials used in this process are cotton for the background and wool for the main pattern. The fabric can then be fashioned into floor coverings, bed coverlets, and runners.

One bedcover pattern, Kump, was originally produced in 1838. It has a border of birds and bushes with a cluster of four roses and an outer row of snowflakes.

The Seifert pattern, c. 1848, has a picket fence, rooster, water pump, houses, geese, and a dog with a cat up a tree. It, too, makes an appropriate country bedcovering.

Woven into the fabric of each coverlet is the weaver's name and the year in which the coverlet was made. There's also room for a two-line message selected by the customer.

Jacquard coverlets are designed for twin, double, queen- or king-size beds. The background color is always a natural cotton, but the customer can select a combination of one, two, or three wool colors for the main pattern.

Brochure, $1.

Family Heir-Loom Weavers
RD 3, Box 59E
Red Lion, PA 17356
(717) 246-2431

Greeff

European and American designs adapted from 18th- and 19th-century documents define Greeff's line of high-quality papers and fabrics. This company has been a respected name in both fields for more than fifty years. Greeff's Shelburne Museum collection offers coordinated and carefully documented papers and fabrics that enhance the character of most period settings.

The Vermont House Floral fabric (on sofa), is taken from a 19th-century dress pattern. The pattern is printed on 55"-wide strips of 100 percent cotton fabric; colors include chamois, brick, ruby, walnut, sapphire, and laurel.

The paisley-and-stripe Harrieta fabric is derived from an 1870s

men's dressing gown. It comes in 56"-wide strips of 100 percent cotton. Colorways include taupe and turquoise, rust and green, blue and red, and green and cherry.

Greeff's Clementine fabric (on settee) is a traditional trailing floral pattern derived from a 19th-century tree-of-life document. The design is printed on 100 percent cotton fabric in 56"-wide strips. Colorways offered are pink on cream, coral on mint, coral on pink, coral on blue, and rust on sand.

Greeff products are available through showrooms around the U. S., Canada, and Europe. Contact the firm for further information.

Greeff Fabrics, Inc.
200 Garden City Plaza
Garden City, NY 11530
(516) 741-9440

Linen and Lace

Blending old-world design with modern convenience, Linen and Lace offers eighteen lace curtain designs that capture the flavor of the past. Most of the material used is a polyester-cotton blend, completely machine washable. This lace can be used for more than just curtains. Other uses include bed canopies and dust ruffles.

The look of hand-crocheted lace is re-created in the delicate floral motif, Victorian Rose. The generously scalloped border is a handsome bonus. Victorian Rose comes in 12″, 24″, and 32″ lengths.

For a more formal appearance, there is the Catherine design, a delicate Scottish lace. A cascade of flowers adorns the scalloped border running along three edges of each panel. Catherine is available in 60″ widths and in lengths of 18″, 63″, 84″, and 90″.

Romantic Bavarian roses framed in lace and bordered with lavish bows give the Roses and Bows pattern an unusual texture and richness. Panel lengths include 12″, 24″, 32″, and 72″.

Catalogue, $2.

Linen and Lace
#4 Lafayette
Washington, MO 63090
(800) 332-5223
(314) 239-6499 (MO)

Lovelia

Lovelia has been selling the highest-quality reproduction Gobelin, Aubusson, and Beauvais tapestry weaves in North America for over twenty-five years. With more than five hundred different sizes and styles in stock, the firm can meet anyone's needs, whether they be for 10″-square pillows or 14′ nonrepeating murals. All tapestries are imported from France, Belgium, and Italy, the only countries where tapestries are woven exactly as the originals were years ago.

The vertical tapestry, 304A, the Horseman's Companion, is an example of a Beauvais French machine-woven wall hanging. Woven in natural colors of 100 percent cotton, its size is 52″ by 64″.

Lovelia also serves as consultants to museums, interior designers, architects, and others in related trades, advising them on period tapestries for the proper decor.

A visit to the company's showroom is recommended and is by appointment only.

Catalogue, $5.

Lovelia Enterprises, Inc.
356 E. 41st
New York, NY 10017
(212) 490-0930

Old Abingdon Weavers

The Goodwins were silk weavers in England prior to their move to the United States in 1837. Robert Harmon is a sixth-generation descendant who continues the family tradition of overshot coverlet weaving, creating fabrics in a 50-50 wool-cotton blend. Turn-of-the-century looms are still used, although they are no longer water powered.

The Whig Rose pattern is thought to have been created by the mountain women of Tennessee to honor Andrew Jackson, the first Whig to become president of the United States. Actually slightly altered from an old European draft, the Whig Rose is pattern is notable for its precise, symmetrical design. It is offered in two sizes, 80″ by 105″ and 108″ by 110″. Colors include navy, red, burgundy, forest green, brown, and more—all on a natural background.

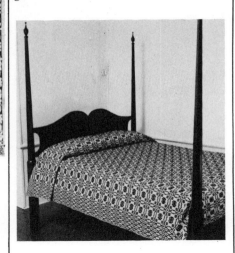

Brochure and color swatches, $3.

Old Abingdon Weavers
PO Box 786
Abingdon, VA 24210
(703) 628-4233

Partridge Replications

Former head of the costume and furnishings department at the famous Plimoth Plantation, Nancy Cook now works solely for Partridge Replications as an interior designer and consultant. Skilled in selecting and crafting appropriate accessories for 18th- and 19th-century homes, she offers her expertise in the selection of appropriate colors, wallpapers, fabrics, architectural treatments, curtain styles, lighting, and carpets.

Cook's speciality is custom draperies and bed hangings in a variety of styles using museum-documented reproduction fabrics from some of the country's premier manufacturers. The Sheraton field bed with the serpentine tester is dressed in an 18th-century fashion using Schumacher's Williamsburg Lozenge Floral patterned fabric.

Brochure available.

Partridge Replications
63 Penhallow St., Box 4104
Portsmouth, NH 03801
(603) 431-8733

Rue de France

Pamela Kelly selects all the lace patterns offered by her company on periodic trips to the Continent. Many different types of curtains and other decorative lace items are crafted from a machine-washable synthetic designed to simulate the delicate cotton originals.

Bands of white daisies contrast

with a delicate point d'esprit pattern in the company's most refined lace, appropriately named Marguerite after the French term for the daisy. Colors include beige or pure white.

Lilas is a pattern offered exclusively by Rue de France. A bouquet of delicate lilacs gathered with a ribbon of lace recalls the romance of the Victorian era.

In the Josephine lace pattern, garlands of flowers are gracefully gathered with bows, an effect that would have pleased Napoleon's Empress, for whom it was named.

A range of standard sizes is available for all the company's laces. The firm will also supply custom lengths and widths.

Catalogue, $2.

Rue de France
78 Thames St.
Newport, RI 02840
(401) 846-2084

Schumacher

As interest in preserving and restoring Art Deco buildings has grown in recent years, companies like Schumacher have begun producing fabrics and papers in patterns and colors that recall the 1930s. Schumacher's Radio City Music Hall collection of woven and printed fabrics adds to the company's highly-respected selection of period designs. There is a wide range of colorways to complement any setting.

The skyscraper, with its soaring lines, was a strong force in the development of 20th-century architecture. The motif is repeated in Metropolis, series 161940. A 58 percent linen-42 percent cotton blend, it is available in 54"-wide panels. Colorways include sunset, December morn, and blue dusk.

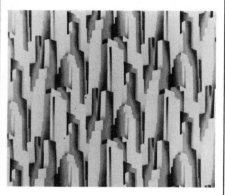

Proscenium, series 161850, was inspired by the great sunburst arch in the hall's auditorium. Made of 100 percent cotton in 54" widths, this pattern is offered in combinations of slate and shell, midnight, azure and amythest, and sea green and oyster.

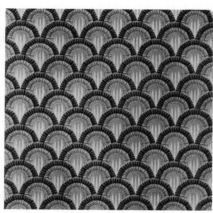

Deco Tulips, series 161900, a design drawn from the hall's archives, combines two important Deco elements—natural imagery and streamlined geometrics. It is printed on 100 percent cotton in 54″ widths and is offered in terra cotta, mauve, carnation red and blue, and gold and blue.

Showtime, series 161860, is a 58 percent linen-42 percent cotton blend on 54″-wide panels. The design is an adaptation of the original hand-blocked linen used in the hall's auditorium. Colorways include ebony, red, and navy. For more information on Schumacher fabrics, contact designers, select retail stores, or the firm itself.

F. Schumacher & Co.
79 Madison Ave.
New York, NY 10016
(212) 213-7900

Kathleen B. Smith

Kathleen B. Smith will develop and execute a complete period furnishings plan for a home or museum or simply supply the necessary elements. Her specialty is the reproduction of 18th-century fabrics. With experience as textiles curator at Colonial Williamsburg, she has a strong background in colonial weaving and needlework.

Smith selects all her tools, fibers, and dyes on the basis of their authenticity. Her skills in this area have been recognized by a number of historical museums that have used her custom-dyed fabrics in period rooms.

Smith has a number of hand-woven 18th-century reproduction textiles in stock, including plain and striped ticking, plain and patterned cottons, canvas, fustian, worsted and woolen twills, worsted tabby, linens in various weights and textures, linsey-woolsey, silk in a number of weights, and a wool-linen coverlet fabric. Wools are dyed in any one of fifty vegetable dye colors, while linens are left natural or bleached in her shop.

All Smith's threads are hand dyed with vegetable colors. She dyes two-ply and seven-strand silk for embroidery and sewing in a range of thirty-four colors. Since colors vary between dyeings, however, the customer should order enough for an entire project.

Smith also sells worsted yarns in two weights and fifty colors, including crimson, coral, black, walnut, blue, purple, and green. Perfect for canvas work, fine knitting, and crewelwork, this yarn comes in 120′, 240′, 480′, and 960′ skeins.

Linens, cotton, and wool trimming tapes and other hard-to-find sewing notions and accessories are also available in addition to a spectrum of other period furnishings. She is an expert at selecting appropriate period bed and table linens.

Literature available. Needlework catalogue, $3; reproduction fabric samples, $2.50; samples for fifty vegetable-dyed wools, $3; samples of thirty vegetable-dyed silks, $3; trimming tape samples, $3.

Kathleen B. Smith
PO Box 48
W. Chesterfield, MA 01084
(413) 296-4437

Sterling Prints

Mario Buatta's distinctive English country chintz style marries elegant comfort and British civility. It is a style appropriate for many period rooms. Sterling Prints offers his collection of wallpapers, companion borders, and coordinating fabrics.

The Peggy's Bouquet coordinating wallpaper and 100 percent cotton fabric features colorful, homey florals, large in scale yet surprisingly down to earth and unaffected in feeling. Ribbons are scattered in an expansive mazelike trail throughout.

Colorways for this pattern and others in the collection include pink, coral, geranium, claret, pewter, aqua, and other shades. There are a total of thirty-seven designs. There are also eighty-nine coordinating papers and thirteen border patterns.

Literature available.

Richard E. Thibaut

Now celebrating its centennial, Thibaut has more than earned its reputation as a supplier of high-quality papers and fabrics suitable for period rooms. Although most of the designs are not precise copies of historic documents, the papers and fabrics do capture the form and spirit of past styles.

Three fabrics from the firm's Waterford VI book are, in order of appearance: Wakefield damask, Buckingham, and Saratoga. Each is produced as a 100 percent cotton chintz in 54″ widths. There are four color schemes for each. Wakefield is available in navy and gold, pearl and off-white, pearl and mauve, and pearl and yellow; Saratoga in background colors of dark green, black, jade, or cream; and Buckingham, a paisley, in mauve and jade, peach and jade, rust and blue, and green-red-black.

The next pattern illustrated, Birmingham, is taken from an antique papier maché tray. The 54″-wide cotton print, part of the American Colonial XII collection, has been produced in collaboration with the Historical Society of Early American Decoration. The fabric is offered in four background colors: dark green, jade, navy, and terra cotta.

Hangar House Garden, the final fabric shown, is an example of the fine, historically documented materials that make up the Historic Homes of America collection. Recently introduced, this selection includes papers and fabrics used in nineteen American homes ranging in style from Federal to late Victorian. The original documents copied were selected by experts from the National Preservation Institute.

Hanger House is located in Little Rock, Arkansas, and is a Queen Anne residence built in 1870 and remodeled in 1889. The design is based on a paper used in the parlor. Fabric and paper are available in four background colors; cream, dark green, sky blue, and navy. As with the other examples from Thibaut, the fabric is 100 percent cotton and is produced in 54″ widths.

Thibaut fabrics are distributed nationally. If help is needed in locating a dealer, contact the company's home office.

Richard E. Thibaut, Inc.
706 S. 21st St.
Irvington, NJ 07111
(201) 399-7888

Tioga Mill Outlet

Anyone looking for a hard-to-find fabric or intending to purchase a large amount of material is advised to contact Tioga Mill Outlet. The outlet's prices are reasonable, a situation that may not be duplicated elsewhere. Tioga offers upholstery fabrics and supplies, as well as drapery fabrics of all makes and designs. These include muslin; osnaburg; plain and printed sheers; damask; moiré; linen; cotton, rayon, and nylon prints; plain, antique, and crushed velvet; and many others.

Out-of-town customers can order through the mail, first requesting a price estimate for the items on their shopping lists. If there is a need for information on various types of available fabrics, Tioga's designers can help out. They will send swatches of several fabrics to prospective customers who provide an idea of what they are looking for.

Literature available. Swatches, $2.

Tioga Mill Outlet
200 S. Hartman St.
York, PA 17403
(717) 843-5139

Van Luit

Albert Van Luit made a name for himself and his company by designing and manufacturing fabrics and wallcoverings in elegant, large-scale floral patterns printed over textured backgrounds. Soft translucent colors have always completed the Van Luit look that connoisseurs have come to appreciate.

Eugenie, series 172, is featured in Van Luit's Select Wovens series. It is a damask appropriate for upholstery, and is printed in 54"-wide strips of a cotton-rayon blend. Colorways include garnet, blossom pink, Flemish blue, cafe au lait, ivory, maize, peach, blue, or antique rose.

The tone-on-tone satin Cortley pattern, series 174, is composed of stripes varying in width. It is available in six subtle colorways, including camellia, champagne, blush, pistachio, Holland blue, or rosewood. This fabric is 100 percent cotton and is also made in 54"-wide strips.

The firm's showrooms are located in Boston, New York, Chicago, San Francisco, and Los Angeles. Contact the main office for further information regarding the availability of these fabrics.

Albert Van Luit & Co.
200 Garden City Plaza
Garden City, NY 11530
(516) 741-9440

Vintage Valances

Vintage Valance's selection of window draping ranges from styles of the late 1700s through the 1800s, with an emphasis on Greek Revival and Victorian valances. The company's artisans take measurements supplied, individually translate the size, and cut the fabric into the proper shapes. Valances are shipped ready to hang.

Valance style P1034 is a typical Greek Revival form dating to the early 1800s. The unusual shield-like escutcheon swag with fringe provides all the ornamentation necessary.

Style P712 epitomizes the neoclassical spirit of this same period. The "toga tossed over a pole" valance was sometimes supported by quarter-moon-shaped brackets, the valance being hung from the horns of the moon.

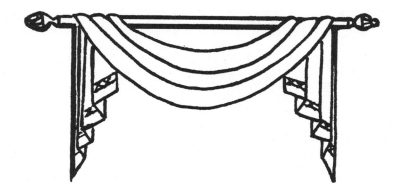

Valance design B204 dates to 1839. Shown beneath a gilt cornice, it is decorated only with a band and lush fringe along its straight edge. Only on the returns does the valance cascade into long tails.

The space between the pleats is taut to create a crisper appearance, and floor-length side curtains are tied up with cord and tassles.

Model P1058 is a flamboyant design waiting to be tossed over spear poles, as was done with many Empire-inspired valances.

The central swag hangs over the pole while side sways dip below it before joining the tails. The long fringe adds to the reserved frivolity of this late-Victorian design.

Vintage Valances offers decorative domestic and European trim, and the company also fashions window shades in the old style, with wooden rollers and firm cotton fabrics in several colors.

Catalogue with sketches, photographs, and fabric swatches, $12.

Vintage Valances
PO Box 43326-C
Cincinnati, OH 45243
(513) 561-8665

Other Suppliers of Fabrics

Consult List of Suppliers for addresses

Angel House
Larua Ashley
Louis W. Bowen
Nina Campbell
Clarence House/Colefax and Fowler
Cowtan and Tout
Design Archives
Lee Joffa
Museum of American Textile History
Osborne and Little
Raintree Designs
Ramm, Son & Crocker, Ltd.
Sanderson
Scalamandré
Shaker Workshops
Standard Trimming
John Stefandis & Associates
Victorian Collectibles
Warner Fabrics
Watts & Co.
Waverley Fabrics
Zoffany

8.
Outdoor and Garden Areas

An old-fashioned garden and handsomely landscaped grounds greatly enhance the pleasure and value of an old house. Such simple amenities as a path lined with mature trees, a well-tended perennial bed, and pines that shelter birds in winter do not usually come with a new house. These features are as much a result of the workings of time and nature as they are of human design. Yet, there are still rules and methods which guide the activity of the successful home gardener. This is particularly true of planning period gardens and other elements of historic landscape design.

Our knowledge of the kind of plant materials and forms used in times past is still being gathered by horticultural historians. The propagation of new forms of old-fashioned flowers, for example, remains an industry in its infancy. Most period gardens are informal attemps at creating old-fashioned effects. To add to the period appearance, decorative objects such as urns and vases, birdbaths and fountains, benches and statuary are used. Unless the grounds of an old house are well documented in photographs or drawings, however, there is no way to know for sure whether the present plantings are historically accurate or not. Anyone planning or re-creating a period garden must gain a knowledge of what plant types were common at various times in the region in which they live and how they were used.

The use of period garden ornaments, fencing, and various kinds of outbuildings is somewhat easier to ascertain. The design of these objects has not changed greatly over the years. Today many attractive and useful garden ornaments are being reproduced. Even old-fashioned types of outdoor furniture are coming back into use. Gazebos and conservatories—not seen since the early 1900s—are very much in vogue. The proper design and placement of these structures, however, is still being studied. Buildings of this sort, while decorative, served a practical function as well as an aesthetic one. The gazebo, for example, was often centered on a grassy knoll or rocky promontory so as to receive the cooling effects of a breeze. The structure was not plunked down in the middle of a backyard as a type of miniature bandstand or shelter for a hot tub.

The suppliers of period products, services, and materials described in the following pages are recommended for their reliability and quality. They range from landscape architects to manufacturers of cast-stone ornaments. Each individual or firm has a special interest in creating attractive outdoor settings of historic character.

Cast- and wrought-iron fencing, Salem, Massachusetts, restored by Cassidy Brothers Forge, Rowley, Massachusetts.

201

Outdoor Furniture

Demand for solid, well-designed lawn and garden furnishings has increased dramatically in recent years. Polyvinyl chairs and settees are an improvement over the rickety metal tubular models of the 1950s and '60s, but nothing can replace pieces made according to old-fashioned methods and using authentic designs. Unfortunately, because of the high cost of cast iron, most reproductions are fashioned of cast aluminum, but this material can be given sufficient strength in the manufacturing process to approximate the solidity, but not the weight, of iron.

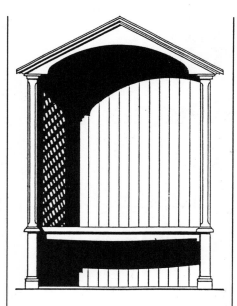

Architectural Iron

One of Architectural Iron's many successfully reproduced historic ironwork designs is the Gramercy Park bench. The firm has been licensed to build the bench by the trustees of Gramercy Park in New York City.

Architectural Iron will reproduce any piece of cast or wrought ironwork from fragments, photographs, or measured drawings. In addition to making cast- and wrought-iron reproductions, the company provides consultation and will produce custom designs. The firm also restores ironwork at its large foundry complex in Pennsylvania.

Visits to the foundry in the upper Delaware valley are welcome. Call or write for specific information and project estimates.

Literature available.

Architectural Iron Co.
PO Box 126, Schocopee Rd.
Milford, PA 18337
(717) 296-7722
(212) 243-2664

Cumberland General Store

Once a fixture in Victorian neighborhoods, the porch swing has come back into fashion. The pleasure of sitting outdoors, swaying slowly in the gentle summer breeze, is still the same. Cumberland General Store offers several varieties of old-fashioned porch swings.

The standard swing is constructed of solid hardwood with tenoned joints and a contoured seat. Each swing package comes complete with ceiling hooks and chain (two 4½' leaders with 2½' branches). Minor assembly is required since the swing is shipped flat for easy handling. All the necessary hardware is included.

With over 200 pages of diverse merchandise to choose from, this company's extensive catalog will interest most mail-order fans.

Catalogue, $3.

Cumberland General Store
Rte. 3
Crossville, TN 38555
(800) 334-4640
(615) 484-8481 (TN)

The English Garden

If a bench does not provide enough comfort and a pavilion occupies too much space, English Garden offers the alternative of a covered seat. The seat easily blends with most settings, formal or country. The covered piece gives a sense of privacy and provides protection from the elements. With a pewter-colored fiberglass roof, each model is fashioned of strong Swedish pine. The side trellising is also sturdy pine.

The Classic covered seat is 6'6" high and 4'6" wide, with a symmetrically sloped roof design. The seat is available in a variety of natural colors, including white, brown, gray, red, and blue.

Catalogue, $6.

The English Garden, Inc.
652 Glenbrook Rd.
Stamford, CT 06906
(203) 348-3048

Gloster

Is there a special place in the yard for relaxation? If so, make it a little more comfortable without spoiling any of its natural charm, with one of Gloster's outdoor benches. Constructed in England of solid teak, one of the finest hardwoods in the world, this outdoor furnishing is extremely durable and impervious to sun, rain, snow, or frost, and needs no paint or preservatives. Teak ages to a soft silvery-gray or it may be oiled to retain its original coloration.

The Gloster model is one of the company's sturdiest. This seat blends in with any setting. The lengths run from 4' to 8', and the other proportions vary accordingly.

The Marlborough model is built from a much more decorative, Victorian design. With the same strength and lasting qualities of teak, this bench will be the focal

point of any garden setting. It is 6' long, 41¼" high, and 21" deep.

Steptoe and Wife Antiques Ltd. serve as Gloster's North American distributor.

Literature available.

Gloster Leisure Furniture Ltd.
Steptoe & Wife Antiques, Ltd.
322 Geary Ave.
Toronto, Ontario, Canada M6H 2C7
(416) 530-4200

Irreplaceable Artifacts

Wreckage entrepreneur Evan Blum's company, Irreplaceable Artifacts, stocks over fifteen floors of rescued and restored architectural artifacts at three locations in downtown Manhattan. If the company does not have a particular item, Blum and his team will search out and usually discover what is needed to fill a specific request. Of course, certain original designs are so highly sought that there aren't enough to accommodate all customers. The company has therefore begun reproducing select designs, particularly garden ornaments and outdoor furniture.

One of the company's most popular dining sets is the Oakwood, with its delicate tracery of vines and grapes. Cast of lightweight and durable aluminum, each chair is 30" high and 21" wide. Finishes include gloss white, satin black, and antique verdigris, and the set is shipped assembled.

The company fashions a line of benches in stone and metal. The Lily bench is 60" wide and 32" high. Matching chairs are available, too. Modeled after a 19th-century British original, it is made

of cast aluminum. Available in gloss white or satin black, this bench has optional fitted cushions.

Catalogue, $3.

Irreplaceable Artifacts
14 Second Ave.
New York, NY 10003
(212) 777-2900

Robinson Iron

Each piece of Robinson Iron's handsome ornamental cast iron-work is reproduced from authentic pre-Civil War patterns. Since 1946 the company's skilled craftsmen have been pouring molten iron into sand molds made from hand-carved wooden patterns. Robinson Iron produces everything from fountains and furniture to urns and vases.

The Fern furniture group, consisting of settee and chair, brings an antique look and solid craftsmanship to any garden or patio.

Intricately detailed, the settee is almost 3' high and 4'10" long. The chair is 2'8" high and just about 2' wide.

Robinson Iron offers a range of finishes, including gloss black, gloss white, matte black, verdigris, Pompeiian green, and bronze. Custom work of all kinds is undertaken, too.

Catalogue, $3.

Robinson Iron Corp.
Robinson Rd.
Alexander City, AL 35010
(205) 329-8486

There are various motifs and symbols such as Cherub, Lion, Sun, Zodiac Signs, and Celtic Design, all of which are generally interchangeable among the many styles of dials. Inscriptions are a common feature of antique sundials, and Abbey Garden will include one of your choice if requested.

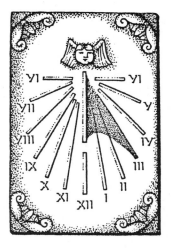

Cast bronze is used for all models, and each is given a satin polish finish which will weather naturally.

Lawn and Garden Ornaments

No garden is truly complete without some type of sculpture or ornament. Even an object as simple as a pedestal birdbath can give an outdoor space a special character. Urns, vases, sundials, wall and freestanding fountains—the choices are many. The available amount of outdoor space will determine to some degree just how extensively durable objects of stone and iron may be employed. But even in the limited outdoor area found around the typical town house, ornamental objects can be effectively used.

Abbey Garden Sundials

Sundials have existed since prehistoric times. Among the first permanent forms were those was used in the Egypt of the Pharoahs. When properly constructed, sundials are still the perfect time-keepers for the natural world. They are Abbey Garden's sole product and are made in Wales by bronze founder Andrew Evans and sculptor Christopher Tynan.

Illustrated are, in order of appearance, the Zodiac Convoluted Round dial, one foot in diameter;

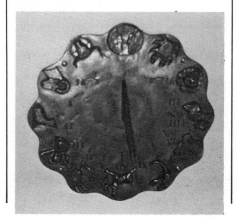

the Sun Square, 9" square; the Cherub Scroll, 8" wide and one foot tall; and the Lion armillary, 10" high.

All models are custom made for the latitude in which the customer lives. (The standard for Canada, for example, is Latitude 45° North.) The customer must also indicate whether a model is to be mounted horizontally or on a wall and, for wall sundials, the direction the wall faces.

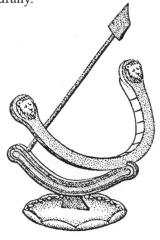

Catalogue, $1.

Abbey Garden Sundials
PO Box 102, Indian Hill Rd.
Pakenham, Ontario, Canada K0A 2X0
(613) 256-3973

The English Garden

Although The English Garden's clientele is mostly interested in pavilions, trellises, porches, and covered seats, the company also provides housing for birds. An integral part of many British gardens is a birdhouse or dovecote. Several bird feeders and birdhouses in various styles are offered, crafted of the same materials and with the same care and quality as all English Garden products.

The bird table, EG910P, is 3' wide at its base and 7'9" tall. With a lead-colored fiberglass roof and finial, it is carefully detailed and then finished with a white preservative paint. The package includes pegs for properly securing the bird table to the ground or deck on which it stands.

The dovecote is 72" high, 29½" wide, and 16½" deep, fashioned of Swedish pine. It is available in a natural or white-painted finish.

Catalogue, $6.

The English Garden, Inc.
652 Glenbrook Rd.
Stamford, CT 06906
(203) 348-3048

Irreplaceable Artifacts

Rescuing parts of old buildings for recycling into new structures, Irreplaceable Artifacts stocks decorative garden objects among its many treasures. Having collected many 19th-century patterns from foundries across North America and in Europe, Irreplaceable Artifacts has recently responded to the incredibly high demand for these products by reproducing them.

Cast in aluminum, the outdoor furnishings and ornaments are lightweight, strong, easy-to-move,

and rustproof. The Italian urn is one of several containers offered. It is 20" high and 16" in diameter.

Lazy Hill Farm Designs

What garden or yard would be complete without its complement of animals and birds? Lazy Hill Farm Designs' birdhouse and bird feeders ensure that at least the birds will always be present. Constructed of North Carolina cypress with cedar shingles, each design is handcrafted for strength, beauty, and lasting pleasure.

The company's birdhouse is an adaptation of an English dovecote design. Measuring 28" tall and 14" in diameter, each house has eight individual compartments. The focal point of any garden, the

The Large Lion lavabo is 29½" high and 18¼" wide. It can function as a planter, ash urn, or wall decoration. It also may be fitted with piping and a water pump to make a beautiful fountain.

All pieces are offered in a glossy white, satin black, or antique verdigris finish.

Catalogue, $3.

Irreplaceable Artifacts
14 Second Ave.
New York, NY 10003
(212) 777-2900

...se is available painted
... or stained gray.

...he pentagonal feeding station has octagonal posts and fits into any garden setting. It measures 28" tall and 16" wide. Seeds may be scattered along the flat base of the feeding station, which is finished in either white or gray stain.

Optional with all orders is a 4" square treated cypress post with chamfered corners at the top. This post comes painted white, stained, or unfinished. Mounting brackets are included with every order.

Catalogue, $1.

Lazy Hill Farm Designs
Lazy Hill Rd.
Colerain, NC 27924
(919) 356-2828

Kenneth Lynch & Sons

The venerable firm of Kenneth Lynch & Sons has one of the broadest selections of lawn and garden ornaments ever assembled. Lynch's craftsmen have produced items in shapes, sizes, and designs that would be impossible for any other single company to stock. Some of the materials used in making these ornaments include cast stone, bronze, lead, fiberglass, and wrought iron.

The company's garden statuary seems to include every figurative subject from birds to animals, classic busts, fish, frogs, and even

a statue of Teddy Roosevelt. The cast-stone figure of a child, number 4929, is available in two sizes: 34" long, 17" wide, and 22½" high; or 15" long, 6½" wide, and 10½" high.

Another manner of garden ornament manufactured by Lynch is a line of birdbaths. Model 88 can also be used as a feeder. It is 28" high and 24" in diameter and is made of cast stone with an antique finish. For the devoted bird lover, the company also offers a heated model.

Literature, $6.

Kenneth Lynch & Sons
Box 488
Wilton, CT 06897-0488
(203) 762-8363

Lehman Hardware

End the nuisance of muddy shoes and tracked-in dirt the old-fashioned way with a cast-iron bootscraper. Handsome and extremely practical, the scrapers made by Lehman Hardware come in different sizes and styles, including a very plain deck model and several more ornate Victorian designs.

The company's Garden bootscraper is the only one designed

to be mounted in the ground. The others are meant for placement on a porch or in an entryway. Measuring 8½" wide by 12½" high, the "H"-shaped scraper gets mud off both the sides and the bottoms of boots. It is mountable anywhere outside to prevent unsightly scrapings on the doorstep or mud in the house.

Lehman Hardware offers a huge collection of other items, too. The company's catalogue is well worth investigating.

Catalogue, $2.

Lehman Hardware and Appliance, Inc.
PO Box 41, 4779 Kidron Rd.
Kidron, OH 44636
(216) 857-5441

Stewart Iron Works

Iron fencing, gates, and ornamental metal decorations of all kinds have been Stewart Iron's specialty for over a century. Whether restoring an original work, reproducing a period design, or creating and forging an original pattern, this company has the facilities and experience to ensure a quality product.

The company's ornamental wellheads are interesting iron decorations. Offered in various styles and sizes, they are suitable for sheltering old open wells with style and grace.

Literature, $2.

Stewart Iron Works Company
PO Box 2612, 20 W. 18th St.
Covington, KY 41012
(606) 431-1985

United House Wrecking

Who knows where United House Wrecking finds all of its lawn and garden furniture and ornamentation. In throw-away America, however, there never seem to be a dearth of reusable salvage. Everything from the unusual to the outrageous can be found in the company's 30,000 square feet of display space. Pottery, statuary, furniture, fountains, birdbaths, planters, urns, benches, pedestals, tables, gargoyles, fencing, gates, and gazebos are available. The company travels the globe seeking interesting and attractive items to meet all decorating and restoration needs.

Visits to the warehouse and grounds in Stamford are recommended, and phone calls are welcome. No catalogue is available, however, since the firm's substantial inventory is in constant flux.

United House Wrecking
535 Hopt St.
Stamford, CT 06906
(203) 348-5371

Fences, Gates, Trellises, and Grates

Attractive fences and gates can add immeasurably to a property's ambiance. Used to define a garden, a yard, or a complete city lot, a fence provides a modicum of protection from human and animal predators as well. At one time almost all small town and rural properties made some use of fencing. Wood picket fences were the most popular; more ambitious designs were fabricated of iron. Because it is subject to harsh outdoor conditions, most antique fencing has not weathered well, and the same problems of deterioration affect reproductions of antique designs. Fencing that will last for more than a generation or two must be fabricated of the best possible materials, among them redwood and well-tempered iron.

Architectural Iron

Commissioned by the United States State Department, Architectural Iron is restoring the cast-iron fence surrounding historic Blair House. Located directly across from the White House, Blair House, built in 1822, has served recently as a guest house for visiting heads of state and other dignitaries.

Since 1984 the nation's foremost craftsmen have been restoring this dwelling to its original condition. Architectural Iron's task involves making patterns and new castings for the fence sections that were lost in storage or damaged over the years.

in mind, Architectural Iron has the craftsmen and facilities to meet such needs. The company also stocks a wide selection of standard items and designs, planned and crafted with the same high standards that custom orders receive.

Cassidy Brothers Forge

Cassidy manfuactures original wrought ironwork, but the company also restores both cast and wrought iron. Fencing, gates, and grille work are Cassidy's forte. From Gothic to contemporary designs, solid constructon provides safety and ensures privacy, while attractive ornamentation adds a refined, stately touch to any building.

In Salem, Massachusetts, Cassidy's workmen restored over half a mile of cast- and wrought-iron fence around the town common, using custom patterns designed to duplicate exactly the original missing components. Over twenty-five tons of new cast iron was needed to complete the project.

In restoration work, the company uses the same methods of hand-forging and fastening that were originally employed. Color galvanizing preserves the work for the future.

Be it Blair House or your house, Architectural Iron takes on projects of any size. The firm works not only in cast iron, but in wrought iron and combinations of cast and wrought iron. If there is a particular fence pattern that needs reproducing or if a customer has a specific, original design

Literature available.

*Architectural Iron Company
PO Box 126, Schocopee Rd.
Milford, PA 18337
(717) 296-7722
(212) 243-2664*

Cassidy Brothers' gate hinges and latches are stainless steel with long-wearing bronze bushings to ensure lasting strength. All exterior ironwork is given a protective finish against rust.

In addition to custom manufacturing, Cassidy Brothers will help design specific projects. Ironwork can be shipped anywhere in the country or abroad.

Catalogue available.

Cassidy Brothers Forge, Inc.
US Rte. 1
Rowley, MA 01969-1796
(508) 948-7303

Cross

Latticework is an integral part of many outdoor architectural forms, and it is an attractive addition to most settings. Normally constructed of wood, lattice can be inconvenient, however, since it is subject to the ravages of the elements. Cross's latticework is fashioned of a vinyl compound. Lasting much longer than wood lattice, Cross's product is available in a number of styles and sizes and is easy to install. It can be sawed or drilled at home and attached without pre-drilling nail holes.

The designs provide an excellent selection for the homeowner looking to replace existing wood lattice at a low cost or to enhance the style of a house with the addition of new latticework on a porch or stairway.

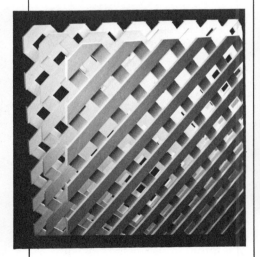

Scale drawings of all Cross's stock designs are available on request. The vinyl lattice comes in several standard colors, including white, Dominion blue, Williamsburg green, and acorn. Custom colors can also be ordered.

Literature available.

Cross Industries
3174 Marjan Dr.
Atlanta, GA 30340
(404) 451-4531

Custom Ironworks

Fencing and gates are the sole concern of the ironworkers at Custom Ironworks. Styles range from simple and functional to ornate high-Victorian designs. The company's huge collection of patterns allows for an exact match with most fencing requests, but, if

wide and 5' high, 14' wide and 6' high, and 16' wide and 7' high.

Literature available.

Custom Ironworks, Inc.
PO Box 99
Union, KY 41091
(606) 384-4486

this is not possible, custom fence or gate fabricating is an option.

Fence style 112 is fashioned with straightforward individual components, but the overall effect is imaginative. Each fence panel comes 80" long and is easily bolted to the next section. The fence height when set is either 36" or 48".

Much more decoratively crafted is estate gate 500, with its scrollwork and intricate detailing. This gate is ideal for any Victorian home, and it is available in three sizes—12'

The English Garden

The English Garden's Traditional Trellis designs are the direct successors of the classical forms of the great European gardens and terraces. Widely used since Roman times, a trellis serves as a framework to support vines, fruit trees, or climbing plants. Trellising is also used in arbors and to form natural tunnels and other landscaping effects. Whether installed inside or out, freestanding or mounted panels can also disguise unsightly views, extend walls, or create alcoves in which to display statuary.

finish, each panel will accept most stains or can be painted white.

The Roman trellis panels have curved upper portions and stand 90″ high and 37¼″ wide. The posts with spear finials are 3″ wide and stand 85″ high. Detailed

Marmion Plantation

Using a 17th-century picket fence design, Marmion Plantation reproduces the wood Diamondtop pickets that will fit many architectural settings. As versatile and sturdy as the more common and much less attractive stockade fencing popular today, the pickets feature a diamond pattern which creates an interesting architectural effect.

Traditional Trellis latticework is all fashioned in a standard diamond pattern and is both durable and elegant. The collection consists of seven panel shapes and two complete arbors. Constructed of European redwood and given a natural

instructions are included with each order so that assembly will be efficient and easy.

Catalogue, $6.

The English Garden, Inc.
652 Glenbrook Rd.
Stamford, CT 06906
(203) 348-3048

At ¾″ thick, 4½″ wide, and 60″ tall, these pickets will form a 5′-high fence when set 3″ below ground level, high enough to keep pets and children within the yard. Marmion also makes this same style of fencing in 72″-high pickets that may be placed edge to edge to guarantee extra privacy.

Literature available.

Marmion Plantation Co.
RD 2, Box 458
Fredericksburg, VA 22405
(703) 775-3480

Neenah Foundry

Tree grates are a welcome addition to an urban streetscape. These devices are both practical and decorative. Neenah Foundry's selection of cast-iron grates is quite large; custom designs can be fabricated as well.

The R-8714 grate is 60″ square with an 18″ inner diameter for the tree trunk and ⅜″ slot openings. Four 1′-diameter holes are left for staking the tree. A cast-iron frame is optional.

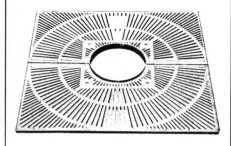

The R-8730 grate is 48″ square with a 17″ inner diameter. The special leaf pattern adds a complementary decorative touch. The grate is nonexpandable and also comes with an optional cast-iron frame.

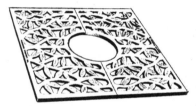

The R-8831-1 grate has a 48″ outer diameter and an 18″ inner diameter. Designed for use with subgrade light fixtures, this three-piece grate requires support at the section joints and is nonexpandable.

The foundry also makes expandable grates for trees and light fixtures. To complement the firm's line of grates are five tree guard designs, cast in a way that allows them to be attached to any type of grate. Available preassembled or not, each guard is 4′, 5′, or 6′ high. The diameter must be specified by the customer.

Catalogue available.

Neenah Foundry
Box 729, 2121 Brooks Ave.
Neenah, WI 54956
(414) 725-7000

Nostalgia

Beautifully patterned and carefully detailed cast-iron grillwork decorates many balconies, fences, and gates in old Savannah and other historic American cities. Nostalgia has spent years researching and locating the most beautiful of these designs. They are reproduced today with all the elegance of the past.

The Taylor Street and Gordon Street panels are two of the most attractive of Nostalgia's extensive

collection of intricately formed panels. They are available in cast iron, as were the originals, or in cast aluminum.

In addition to these panels, Nostalgia offers a vast selection of reproduction Southern architectural antiques. The firm also undertakes custom decorative ironwork and brasswork. Contact Nostalgia for a firm quotation for any project, large or small.

Catalogue, $2.50.

Nostalgia, Inc.
307 Stiles Ave.
Savannah, GA 31401
(800) 874-0015
(912) 232-2324 (GA)

Schwartz's Forge

Joel Schwartz's iron- and metalwork have been displayed at such prestigious institutions as the Smithsonian Institution in Washington, D. C., and the Museum of Contemporary Crafts in New York City. Schwartz is an artist as well as a respected craftsman. His best work is of his own design, whether closely modeled on original period metalwork or on more modern lines.

Schwartz was commissioned by the United States State Department to work with a group of the nation's finest craftsmen on the White House guest residence, Blair House, home to visiting dignitaries and heads of state. Drawing on period designs from the Philadelphia area, Schwartz's authentically crafted ironwork makes up the second-story balcony of an addition to the building on two sides of a courtyard. The total length of this project is 80' and the height is 3'. Each side has two curved balconies in addition to a straight walkway in between.

Anyone seeking fine metalwork such as fences, gates, railings, or ornamental window grilles is advised to contact Joel Schwartz. Everything he undertakes is a custom job and receives the

special attention it deserves. He can provide original designs, adaptations of traditional pieces, or faithful reproductions.

Literature, $4.

Schwartz's Forge and Metalworks
PO Box 205, Forge Hollow Rd.
Deansboro, NY 13328
(315) 841-4477

Stewart Iron Works

Stewart fabricates all sorts of work in cast and wrought iron, but specializes in fence and gate designs which are unexcelled in variety of design and size. The company's newel posts, for example, offer ornamental relief and highly decorative styling in addition to practicality and versatility. Constructed as flat newels, these may be used in pairs as two-way posts for corners, or they may be used in groups of four as square posts for ends or gateways.

Newel style 31, with its circular cast-iron top ornament, is 10" wide. Style 32, slightly more ornate, is 12" wide. Style 34, 12½" wide, is the most intricate of all the designs.

Interior and exterior gates have been manufactured by Stewart for over fifty years. Romantically flowing curves make design L-964 one of the company's most popular. It comes in various custom sizes.

Literature, $2.

Stewart Iron Works Company
PO Box 2612, 20 W 18th St.
Covington, KY 41012
(606) 431-1985

To match the gates, Stewart fashions gateway arches in an infinite number of custom styles from simple to elaborate. The company can affix logos, letters, or numbers on request. Model number one is an example of the company's more standardized designs and is frequently requested.

Outdoor Structures

Outbuildings such as the gazebo and pavilion and add-ons like a conservatory or greenhouse have attracted more and more attention in the past few years. Back in the early 1900s, a prosperous country property might have contained a number of outbuildings and an attached greenhouse. There is very little practical need for some of these auxiliary structures today, but they do form part of an historical record. Lack of utility notwithstanding, a gazebo or pavilion can provide a welcome shady nook on a hot summer day. Attractive outbuildings of almost every style and historic character are offered today in plan, kit, or assembled form.

Amdega

Conservatories are almost as popular today as they were in Victorian times. Greenhouses, as conservatories are usually called, are no longer just for plants, but are places for people, too. With graceful lines and an air of romance, these buildings are timeless; they are suitable additions to almost any style home. Amdega Conservatories, an English company, designs a variety of energy-

saving models easily adapted to a client's needs.

In the United States the company has representatives who will visit serious customers to discuss ideas and draw up sketches. The modular conservatories can be installed within fourteen weeks from the date that they are ordered.

The brick or stone bases for all Amdega additions must be constructed prior to the erection of the structure itself. Once an order is received, the plans for the base are sent ahead so that a local builder can begin this construction.

Amdega offers two basic modular designs which can be combined in an infinite variety of ways for as many different effects. These two types are the octagonal and the rectangular (lean-to), the former freestanding and the latter requiring some type of structural support. Illustrated is a standard octagonal model measuring 15'1"

by 19'2⅛". All Amdega frames are fashioned from Western red cedar, a wood prized for its durability. Double-glazing is standard in all conservatories sold in North America.

All materials—frame, glass, and finishing paint—are shipped in easy-to-handle sections; shipping costs are included in the initial estimate. An installation service is also available, if necessary, on a fee basis.

Literature available.

Amdega Conservatories
Boston Design Center
One Design Center Plaza, Suite 624
Boston, MA 02210
(617) 951-2755

struction with a raised patterned deck and a cedar shake roof. Each plan package comes with three detailed drawings, 17" by 22", which contain all the information that a customer or his contractor will need for estimates and construction. A materials list is also included.

Literature, $10.

A. S. L. Associates, Architects
5182 Maple
Irvine, CA 92715
(415) 344-5044

Building Conservation

For the ambitious amateur builder, Building Conservation has developed a number of plans for additions, alterations, and completely new structures. Building Conservation provides imaginative project designs. Shown are the Eastlake carriage shed, the Gothic kennel, and the Gothic garden shed.

The Eastlake carriage shed is 12' wide and 20' long, with a 6' by 14' porch. It is named for the style of wood ornamentation which embellished many plain Victorian

A. S. L. Associates

For the home handyman or for anyone wishing to supervise the construction of his own gazebo, A. S. L. Associates has just the service required. A gazebo can serve to enhance a garden or other outdoor setting in a variety of ways, including acting as a shady resting place and winter storage area.

A. S. L. Associates provides plans for a six-sided gazebo with posts on each corner and an 8' diameter. The inside height is 7'4", and the design calls for wood con-

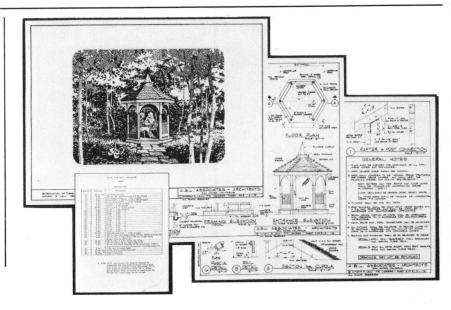

213

buildings, from barns to train stations. The Gothic kennel, only for the discerning dog, is designed in a style similar to its namesake and is 3' wide and 4' long. The Gothic garden shed, designed in a style popular from about 1830 to 1880, is 8' by 8', large enough to serve a variety of purposes and small enough to fit nicely in most yards.

All of Building Conservation's plans are designed for assembly with easily attainable materials and common tools.

Catalogue, $5.

Building Conservation
2204 Ludington Ave.
Wauwatosa, WI 53226
(414) 475-1896

Dalton Pavilions

Dalton offers gazebo kits in several styles and many sizes for any homeowner who wishes to add an outdoor living space for relaxation. Constructed entirely of Western red cedar, each gazebo can be assembled by two people in one day. The designs are carefully worked out so that one would never suspect that the finished product was fashioned

from a kit. Screening and matching tables and benches are optional with every model. Dalton Pavilion's gazebos may be stained, painted, or left to weather naturally.

The Williamsburg gazebo is based on a colonial design. Thirteen feet wide, this model is completely screened. The standard wooden flooring was omitted from the model illustrated so that the gazebo could be placed on the customer's brick patio.

Dalton gazebos are available through landscape architects and designers nationwide. Many dealers will also provide construction services.

Brochure available.

Dalton Pavilions, Inc.
7260-68 Oakley St.
Philadelphia, PA 19111
(215) 342-9804

The English Garden

The British are world-famous for their appreciation and care of gardens and parks. Ornamental

garden buildings not only add to the beauty of these settings, attractively mingling the man-made and the natural, but they provide a place for reflection and contemplation of the surrounding environment.

English Garden's Hexagonal pavilion is styled in the classic British gazebo tradition. The graceful bell-shaped roof and ball finial are both made of fiberglass, naturally colored to look like lead. The generous overhang protects the wood structure and decorative elements. Trellis screens shelter the interior on three sides, below which are fitted comfortable

214

bench seats. This structure is 7' 2" wide and 10' 6" high, including the finial. A level base is required for properly erecting the pavilion.

The company's Gothic porch is an aesthetically pleasing way in which to protect a doorway from the elements. With a fiberglass roof and latticed sides, this porch comes either in a natural finish or painted. It is 77½" wide, 52" high, and 28" deep.

Catalogue, $6.

The English Garden, Inc.
652 Glenbrook Rd.
Stamford, CT 06906
(203) 348-3048

Everlite Greenhouses

Everlite has developed a line of period conservatories that combines traditional elegance and romantic lines with modern reliability and efficiency.

Recognizing the considerable investment undertaken by a customer, Everlite suggests that a client begin working out his solarium design with an Everlite representative. Once early design and siting plans have been set, a professional architect or designer, chosen by either the customer or the company, will step in.

Everlite conservatories are fashioned of Brazilian mahogany as a rule, but custom orders in other woods are welcome. A list of some 200 different woods, among them white oak, black walnut, and cherry, is available. The exterior wood surface is treated with a patented glazing material so that it needs little maintenance. The interior retains the traditional character of a conservatory. All Everlite solariums are provided with 1"-thick bronze-tinted, insulated glass panels.

Catalogue, $5.

Everlite Greenhouses, Inc.
9305 Gerwig Ln., Suite H
Guilford Industrial Park
Columbia, MD 21046
(301) 381-3880

Gazebo Woodcrafters

Looking for a weekend project? How about building a gazebo? With a kit from Gazebo Woodcrafters and a base in place, an outdoor pavilion can be put together in forty-eight hours.

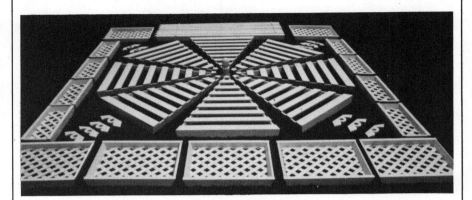

Three versions of the standard octagonal design are available. Each is made from kiln-dried Western red cedar, an exceptionally sturdy wood. The gazebo parts are precut (as shown in this picture), presanded, and ready for paint, stain, or varnish. In addition to exterior finishing, a level surface or base platform on which to set the gazebo will have to be provided. The kit comes complete with hardware, including a screwdriving bit and easy-to-follow instructions.

Shown is the completed Country model with 2" by 2" railings, slatted top and bottom panels, and a slatted roof. Variations include a choice of slatted or lattice top, bot-

tom, and roof sections. Shakes or shingles can be added to the roof. Gazebos are made in diameters of 8', 9', 10', or 12'. Entryways for each model are 6'6", leaving ample head room and no feeling of being hemmed in.

Kits can be ordered directly from the company or through area dealers.

Brochure available.

Gazebo Woodcrafters
205 Virginia St.
Bellingham, WA 98225
(206) 734-0463

New England Outbuildings

Dotting the New England countryside are many farms that have existed for centuries. These farms consist of farmhouses and a wide assortment of practical outbuildings. New England Outbuildings reproduces a variety of these structures in the form of frame kits for the modern do-it-yourselfer.

Each frame is hand-built, carefully preserving the original lines, proportions, and details so that an exact copy always results. All framing is of post-and-beam construction with mortise-and-tenon joinery fastened by wooden pegs. Hand-finished joints and housings are carved by craftsmen skilled in the techniques of 18th-century housewrights.

The Three-Bay wagon shed is one of the company's most popular designs. The large 18' by 36' size makes it extremely practical, and its appearance allows it to blend in almost any setting.

with 177 square feet of floor space; 12½' square and 12'1" high with 130 square feet; and 10' square and 11'1" high with 83 square feet of floor space.

The Daniel Meigs corn crib is an attractive, though slightly smaller, outbuilding. It can serve as a tool or garden shed. The entire structure measures 10' by 16'.

Each of New England Outbuildings' frame kits comes with all the necessary timber and pegs; written, illustrated instructions are also included. In addition, if there

The wood may be stained, painted, or left to weather naturally. Several skirting options are offered. Interior paneling can be made up of 1' by 4' tongue and groove boards. Another choice is the use of pickets and full screening on the inside. A cupola is standard, but an 8" standing-seam copper roof is also available.

Hardware is included with the package for easy assembly at home. Outdoor Designs also provides assembly services. Contact the firm to work out all the details.

Literature available.

Outdoor Designs
197 George St.
Excelsior, MN 55331
(612) 474-8328

Palm Rooms Ltd.

Anyone looking for a reproduction Victorian or Edwardian conservatory will be interested to know about Palm Rooms Ltd., an English firm. The company has recently begun marketing its greenhouses in the United States. Manufacturing weather-resistant, aluminum-framed room additions, Palm Rooms offers several attractive styles with numerous options, such as choice of doorway, glass paneling, ridge cresting, finials, and period lighting. The ridge detail and various glass panel options are illustrated here.

is a particular type of outbuilding needing reproduction, the company will document and duplicate the design on a custom-order basis.

Catalogue available.
New England Outbuildings
152 Old Clinton Rd.
Westbrook, CT 06498
216 *(203) 669-1776*

Outdoor Designs

Outdoor Designs' Lakeline gazebos are constructed of Western red cedar as either freestanding structures or as additions to decks or patios. The basic model is reminiscent in style of resort-camp buildings of the early 1900s. There are three standard octagonal sizes: 14'7" square, 13'3" high

The basic architectural types are determined by the style of roofing and by the shape of the conservatory wall furthest from the room to which it is added. The roofs can be sloped in any number of directions, barrel-shaped, or designed as a combination of the two.

Likewise, the ends of the greenhouse additions can be squared or rounded or both, if desired. Pictured is the Garden Room model, characterized by a sloped roof and rounded closure. This style is also available with arched glass panels and roof cresting.

Palm Rooms Ltd. does no direct selling. The company's marketing is done through authorized "sun space" or greenhouse dealers. Each conservatory is preconstructed to individual specifications, but the base must be built by the customer before the structure can be erected.

Brochure available.

Palm Rooms Ltd.
10 Farrell St.
South Burlington, VT 05403
(802) 863-0001

Sun Room

If the Shakers had designed a conservatory, it probably would have been similar in style to those of Sun Room. The simple elegance and beauty of Sun Room's designs allow each solarium to blend attractively with almost any exterior and simultaneously bring to the interior of a house a fresh and invigorating atmosphere.

Each greenhouse is custom designed and produced of clear-heart redwood, with double-layered glass panes in a variety of styles, including laminated and tempered safety glass and tinted glass. Doorways and windows are located where desired, and Sun Room's special ventilation system, keeping the room cooled in the summer, is standard.

Literature available.

Sun Room Company, Inc.
PO Box 301, 2761 Creek Hill Rd.
Leola, PA 17540
(800) 426-2737
(717) 656-8018 (PA)

Landscape Architects

Owners of old properties enjoy the luxury of a landscape of mature plantings. There is no need to wait years for a variety of trees and shrubs to develop their full form. Shade is already provided; perennial beds are well-established. The one problem may be that of overgrowth which can distort and eventually overwhelm any semblance of landscape design. For professional assistance in restoring or re-creating period grounds, consider using a landscape architect who understands both horticulture and history. If there is not a recognized authority in your area, contact the nearest school of architecture for its recommendations.

Jamie Gibbs and Associates

With degrees in architecture, landscape architecture, horticulture, and historic preservation, Jamie Gibbs has established his name in the field of landscape architecture and design. Specializing in the restoration and re-creation of period gardens and traditional interiors, Gibbs has over ten years experience in his field, experience which has taken him throughout the United States and to Europe and South America.

In addition to design, however, Gibbs is a sought-after lecturer and has written three books. In the past, he has led many study tours of gardens and homes, and he has been published in magazines such as *Landscaping Homes and Gardens* and *Garden*.

Literature available.

Jamie Gibbs and Associates
Landscape Architects and Interior
 Designers
340 East 93rd St., Suite 14C
New York, NY 10128
(212) 722-7508

Old House Gardens

Through years of research and applied experience, Scott Kunst has developed his expertise in period landscaping and landscape design. Having founded Old House Gardens, Kunst now teaches, lectures, consults, and writes on his chosen field. In addition to landscaping the ground of private homes, he has completed public, commercial, and museum projects, working with a diverse clientele, including preservationists, developers, landscape architects, and do-it-yourself gardeners.

Although anyone can enjoy period landscape design, its application is particularly suited to owners of older homes. Whatever the interest—formal espaliered fruit trees or a rustic summerhouse, a blazing crescent of coleus or an herb garden—expert advice is provided by Old House Gardens.

Brochure available.

Old House Gardens
536 3rd St.
Ann Arbor, MI 48103
(313) 995-1486

Other Suppliers for Outdoor and Garden Areas

Consult List of Suppliers for addresses.

Outdoor Furniture

Alfresco
Architectural Antique Warehouse
Gazebo and Porchworks
Governor's Antiques
Gravity-Randall
Whit Hanks
Irreplaceable Artifacts
Schwartz's Forge and Metalworks
Silver Dollar Trading
United House Wrecking

Lawn and Garden Ornaments

Architectural Salvage
Robert Bourdon, The Smithy
Cassidy Brothers
Country Loft
Good Directions
Governor's Antiques
Marian Ives
Period Furniture Hardware
Remodelers' and Renovators' Supply
Robinson Iron
Schwartz's Forge and Metalworks
Silver Dollar Trading
Travis Tuck
United House Wrecking

Fences, Gates, Trellises, and Grates

Architectural Antique Warehouse
Architectural Antiques Exchange
Architectural Salvage
The Bank
E. Cohen's Architectural Heritage
Governor's Antiques
Great American Salvage Co.
Mad River Woodworks
Nye's Foundry
Pelnik Wrecking
Robinson Iron
Silver Dollar Trading
United House Wrecking
Wrecking Bar

Outdoor Structures

Cape Cod Cupolas
Cumberland Woodcraft
Gazebo and Porchworks
Historical Replications
Silver Dollar Trading
Vintage Wood Works

Landscape Architects

Richard N. Hayton and Associates
Philip M. White and Associates

9.

Furniture

A period house looks best furnished with complementary antique furniture. Few people, nonetheless, are able to find—or afford—to match a furnishings scheme with an architectural style. As a result, a reproduction furniture industry has developed in the United States that rivals the contemporary furnishings business. Reproduction chairs and tables in the American colonial style were made more than one hundred years ago, and the variety of period styles offered has kept pace with changing tastes in decoration ever since. Today, Art Deco reproductions are offered along with Pilgrim Century pieces. There are even reproductions of early reproductions such as the neo-colonial chairs first produced for the American Centennial in the 1870s.

The emphasis in the following pages is on individual woodworkers who use antique tools and follow traditional methods of cabinetmaking. Their reproductions are more costly than those turned out en masse by manufacturers, but prices are not that much higher for the average handmade piece. A handcrafted chair or table, for example, is more than likely to be worth the extra investment. It will have been made from a carefully selected hardwood, hand assembled, and perhaps even hand carved or turned. Each piece will be finished in an appropriate manner and not simply given a fast coat of shiny polyurethane.

The art of cabinetmaking and chair making has undergone a revival in the past twenty years. Skilled woodworkers can be found in all areas of North America. New England, the mid-Atlantic states, and the Carolinas, nevertheless, are still major centers of fine woodworking. Anyone seeking the best craftsmanship is encouraged to tour the workshops of these artisans. Many of the craftsmen are also skilled in architectural woodworking and can be a source of handsome and authentic cabinetry.

Pine cupboard and a reproduction Shaker rocking chair from Smith Woodworks & Design, Califon, New Jersey.

Alexandria Wood Joinery

The craftsmen at Alexandria Wood Joinery repair and restore furniture. Among the special services offered is the replacement of all types of caning.

If a customer is looking for artisans who can also reproduce a piece to complete a set, Alexandria may be able to help. The firm is equipped to draw up plans and produce whatever is needed. No catalogue is available, but a letter or phone call will bring a quick response to an inquiry.

Alexandria Wood Joinery
PO Box 92, Plummer Hill Rd.
Alexandria, NH 03222
(603) 744-8243

Alfresco

As the name suggests, Alfresco specializes in the outdoors—in particular, porch swings. Owner Paul Wilbert, a woodworker and landscape architect, devotes all of his skill to the production of this old-fashioned design.

Made of solid redwood, fastened with dowels, and given an oil finish, the swing is hung with 80' of sisal rope for a cushioned glide. Each swing is 52" wide, 30" deep, and 24" high.

Brochure available.

Alfresco
PO Box 1336
Durango, CO 81302
(303) 247-9739
(303) 259-5743

Angel House Designs

Among the many aspects of the Angel House enterprise is the design and production of simple colonial furniture. Based on antiques, almost all the pieces in the company's collection were originally designed for the restoration of the John Watson House, dating to 1731, now the company's main shop.

Among the sofas in the Angel House collection, the Country Heart-Back stands out. With a straight back, this model is available in 54", 66", 72", 76", or custom lengths. The legs are fashioned of maple, with the remainder of select hard and semi-hard woods. Seat depth is 21", and the height varies between 33" and 36", depending on the length.

The Salem Hooded settle design dates between 1690 and 1720, and it comes complete with a tavern arm and Bible drawer, an interesting combination. The Concord Tavern chair also has a tavern arm and Bible drawer. It is a later variation of the Salem Hooded settle. The seat is 21" wide and 19½" deep, and the overall height is 48".

All cushions are Dacron-wrapped foam. Tight seats for a period look are available on request. Stock or custom-ordered fabrics are available.

Brochure, $2.

Angel House Designs
RFD 1, Rte. 148
Brookfield, MA 01506
(508) 867-2517

Stephen P. Bedard

Stephen Bedard individually steam bends each bow of select ash for his Windsor chairs. The remaining sections are crafted of native pine and maple. Specializing in chairs of the late 18th century, Bedard hand carves and planes each seat. Spindles and legs are hand turned, and the joinery is mortise and tenon.

The fanback armchair is comfortable enough to use at the kitchen table and attractive enough to use as a desk chair in the office. Each seat is 17½" high, and all chairs come with a painted, hand-rubbed finish.

Bedard recommends a painting process for the chairs in which the "alligatored" appearance of the original models is reproduced.

Bedard's cradles are exceptional. Any nursery would benefit from the restrained design and classical beauty of the handcrafted pine base, ash bows, and maple spindles. Standard dimensions are 18½" high, 39" long, and 24" wide, including the rockers.

Custom orders are welcome.

Catalogue, $3.

Stephen P. Bedard
Durrell Mountain Farm, PO Box 2H
Gilmanton Iron Works, NH 03837
(603) 528-1896

John K. Buchanan

John Buchanan works alone and, for the most part, by hand, creating one piece at a time. Accurate, detailed reproductions of 18th- and early 19th-century furniture are his specialty. He has been involved in cabinetmaking for more than sixteen years and has amassed a large deal of knowledge and experience regarding the materials and methods used by early American furniture craftsmen.

The cherry Queen Anne flat-top highboy of New England origin, c. 1750, is one of Buchanan's most popular pieces. It is 57½" high, 33½" wide, and 20" deep.

After the wood stock—clear and kiln-dried cherry, maple, or walnut—has been sized, Buchanan hand planes all surfaces, with secondary surfaces left to reflect the use of the plane. The primary surfaces are later hand scraped before finishing. All joinery is with hand-cut dovetail and mortise and tenon joints, pinned for extra durability.

A blend of oils finishes each piece, carefully rubbed into the wood with many coats. This finish is in keeping with period styling, and it affords protection and beauty. Pieces of a formal nature are given a coating of shellac, as was used historically.

John Buchanan designs and produces custom work of all kinds. Inquiries are welcome.

Brochure, $2.

John K. Buchanan, Cabinetmaker
PO Box 696, Sugarland Rd.
Washington, IN 47501
(812) 254-7424

Marion H. Campbell

Once an engineer planning and managing the construction of steel bridges and buildings, Marion Campbell is now a cabinetmaker who re-creates and restores American period furniture and architectural woodwork. Operating his own woodworking shop in Bethlehem, Pennsylvania, he is known widely in the Philadelphia area for fine custom recreations and original designs. Campbell has worked on projects all over the East Coast from Massachusetts to Florida.

Campbell has a large assortment of woods with which to work, including Honduran mahogany, walnut, and cherry. One of his

most requested items, typical of all his woodwork, is a mahogany Queen Anne lowboy. It is available with drawers as shown or with a decorated centerpiece at the lower edge.

For designing and building architectural woodwork or casework and other furniture, Campbell is highly recommended.

Catalogue, 50¢.

Marion H. Campbell
39 Wall St.
Bethlehem, PA 18018
(215) 865-3292
(215) 837-7775 (workshop)

Candlertown Chairworks

The Steingresses specialize in chairs and painted country furniture designed to imitate hard-to-find or prohibitively expensive originals. Proprietors of Candlertown Chairworks, they aim to fashion furniture that can be easily mixed with antique originals.

The chairs are crafted of hickory and red oak and feature hand-woven split seats. Many styles, shapes, and sizes are available. Each is finished with the company's worn milk paint in red, blue, green, black, gray, mustard, or pumpkin.

The Mule Ear chair (top left and bottom right) features back posts that are flattened above the seat, while the chair back is steam bent for a comfortable fit. Chairs of this simple country style were common throughout the South in the 19th century. The overall height is 32", with a 23" seat height, and a base that is 16" by 18".

height is 32", and the chair has a 23" seat height and an 11" width. The base is 16" by 18".

Constructed of Southern yellow pine, Candlertown's hanging corner cupboard is available in combinations of any two standard colors. This 19th-century design is 32" tall and takes a 16" corner. It features a mellow whitewash interior and can be left open or fitted with a door. The cupboard can be used in combination with a corner table, 30" high, also made for a 16" corner.

Candlertown's country stand features mortise and tenon pegged construction and gracefully tapered legs. Its 19" square top is undercut in a simple 19th-century country manner. At 27" high, it is available in any combination of two of the company's standard colors.

The Knobby chair (lower left) has the same generously bowed back slats for comfortable seating, but the back posts are canted forward. Each post is topped with a hand-turned knob finial. The overall

Brochure, $1.

Candlertown Chairworks
PO Box 1630
Candler, NC 28715
(704) 667-4844

G. R. Clidence

Although G. R. Clidence makes every effort to match his 18th-century reproductions to their antique counterparts, he is equally skilled at adapting his furniture for practical living and personal tastes.

Clidence's standard offerings are all reproductions, crafted in his 18th-century woodworking mill equipped with antique machinery.

Cherry and maple are his woods of choice, but other hardwoods may be requested. All lathe work is done by hand, and, although roughing of the sideboards and rails is done with power equipment, all fitting and finishing is done with hand tools.

Beds are Clidence's most popular pieces. Offered in various styles and sizes, each design is carefully studied in the original for proper measurements and other specifications before work commences. All pieces are assembled with bed bolts and fitted with decorative bedcovers.

The Sheraton field bed features an elegant serpentine canopy. This style was found in New England homes during the late 1800s and was designed by Thomas Sheraton for use at military camps, "in the field."

The pencil post bed has been popular since colonial times and is still so today. Decorative details

on the posts and headboards take many imaginative forms. Clidence has six standard post and headboard styles from which to choose.

The low post bed was also known as a common or workman's bed. The original is from Cape Cod and offers solid design with attractive but simple ornamentation.

In addition to his beds, Clidence offers several styles of tables and other furniture, not to mention the infinite possibilities when custom ordering.

Brochure, $2, and photos of specific pieces or finishes will be sent on request.

G. R. Clidence
Box 272, James Trail
West Kingston, RI 02892
(401) 539-2558

Cornucopia

Typical of Cornucopia's reproduction furniture is the Windsor continuous arm chair. First built by English wheelwrights, Americans began reproducing them in about 1725 in Philadelphia. By the end of the 18th century, New England chairmakers had improved the design with vase-and-ring turnings, bamboo turnings, and other variations.

Cornucopia's Windsors are constructed in the manner and detail of the originals; bows are fashioned of steamed oak, hand formed and bent, with birch or

maple spindles and turnings. The hand-saddled seat is Eastern white pine, and all joints are fox wedged and glued. The chair is 38" tall.

Cornucopia also deals in other period home furnishings. The company offers several hutches modeled on original pieces in a number of shapes and sizes. Cornucopia even has a corner hutch for more efficient use of space. All are fashioned of Eastern white pine, and a number of finishes are offered—dark pine, antique pine, antique maple, cherry, and dark cherry. Custom color matching is also available.

Catalogue, $2.

Cornucopia, Inc.
Westcott Rd., Box 44
Harvard, MA 01451-0044
(508) 772-7733

Country Accents

Many pieces of 19th-century country furniture make use of pierced-tin panels. Country Accents can supply replacement panels for such old pieces as pie safes and kitchen cupboards as well as panels that can be used for new cabinets. The company's pierced-tin paneling kits are practical to use and contain designs that are aesthetically pleasing.

The kits include panels in a standard size of 16" x 28". Custom-ordered sizes are also available. Metal finishes include bright tin, pewter-tone tin, antique tin, zinc plate, copper foil, brass foil, and many more. A punching tool, chisel, patterns, and instructions are sent with the panels.

A large selection of patterns is offered for standard and custom panels. The Double Rosette, RBA 1074, for example, is one of many designs available.

Doing the piercing work is easy. The metal is then hand rubbed and given two coats of protective finish.

Catalogue available.

Country Accents
PO Box 437
Montoursville, PA 17754
(717) 478-4127

Country Bed Shop

Founded in 1972 in historic Groton, Massachusetts and now transplanted to Ashby, The Country Bed Shop re-creates 17th- and 18th-century beds, chairs, and tables, and handcrafts them in the old manner. All joints, carvings, and flat surfaces are worked with traditional tools, and only construction techniques and materials found in furniture of the period are used. All the traditional hardwoods are available, including curly maple.

The Ephraim Haines field bed is one of the finest beds in the Sheraton style, and it dates to 1806 from Philadelphia. It features hand-carved festooned and tasseled drapery on the reeded posts.

The oldest known bedstead to survive from 17th-century New England is the turned Pilgrim bed, the original of which is owned by the Museum of Fine Arts in Boston. The original is ash, 46½" high, 49¾" wide, and 72⅝" long. The Country Bed Shop's ash reproduction is slightly smaller to accommodate a modern twin mattress.

Trundle beds are ideal for children's or guest rooms, saving space without sacrificing that often-needed extra bed. Country Bed Shop will make a bed to fit under its own standard beds or one to fit the customer's specifications.

The Country Bed Shop offers a large variety of antique bed styles

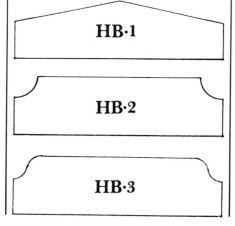

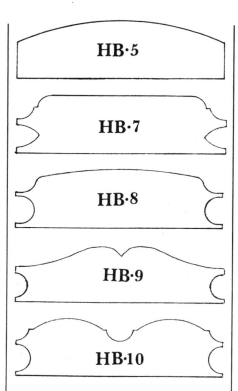

to choose from, a pleasant "problem" multiplied by its wide range of headboard styles. Since the firm will custom produce almost any item of antique furniture, inquiries are welcome.

Catalogue, $4.

The Country Bed Shop
RR 1, Richardson Rd., Box 65C
Ashby, MA 01431
(508) 386-7550

Decorum

Complete with secret compartments, Decorum's oak desks are designed in a Victorian style and adapted to suit modern needs. These desks are particularly suitable for people with lots of things to hide away. More than twenty-five small compartments are attractively arranged in the typical desk's top half. There are brass-covered grommets on the top of the desk to hide electrical wiring for a lamp, calculator, and the like.

Raised panels are complemented by solid-brass, lacquered hardware and fully finished dovetailed drawers. Options include tops in rich forest-green leather with gold-leaf tooling, felt-lined center drawers, and more. Each roll curtain is made as the original was, tracking smoothly in its own groove. Most models are designed so that all the drawers in the desk will lock when the curtain is closed.

The company also offers file cabinets in the same style as the desk to complete the Victorian appearance of an office.

Catalogue available.

Decorum
235-237 Commercial St.
Portland, ME 04101
(207) 775-3346

Ezra G.

Who is Ezra G.? No one knows. But what does it matter if you're looking for reproduction furniture that is reasonably priced? Ezra G. is the place where the budget-minded seek assorted pieces in the colonial and Federal styles.

The wood of choice for this company's craftsmen is ponderosa pine, but sugar pine is used for all table tops, maple for all turnings, and yellow pine for most furniture legs that are not turned. From dressers to chairs, tables, shelves, and more, each piece is finished in the company's unique distressed painting process, giving the furniture its antique look.

The architectural corner cupboard, C95, is one of the most detailed models. It is 44½″ wide and comes in heights of 55″, 57″, and 64″.

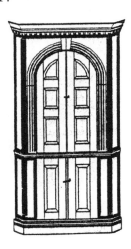

The hooded cupboard, C80, is another corner model, less

decorative but equally useful. It is 72″ high and 30½″ wide.

The armoire, C15, is still another variation on the corner cupboard theme. It is 39½″ wide and 76¼″ high.

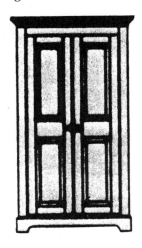

Literature available.

Ezra G.
1120 E. Sandusky St.
Fostoria, OH 44830
(419) 435-7707

Fireside Reproductions

Dating back to the 17th century in colonial New England, the versatile benchtable could be found in many households. Once the evening meal was finished and the table cleared, family members could turn up the table top to create a high-back bench similar to a settee. This bench would then be positioned in front of the fire, the back serving to protect the family from chilly drafts while simultaneously retaining heat from the fire.

Cabinetmaker John Glenn produces these benchtables exactly as they were first crafted, using original tools and materials including one-hundred-and-fifty- to two-hundred-year-old pine.

Glenn's benchtables are constructed with wedged mortise and tenon joints; Each mortise is hand cut using mallet and chisel, and the pins are hand turned. Each apron and seat-board edge is hand beaded using original beading planes.

Table top lengths range from 4′ to 7′ and the widths from 38″ to 40″. The finish is shellac and lacquer. The bench length is 2′ shorter than the top, and the seat height is 16½″ with a 15½″ width.

Brochure, $2.

Fireside Reproductions
4727 Winterset Dr.
Columbus, OH 43220
(614) 451-7695

Peter Franklin

The bow back stool and the sack stool are typical of the many pieces crafted by Peter Franklin at his workshop in the heart of New England. The sack stool, right, features a solid pine seat, carved and shaped by hand for the sitter's comfort. The hand-turned legs are maple for added strength. It is 28½″ tall.

The bow back stool is similar except for the legs and added back rest. It features an ash bow with red oak spindles in addition to the hand-formed pine seat and maple legs. It is 28½″ high to the seat and 46″ tall overall.

Other types of furniture crafted by Peter Franklin include a tavern table for dining. It is made of solid maple for durability and beauty. The standard finish for this model is stain and varnish, but the base is available in Franklin's milk paint. Colors include mustard, juniper, ash blue, black, garnet brown, and others. It is 79″ long, 36″ wide, and 29⅝″ high.

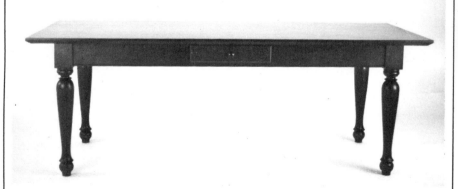

Custom orders are welcome, too.

Brochure, $3.

Peter Franklin
1 Cottage St., Box 1166
Easthampton, MA 01027
(413) 527-4004

Edward Ludlow

Specializing in the restoration and conservation of 18th- and early 19th-century furniture, Edward Ludlow will also build period pieces to order, often copying a preexisting piece to complete a set.

This 18th-century chair is reproduced from an original from England or Ireland. Its owner wanted to complete a set of the same pattern. Since Ludlow never uses dowels or machine-cut dovetails, the chair is joined by mortise and tenon, as is the original. Of special interest are the ball-and-claw legs ornamented with leaves and a shell, as well as the harp chair back with scrollwork.

Because all work is done on a custom-order basis, no catalogue is available. Call for information and photographs.

Edward Ludlow, Cabinetmaker
PO Box 646
Pluckemin, NJ 07978
(201) 658-9091

North Woods Chair Shop

Although only a few Shakers are alive today, the aesthetic ideals of the sect are being upheld by admiring and skilled craftsmen. North Woods Chair Shop copies only original Shaker designs, incorporating classical lines, elegant curves, and restrained ornamentation.

All of North Woods' furniture and home furnishings are handmade, including standard as well as custom-ordered pieces. The company now does mostly custom work, and a line of occasional tables and dining tables has been added. In addition, the gallery includes other craftsmen's home furnishings—upholstered furniture, pottery and table linens, tinware, baskets, and more.

Shown to the left of the drop-leaf table is the Enfield side chair, a classic Shaker ladderback design dating from the early 1800s. It was originally created by residents of the Shaker community at Enfield, New Hampshire. To the right of the table is an Enfield armchair available with three or four slats. The curved arms of this chair are pleasing to the eye and to the body. All seats are 17¼" high, with the width and depth varying according to the model.

The drop-leaf table has a single large drawer and a practical, folding leaf, allowing it to serve as anything from a simple side table to a larger writing or breakfast table.

All North Woods furniture is made from cherry, although any type of wood may be used for a custom project. Customers can choose a natural oil finish or any number of custom-blended stains. Chair seats can be caned or woven with fabric in a wide range of colors—from black to red and green stripes to beige to white—and patterns similar to those used by the Shakers themselves.

All furniture is signed, dated, given a serial number, and registered to the buyer. Visits to the gallery are recommended during normal business hours, but individual appointments can also be arranged.

Catalogue only, free. Photos and color tape samples, $3.

North Woods Chair Shop
RFD 1, Old Tilton Rd.
Canterbury, NH 03224
(603) 783-4595

Olde Virginea Floorcloth & Trading Co.

Elegant simplicity best describes Olde Virginea's pencil post beds. Their clean lines and fine woods enable these beds to blend attractively in any setting, from casual country to highly traditional.

Each bed is crafted by an individual woodworker using antique planes and shaping tools. A combination of woods is used: maple for the rails and posts and clear pine for the headboard are the standard. But combinations of mahogany, cherry, and American black walnut are also available. A variety of headboard styles is offered, as are several post styles. All four posts are usually cut from the same tree.

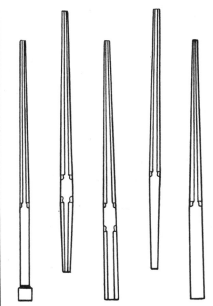

Beds can be delivered unfinished or finished by the company, hand-rubbed with oil for a natural look, or painted with Olde Virginea's own milk paints in a variety of early American colors.

The beds can be arranged for the use of rope springs, box springs, or even lightweight water mattresses. Assembly of the beds

should take two people about a half hour. The pieces are numbered to match and have been pretested in the shop for fit.

For those who have trouble climbing up to bed, Olde Virginea makes a set of old fashioned bed steps in cherry, maple, walnut, or mahogany. They can be painted or finished with oil to coordinate with any bed.

Catalogue, $3.

Olde Virginea Floorcloth
*   & Trading Co.*
PO Box 3305
Portsmouth, VA 23701
(804) 397-0948

William James Roth

The hand scraper was the preferred smoothing tool of 18th-century cabinetmakers. Its use requires substantial physical effort and a good deal of skill learned only through experience. Despite the problems all this may cause many modern woodworkers, William James Roth refuses to replace the hand scraper with today's power tools, which do not live up to traditional standards. All his extra work pays off when

chair has crest rails, bows, and arms that are steam bent from hand-split white oak. A spokeshave is used to shape each oak spindle. The back height is 37", and the seat height is 17½". The chair may be painted, as was the original, or stained.

The stretcher base dining table was used throughout the 17th and early 18th centuries. The stretchers and aprons are all ogee mold-

Catalogue, $3.

William James Roth
PO Box 355
Yarmouth Port, MA 02675
(508) 362-9235

Shaker Workshop

A furniture kit provides a handy and inexpensive means of producing simple, useful furniture. It is important that the pieces supplied be well turned out and that proper instructions and fittings be included with the kit. Each Shaker Workshops kit is produced by skilled craftsmen and each design is based on a specific Shaker piece in a museum or private collection. The wood supplied is carefully seasoned and dried, and no knots are permitted to mar the clean wood grain, which comes ready for the final sanding and finishing. Only common hand tools are needed for kit assembly.

When ordering a kit, stain color—light, medium, mahogany, ebony, or a simple oil finish—must be specified along with the final finish, a choice of hand-rubbed oil and wax or semi-gloss lacquer. For chair kit orders, the colors of the tape and the weaving pattern need to be selected.

Shaker Workshops offers several types of chairs, tables, benches, stools, settees, a bed, and various other kinds of objects in kit form. These are also produced in assembled and finished form for the all-thumbs home owner.

Catalogue, $1.

Shaker Workshops
PO Box 1028
Concord, MA 01742
(508) 646-8985

Smith Woodworks & Design

the final piece is complete. A William James Roth reproduction is most definitely an antique of tomorrow.

The continuous arm Windsor chair illustrates his devotion to tradition. Featuring a hand-shaped seat of white pine, the

ed, and the top is removable. Offered in cherry, maple, or tiger maple, the height is 29" with lengths ranging from 4' to 9' and widths varying accordingly. Drawers are optional. This piece is most attractive with a painted base and a scrubbed and polished top.

Each piece of Todd Smith's Shaker-style furniture is custom tailored to meet a discriminating buyer's requirements. Whether the subtle beauty and grace of a classic Shaker chair or a more primitive country-looking cabinet is desired, Smith will work with the customer, drawing up detailed plans, and then he will craft each piece completely by hand.

Shown is one of his straight cupboard designs, 72" tall, 27¼" wide, and 11¾" deep. This one is made of hand-planed pine with cut nails for a casual rugged look. The knob and latch are normally cut of

any project from the initial planning stage to the final waxing.

Catalogue, $2.

*Smith Woodworks & Design
Box 42, RR 1, Farmersville Rd.
Califon, NJ 07830
(201) 832-2723*

only native Pennsylvania-German styling but also the designs of the Shakers, the English, and others. The items range from stools to cupboards, tables, candlestands, presses, and Pennsylvania-German schranks. Every item is offered in tulip poplar, wild cherry, or black walnut, although some styles may be crafted of Eastern white pine on request

Although the company's table collection could be called Shaker in styling, the candlestand is from a design found in central Penn-

sylvania. An original is in the company's collection. Simple and straightforward in design, this piece is pleasing to the eye. It is 28" high, 12" wide, and 12" deep.

select hardwood for extra durability. It is lacquered as shown, but the finish that Smith employs depends on the piece's intended use; finishes include oil, paint, varnish, and lacquer. Regardless of the finish, each piece is hand waxed to a satiny patina.

For custom work in the Shaker style, Smith will handle almost

Spring House Classics

In the heart of the Pennsylvania-German farm country of Lancaster and Lebanon counties lies Buffalo Springs, a hamlet not even noted on most maps. Just over one mile west of historic Schaefferstown, this village is home to Spring House Classics. The company's furniture collection reflects not

Sometimes decorated with a simple inlay, the Pennsylvania-German hanging wall cupboard is normally fashioned of native black walnut, oiled both inside and out. Spring House Classics also offers a version in tulip poplar with a walnut stain and an attractive, blue-painted interior. It is 14½" deep, 25" wide, and 37" high.

Catalogue available.

Spring House Classics
PO Box 541
Schaefferstown, PA 17088
(717) 949-3902

Chapin Townsend

Chapin Townsend reproduces most of its 18th-century furniture from designs by the leaders of two notable schools of American cabinetmakers: the Chapin family of Connecticut and the Goddard and Townsend families of Rhode Island. Typically, the original pieces are priceless and not available even to the most affluent collectors because of their rarity.

Each piece is reproduced in exactly the same manner as that used by the master who originally created it. Only handcrafted hardware of the highest quality is used, including the forged rosehead and finish nails on the backs and moldings. All joinery utilized is authentic, and all carving is done by hand. Each piece is finished in a manner corresponding to that of the original, and no "antiquing" is performed since only nature can do that properly.

The Queen Anne desk on frame, DK6, is offered in cherry,

mahogany, maple, tiger maple, and curly maple. It dates to the early 1750s and is 36" wide, 20" deep, and 40" high.

The Chippendale chair, CR2, dates to 1760. Shown with stop-fluted legs (bead molded and ball and claw feet are also available), this model has carved ears, crest shell, and pierced splat. With optional arms, it is 38½" high.

Chapin Townsend also undertakes custom work. Photographs of specific pieces will be sent on request.

Brochure, $2.

Chapin Townsend
PO Box 628, James Trail
West Kingston, RI 02892
(401) 783-6614

Eldred Wheeler

Two exceptional historic museums have licensed Eldred Wheeler to reproduce furniture from their collections: the Colonial Williamsburg Foundation and the Nantucket Historical Association. Each piece is created by hand in the best tradition of 18th-century craftsmen. The company's cabinetmakers work with cherry, maple, and tiger maple when fashioning their magnificent tables, chairs, desks, beds, dressers, and other objects.

The Nantucket tea table, model 3520, is one of the most sought after of all New England antiques. This and other molded-top Queen Anne tea tables represent the ultimate integration of elegant curves and classically geometrical lines. The graceful cabriole legs and delicately scrolled skirt har-

monize to produce a flowing sculpture. The rare pull-out candle slides add to the tea table's attractiveness and usefulness. It is 26¼" high, 28" wide, and 16¾" deep.

Catalogue, $4.

Eldred Wheeler
% Partridge Replications
63 Penhallow St.
Portsmouth, NH 03801
(603) 431-8733

The Wicker Garden

The Victorians certainly had a way with wicker. Wonderfully sculpted in all shapes and sizes, these turn-of-the-century pieces are far more durable than most of their descendants. The Wicker Garden has amassed a sizable collection of such vintage pieces. (The Metropolitan Museum of Art recently accepted one of the store's Heywood-Wakefield examples for its renovated American wing.)

Antique wicker furniture can make a lively addition to any home, and you can be certain that no piece will ever bore you. Visit the shop if only to see the huge range of furniture shapes and styles that once filled many homes in America and Europe and to select the piece that would best suit your house. Information on available pieces is also offered by mail.

Catalogue, $7.50

The Wicker Garden
1318 Madison Ave.
New York, NY 10128
(212) 410-7001 (store)
(212) 410-2777 (office)

Other Suppliers of Furniture

Consult List of Suppliers for addresses.

Furniture

Aged Woods
Alfresco
Angel House
Caning Shop
Cohasset Colonials
Dovetail Woodworking
Historic Charleston Reproductions

Hitchcock Chair Co.
Joinery Co.
James Lea
Lehman Hardware
Craig Nutt
Traditional Line
Robert Whitley
Winterthur Museum and Gardens

234

10.
Decorative Accessories

As any dictionary will tell you, an accessory is a supplement; an adjunct, rather than a primary object. Decorative accessories—mirrors, pillows, baskets, weather vanes, pottery objects, etc.—can provide just the right finishing touch in a period decor. Unfortunately, they tend to be the last thing we think about when decorating a home, and we may have a tendency to buy such objects on impulse—from a flea market or garage sale, perhaps. Items bought in that way, however, frequently find their way back to the same type of sale a year or two later. But that doesn't have to be the case. There are many beautifully designed, well-made objects to enhance a period setting while serving a useful function as well. Some are illustrated in this chapter; many others are available from craftsmen and established firms listed in previous chapters.

Most of the objects recommended in the following pages are made by modern artisans. They are not antiques, although the methods and patterns followed are thoroughly based on tradition. Forms, too, resemble those from the past to a striking degree. The materials used are natural, not synthetic. The personal commitment to imaginative, well-wrought work is clearly evident in the objects themselves. There are far easier ways to make a good living than laboring at the forge, kiln, or workbench.

Antique accessories of the same quality and form may be priced several times more than reproductions or adaptations of old designs, and the profit therefrom keeps the dealer in business. We have no argument with those who make their livelihood by saving and selling such treasures, but there is a special kind of satisfaction that comes from helping to support present-day artistry. It is easy to decry most of the products of our materialistic society; the average gift shop is stuffed to the brim with absolutely worthless trash that cannot even be recycled. That is why it is such a pleasure to collect the work of living craftsmen whether they are employed by large companies or in workshops.

Copper and brass rooster vane by Good Directions, Inc., Stamford, Connecticut.

Black Ash Baskets

Jonathan Kline finds his valuable materials in the swampy woodlands near his home in New York's Finger Lake region. Here are located black ash trees, strips from which he weaves all his baskets. The strips are cut to narrow widths and shaved for a smooth finish.

Basket handles and rims are of steam-bent hickory for extra strength. The ash strips are woven over the hickory frames. The patterns, while not exact reproductions, are based on Shaker and Tagkanic patterns from basket makers in the upper Hudson valley region. Since each basket is completely handmade, minor variations are expected among various pieces.

No finishes are applied since they tend to prevent the wood from breathing and make it brittle. The baskets are left to darken naturally with age.

The harvest basket with a rigid handle is one of Kline's standard designs. It is versatile and attractive and is available in diameters ranging from 2" to 14".

Kline's kindling basket is of especially heavy construction and comes with hickory shoes. Its rectangular shape makes it ideal for storing many things from kindling to magazines and blankets. It is offered in either 28" or 33" lengths, with the remaining dimensions varying accordingly.

Brochure, $1.

Black Ash Baskets
RD 2, Box 252
Trumansburg, NY 14886
(607) 387-5718

The Candle Cellar

The proprietors of the Candle Cellar first began to experiment with candlemaking using an antique mold. After trial and error, the Silvias began making tapers professionally. They have been at it for fifteen years and have mastered other traditional crafts as well. Recently they added an imaginative selection of wood objects to their line of products. These useful and attractive pieces are made of native pine, stained, and given a satin finish.

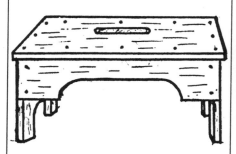

The company's bench is the type of object which is useful for several purposes. It is sturdy enough for an adult to use for reaching hard-to-get places or a child to use as his own personal seat. With a handy carrying handle, the bench is available in antique pine, country red, or blue. It measures 16" by 10" by 10".

Catalogue, $1.

The Candle Cellar and Emporium
PO Box 135, South Station
Fall River, MA 02724
(401) 624-9529

Cumberland General Store

With a fine selection of churns, jars, pitchers, and more, Cumberland General Store offers old-fashioned stoneware that is more than just functional. Cumberland has sets of well-designed, durable stoneware in all shapes and sizes for almost any purpose. Individual items are available in matching patterns. The different designs and styles will blend with any setting and are simple without being pedestrian.

The blue and white stoneware crock with its chrome button faucet, for example, is attractive and unassuming. In either two- or four-gallon sizes, the striped crock is ideal for iced tea or punch.

All the company's stoneware is completely safe for any foods and can be used in a conventional oven or in a microwave unit.

Catalogue, $3.

Cumberland General Store
Rte. 3
Crossville, TN 38555
(800) 334-4640
(615) 484-8481 (TN)

Good Directions, Inc.

Whatever the reason for wanting a weather vane, these classic objects of functional folk art make pleasing additions to a period house. Good Directions specializes in all-copper-and-brass decorative devices like the rooster vane shown. The figure is 20" high and crafted of solid copper. The directionals are solid brass, with copper spacer balls and a steel mounting rod. A variety of brackets make installation possible on a roof of any pitch or on a flat roof.

The rooster is one of forty models. All are available in an antique, weathered green finish, and most are also made in a highly polished finish. Other figures include a squirrel, eagle, grasshopper, cherub, and sulky.

The company also manufactures wood cupolas, with or without copper-topped roofs, and a variety of brass sundials.

Catalogue, $1.

Good Directions, Inc.
Dept. OH8C
24 Ardmore Rd.
Stamford, CT 06902
(203) 348-1836
(800) 346-7678

Hephaestus Pottery

Jeff White first began throwing pots in 1966, and three years later he set up his own working pottery for making colonial-style stoneware and salt-glaze pieces. He now produces redware exclusively at his company—Hephaestus Pottery.

Redware has been made in America since the colonial period and was particularly popular through the 1850s. White's specialty is the hand-decorating of each piece. Two forms of decoration are used. Slipware is made by painting or trailing yellow slip over red clay; sgrafitto ware is made by covering red clay with yellow slip and then carving through to expose the red clay underneath. Manganese black and copper green are then added for highlights. Each piece is glazed in the last stage to set the design.

All Hephaestus pieces are completely safe for cooking and dining.

Illustrated is a sgrafitto jar, 10" tall, and a slip-trailed plate, a copy of a piece from the late 1700s, 11½" in diameter.

The remaining illustrations are of a slip-trailed dinner plate and a sgrafitto plate. Each is 11½" in diameter.

Catalogue, $3.

Hephaestus Pottery
2012 Penn St.
Lebanon, PA 17042
(717) 272-0806

Hurley Patentee

Each Hurley Patentee lighting device is carefully copied from an original 17th- or 18th-century piece now found in a museum or private collection. Devotees of fine reproduction fixtures and accessories rarely look further than Hurley for authentic pieces. All metal parts used are shaped with simple hand tools as of old, and only solder and rivets are used to join the individual parts. Most of the lighting devices are of tin, but Hurley also makes use of iron and brass. The finish given each piece is of a mellow, antique appearance.

The courting mirror is a Hudson Valley design and is available either electrified or for use with candles. It is approximately 15" tall and 10" wide and is made completely of tin. The mirror is given an antique tin finish.

237

Catalogue available.

Hurley Patentee Lighting
RD 7, Box 98A
Kingston, NY 12401
(914) 331-5414

Marian Ives

Weather vanes make up the majority of Marian Ives's projects. Nearly two dozen designs are offered on a regular basis, and these include such figures as a sheep, cow, horse, fox, grasshopper, Canadian goose, peacock, two-masted schooner, and pineapple. Each vane is supplied with a rod and one copper ball. The rod is fitted with a lock groove for the setting screw.

Ives will also undertake special designs. One of her most interesting projects is a 5½' copper lobster that is mounted as a vane on the James Hook & Co. building in Boston. It is gold-leafed, an option with all of her work. In addition to copper, she will also make up vanes in brass or steel. Copper and brass vanes are left to weather naturally, but the flat steel types are painted.

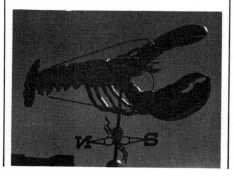

In her custom work, Ives will follow real models (as in the case of the highly detailed lobster, originally worked in wood), plans, blueprints, photographs, drawings, and whatever else can be supplied.

Ives is also a skilled jeweler and gemologist. She brings these talents into play in other types of metalwork—from a six-foot steel flamingo, complete with tennis shoes and socks, to tiny brass Christmas tree ornaments, mainly in the form of animals.

Literature available.

Marian Ives
Box 101A, RR 1
Charlemont, MA 01339
(413) 339-8534

Lehman Hardware

Throughout the ages the ringing of bells has been part of daily life. Whether ringing out an alarm or just announcing dinner, the sound of a bell is striking and appealing. Lehman's old-fashioned farm and patio bells are cast in an iron alloy called "crystal" metal for a rich tone.

Three basic sizes of farm bells are offered. The largest model weighs fifty pounds and rings loud enough to carry up to a mile on a clear day. It is 24½" high and 15½" in diameter. The other bells measure 23" high and 13¾" around and 16½" high and 11¼" around. All the farm bells are designed for post mounting with flat-black bracket and a bronze-colored bowl.

The company's two patio bell models are smaller than the farm bells and are of a slightly different design. Decorative and practical, these bells are cast to carry sound a shorter distance. The larger model is 9" high and 7½" in diameter; the smaller is 8¼" high and 5¾" in diameter. Each bell comes with a bracket for wall mounting, and the height includes the iron eagle finial.

Catalogue, $2.

Lehman Hardware & Appliances, Inc.
4779 Kidron Rd., PO Box 41
Kidron, OH 44636
(216) 857-5441

Kenneth Lynch & Sons

Cast-stone, iron, bronze, lead, and wrought-iron lawn and garden ornaments are an important part of the Lynch collection. For gardeners of all sorts, or for the home handyman who simply wants to improve his yard's appearance, however, this company also makes decorative accessories of other kinds that call for additions by the homeowner.

Lynch's topiary frames, for example, serve as only the start of what can become the centerpiece of any garden setting. Iron frames in various shapes and almost any size are provided; the homeowner must provide the greenery. Model 4136, a topiary mushroom frame, is 6' tall as illustrated.

Ornamental steel forms, serving a function similar to topiary, are extremely useful, too. Number 4356 is a typical garden design made in any size. By using curbing of this sort, the home gardener can re-create various types of raised geometric beds similar to those found in Victorian gardens.

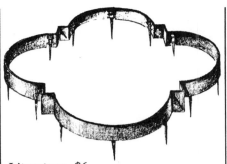

Literature, $6.

Kenneth Lynch & Sons
Box 488
Wilton, CT 06897-0488
(203) 762-8363

Sandra McKenzie Schmitt

Sandra Schmitt's unusual terra cotta and stoneware sculptures are for enjoyment only. That they serve no practical function, however, should not deter anyone from admiring their artistry. Each sculpture is a miniature building, often a Victorian house or cottage. Schmitt captures what she calls the "gingerbread quality of these structures" in the highly malleable medium of clay.

Sandra Schmitt will undertake other types of house portraits in clay and has executed colonial and Federal buildings as well as Victorian. She especially enjoys this type of custom work and will work from photographs or drawings of a building. Most of the sculptures are freestanding, but they can be made to fit on top of a stoneware casserole. Nothing surprises the artist: "Some people want their entire farm on the tip of the casserole, with the barn, the corncrib and any outbuildings."

Schmitt's work has been exhibited across the country. She now sculpts her exceptional models in the small Delaware valley village of Frenchtown, New Jersey. Orders require six months to a year for delivery.

Literature available.

Sandra McKenzie Schmitt
25 Fifth St.
Frenchtown, NJ 08825
(201) 996-3214

Smith Woodworks and Design

Todd Smith's Shaker-style furniture, with its fine lines and excellent proportions, is crafted not only to be used, but to be admired.

Pictured is one of his most popular Shaker clocks, 37½″ high, 13⅜″ wide, and 5⅞″ deep. Made of cherry, it has works which are key-wound and spring-driven. Chimes are standard. The clock is also available with another type of face using Roman numerals rather than Arabic, and an inscribed date—1840.

Various finishes include oil, varnish, lacquer, and polyurethane. Each piece is hand waxed and polished to a satiny patina similar to the look of most quality antiques.

Catalogue, $2.

Smith Woodworks and Design
Box 42, RR 1, Farmersville Rd.
Califon, NJ 07830
(201) 832-2723

Chapin Townsend

Who wouldn't enjoy looking at Chapin Townsend's Chippendale mirror? The phoenix ornament, flame-like carvings, and scrollwork give the piece a solid character and elegant flair. The design dates to 1760 and originated in Massachusetts. The mirror comes in a standard 20½″ width and 41½″ height.

Each Chapin Townsend piece is fashioned exactly as the original with respect to design, materials, joinery, carving, and finishing. Only wide, seasoned cherry, maple, tiger maple, or mahogany are used for primary surfaces. Poplar, pine, maple, birch, or oak are appropriate secondary woods used. All brass hardware is historically accurate. Each piece of fine yellow brass is hand-filed, scraped, and polished.

Brochure, $2. Larger glossies are sent to those interested in specific pieces.

Chapin Townsend
PO Box 628, James Trail
West Kingston, RI 02892
(401) 783-6614

Travis Tuck

Sculptor Travis Tuck was commissioned to fashion eight large weather vanes for buildings at the Gainsborough Farm, an important horse farm in the heart of Woodford County, Kentucky. Seven designs were variations of a horse and jockey, each over 5' long. The eighth is this 5' mare and foal.

All Tuck's work is executed in copper—including weather vanes, outdoor lanterns, and wall sculptures of all shapes and sizes. Beginning with sheets and tubes of copper, the artist uses the ancient technique of *repoussé* to shape the metal. After heating, each sheet of copper is hammered on a concave wooden block to give it general form and shape. Details are then chiseled with a variety of metalworking tools. No finish is applied; the copper will weather naturally to an antique hue.

Each vane is a three-dimensional sculpture characterized by sharpness of outline and exactness of detail. Tuck signs, dates, and numbers each work. If you're ever on Martha's Vineyard, a visit to the artist's studio is recommended.

Brochure available.

Travis Tuck, Metal Sculptor
Box 1832
Martha's Vineyard, MA 02568
(508) 693-3914

Victorian Reproduction Lighting

Lightning rods have been used on buildings for several centuries. Practicality alone makes a rod worth installing, but, with some of the more ornamental styles, aesthetics are as appealing as function. A well-designed lightning rod also serves as an attractive finial.

Victorian Reproduction Lighting offers several lightning rod designs in kit form and also makes individual parts available for the homeowner who wants to design and construct his own unique lightning rod.

Model LR-101 is centered on a copper rod with a nickel-plated tip. It comes with a four-legged scroll brace. The top star ornament is bronze-finished aluminum. The diamond-quilt glass ball comes in several colors, including blue, white, red, and green. The overall height of the assembled rod is 30".

Model LR-104 is also a copper rod with a nickel-plated tip. The glass globe is offered in the same range of colors, but this model uses a three-legged brace. The model is 36" high when mounted.

For a complete lightning protection system, provide Victorian Reproduction Lighting with blueprints of the top roof view and side elevation of your building, and the company's design team will fashion a system for you, including necessary parts and prices. All installation is done by the customer or a local contractor.

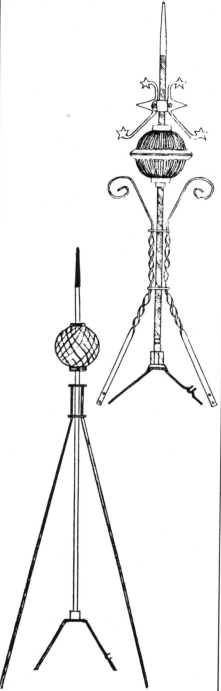

Literature available.

Victorian Reproduction Lighting Co.
PO Box 579
Minneapolis, MN 55458
(612) 338-3636

Westmoore Pottery

Although Westmoore Pottery offers a number of reproductions of old redware, most of the designs are uniquely its own. Both new and old models, however, look and feel like antiques. Designs range from simple to very fancy. Slip is used to decorate plates, crocks, and jugs in various colors. Each piece is finished with a clear glaze to enable the true clay colors to show through.

Since the pieces are handmade, natural variations will occur in each. This difference is also the result of firing the salt-glazed stoneware in an old style wood-burning Groundhog kiln, as did earlier potters.

The plates illustrated exhibit various slip-trail decorations. Each piece is 13″ in diameter.

Literature available.

Westmoore Pottery
Rte. 2, Box 494
Seagrove, NC 27341
(919) 464-3700

Martha Wetherbee

The basket weavers at Martha Wetherbee not only fashion traditional American baskets at their New Hampshire studio, but they teach the art of Shaker basket weaving in workshops throughout the country. Their thorough knowledge has come through a combination of research and experience since the founding of the business thirteen years ago.

One of the most interesting baskets added recently to the line has been produced in a limited edition of ten. It is the largest basket made, a two-bushel round-bottomed Shaker apple basket from the Canterbury, New Hampshire, community. It is made of brown ash, as are all the company's baskets.

Wetherbee also carries a line of books on basket weaving and its history, and a supply of tools that are useful for the home enthusiast.

Literature available.

Martha Wetherbee Basket Shop
Star Rte., Box 35
Sanborntown, NH 03269
(603) 286-8927

Other Suppliers of Decorative Accessories

Consult List of Suppliers for addresses.

Accessories

Amazon Drygoods
American Wood Column
Angel House
Laura Ashley
Baldwin Hardware
Colonial Weavers
Country Loft
Curran Glass and Mirror
The Fan Man
Ferguson's Cut Glass Works
Granville Manufacturing
Historic Charleston Reproductions
Import Specialists
M-H Lamp & Fan
Moravian Pottery and Tile Works
The Old Wagon Factory
Shaker Workshops
Sunflower Glass Studio
Eldred Wheeler
Winterthur Museum and Gardens
Woodstock Soapstone

List of Suppliers

AA-Abbingdon Affiliates Inc.
2149-51 Utica Ave.
Brooklyn, NY 11234
(718) 258-8333

A-Ball Plumbing Supply
1703 W. Burnside
Portland, OR 97209
(503) 228-0026

AMS Imports
23 Ash Ln.
Amherst, MA 01002
(800) 648-1816
(413) 253-2644 (MA)

ARJ Associates, Inc.
310 Washington St.
Brighton, MA 02135
(617) 783-0467

A. S. L. Associates, Architects
5182 Maple
Irvine, CA 92715
(415) 344-5044

Abatron Inc.
141 Center Dr.
Gilberts, IL 60136
(312) 426-2200

Abbey Garden Sundials
PO Box 102, Indian Hill Rd.
Pakenham, Ontario
K0A 2X0, Canada
(613) 256-3973

Acorn Manufacturing Co.
PO Box 31, School St.
Mansfield, MA 02048
(800) 835-0121
(508) 339-4500 (MA)
(508) 339-2977 (MA)

Aetna Stove Co.
S. E. corner 2nd
& Arch Sts.
Philadelphia, PA 19106
(215) 627-2008

Aged Woods
RD 3, Box 80
Delta, PA 17314
(800) 233-9307

Alexandra's Textile
5606 State Rt. 37
Delaware, OH 43015
(614) 369-1817

Alexandria Wood Joinery
PO Box 92, Plummer Hill Rd.
Alexandria, NH 03222
(603) 744-8243

Allentown Paint Manufacturing Co., Inc.
Box 597, E. Allen and
N. Graham Sts.
Allentown, PA 18105
(215) 433-4273

Alfresco
PO Box 1336
Durango, CO 81302
(303) 247-9739
(303) 259-5743

Amazon Drygoods
2218 E. 11th St.
Davenport, IA 52803
(319) 322-6800

Amdega Conservatories
Boston Design Center
One Design Center Plaza,
Suite 624
Boston, MA 02210
(617) 951-2755

American Architectural Art
PO Box 904
Adamstown, PA 19501

American Building Restoration
9720 S. 60th St.
Franklin, WI 53132
(414) 761-2440

American Heirlooms, Inc.
Rt. 2, Box 347A
Bean Station, TN 37708

American Heritage Shutters
2549 Lamar Ave.
Memphis, TN 38114
(901) 743-2800

American Olean Tile Co.
1000 Cannon Ave., Box 271
Lansdale, PA 19446
(215) 855-1111

American Wood Column
913 Grand St.
Brooklyn, NY 11211
(718) 782-3163

Anderson Building Restoration
923 Marion Ave.
Cincinnati, OH 45229
(513) 281-5258

Anderson Pulley Seal
920 W. 53rd St.
Minneapolis, MN 55419
(612) 827-1117

Townsend Anderson
RD 1, Box 860
Moretown, VT 05660
(802) 244-5095

Angel House Designs
RFD 1, Rte. 148
Brookfield, MA 01506
(508) 867-2517

Anthony Wood Products
PO Box 1081
Hillsboro, TX 76645
(817) 582-7225

Antique Baths & Kitchens
2220 Carlton Way
Santa Barbara, CA 93109
(805) 962-8598

Antique Hardware Store
43 Bridge St.
Frenchtown, NJ 08825
(800) 422-9982
(201) 996-4040 (NJ)

Architectural Antique Warehouse
PO Box 3065
Ottawa, Ontario, K1P 6H6,
Canada
(613) 526-1818

Architectural Antiques
121 E. Sheridan Ave.
Oklahoma City, OK 73104
(405) 232-0759

Architectural Antiques Exchange
709-15 N. 2nd St.
Philadelphia, PA 19123
(215) 922-3669

Architectural Antiques West
3117 S. LaCienega Blvd.
Los Angeles, CA 90016
(213) 559-3019

Architectural Color
See Jill Pilaroscia

Architectural Components
Box 249
Leverett, MA 01054
(413) 367-9441

Architectural Iron Co.
PO Box 126, Schocopee Rd.
Milford, PA 18337
(717) 296-7722
(212) 243-2664

Architectural Masterworks
3502 Divine Ave.
Chattanooga, TN 37407
(615) 867-3630

Architectural Paneling, Inc.
979 Third Ave., Suite 1518
New York, NY 10022
(212) 371-9632

Architectural Preservation Trust
152 Old Clinton Rd.
Westbrook, CT 06498
(203) 669-1776

Architectural Reclamation
312 S. River St.
Franklin, OH 45005
(513) 746-8964

Architectural Resources Group
Pier 9, The Embarcadero
San Francisco, CA 94111
(415) 421-1680

Architectural Salvage Co.
103 W. Michigan Ave.,
Box 401
Grass Lake, MI 49240
(517) 522-8516

Architectural Sculpture Ltd.
242 Lafayette St.
New York, NY 10012
(212) 431-5873

Arden Forge
301 Brinton's Bridge Rd.
West Chester, PA 19382
(215) 399-1350

Art Directions
6120 Delmar Blvd.
St. Louis, MO 63112
(314) 863-1895

Artistic License in San Francisco
1489 McAllister St.
San Francisco, CA 94119
(415) 922-5219

Artistry in Veneers, Inc.
450 Oak Tree Ave.
S. Plainfield, NJ 07080
(201) 668-1430

Laura Ashley
Dept. B117 Box 5308
Melville, NY 11747
(800) 367-2000

Association for Preservation Technology
Box 2487, Station D
Ottawa, Ontario K1P 5W6,
Canada
(613) 238-1972

Authentic Design
42 The Mill Rd.
W. Rupert, VT 05776
(802) 394-7713

Authentic Lighting
558 Grand Ave.
Englewood, NJ 07631
(201) 568-7429

Baldwin Hardware
841 Wyomissing Blvd.,
Box 82
Reading, PA 19603
(215) 777-7811

Ball & Ball
463 W. Lincoln Hwy.
Exton, PA 19341
(215) 363-7330
(215) 363-7639 (FAX)

The Balmer Architectural Art Studios
9 Codeco Court
Don Mills, Ontario
M3A 1B6, Canada
(416) 449-2155
(416) 449-3018 (FAX)

The Bank, Architectural Antiques
1824 Felicity St.
New Orleans, LA 70113
(504) 523-2702

Barewood Inc.
106 Ferris St.
Brooklyn, NY 11231
(718) 875-9037

Barnstable Stove Shop
Rt. 149, Box 472
West Barnstable, MA 02668
(508) 362-9913

Bassett & Vollum Inc.
217 N. Main St.
Galena, IL 61036
(815) 777-2460

Bay-Waveland Woodworks
Rt. 4, Box 548
Bay St. Louis, MS 39520
(601) 467-6126

Beachwood Wallcoverings
23645 Mercantile Rd.
Cleveland, OH 44122
(216) 464-3700

Stephen P. Bedard
Durrell Mountain Farm,
PO Box 2H
Gilmanton Iron Works, NH
03837
(603) 528-1896

Beech River Mill Co.
Old Route 16
Centre Ossipee, NH 03814
(603) 539-2636

S. A. Bendheim Co., Inc.
122 Hudson St.
New York, NY 10013
(800) 221-7379
(212) 226-6370 (NY)

Bendix Mouldings, Inc.
235 Pegasus Ave.
Northvale, NJ 07647
(800) 526-0240
(201) 767-8888 (NJ)

Bentley Brothers
918 Baxter Ave.
Louisville, KY 40204
(800) 824-4777
(502) 589-2939 (KY)

Bergen Bluestone Co., Inc.
404 Rte. 17, Box 67
Paramus, NJ 07652
(201) 261-1903

Besco Plumbing
729 Atlantic Ave.
Boston, MA 02111
(617) 423-4535

Biltmore, Campbell, Smith Restorations
One Biltmore Plaza
Asheville, NC 28803
(704) 274-1776

Black Ash Baskets
RD 2, Box 252
Trumansburg, NY 14886
(607) 387-5718

Blaine Window Hardware
1919 Blaine Dr.
Hagerstown, MD 21740
(301) 797-6500

Blenko Glass
PO Box 67
Milton, WV 25541
(304) 743-9081

Blue Ridge Shingle Co.
Montebello, VA 24464
(703) 377-6635 or
(919) 395-5333

Bona Decorative Hardware
3073 Madison Rd.
Cincinnati, OH 45209
(513) 321-7877

Nancy Borden Period Textile Furnishings
PO Box 4381 OH
Portsmouth, NH 03801
(603) 436-4284

Boulder Stained Glass Studios
1920 Arapahoe Ave.
Boulder, CO 80302
(303) 449-9030

Robert Bourdon, The Smithy
Box 2180
Wolcott, VT 05680
(802) 472-6508

Louis W. Bowen, Inc.
950 Third Ave.
New York, NY 10022
(212) 751-4470

Larry Boyce & Associates
Box 421507
San Francisco, CA 94142-1507
(415) 923-1366

Bradbury & Bradbury Wallpapers
PO Box 155-D
Benicia, CA 94510
(707) 746-1900

Bradford Consultants
PO 4020
Alameda, CA 94501
(415) 523-1968

The Brass Finial
2408 Riverton Rd.
Cinnaminson, NJ 08077
(609) 786-9337

The Brass Knob
2311 18th St., N.W.
Washington, DC 20009
(202) 332-3370

Brass Light Gallery
719 S. 5th St.
Milwaukee, WI 53204
(414) 383-0675

Brasslight, Inc.
90 Main St.
Nyack, NY 10960
(914) 353-0567

Briar Hill Stone Co.
PO Box 398
Glenmont, OH 44628
(216) 276-4011

The Brickyard
101 E. Wall, PO Box A
Harrisonville, MO 64701
(816) 884-3218

Bright Star Woodworking
14618 Tyler Foote Rd.
Nevada City, CA 95959
(916) 292-3514

Brill and Walker Associates
PO Box 731, OHC
Sparta, NJ 07871-0731
(201) 729-8876

The Broadway Collection
250 N. Troost
Olathe, KS 66061
(800) 255-6365
(913) 782-6244 (KS)
(800) 468-1219 (Canada)

Broadway Market MRA
79 Bridge St.
Brooklyn, NY 11201
(718) 643-0994

Carol Brown
PO Box C-100
Putney, VT 05346
(802) 387-5875

Brunschwig & Fils
75 Virginia Rd.
North White Plains, NY 10603
(914) 684-5800

Bryant Steel Works
RFD #2, Box 2048
Thorndike, ME 04986
(207) 568-3665

John K. Buchanan, Cabinetmaker
PO Box 748, 15 E. Main St.
Lebanon, OH 45036
(513) 932-0314

Bob Buckter
Color Consultant
3877 20th St.
San Francisco, CA 94114
(415) 922-7444

Building Conservation
2204 Ludington Ave.
Wauwatosa, WI 53226
(414) 475-1896

Burdoch Silk Lampshade Co.
11120 Roselle St., Suite G
San Diego, CA 92121
(619) 458-1005

J. R. Burrows Co.
PO Box 148, Cathedral Station
Boston, MA 02118
(617) 451-1982

C. & H. Roofing, Inc.
1305 E. 39th St. N.
Sioux Falls, SD 57104
(800) 327-8115
(605) 332-5060 (SD)

Samuel Cabot, Inc.
1 Union St.
Boston, MA 02108
(617) 723-7740

California Paints
California Products Corp.
169 Waverly St.
Cambridge, MA 02139
(800) 225-1141
(800) 842-1161 (MA)

Campbell Center
Box 66
Mount Carroll, IL 61053
(815) 244-1173

Marion H. Campbell
39 Wall St.
Bethlehem, PA 18018
(215) 865-3292
(215) 837-7775 (Workshop)

Nina Campbell
9 Walton St.
London SW3 2JD, England
(01) 584-9401

The Canal Company
1612 14th St. N.W.
Washington, DC 20009
(202) 234-6637

The Candle Cellar & Emporium
PO Box 135, South Station
Fall River, MA 02724
(401) 624-9529

Candlertown Chairworks
PO Box 1630
Candler, NC 28715
(704) 667-4844

John Canning
132 Meeker Rd.
Southington, CT 06489
(203) 621-2188

Cape Cod Cupolas
78 State Road
N. Dartmouth, MA 02747
(617) 994-2119

Carefree Wallcoverings
23645 Mercantile Rd.
Cleveland, OH 44122
(216) 464-3700

Carlisle Restoration Lumber
Rte. 123
Stoddard, NH 03464
(603) 446-3937

A Carolina Craftsman
975 Avocado St.
Anaheim, CA 92805
(714) 776-7877

Carpenter and Smith Restorations
Box 504
Highland Park, IL 60035
(312) 831-5047

Carson, Dunlop & Associates
597 Parliament St., Suite B-5
Toronto, Ontario M4X 1W3, Canada
(416) 964-9415

Carter Canopies
Rt. 2, Box 270G, PO Box 808
Troutman, NC 28166-0808
(704) 528-4071

Cassidy Brothers Forge, Inc.
US Rte. 1
Rowley, MA 01969-1796
(508) 948-7303

Cedar Valley Shingle Systems
985 S. 6th St.
San Jose, CA 95112
(408) 998-8550

Century House Antiques
46785 Rte. 18 West
Wellington, OH 44090
(216) 647-4092

Chadsworth, Inc.
PO Box 53268
Atlanta, GA 30355
(404) 876-5410

Chatham Glass Co.
Box 522
N. Chatham, MA 02650
(508) 945-5547

Chelsea Decorative Metal Co.
9603 Moonlight
Houston, TX 77096
(717) 721-9200

The Chicago Faucet Co.
2100 S. Nuclear Dr.
Des Plaines, IL 60018
(312) 694-4400

Chromatic Paint Corp.
PO Box 690
Stony Point, NY 10980
(800) 431-7001
(914) 947-3210 (NY)

Circecast
380 7th St.
San Francisco, CA 94103
(415) 863-8319

City Lights
2226 Massachusetts Ave.
Cambridge, MA 02140
(617) 547-1490

Clarence House/Cole and Son
211 E. 58th St.
New York, NY 10022
(212) 752-2890

Clarence House/Colefax & Fowler
See Clarence House

Classic Accents, Inc.
Dept. L., PO Box 1181
Southgate, MI 48195
(313) 282-5525

Classic Architectural Specialties
5302 Junius
Dallas, TX 75214
(214) 827-5111

Classic Illumination, Inc.
2743 Ninth St.
Berkeley, CA 94710
(415) 849-1842

G. R. Clidence
Box 272, James Trail
West Kingston, RI 02892
(401) 539-2558

Clio Group, Inc.
3961 Baltimore Ave.
Philadelphia, PA 19104
(215) 386-6276

Coco Millwork & Supply
19151 Highland Rd.,
PO Box 2601
Baton Rouge, LA 70821
(504) 291-0950

Cohasset Colonials
643X Ship St.
Cohasset, MA 02025
(617) 383-0110

E. Cohen's Architectural Heritage
1240 Bank St.
Ottawa, Ontario K1S 3Y3, Canada
(613) 729-4427

Colonial Brick Co. Inc.
977 W. Cermak Rd.
Chicago, IL 60623
(312) 927-0700

Colonial Weavers
Box 16
Phippsburg Center, ME 04562
(207) 389-2033

The Color People
1546 Williams St.
Denver, CO 80218
(303) 388-8686

Combination Door Co.
Box 1076, Dept. OH
Fond du Lac, WI 54935
(414) 922-2050

Community Services Collaborative
1315 Broadway
Boulder, CO 80302
(303) 442-3601

Conklin's Authentic Antique Barnwood & Hand-Hewn Beams
RD 1, Box 70
Susquehanna, PA 18847
(717) 465-3832

Cook & Dunn Paint Corp.
Box 117
Newark, NJ 07101
(201) 589-5580

Conant Custom Brass
270 Pine St.
Burlington, VT 05402
(802) 658-4482

Laura Copenhaver Industries, Inc.
PO Box 149
Marion, VA 24354
(800) 227-6797
(703) 783-4663 (VA)

A. J. P. Coppersmith & Co.
20 Industrial Pkwy.
Woburn, MA 01801
(800) 545-1776
(617) 932-3700 (MA)

Josiah R. Coppersmythe
80 Stiles Rd.
Boylston, MA 01505
(508) 869-2769

Cornucopia, Inc.
Westcott Rd., Box 44
Harvard, MA 01451-0044
(508) 772-7733

Country Accents
PO Box 437
Montoursville, PA 17754
(717) 478-4127

The Country Bed Shop
RR 1, Richardson Rd.,
Box 65C
Ashby, MA 01431
(508) 386-7550

Country Comfort Stove Works
Union Road
Wales, MA 01081
(413) 245-7396

The Country Iron Foundry
Box 600-OHC
Paoli, PA 19301
(215) 296-7122

Country Loft
South Shore Park
Hingham, MA 02043
(617) 749-7766

Cowtan & Tout, Inc.
D & D Building
979 Third Ave.
New York, NY 10022
(212) 753-4488

Craftsman Lumber Co.
PO Box 222
Groton, MA 01450
(508) 448-6336

Crawford's Old House Store
550 Elizabeth St.
Waukesha, WI 53186
(800) 556-7878
(414) 542-0685 (WI)

Creative Openings
Box 4204
Bellingham, WA 98227
(206) 671-6420

Cross Industries
3174 Marjan Dr.
Atlanta, GA 30340
(404) 451-4531

Crown Products
See Bentley Brothers

Crystal Mountain Prisms
PO Box 31
Westfield, NY 14787
(716) 326-3676

Cumberland General Store
Rte. 3
Crossville, TN 38555
(800) 334-4640
(615) 484-8481 (TN)

Cumberland Woodcraft Co.
Drawer 609
Carlisle, PA 17013
(717) 243-0063

Curran Glass & Mirror Co.
30 N. Maple St.
Florence, MA 01060
(413) 584-5761

Victor Cushwa & Sons, Inc.
PO Box 160
Williamsport, MD 21795
(301) 223-7700

Custom Ironworks
PO Box 99
Union, KY 41091
(606) 384-4486

Custom Millwork, Inc.
PO Box 562
Berryville, VA 22611
(703) 955-4988

D. E. A./Bathroom Machineries
495 Main St., Box 1020
Murphys, CA 95247
(209) 728-3860

Dahlke Studios
Box 1128
Glastonbury, CT 06033
(203) 659-1887

Dalton-Gorman, Inc.
1508 Sherman Ave.
Evanston, IL 60201
(312) 869-5575

Elizabeth Day
Pippins, Town Row
Rotherfield, East Susex
TN6 3HU, England
(08) 92985 3112

Day Studio-Workshop, Inc.
1504 Bryant St.
San Francisco, CA 94103
(415) 626-9300

The Decorators Supply Corp.
3610-12 S. Morgan St.
Chicago, IL 60609
(312) 847-6300
(312) 847-6357 (FAX)

Decorum
235-237 Commercial St.
Portland, ME 04101
(207) 775-3346

Delaware Quarries, Inc.
River Rd.
Lumberville, PA 18933
(215) 297-5647

Dell Corp.
1045 Taft St., PO Box 1462
Rockville, MD 20850
(301) 279-2612

The Design Archives
79 Walton St.
London SW3 2HP, England
(01) 581-3968

Designs in Tile
Box 4983
Foster City, CA 94404
(415) 571-7122

Devenco Products Inc.
PO Box 700, Dept. OHC
Decatur, GA 30031
(800) 888-4597
(404) 378-4597 (GA)

DeWeese Woodworking
Box 576
Philadelphia, MS 39350
(601) 656-4951

A. L. Diament & Co.
309 Commerce Dr.
Exton, PA 19341
(215) 363-5660

Diamond K. Co., Inc.
130 Buckland Rd.
South Windsor, CT 06074
(203) 644-8486

Duo Dickinson, Architect
70 Wall St.
Madison, CT 06443
(203) 245-0405

Diedrich Chemicals Restoration Technologies, Inc.
300A E. Oak St.
Milwaukee, WI 53154
(800) 323-3565

Donnell's Clapboard Mill
County Rd., RR Box 1560
Sedgwick, ME 04676
(207) 359-2036

Dovetail Woodworking
550 Elizabeth St.
Waukesha, WI 53186
(414) 544-5859

Driwood Moulding Co.
Box 1729
Florence, SC 29503-1729
(803) 669-2478

Dutch Boy
1370 Ontario St.
Cleveland, OH 44101
(216) 566-3140

18th Century Hardware
131 E. 3rd St.
Derry, PA 15627
(412) 694-2708

Eagle Plywood & Door Mfg. Co. Inc.
450 Oak Tree Ave.
South Plainfield, NJ 07080
(201) 668-1460

Eastfield Village
Box 145, RD
East Nassau, NY 12062
(518) 766-2422

Edison Chemical Systems
25 Grant St.
Waterbury, CT 06704
(203) 597-9727

Elcanco, Inc.
Beharrell St.
Concord, MA 01742
(508) 369-7609

Elephant Hill Iron Works
RR 1, Box 168
Tunbridge, VT 05077
(802) 889-9444

Elmira Stove & Fireplace
145 Northfield Dr.
Waterloo, Ontario 2NL 5J3,
Canada
(519) 747-5443
(519) 747-5444 (FAX)

The English Garden, Inc.
652 Glenbrook Rd.
Stamford, CT 06906
(203) 348-3048

Entrances
RFD 1, Box 246A
Westmoreland, NH 03467
(603) 399-7723

Especially Lace
202 Fifth St.
West Des Moines, IA 50265
(515) 277-8778

EverGreene Painting Studios
365 W. 36th St.
New York, NY 10018
(212) 239-1322

Everlite Greenhouses, Inc.
9305 Gerwig Ln., Suite H
Guilford Industrial Park
Columbia, MD 21046
(301) 381-3880

Experi-Metals
524 W. Greenfield Ave.
Milwaukee, WI 53204
(414) 384-2167

Ezra G.
1120 E. Sandusky St.
Fostoria, OH 44830
(419) 435-7707

Family Heir-Loom Weavers
RD 3, Box 59E
Red Lion, PA 17356
(717) 246-2431

The Fan Man Inc.
4614 Travis
Dallas, TX 75205
(214) 559-4440

Faneuil Furniture Hardware
163 Main Street
Salem, NH 03079
(603) 898-7733

Federal Street Lighthouse
38 Market Sq.
Newburyport, MA 01950
(617) 462-6333

Ferguson's Cut Glass Works
4292 Pearl Rd.
Cleveland, OH 44109
(216) 459-2929

David Flaharty
402 Magazine Rd., RD 2
Green Lane, PA 18054
(215) 234-8242

Fireplace Mantel Shop
4217 Howard Ave.
Kensington, MD 20895
(301) 564-1550

Fireside Reproductions
4727 Winterset Dr.
Columbus, OH 43220
(614) 451-7695

Flexi-Wall Systems
PO Box 88
Liberty, SC 29657
(803) 855-0500

Floorcloths Incorporated
920 Edgewater Rd.
Severna Park, MD 21146
(301) 544-0858

Focal Point, Inc.
PO Box 93327
Atlanta, GA 30318
(800) 662-5550
(404) 351-0820 (GA and AK)

Folkheart Rag Rugs
15 Main St.
Bristol, VT 05443
(802) 453-4101

Franklin County Millwork
PO Box 30
St. Clair, MO 63077
(314) 927-5770

Peter Franklin
1 Cottage St., Box 1166
Easthampton, MA 01027
(413) 527-4004

Anna French
343 Kings Rd.
London SW3 5ES, England
(01) 351-1126

Frog Tool Co., Ltd.
700 W. Jackson Blvd.
Chicago, IL 60606
(312) 648-1270

Fuller-O'Brien Paints
PO Box 864
Brunswick, GA 31521
(912) 265-7650

Fypon, Inc.
22 W. Pennsylvania Ave.
Stewartstown, PA 17363
(717) 993-2593

Gainsborough Hardware Industries, Inc.
PO Box 569
Chesterfield, MO 63017
(314) 532-8466

Garrett Wade Co.
161 Ave. of the Americas
New York, NY 10013
(212) 807-1757

Gaslight Time Antiques
823 President St.
Brooklyn, NY 11215
(718) 789-7185

Gates Moore
River Rd., Silvermine RD 3
Norwalk, CT 06850
(203) 847-3231

Gazebo & Porchworks
728 9th Ave. SW
Puyallup, WA 98371-6744
(206) 848-0502

Gazebo Woodcrafters
205 Virginia St.
Bellingham, WA 98225
(206) 734-0463

Jamie Gibbs and Associates
Landscape Architects and
    Interior Designers
340 E. 93rd St., Suite 14C
New York, NY 10128
(212) 722-7508

Glashaus, Inc.
PO Box 517
Elk Grove, IL 60007
(312) 640-6910

Glass Arts
30 Penniman Rd.
Boston (Allston), MA 02134
(617) 782-7760

Glen-Gery Corp.
Rte. 61, PO Box 340
Shoemakersville, PA 19555
(215) 562-3076

The Glidden Co.
925 Euclid Ave.
Cleveland, OH 44115
(216) 344-8000

Gloster Leisure Furniture, Ltd.
See Steptoe and Wife
    Antiques, Ltd.

Golden Age Glassworks
339 Bellvale Rd.
Warwick, NY 10990
(914) 986-1487

Good & Co. Floorclothmakers
Salzburg Sq., Rt. 101
Amherst, NH 03031
(603) 672-0490

Good Directions, Inc.
Dept OH8C
24 Ardmore Rd.
Stamford, CT 06902
(203) 348-1836
(800) 346-7678

Good Time Stove Co.
PO Box 306, Rt. 112
Goshen, MA 01032-0306
(413) 268-3677

Lynn Goodpasture
42 W. 17th St.
New York, NY 10011
(212) 645-5334

Goodwin Lumber Co.
Rte. 2, Box 119-AA
Micanopy, FL 32667
(904) 373-WOOD

Governor's Antiques Ltd.
6240 Meadowbridge Rd.
Mechanicsville, VA 23111
(804) 746-1030

The Grammar of Ornament
2626 Curtis St.
Denver, CO 80205
(303) 295-2431

Grand Era Reproductions
PO Box 1026
Lapeer, MI 48446
(313) 664-1756

Granville Manufacturing Co.
Rte. 100
Granville, VT 05747
(802) 767-4747

Gravity-Randall
208 N. Douty St.,
PO Box 1378
Hanford, CA 93232
(209) 584-2216

Great American Salvage Co.
34 Cooper Sq.
New York, NY 10003
(212) 505-0070

Great Panes Glassworks
2861 Walnut Street
Denver, CO 80205
(303) 294-0927

Greatwood Log Homes
PO Box 707
Elkhart Lake, WI 53020
(800) 558-5812

Greeff Fabrics, Inc.
150 Midland Ave.
Port Chester, NY 10573
(914) 939-6200

Greg's Antique Lighting
12005 Wilshire Blvd.
Los Angeles, CA 90025
(413) 478-5475

H and M Stair Builders, Inc.
4217 Howard Ave.
Kensington, MD 20895
(301) 564-1550

Half-Moon Antiques
Box 141
Fair Haven, NJ 07701
(201) 219-0027

W. J. Hampton Plastering
30 Fisk St.
Jersey City, NJ 07305
(201) 433-9002

Whit Hanks
1009 W. 6th St.
Austin, TX 78703
(512) 478-2101

Richard N. Hayton & Assoc.
501 11th St.
Brooklyn, NY 11215
(718) 499-5299

Hephaestus Pottery
2012 Penn St.
Lebanon, PA 17042
(717) 272-0806

Hearth Realities
PO Box 38093
Atlanta, GA 30334
(404) 377-6852

Heartwood
Johnson Rd.
Washington, MA 01235
(413) 623-6677

Heart-Wood, Inc.
Rte. 1, Box 97-A
Jasper, FL 32052
(904) 792-1688

Judith Hendershot
1408 Main St.
Evanston, IL 60202
(312) 475-6411

Heritage Lanterns
70A Main St.
Yarmouth, ME 04096
(207) 846-3911

Heritage Mantels
PO Box 240
Southport, CT 06490
(203) 335-0552

Allen Charles Hill, AIA
25 Englewood Rd.
Winchester, MA 01890
(617) 729-0748

Hill & Knowles
133 Kew Rd.
Richmond, Surrey,
    TW9 2PN England
(01) 948-4010

Hippo Hardware & Trading
201 S.E. 12th Ave.
Portland, OR 97214
(503) 231-1444

Historic Boulevard Services
1520 W. Jackson Blvd.
Chicago, IL 60607
(312) 829-5562

Historic Charleston Reproductions
105 Broad St., Box 622
Charleston, SC 29402
(803) 723-8292

Historic Hardware Ltd.
PO Box 1327
North Hampton, NH 03862
(603) 964-2280
(Showroom)
821 Lafayette Rd.
Hampton, NH 03842
(603) 926-8315

Historic Housefitters Co.
Dept. 5, Farm to Market Rd.
Brewster, NY 10509
(914) 278-2427

Historic Windows
Box 1172
Harrisonburg, VA 22801
(703) 434-5855

Historical Replications, Inc.
Box 13529
Jackson, MS 39236
(601) 981-8743

Hitchcock Chair Co.
PO Box 369
New Hartford, CT 06057
(203) 379-8531

Pete Holly
3111 2nd Ave.
Minneapolis, MN 55408
(612) 824-2333

Alvin Holm, AIA
2014 Sansom St.
Philadelphia, PA 19103
(215) 963-0747

Pat Hornafius
Lancaster County Folk Art
113 Meadowbrook Ln.
Elizabethtown, PA 17022
(717) 367-7706

House Carpenters
Box 217
Brewster, MA 01072
(617) 896-7857

Humberstone Woodworking
PO Box 104
Georgetown, Ontario
L7G 4T1, Canada
(416) 877-6757

Hurley Patentee Lighting
Hurley Patentee Manor
RD 7, Box 98A
Kingston, NY 12401
(914) 331-5414

Iberia Millwork
500 Jane St.
New Iberia, LA 70560
(318) 365-5644

Illustrious Lighting
1925 Fillmore St.
San Francisco, CA 94115
(415) 922-3133

Import Specialists, Inc.
82 Wall St.
New York, NY 10005-3688
(800) 334-4044
(212) 709-9633 (NY)

The Iron Shop
Dept. OHCF
Box 128, 400 Reed Rd.
Broomall, PA 19008
(215) 544-7100

Irreplaceable Artifacts
14 Second Ave.
New York, NY 10003
(212) 777-2900

Marian Ives
Box 101A, RR 1
Charlemont, MA 01339
(413) 339-8534

Jerard Paul Jordan Gallery
Box 71, Slade Acres
Ashford, CT 06278
(203) 429-7954

The Joinery Co.
Box 518
Tarboro, NC 27886
(919) 823-3306

Lee Joffa
979 Third Ave.
New York, NY 10022
(212) 688-0444

K & D Supply Co.
2717 High Ridge Rd.
Charlotte, NC 28226
(704) 846-4345

Kane-Gonic Brick Co.
Winter St.
Gonic, NH 03867
(603) 332-2861

Howard Kaplan Antiques
827 Broadway
New York, NY 10003
(212) 674-1000

The Kardell Studio Inc.
904 Westminster Dr. N.W.
Washington, DC 20001
(202) 462-4433

Katzenbach & Warren
C & A Wallcoverings
23645 Mercantile Rd.
Cleveland, OH 44122
(216) 464-3700

Kayne & Son
76 Daniel Ridge Rd.
Candler, NC 28715
(704) 667-8868

Kenmore Industries
Box 34, One Thompson Sq.
Boston, MA 02129
(617) 242-1711

Kentucky Wood Floors
4200 Reservoir Ave.
Louisville, KY 40213
(502) 451-6024

King's Chandelier Co.
Highway 14, PO Box 667
Eden, NC 27288
(919) 623-6188

Mark A. Knudsen
1100 E. County Line Rd.
Des Moines, IA 50320
(515) 285-6112

Koeppel/Freedman Studios
386 Congress St.
Boston, MA 02210
(617) 426-8887

Kohler Co.
Kohler, WI 53044
(414) 457-4441

Kraatz Russell Glass
Grist Mill Hill
RFD 1, Box 320C
Canaan, NH 03741
(603) 523-4289

John Kruesel's General
Merchandise
22 Third St. S.W.
Rochester, MN 55902
(507) 289-8049

KU/2 Specialties, Marc
Coutu
Box 618
Munsonville, NH 03457
(603) 847-9749

Kyp-Go, Inc.
PO Box 247, 20 N. 17th St.
St. Charles, IL 60174
(312) 584-8181

Lazy Hill Farm Designs
Lazy Hill Rd.
Coleman, NC 27924
(919) 356-2828

James Lea, Cabinetmaker
Harkness House/9 West St.
Rockport, ME 04856
(207) 236-3632

Lehman Hardware &
Appliances
PO Box 41, 4799 Kidron Rd.
Kidron, OH 44636
(216) 857-5441

Lemee's Fireplace Equipment
815 Bedford St.
Bridgewater, MA 02324
(508) 697-2672

Brian F. Leo
7532 Columbia Ave. S.
Richfield, MN 55423
(612) 861-1473

Linen and Lace
#4 Lafayette
Washington, MO 63090
(800) 332-5223
(314) 239-6499 (MO)

Linoleum City
5657 Santa Monica Blvd.
Hollywood, CA 90038
(213) 469-0063

Littlewood & Maue
PO Box 402
Palmyra, NJ 08065
(609) 829-4615

W. S. Lockhart Designs
112 S. Warren St.
Timmonsville, SC 29161
(803) 346-3531

Lovelia Enterprises, Inc.
356 E. 41st
New York, NY 10017
(212) 490-0930

Edward Ludlow,
Cabinetmaker
PO Box 646
Pluckemin, NJ 07978
(201) 658-9091

Lunenberg Foundry &
Engineering Ltd.
PO Box 1240, 53 Falkland
St.
Lunenberg, Nova Scotia
B0J 2C0, Canada
(902) 634-8827
(902) 455-2461
(902) 634-8886 (FAX)

Kenneth Lynch & Sons
Box 488
Wilton, CT 06897-0488
(203) 762-8363

M-H Lamp & Fan Co.
7231-½ N. Sheridan Rd.
Chicago, IL 60626
(312) 743-2225

Steven P. Mack Associates
Chase Hill Farm
Ashaway, RI 02804
(401) 377-8041

Mad River Wood Works
Box 163
Arcata, CA 95521
(707) 826-0629

Maizefield Mantels
PO Box 336
Port Townsend, WA 98368
(206) 385-6789

Merilyn M. Markham
90 Main St.
Andover, MA 01810
(508) 475-4931

Marmion Plantation Co.
RD 2, Box 458
Fredericksburg, VA 22405
(703) 775-3480

The Martin-Senour Co.
1370 Ontario Ave. N.W.
Cleveland, OH 44113
(216) 566-3140

Marvin Windows
PO Box 100
Warroad, MN 56763
(800) 346-5128
(800) 552-1167 (MN)

Materials Unlimited
2 W. Michigan Ave.
Ypsilanti, MI 48197
(313) 483-6890

Maurer & Shepherd
Joyners, Inc.
122 Naubuc Ave.
Glastonbury, CT 06033
(203) 633-2383

M. J. May Antique Building
Restoration
505 Storle Ave.
Burlington, WI 53105
(414) 763-8822

Mechanick's Workbench
Box 668, Front St.
Marian, MA 02738
(617) 748-1680

Metropolitan Lighting Fixture Co., Inc.
315 E. 62nd St.
New York, NY 10021
(212) 838-2425

Mid-State Tile Co.
PO Box 1777
Lexington, NC 27292
(704) 249-3931

Midwest Wood Products
1051 S. Rolff St.
Davenport, IA 52802
(319) 323-4757

Millbrook Wallcoverings
23645 Mercantile Rd.
Cleveland, OH 44122
(216) 464-3700

Mr. Slate
Smid , Inc.
Sudbury, VT 05733
(802) 247-8809

Benjamin Moore & Co.
51 Chestnut Ridge Rd.
Montvale, NJ 07645
(201) 573-9600

E. T. Moore, Jr., Co.
3100 N. Hopkins Rd.,
Suite 101
Richmond, VA 23224
(804) 231-1823

Tom Moore's Steeple People
21 Janine St.
Chicopee, MA 01013
(413) 533-9515

Moravian Pottery & Tile
Works
Swamp Rd.
Doylestown, PA 18901
(215) 345-6722

Matthew John Mosca
2513 Queen Anne Rd.
Baltimore, MD 21216
(301) 466-5325

Mountain Lumber Co.
Rte. 2, Box 43-1
Ruckersville, VA 22968
(804) 985-3646 or
(804) 295-1922

M. J. Mullane Co.
PO Box 108, 17 Mason St.
Hudson, MA 01749
(508) 568-0597

Museum of American Textile
History
800 Massachusetts Ave.
N. Andover, MA 01845
(617) 686-0191

National Preservation
Institute
Juduciary Square, N.W.
Washington, DC 20001
(202) 393-0038

Neenah Foundry
Box 729, 2121 Brooks Ave.
Neenah, WI 54956
(414) 725-7000

New England Outbuildings
152 Old Clinton Rd.
Westbrook, CT 06498
(203) 669-1776

New England Woodturners
75 Daggett St., PO Box 7242
New Haven, CT 06519
(203) 776-1880

The New Jersey Barn Co.
PO Box 702
Princeton, NJ 08542
(609) 924-8480

New York Marble Works
1399 Park Ave.
New York, NY 10029
(212) 534-2242

W. F. Norman Corp.
Box 323,
214-32 N. Cedar St.
Nevada, MO 64772-0323
(800) 641-4038
(MO call collect)
(417) 667-5552

North Fields Restorations
Box 741
Rowley, MA 01969
(617) 948-2722

North Pacific Joinery
76 W. 4th St., Dept. OHC
Eureka, CA 95501
(707) 443-5788

North Woods Chair Shop
RFD 1, Old Tilton Rd.
Canterbury, NH 03224
(603) 783-4595

Nostalgia, Inc.
307 Stiles Ave.
Savannah, GA 31401
(800) 874-0015
(912) 232-2324

Nowell's, Inc.
490 Gate 5 Road
Sausalito, CA 94965
(415) 332-4933

Craig Nutt, Fine Wood Works
2014 Fifth St.
Northport, AL 35476
(205) 752-6535

Oak Crest Mfg., Inc.
1405 E. Emory Rd.
Knoxville, TN 37938
(615) 938-1315

Oakleaf Reproductions
Lucas G. Leone, Jr.
North American Agent
Stonewalls, Chester
  Springs, PA 19425
(215) 827-9491

Russell Swinton Oatman Design Associates, Inc.
132 Mirick Rd.
Princeton, MA 01541
(508) 464-2360

Oehrlein and Associates
1702 Connecticut Ave., NW
Washington, DC 20009
(202) 387-8040

Ohmega Salvage
2407 San Pablo Ave., Box 2125
Berkeley, CA 94702
(415) 843-7368

Old Abingdon Weavers
PO Box 786
Abingdon, VA 24210
(703) 628-4233

Old Carolina Brick Co.
Rt. 9, Box 77, Majolica Rd.
Salisbury, NC 28144
(704) 636-8850

The Old Fashioned Milk Paint Co.
PO Box 222
Groton, MA 01450
(508) 448-6336

Old Lamplighter Shop
The Musical Museum
Deansboro, NY 13328
(315) 841-8774

Old House Gardens
536 3rd St.
Ann Arbor, MI 48103
(313) 995-1486

The Old Jefferson Tile Co.
PO Box 494
Jefferson, TX 75657
(214) 665-2221

Old Wagon Factory
130 Russell St.
PO Box 1427
Clarksville, VA 23927
(804) 374-5787

Old World Moulding & Finishing Co., Inc.
115 Allen Blvd.
Farmingdale, NY 11735
(516) 293-1789

Olde Virginea Floorcloth & Trading Co.
PO Box 3305
Portsmouth, VA 23701
(804) 397-0948

Olympic Stain
2233 112th Ave., N.E.
Bellevue, WA 98004
(800) 426-6306

Omnia Industries
5 Cliffside Dr., Box 330
Cedar Grove, NJ 07009
(201) 239-7272

Ornamental Mouldings Ltd.
PO Box 336
Waterloo, Ontario N2J 4A4, Canada
(519) 884-4080
(519) 884-9692 (FAX)

Osborne & Little
49 Temperley Rd.
London SW12 8QE, England
(01) 675-2255

Outdoor Designs
197 George St.
Excelsior, MN 55331
(612) 474-8328

Ox-Line Paints
California Products Corp.
169 Waverly St.
Cambridge MA 02139
(800) 225-1141
(800) 842-1161 (MA)

Pagliacco Turning & Milling
Box 225
Woodacre, CA 94973
(415) 488-4333

Palm Rooms Ltd.
10 Farrell St.
S. Burlington, VT 05403
(802) 863-0001

William H. Parsons & Assoc.
420 Salmon Brook
Granby, CT 06035
(203) 653-2281

Partridge Replications
63 Penhallow St., Box 4104
Portsmouth, NH 03801
(603) 431-8733

Pasvalco
Bogert St.
Closter, NJ 07624
(201) 768-2133

Patterson, Flynn & Martin
950 Third Ave.
New York, NY 10022
(212) 751-6414

Paxton Hardware Ltd.
7818 Bradshaw Rd.
Upper Falls, MD 21156
(301) 592-8505

Pelnik Wrecking Co., Inc.
1749 Erie Blvd. E
Syracuse, NY 13210
(315) 472-1031

Pemaquid Floorcloths
Round Pond, ME 04564
(207) 529-5633

Pennsylvania Firebacks, Inc.
308 Elm Ave.
North Wales, PA 19454
(215) 699-0805

Period Furniture Hardware
Boxc 314
Charles St. Station
Boston, MA 02114
(617) 227-0758

Period Lighting Fixtures
1 West Main Street
Chester, CT 06412
(203) 526-3690

Perkins Architectural Millwork
Rte. 5, Box 264-W
Longview, TX 75601
(214) 663-3036

Perkowitz Window Fashions
136 Green Bay Rd.
Wilmette, IL 60091-3375
(312) 251-7700

Perma Ceram Enterprises
65 Smithtown Blvd.
Smithtown, NY 11787
(800) 645-5039
(516) 724-1205

Edward K. Perry Co.
322 Newbury St.
Boston, MA 02115
(617) 536-7873

Jill Pilaroscia Architectural Color
220 Eureka St.
San Francisco, CA 94114
(415) 861-8086

Pittsburgh Paints
One PPG Plaza
Pittsburgh, PA 15272
(412) 434-2400

Pompei & Company
454 High St.
West Medford, MA 02155
(617) 395-8867

Portland Stove Co.
PO Box 377, Fickett Rd.
N. Pownal, ME 04069
(207) 688-2254
(207) 775-6424

Pratt & Lambert Paints
PO Box 22, Dept. GV
Buffalo, NY 14240
(716) 873-6000

Preservation Associates
207 S. Potomac St.
Hagerstown, MD 21740
(301) 791-7880

The Preservation Partnership
345 Union St.
New Bedford, MA 02740
(508) 996-3383

Preservation Resources Group (PRG)
5619 Southampton Dr.
Springfield, VA 22151
(703) 323-1407

Preservation Services
1445 Hampshire
Quincy, IL 62301
(217) 224-2300

Price Glover, Inc.
817½ Madison Ave.
New York, NY 10021
(212) 772-1740

Q R B Industries
3139 N. U.S. 31
Niles, MI 49120

Queen City Architectural Salvage
4750 Brighton Blvd.
Denver, CO 80216
(303) 296-0925

Ramase
Rte. 47
Woodbury, CT 06798
(203) 263-3332 (office)
(203) 263-4909 (home)

Rambusch
40 W. 13th St.
New York, NY 10011
(212) 675-0400

Ramm, Son & Crocker Ltd.
13-14 Treadway Technical
  Centre
Treadway Hill, Loudwater,
  High Wycombe
Buckinghamshire HP10 9PE
England

Rejuvenation Lamp & Fixture
901 N. Skidmore
Portland, OR 97217
(503) 249-0774

Remodelers' and Renovators' Supply
1920 N. Liberty St.
Boise, ID 83704
(208) 323-1089

Renaissance Marketing, Inc.
PO Box 360
Lake Orion, MI 48035
(313) 693-1109

The Renovation Source, Inc.
3512 N. Southport Ave.
Chicago, IL 60657
(312) 327-1250

Restoration Supply
Box 253
Hawesville, KY 42348
(502) 927-8494

Restorations Unlimited, Inc.
24 W. Main St.
Elizabethville, PA 17023
(717) 362-3477

J. Ring Glass Studio
2724 University Ave. S.E.
Minneapolis, MN 55414
(612) 379-0920

Rising and Nelson Slate Co.
West Pawlet, VT 05775
(802) 645-0150

River City Restorations
PO Box 1065
623 Collier Rd.
Hannibal, MO 63401
(314) 248-0733

Riverbend Timber Framing
Box 26
Blissfield, MI 49228
(517) 486-4566

Robinson Iron Corp.
Robinson Rd.
Alexander City, AL 35010
(205) 329-8486

Robinson Lumber
Suite 202, 512 S. Peters St.
New Orleans, LA 70130
(504) 523-6377

Robson Worldwide Graining
4308 Argonne Dr.
Fairfax, VA 22032
(703) 978-5331

Barry Rose
1450 Logan
Denver, CO 80203
(303) 832-3250

McKie Wing Roth, Jr., Associates
PO Box 130
Gardiner, ME 04345
(207) 582-3718

William James Roth
PO Box 355
Yarmouth Port, MA 02675
(508) 362-9235

Roy Electric Co., Inc.
1054 Coney Island Ave.
Brooklyn, NY 11230
(718) 434-7002

Rue de France
78 Thames St.
Newport, RI 02840
(401) 846-2084

Russell Restoration of Suffolk
5550 Bergen Ave.
Mattituck, New York 11952
(516) 765-2481

Rye Tiles
The Old Brewery
Wishward, Rye TN31 7DH
England
(0797) 223038

S. P. N. E. A. Conservation Center
185 Lyman Street
Waltham, MA 02154
(617) 891-1985

Samuel B. Sadtler & Co.
340 S. Fourth St.
Philadelphia, PA 19106
(215) 923-3714

St. Louis Antique Lighting
801 N. Skinker
St. Louis, MO 63130
(314) 863-1414

St. Thomas Creations Inc.
79-25 Denbrook Rd.,
Suite D
San Diego, CA 92126
(619) 530-1940

Arthur Sanderson & Sons
979 Third Ave., Suite 403
New York, NY 10022
(212) 319-7220

San Francisco Victoriana
2245 Palou Ave.
San Francisco, CA 94124
(415) 648-0313

Saxe-Patterson
Taos Clay Products, Inc.
Box 15, Camino de la
 Merced
Taos, NM 87571
(505) 758-9513

Sandra McKenzie Schmitt
25 Fifth St.
Frenchtown, NJ 08825
(201) 996-3214

F. Schumacher & Co.
79 Madison Ave.
New York, NY 10016
(212) 213-7900

Schwartz's Forge and Metalworks
PO Box 205,
Forge Hollow Rd.
Deansboro, NY 13328
(315) 841-4477

Shaker Workshop
PO Box 1028
Concord, MA 01742
(508) 646-8985

Sheppard Millwork
21020 70th Ave. W.
Edmonds, WA 98020
(206) 771-4645
(206) 672-1622 (FAX)

Shuttercraft
282 Stepstone Hill Rd.
Guilford, CT 06437
(203) 453-1973

Silver Dollar Trading
1591 Main St., PO Box 394
San Elizario, TX 79849

Silverton Victorian Mill Works
PO Box 2987-OCE
Durango, CO 81302
(303) 259-5915

The Sink Factory
2140 San Pablo
Berkeley, CA 94702
(415) 540-8193

Skyline Engineers of Maryland, Inc.
PO Box 671
Frederick, MD 21701
(301) 831-8800

Kathleen B. Smith
PO Box 48
W. Chesterfield, MA 01084
(413) 296-4437

Smith Woodworks & Design
Box 42, RR 1,
Farmersville Rd.
Califon, NJ 07830
(201) 832-2723

Somerset Door & Column
Box 328
Somerset, PA 15501
(800) 242-7916
(800) 242-7915 (PA)

William Spencer
Creek Rd.
Rancocas Woods, NJ 08060
(609) 235-1830

Spring House Classics
PO Box 541
Schaefferstown, PA 17088
(717) 949-3902

Spiess Antique Building Materials
228-230 E. Washington
Joliet, IL 60433
(815) 722-5639

Standard Trimming
1114 First Ave. (61st St.)
New York, NY 10021
(212) 755-3034

Stair Specialist
2257 W. Columbia Ave.
Battle Creek, MI 49017
(616) 964-2351

Stark Carpet Co.
979 Third Ave.
New York, NY 10022
(212) 752-9000

States Industries, Inc.
29545 Enid Rd. E.
PO Box 7037
Eugene, OR 97401
(800) 537-0419

John Stefandis & Associates
Unit 7, Charles Wharf,
Lots Rd.
London SW10, England
(01) 376-3999

Stencilsmith
71 Main St.
Cold Spring, NY 10156
(914) 265-9561

Steptoe & Wife Antiques
322 Geary Ave.
Toronto, Ontario M6H 2C7,
Canada
(416) 530-4200

Sterling Prints
23645 Mercantile Rd.
Cleveland, OH 44122
(216) 464-3700

Stewart Iron Works Co.
PO Box 2612, 20 W. 18th St.
Covington, KY 41012
(606) 431-1985

Structural Slate Co.
222 E. Main St.
Pen Argyl, PA 18072
(215) 863-4141

Sturbridge Studio
114 E. Hill
Brimfield, MA 01010
(413) 245-3289

Donald Stryker Restorations
154 Commercial Ave.
New Brunswick, NJ 08901
(201) 828-7022

Sun Room Company, Inc.
PO Box 301
2761 Creek Hill Rd.
Leola, PA 17540
(800) 426-2737
(717) 656-8018 (PA)

Sunflower Glass Studios
Box 99, RD 3
Sergeantsville, NJ 08557
(609) 397-1535

Sunrise Specialty
2204 San Pablo Ave.
Berkeley, CA 94702
(415) 845-4751

Sunshine Architectural Woodworks
Rte. 2, Box 434
Fayetteville, AR 72701
(501) 521-4329

Superior Clay Corp.
Box 352
Uhrichsville, OH 44683
(800) 848-6166

Tennessee Tub Inc. & Tubliner Co.
6682 Charlotte Pk
Nashville, TN 37209
(615) 352-1939

Terra Cotta Productions, Inc.
Box 99781
Pittsburgh, PA 15233
(412) 321-2109

Richard E. Thibaut, Inc.
706 S. 21st St.
Irvington, NJ 07111
(201) 399-7888

Timberpeg, East Inc.
Box 1500
Claremont, NH 03603
(603) 542-7762

Tioga Mill Outlet
200 S. Hartman St.
York, PA 17403
(717) 843-5139

Tiresias, Inc.
PO Box 1864
Orangeburg, SC 29116
(803) 534-8476

Chapin Townsend
PO Box 628, James Trail
West Kingston, RI 02892
(401) 783-6614

Traditional Line Architectural Restoration Ltd.
35 Hillside Ave.
Monsey, NY 10952
(914) 425-6400

Tremont Nail Co.
PO Box 111
Wareham, MA 02571
(617) 295-0038

Tromploy Inc.
400 Lafayette St.
New York, NY 10003
(212) 420-1639

Tsigonia Paints & Varnishes
568 W. 184th St.
New York, NY 10033
(212) 568-4430

Travis Tuck, Metal Sculptor
Box 1832
Martha's Vineyard, MA
 02568
(508) 693-3914

Tullibardine Enterprises
5900 Dublin Rd.
Dublin, OH 43017
(614) 889-6307

United House Wrecking
535 Hope St.
Stamford, CT 06906
(203) 348-5371

Urban Archaeology
137 Spring St.
New York, NY 10012
(212) 431-6969

Urfic, Inc.
1000 S. Broadway
Salem, OH 44460
(216) 332-9500

Van Luit & Co.
200 Garden City Plaza
Garden City, NY 11530
(516) 741-9440

Vermont Cobble Slate
Smid, Inc.
Sudbury, VT 05733
(802) 247-8809

Vermont Marble Co.
61 Main St.
Proctor, VT 05765
(802) 459-3311

Vermont Soapstone Co.
PO Box 168, Stoughton
 Pond Rd.
Perkinsville, VT 05151-0168
(802) 263-5404

Victorian Collectibles, Ltd.
845 E. Glenbrook Rd.
Milwaukee, WI 53217
(414) 352-6910

Victorian Lightcrafters, Ltd.
PO Box 350
Slate Hill, NY 10973
(914) 355-1300

Victorian Reproduction
Lighting Co.
PO Box 579
Minneapolis, MN 55458
(612) 338-3636
Victorian Warehouse
190 Grace St.
Auburn, CA 05603
(916) 823-0374
Vintage Lumber & Construc-
tion Co., Inc.
9507 Woodsboro Rd.
Frederick, MD 21701
(301) 898-7859
Vintage Plumbing &
Sanitary Specialties
9645 Sylvia Ave.
Northridge, CA 91324
(818) 772-6353
Vintage Valances
PO Box 43326-C
Cincinnati, OH 45243
(513) 561-8665
Vintage Wood Works
513 S. Adams, #1276
Fredericksburg, TX 78624
(512) 997-9513

Warner Fabrics
7-11 Noel St.
London W1V 4AL, England
(01) 439-2411
E. G. Washburne & Co. Inc.
85 Andover St., Rte. 114
Danvers, MA 01923
(617) 774-3645
The Washington Copper
Works
Washington, CT 06793
(203) 868-7637 (workshop)
(203) 868-7527 (residence)
Watercolors, Inc.
Garrison, NY 10524
(914) 424-3327

Waterman Works
266B Oxford Pl., NE
Atlanta, GA 30307
(404) 373-9438
Watertower Pines
Rte. 1 South, PO Box 1067
Kennebunk, ME 04043
(207) 985-6868
Watts & Co. Ltd.
7 Tufton St. Westminster
London SW1P 3QB,
England
Waverly Fabrics
79 Madison Ave.
New York, NY 10016
(212) 644-5900
J. P. Weaver
2301 W. Victory Blvd.
Burbank, CA 91506
(818) 841-5700
Wendall's Wood Stoves
19964 Inks Dr.
Tuolumne, CA 95379
(209) 928-4508
Westmoore Pottery
Rt. 2, Box 494
Seagrove, NC 27341
(919) 464-3700
Martha Wetherbee Basket
Shop
Star Rte., Box 35
Sanborntown, NH 03269
(603) 286-8927
Eldred Wheeler
c/o Partridge Replications
63 Penhallow St.
Portsmouth, NH 03801
(603) 431-8733
Philip M. White and Assoc.
Box 47
Mecklenburg, NY 14863
(607) 387-6370

Robert Whitley Furniture
Studios
Laurel Rd.
Solebury, PA 18963
(215) 297-8452
Whitten Enterprises, Inc.
PO Box 1121
Bennington, VT 05201
(802) 442-8344
The Wicker Garden
1318 Madison Ave.
New York, NY 10128
(212) 410-7001 (store)
(212) 410-2777 (office)
Wiggins Brothers
Hale Rd., Box 420
Tilton, NH 03276
(603) 286-3046
Frederick Wilbur
PO Box 425
Lovingston, VA 22949
(804) 263-4827
Williams Art Glass Studios
Sunset Antiques, Inc.
22 N. Washington (M-24)
Oxford, MI 48051
(313) 628-1111
Helen Williams/Rare Tiles
12643 Hortense St.
Studio City, CA 91604
(818) 761-2756
Williamsburg Blacksmiths
1 Buttonshop Rd.
Williamsburg, MA 01096
(413) 268-7341
Winans Construction
2004 Woolsey St.
Berkeley, CA 94703
(415) 843-4796
Windy Hill Forge
3824 Schroeder Ave.
Perry Hall, MD 21128-9783
(301) 256-5890

Winterthur Museum and
Gardens
Winterthur, DE 19735
(302) 656-8591
Woodbury Blacksmith &
Forge Co.
Box 268
Woodbury, CT 06798
(203) 263-5737
Wooden Nickel Antiques
1400-1414 Central Pkwy.
Cincinnati, OH 45210
(513) 241-2985
Woods Co.
123 S. Main St.
Brownsville, MD 21715
(301) 432-8419
The Woodworkers' Store
21801 Industrial Blvd.
Rogers, MN 55374
(612) 428-4101
The Wrecking Bar
292 Moreland Ave., N.E.
Atlanta, GA 30307
(404) 525-0468

Yankee Craftsmen
357 Commonwealth Rd.,
Rt. 30
Wayland, MA 01778
(617) 653-0031
Wick York
PO Box 334
Stonington, CT 06378
(203) 535-1409

Zoffany
63 S. Audley St.
London W1, England
(01) 629-9262

Geographical Directory of Suppliers

ALABAMA

Alexander City
Robinson Iron Corp.
Northport
Craig Nutt, Fine Wood Works

ARKANSAS

Fayetteville
Sunshine Architectural
Woodworks

CALIFORNIA

Alameda
Bradford Consultants
Anaheim
A Carolina Craftsman

Arcata
Mad River Woodworks
Auburn
Victorian Warehouse
Benicia
Bradbury & Bradbury
Wallpapers
Berkeley
Caning Shop
Classic Illumination, Inc.
Ohmega Salvage
The Sink Factory
Sunrise Specialty
Winans Construction
Burbank
J. P. Weaver
Eureka
North Pacific Joinery
Foster City
Designs in Tile
Hanford
Gravity-Randall
Hollywood
Linoleum City
Irvine
A. S. L. Associates

Los Angeles
Architectural Antiques
Warehouse
Greg's Antique Lighting
Murphys
D. E. A./Bathroom
Machineries
Nevada City
Bright Star Woodworking
Northridge
Vintage Plumbing and
Sanitary Specialties
San Diego
Burdoch Silk Lampshade Co.
St. Thomas Creations
San Francisco
Architectural Color
Architectural Resources
Group
Artistic License
Larry Boyce & Associates
Bob Buckter
Cirecast
Day Studio-Workshop
Illustrious Lighting
San Francisco Color Service
San Francisco Victoriana

San Jose
Cedar Valley Shingle Systems
Santa Barbara
Antique Baths & Kitchens
Sausalito
Nowell's, Inc.
Studio City
Helen Williams/Rare Tiles
Tuolumne
Wendell's Wood Stoves
Woodacre
Pagliacco Turning and Milling

COLORADO

Boulder
Boulder Stained Glass
Studios
Denver
The Color People
Grammar of Ornament
Queen City Architectural
Salvage
Barry Rose
Durango
Alfresco Fine Furniture
Silverton Victorian Millworks

249

CONNECTICUT

Ashford
Jerard Paul Jordan Gallery
Chester
Period Lighting Fixtures
Glastonbury
Dahlke Studios
Maurer and Shepherd
  Joyners
Granby
William H. Parsons &
  Associates
Guilford
Shuttercraft
Madison
Duo Dickinson, Architect
New Hartford
Hitchcock Chair Co.
New Haven
New England Woodturners
Norwalk
Gates Moore
South Windsor
Diamond K. Co.
Southington
John Canning
Southport
Heritage Mantels
Stamford
The English Garden, Inc.
Good Directions, Inc.
United House Wrecking
Stonington
Wick York
Washington
The Washington Copper
  Works
Waterbury
Edison Chemical Systems,
  Inc.
Westbrook
Architectural Preservation
  Trust
New England Outbuildings
Wilton
Kenneth Lynch & Sons
Woodbury
Ramase
Woodbury Blacksmith &
  Forge Co.

DELAWARE

Winterthur
Winterthur Museum and
  Gardens

DISTRICT OF COLUMBIA

The Brass Knob
The Canal Co.
The Kardell Studio
National Preservation
  Institute
Oehrlein and Associates

FLORIDA

Jasper
Heart-Wood, Inc.
Micanopy
Goodwin Lumber Co.

GEORGIA

Atlanta
Chadsworth, Inc.
Cross Industries
Focal Point, Inc.
Hearth Realities
Waterman Works
The Wrecking Bar
Brunswick
Fuller O'Brien Paints
Decatur
Devenco Products
Savannah
Nostalgia

IDAHO

Boise
Remodelers' & Renovators'
  Supply

ILLINOIS

Chicago
Colonial Brick Co.
Decorators Supply Corp.
Frog Tool Co.
Historic Boulevard Services
M-H Lamp & Fan Co.
Renovation Source
Des Plaines
The Chicago Faucet Co.
Elk Grove
Glashaus, Inc.
Evanston
Dalton-Gorman, Inc.
Judith Hendershot
Galena
Bassett & Vollum, Inc.
Gilberts
Abatron, Inc.
Highland Park
Carpenter and Smith
  Restorations
Joliet
Spiess Antique Building
  Materials
Mount Carroll
Campbell Center
Quincy
Preservation Services
St. Charles
Kyp-Go, Inc.
Wilmette
Perkowitz Window Fashions

IOWA

Davenport
Amazon Drygoods
Midwest Wood Products
Des Moines
Mark A. Knudsen
West Des Moines
Especially Lace

KANSAS

Olathe
The Broadway Collection

KENTUCKY

Covington
Stewart Manufacturing Co.

Hawesville
Restoration Supply
Lexington
Central Kentucky Millwork
Louisville
Bentley Brothers
Kentucky Wood Floors
Union
Custom Ironwork, Inc.

LOUISIANA

Baton Rouge
Coco Millwork & Supply Co.

New Iberia
Iberia Millwork
New Orleans
The Bank, Architectural
  Antiques
Robinson Lumber

MAINE

Gardiner
McKie Wing Roth, Jr.,
  Associates
Kennebunk
Watertower Pines
North Pownall
Portland Stove Co.
Phippsburg Center
Colonial Weavers
Portland
Decorum
Rockport
James Lea, Cabinetmaker
Round Pond
Pemaquid Floorcloths
Sedgwick
Donnell's Clapboard Mill
Thorndike
Bryant Stove Works
Yarmouth
Heritage Lanterns

MARYLAND

Baltimore
Matthew John Mosca
Brownsville
The Woods Co.
Columbia
Everlite Greenhouses
Frederick
Skyline Engineers
Vintage Lumber and Con-
  struction Co.
Hagerstown
Blaine Window Hardware
Preservation Associates
Kensington
Fireplace Mantel Shop
H and M Stair Builders, Inc.
Perry Hall
Windy Hill Forge
Rockville
Dell Corp.
Severna Park
Floorcloths, Inc.
Upper Falls
Paxton Hardware Ltd.
Williamsport
Victor Cushwa and Sons

MASSACHUSETTS

Andover
Merilyn M. Markham
Amherst
AMS Imports
Ashby
The Country Bed Shop
Boston
Amdega Conservatories
Besco Plumbing
J. R. Burrows Co.
Samuel Cabot, Inc.
Glass Arts
Kenmore Industries
Koeppel/Freedman Studios
Period Furniture Hardware
Edward K. Perry Co.
Boylston
Josiah R. Coppersmythe
Brewster
House Carpenters
Bridgewater
Lemee's Fireplace Equipment
Brighton
ARJ Associates
Brimfield
Sturbridge Studio
Brookfield
Angel House Designs
Cambridge
California Paints
City Lights
Ox-Line Paints
Charlemont
Marian Ives
Chicopee
Tom Moore's Steeple People
Cohasset
Cohasset Colonials
Concord
Elcanco, Inc.
Shaker Workshops
Danvers
E. G. Washburne & Co.
Easthampton
Peter Franklin
Fall River
The Candle Cellar and
  Emporium
Florence
Curran Glass & Mirror Co.
Goshen
Good Time Stove Co.
Groton
Craftsman Lumber Co.
Old-Fashioned Milk Paint Co.
Harvard
Cornucopia, Inc.
Hingham
Country Loft
Hudson
M. J. Mullane Co.
Leverett
Architectural Components
Lunenburg
Antique Color Supply, Inc.
Mansfield
Acorn Manufacturing Co.
Marion
The Mechanick's Workbench

Martha's Vineyard
Travis Tuck

New Bedford
The Preservation Partnership

Newburyport
Federal Street Lighthouse

North Andover
Museum of American Textile
History, Conservation
Center

North Chatham
Chatham Glass Co.

North Dartmouth
Cape Cod Cupola Co.

Princeton
Russell Swinton Oatman
Design Associates

Rowley
North Fields Restorations

Wales
Country Comfort Stove
Works

Waltham
S.P.N.E.A. Conservation
Center

Wareham
Tremont Nail Co.

Washington
Heartwood

Wayland
Yankee Craftsman

West Barnstable
Barnstable Stove Shop

West Chesterfield
Kathleen B. Smith

West Medford
Pompei & Co.

Williamsburg
Williamsburg Blacksmiths

Winchester
Allen Charles Hill, AIA

Woburn
A. J. P. Coppersmith & Co.

Yarmouth Port
William James Roth

MICHIGAN

Ann Arbor
Old House Gardens

Battle Creek
Stair Specialist

Blissfield
Riverbend Timber Framing,
Inc.

Grass Lake
Architectural Salvage Co.

Lake Orion
Renaissance Marketing, Inc.

Lapeer
Grand Era Reproductions

Niles
QRB Industries

Oxford
Williams Art Glass Studios

Southgate
Classic Accents, Inc.

Ypsilanti
Materials Unlimited

MINNESOTA

Excelsior
Outdoor Designs

Minneapolis
Anderson Pulley Seal
Pete Holly
J. Ring Glass Studio
Victorian Reproduction
Lighting Co.

Richfield
Brian F. Leo

Rochester
John Kruesel's General
Merchandise

Rogers
Woodworkers' Store

Warroad
Marvin Windows

MISSISSIPPI

Bay St. Louis
Bay-Waveland Woodworks

Jackson
Historical Replications, Inc.

MISSOURI

Chesterfield
Gainsborough Hardware
Industries

Hannibal
River City Restorations

Harrisonville
The Brickyard

Nevada
W. F. Norman Corp.

St. Clair
Franklin County Millwork

St. Louis
Art Directions
St. Louis Antique Lighting
Co.

Washington
Linen and Lace

NEW HAMPSHIRE

Alexandria
Alexandria Wood Joinery

Amherst
Good and Co.

Canaan
Kraatz Russell Glass

Canterbury
North Woods Chair Shop

Center Ossipee
Beech River Mill Co.

Claremont
Timberpeg, East Inc.

Gilmanton Iron Works
Stephen P. Bedard

Gonic
Kane-Gonic Brick Corp.

Hampton
Historic Hardware Ltd.

Munsonville
KU/2 Specialties

Portsmouth
Nancy Borden Period Textile
Furnishings
Partridge Replications
Eldred Wheeler

Salem
Faneuil Furniture Hardware

Sanborntown
Martha Wetherbee Basket
Shop

Stoddard
Carlisle Restoration Lumber

Tilton
Wiggins Brothers

Westmoreland
Entrances, Inc.

NEW JERSEY

Bayonne
The Muralo Co.

Califon
Smith Woodworks and
Design

Cedar Grove
Omnia Industries

Cinnaminson
The Brass Finial

Closter
Pasvalco

Englewood
Authentic Lighting

Fair Haven
Half Moon Antiques

Frenchtown
Antique Hardware Store
Sandra McKenzie Schmitt

Irvington
Richard E. Thibaut, Inc.

Jersey City
W. J. Hampton Plastering

Montvale
Benjamin Moore & Co.

New Brunswick
Donald Stryker Restorations

Newark
Cook & Dunn Paint Corp.

Northvale
Bendix Mouldings, Inc.

Palmyra
Littlewood & Maue Museum
Quality Reproductions

Paramus
Bergen Bluestone Co.

Pluckemin
Edward Ludlow,
Cabinetmaker

Princeton
New Jersey Barn Co.

Rancocas
William Spencer

Sergeantsville
Sunflower Glass Studio

Sparta
Brill and Walker Associates

NEW MEXICO

Taos
Saxe-Patterson

NEW YORK

Brewster
Historic Housefitters Co.

Brooklyn
AA-Abbingdon Affiliates, Inc.
American Wood Column

Barewood, Inc.
Broadway Market MRA
Gaslight Time Antiques
Richard N. Hayton and
Associates
Roy Electric Co.

Buffalo
Pratt & Lambert Paints

Cold Spring
Stencilsmith

Corona
George Studios

Deansboro
Old Lamplighter Shop
Schwartz's Forge and
Metalworks

East Nassau
Eastfield Village

Farmingdale
Old World Moulding and
Finishing Co.

Garden City
Albert Van Luit & Co.

Garrison
Watercolors, Inc.

Kingston
Hurley Patentee Lighting

Mattituck
Russell Restoration of Suffolk

Mecklenburg
Philip M. White and
Associates

Melville
Laura Ashley (mail order)

Monsey
Traditional Line Architectural
Restoration Ltd.

New York City
Architectural Paneling
Architectural Sculpture, Ltd.
S. A. Bendheim Co.
Louis W. Bowen, Inc.
Clarence House/Cole and
Son/Colefax and Fowler
Cowtan & Tout
EverGreene Painting Studios
Garrett Wade Co.
Jamie Gibbs and Associates
Lynn Goodpasture
Great American Salvage Co.
Import Specialists
Irreplaceable Artifacts
Howard Kaplan Antiques
Lee Joffa
Lovelia Enterprises
Metropolitan Lighting Fixture
Co.
New York Marble Works, Inc.
Osborne and Little
Patterson, Flynn & Martin
Price Glover, Inc.
Rambusch
Raintree Designs, Inc.
Arthur Sanderson & Sons
Scalamandré, Inc.
F. Schumacher & Co.
Standard Trimming Co.
Stark Carpet Corp.
Tromploy
Tsigonia Paints & Varnishes
Urban Archaeology
Waverly
The Wicker Garden

North White Plains
Brunschwig & Fils
Nyack
Brasslight, Inc.
Port Chester
Greeff Fabrics, Inc.
Slate Hill
Victorian Lightcrafters, Ltd.
Smithtown
Perma Ceram Enterprises
Stony Point
Chromatic Paint Corp.
Syracuse
Pelnik Wrecking Co.
Trumansburg
Black Ash Baskets
Warwick
Golden Age Glassworks
Westfield
Crystal Mountain Prisms

NORTH CAROLINA

Asheville
Biltmore, Campbell, Smith Restorations, Inc.
Candler
Candlertown Chairworks
Kayne & Son
Charlotte
K & D Supply Co.
Colerain
Lazy Hill Farm Designs
Eden
King's Chandelier Co.
Lexington
Mid-State Tile Co.
Seagrove
Westmoore Pottery
Tarboro
The Joinery Co.
Troutman
Carter Canopies

OHIO

Cincinnati
Anderson Building Restoration
Bona Decorative Hardware
Old World Restorations, Inc.
Vintage Valances
Wooden Nickel Antiques
Cleveland
Beechwood Wallcoverings
Carefree Wallcoverings
Dutch Boy Paints
Ferguson's Cut Glass Works
The Glidden Co.
Katzenbach & Warren
The Martin-Senour Co.
Millbrook Wallcoverings
Sterling Prints
Columbus
Fireside Reproductions
Delaware
Alexandra's Textiles
Dublin
Tullibardine Enterprises
Fostoria
Ezra G.
Franklin
Architectural Reclamation

Glenmont
Briar Hill Stone Co.
Kidron
Lehman Hardware & Appliances, Inc.
Lebanon
John K. Buchanan, Cabinetmaker
Salem
Urfic, Inc.
Uhrichsville
Superior Clay Corp.
Wellington
Century House Antiques

OKLAHOMA

Oklahoma City
Architectural Antiques

OREGON

Eugene
States Industries
Portland
A-Ball Plumbing Supply
Hippo Hardware & Trading Co.
Rejuvenation Lamp & Fixture

PENNSYLVANIA

Adamstown
American Architectural Art Co.
Allentown
Allentown Paint Manufacturing Co.
Ardmore
Finnaren & Haley, Inc.
Bethlehem
Marion H. Campbell
Broomall
The Iron Shop
Carlisle
Cumberland Woodcraft Co.
Chester Springs
Oakleaf Reproductions
Delta
Aged Woods
Derry
18th Century Hardware
Doylestown
Moravian Pottery & Tile Works
Elizabethtown
Pat Hornafius
Elizabethville
Restorations Unlimited, Inc.
Exton
Ball and Ball
A. L. Diament & Co.
Green Lane
David Flaherty
Lansdale
American Olean Tile Co.
Lebanon
Hephaestus Pottery
Leola
Sun Room Co.
Lumberville
Delaware Quarries

Milford
Architectural Iron Co.
Montoursville
Country Accents
North Wales
Pennsylvania Firebacks, Inc.
Paoli
Country Iron Foundry
Pen Argyl
Structural Slate Co.
Philadelphia
Aetna Stove Co.
Architectural Antiques Exchange
Clio Group, Inc.
Dalton Pavilions, Inc.
DeWeese Woodworking
Alvin Holm, AIA
Samuel B. Sadtler & Co.
Pittsburgh
Pittsburgh Paints
Terra Cotta Productions, Inc.
Reading
Baldwin Hardware Manufacturing Corp.
Red Lion
Family Heir-Loom Weavers
Schaefferstown
Spring House Classics
Shoemakersville
Glen-Gery Corp.
Solebury
Robert Whitley Furniture Studios
Somerset
Somerset Door & Column Co.
Stewartstown
Fypon, Inc.
Susquehanna
Conklin's
West Chester
Arden Forge
Monroe Coldren & Son's Antiques and Restorations
York
Tioga Mill Outlet

RHODE ISLAND

Ashaway
Steven P. Mack Associates
Newport
Rue de France
West Kingston
G. R. Clidence
Chapin Townsend

SOUTH CAROLINA

Charleston
Historic Charleston Reproductions
Florence
Driwood Moulding Co.
Liberty
Flexi-Wall Systems
Orangeburg
Tiresias, Inc.
Timmonsville
W. S. Lockhart Designs

SOUTH DAKOTA

Sioux Falls
C. & H. Roofing, Inc.

TENNESSEE

Bean Station
American Heirlooms, Inc.
Chattanooga
Architectural Masterworks
Crossville
Cumberland General Store
Knoxville
Oak Crest Manufacturing, Inc.
Memphis
American Heritage Shutters, Inc.
Nashville
Tennessee Tub & Tubliner Co.

TEXAS

Austin
Whit Hanks
Dallas
Classic Architectural Specialties
The Fan Man
Hillsboro
Anthony Wood Products
Houston
Chelsea Decorative Metal Co.
Jefferson
Old Jefferson Tile Co.
Longview
Perkins Architectural Millwork

VERMONT

Bennington
Whitten Enterprises, Inc.
Burlington
Conant Custom Brass
Granville
Granville Manufacturing Co.
Moretown
Townsend Anderson
Perkinsville
Vermont Soapstone Co.
Proctor
Vermont Marble Co.
Putney
Carol Brown
South Burlington
Palm Rooms Ltd.
Sudbury
Mister Slate
Vermont Cobble Slate
West Pawlet
Rising and Nelson Slate Co.
Wolcott
Robert Bourdon, The Smithy

VIRGINIA

Abingdon
Old Abingdon Weavers
Berryville
Custom Millwork, Inc.

Index